Entropy Method for Decision Making with Uncertainty

Entropy Method for Decision Making with Uncertainty

Guest Editor

Małgorzata Przybyła-Kasperek

MDPI

Basel • Beijing • Wuhan • Barcelona • Belgrade • Novi Sad • Cluj • Manchester

Guest Editor
Małgorzata Przybyła-Kasperek
Institute of Computer Science
University of Silesia in Katowice
Sosnowiec
Poland

Editorial Office
MDPI AG
Grosspeteranlage 5
4052 Basel, Switzerland

This is a reprint of the Special Issue, published open access by the journal *Entropy* (ISSN 1099-4300), freely accessible at: https://www.mdpi.com/journal/entropy/special_issues/1LL73O0C58.

For citation purposes, cite each article independently as indicated on the article page online and as indicated below:

Lastname, A.A.; Lastname, B.B. Article Title. *Journal Name* **Year**, *Volume Number*, Page Range.

ISBN 978-3-7258-7032-5 (Hbk)
ISBN 978-3-7258-7033-2 (PDF)
https://doi.org/10.3390/books978-3-7258-7033-2

Contents

About the Editor

Małgorzata Przybyła-Kasperek

Małgorzata Przybyła-Kasperek is currently a Professor with the Faculty of Science and Technology, Institute of Computer Science, University of Silesia in Katowice. She received the Ph.D. degree in computer science and the Habilitation degree from the Polish Academy of Sciences, in 2011 and 2018, respectively. She has authored more than 100 scientific articles. She also leads the Complex Decision Systems Group and mentors Ph.D. students in AI. Her research interests include data mining, decision support systems, and AI. Her academic interests center on artificial intelligence, machine learning, and data-driven decision making, with particular interest in distributed learning, dispersed data, and decision support systems. She has actively contributed to theoretical research and practical applications of AI, with a strong focus on educational initiatives and interdisciplinary collaboration. She honed modern higher education practices at the University of Groningen, Aarhus University, and the University of Alicante.

entropy

MDPI

Editorial

Entropy Method for Decision Making with Uncertainty

Małgorzata Przybyła-Kasperek

Institute of Computer Science, University of Silesia in Katowice, Bedzinska 39, 41-200 Sosnowiec, Poland;
malgorzata.przybyla-kasperek@us.edu.pl; Tel.: +48-32-269-17-56

1. Introduction

In complex socio-technical systems, uncertainty is the rule rather than the exception. Decisions depend on partial, ambiguous, or noisy evidence; data are distributed or privacy-sensitive; and stakeholders operate in cooperative–competitive environments. In this Special Issue, we bring together entropy-based methods, rough and fuzzy set formalisms [1], expert and distributed learning systems [2], and game-theoretic models to develop interpretable, robust, and privacy-aware decision support spanning areas of medicine [3], cybersecurity, and environmental risk [4].

The articles selected for this Special Issue reflect a noticeable shift in current research: from isolated modelling techniques to integrated uncertainty pipelines capable of combining robustness, interpretability, privacy awareness, and mathematical rigour. A clear example of this integration is found in the paper on interval-valued entropy measures for interval-valued fuzzy sets, where uncertainty is treated not as a nuisance but as an explicit, structured signal [5]. By embedding these interval entropies into a federated learning framework, the authors demonstrate that medical risk prediction can remain privacy-preserving while achieving high sensitivity even under heterogeneous, non-IID data distributions. The study illustrates how epistemic uncertainty, often flattened into scalar indicators, can become a valuable and interpretable component of diagnostic reasoning. A similar orientation toward uncertainty as a guiding principle appears in the paper [6], focused on entropy-based mimic-defence scheduling. Here, entropy serves not only as a statistical descriptor but also as a strategic tool. The REWS algorithm developed by the authors is grounded in incomplete-information game theory and addresses the realistic scenario of memory-based attackers operating under tight resource constraints. The paper [7] on urban flood resilience builds on this thread by showing how heterogeneous data modalities—numerical, interval, and linguistic—can be naturally merged into a unified evaluation framework. By combining SW-GAHP weighting with cloud-model fusion, the authors capture interpersonal and intrapersonal consistency while preserving the inherent semantic uncertainty in expert assessments. Uncertainty also lies at the heart of the hybrid weighting scheme [8], which responds to a long-standing problem in multi-criteria decision making: entropy weights are sensitive to outliers, while purely statistical dispersion measures may disregard meaningful variability. By integrating IQR-based robustness and entropy-based information, the authors create a weighting model that adapts smoothly to the level of contamination within the data. Recent investigations have further illuminated the critical role of normalization choices in entropy-based multi-criteria decision analysis, particularly their impact on ranking stability amid data variability. Such data-driven perspectives underscore the need for preprocessing strategies that enhance empirical robustness, ensuring that entropy weights remain reliable across diverse and uncertain decision scenarios. A more fundamental

 https://doi.org/10.3390/e28020141

analysis of uncertainty appears in [9], where a method for cloud-model similarity is presented. This enhancement corrects systematic similarity overestimation, improves concept discrimination, and yields more reliable performance in multi-expert decision settings and time-series classification. Its conceptual cornerstone is straightforward yet powerful: uncertainty should be decomposed, not collapsed. The contribution on coalition-based decision trees [10] provides a compelling perspective on distributed decision making, where conflicts between independently maintained data sources are inevitable. By combining Pawlak's conflict analysis, coalition formation, decision tree induction, and decision-template fusion, the authors develop a transparent and powerful methodology for reducing global decision entropy in multi-source environments.

In conclusion, this collection of papers serves as a coherent response to the growing need for decision-support systems that acknowledge and exploit uncertainty rather than suppress it. Across various domains—including medical diagnostics, cyber defence, environmental assessment, statistical weighting, cloud-model reasoning, and distributed classification—the authors show that entropy and related constructs provide not only mathematical elegance but also operational value.

2. Key Research Gaps

Contemporary research on uncertainty-aware decision making often confronts limitations that stem from oversimplified representations of uncertainty, insufficient robustness to data imperfections, or a lack of mechanisms that reconcile heterogeneous or conflicting information. A recurring challenge is the difficulty of capturing epistemic uncertainty in a form that preserves its structure rather than collapsing it into single-point indicators. Approaches based on interval entropies demonstrate how uncertainty can be quantified without losing the nuance of incomplete or imprecise evidence, particularly in settings where privacy constraints and fragmented information make classical aggregation impractical.

A further obstacle for complex decision problems arises from heterogeneous data sources, inconsistent expert judgments, and mixed information formats. Real-world systems rarely rely on a single data modality, and traditional multi-criteria methods have struggled to combine numerical precision, linguistic descriptions, and interval uncertainty in a principled way [11,12]. Methodologies that fuse weighting schemes with cloud-model reasoning offer a pathway toward unified treatment of multi-modal evidence, ensuring that ambiguity, vagueness, and variability are not treated as noise but as meaningful components of the decision process.

Equally important is the tendency for information-theoretic weights to become unstable in the presence of noise or outliers [13]. Pure entropy weighting is highly sensitive to numerical irregularities, while dispersion-based weights such as those derived from variability measures often disregard valuable informational structure. Hybrid approaches that explicitly balance robustness and information sensitivity create a more adaptive weighting mechanism—one capable of responding to contamination levels and shifting data distributions in a controlled and interpretable way.

Distributed decision-making environments often rely on implicit or opaque aggregation mechanisms, making it difficult to trace how conflicting or incomplete data influence the final outcome [14]. Structured approaches that combine conflict analysis, coalition formation, and interpretable model fusion address this gap by offering transparent mechanisms for understanding how individual data sources contribute to collective decisions, especially when these sources disagree or vary in reliability.

Closing these gaps requires viewing uncertainty not as a residual quantity to be suppressed, but as a foundational principle that shapes how information is represented,

https://doi.org/10.3390/e28020141

combined, and interpreted. By embracing this richer and more structural understanding of uncertainty, future methods can advance toward decision processes that are not only more accurate, but also more transparent, resilient, and attuned to the complexity of real-world environments.

3. Future Research Directions

Looking ahead, several broad research trajectories appear increasingly important for the evolution of uncertainty-aware decision making—directions that extend well beyond the methods and case studies explored so far, and that will likely shape the next decade of developments in this field. A first direction involves the construction of multi-layered uncertainty architectures capable of operating seamlessly across scales, modalities, and degrees of abstraction [15]. Future systems will need to integrate probabilistic inference, fuzzy semantics, interval representations, causal reasoning, and learning-based uncertainty estimates into an integrated conceptual and computational framework.

A second major opportunity lies in developing autonomous systems that can negotiate uncertainty, not just model it. As AI agents increasingly interact with one another—and with human decision makers—mechanisms for uncertainty-aware negotiation, coordination, and conflict resolution will become indispensable [16]. Research is needed on protocols in which agents exchange uncertainty-qualified information, justify their recommendations, and collaboratively decide when to defer, escalate, or abstain. These mechanisms must be flexible enough to operate in mixed human–machine teams and robust enough to withstand adversarial manipulation.

Equally significant is the emerging need to rethink data quality and trustworthiness in environments where data may be incomplete, strategic, corrupted, or intentionally deceptive. Traditional assumptions of stationarity and benign noise no longer hold. Future work will need to integrate provenance tracking, explainable uncertainty diagnostics, trust scores, and mechanisms for detecting epistemic anomalies. This includes designing learning systems capable of identifying when uncertainty arises from insufficient evidence, when it signals concept drift, and when it reflects adversarial activity [17].

In parallel, the rise of complex, high-dimensional data streams—sensor networks, multimodal monitoring, autonomous vehicles, remote healthcare—demands advances in real-time uncertainty quantification [18,19]. Future systems must be capable of updating uncertainty assessments not just at inference time but continuously, reflecting evolving contexts, shifting environmental conditions, and newly acquired evidence. Lightweight yet expressive representations of uncertainty will be crucial for enabling such dynamic adaptation under computational constraints.

Taken together, these research directions suggest a future in which uncertainty is not something to be avoided but something to be used. In such a future, intelligent systems will recognize uncertainty as a source of information and context rather than a weakness. This shift can lead to decision-making approaches that are not only more advanced technically, but also better suited to the complexity, unpredictability, and interconnected nature of the real environments in which they operate.

Funding: This research received no external funding.

Acknowledgments: The Guest Editor extends their sincere gratitude to all contributing authors for their excellent work, to the anonymous reviewers for their insightful and constructive feedback, and to the Editorial Team of *Entropy* for their professional support on this Special Issue.

Conflicts of Interest: The author declares no conflicts of interest.

https://doi.org/10.3390/e28020141

References

1. Singh, J.; Ray, S.S. Integrating fuzzy rough set-based entropies for identifying drug-resistant miRNAs in cancer. *J. Comput. Sci.* **2025**, *91* , 102673. [CrossRef]
2. Kalakoti, R.; Nõmm, S.; Bahsi, H. Federated Learning of Explainable AI (FEDXAI) for deep learning-based intrusion detection in IoT networks. *Comput. Netw.* **2025**, *270*, 111479. [CrossRef]
3. Reis, M.I.; Gonçalves, J.N.; Cortez, P.; Carvalho, M.S.; Fernandes, J.M. A context-aware decision support system for selecting explainable artificial intelligence methods in business organizations. *Comput. Ind.* **2025**, *165*, 104233. [CrossRef]
4. Islam, S.; Basheer, N.; Papastergiou, S.; Ciampi, M.; Silvestri, S. Intelligent dynamic cybersecurity risk management framework with explainability and interpretability of AI models for enhancing security and resilience of digital infrastructure. *J. Reliab. Intell. Environ.* **2025**, *11*, 12. [CrossRef] [PubMed]
5. Pękala, B.; Kosior, D.; Rząsa, W.; Garwol, K.; Czuma, J. Unique Method for Prognosis of Risk of Depressive Episodes Using Novel Measures to Model Uncertainty Under Data Privacy. *Entropy* **2025**, *27*, 162. [CrossRef] [PubMed]
6. Wu, X.; Wang, M.; Cai, Y.; Chang, X.; Liu, Y. Improving the CRCC-DHR Reliability: An Entropy-Based Mimic-Defense-Resource Scheduling Algorithm. *Entropy* **2025**, *27*, 208. [CrossRef] [PubMed]
7. He, X.; Hu, Y.; Yang, X.; Wang, S.; Wang, Y. Urban Flood Resilience Evaluation Based on Heterogeneous Data and Group Decision-Making. *Entropy* **2024**, *26*, 755. [CrossRef] [PubMed]
8. Erbey, A.; Fidan, Ü.; Gündüz, C. A robust hybrid weighting scheme based on IQRBOW and Entropy for MCDM: Stability and advantage criteria in the VIKOR framework. *Entropy* **2025**, *27*, 867. [CrossRef] [PubMed]
9. Pu, J.; Liu, Z. HECM-Plus: Hyper-Entropy Enhanced Cloud Models for Uncertainty-Aware Design Evaluation in Multi-Expert Decision Systems. *Entropy* **2025**, *27*, 475. [CrossRef] [PubMed]
10. Kusztal, K.; Przybyła-Kasperek, M. Distributed Data Classification with Coalition-Based Decision Trees and Decision Template Fusion. *Entropy* **2025**, *27*, 1205. [CrossRef] [PubMed]
11. Xiao, Y.; Ma, X.; Zhan, J. Group decision-making in heterogeneous multi-scale information fusion: Integrating overconfident and non-cooperative behaviors. *Inf. Fusion* **2026**, *125*, 103401. [CrossRef]
12. Libório, M.P.; Ekel, P.; D'Angelo, M.F.S.V.; Martínez, L.; Pedrycz, W. Dealing with heterogeneous information in multi-criteria group decision-making problems: A comprehensive design framework. *IEEE Access* **2025**, *13*, 114444–114459. [CrossRef]
13. Alastal, H.; Sharaf, A.; Mahmoud, S.; Alsaidi, O.; Bahroun, Z. Integrating Multiple Criteria Decision-Making Techniques in Sustainable Supplier Selection: A Comprehensive Review. *Decis. Mak. Appl. Manag. Eng.* **2025**, *8*, 380–400.
14. Tong, S.; Sun, B.; Zhang, L.; Chu, X. An approach of multi-criteria group decision making with incomplete information based on formal concept analysis and rough set. *Expert Syst. Appl.* **2024**, *248*, 123364. [CrossRef]
15. Krishankumar, R.; Ravichandran, K.S.; Gandomi, A.H.; Kar, S. Interval-valued probabilistic hesitant fuzzy set-based framework for group decision-making with unknown weight information. *Neural Comput. Appl.* **2021**, *33*, 2445–2457. [CrossRef]
16. Rowe, F.; Jeanneret Medina, M.; Journé, B.; Coëtard, E.; Myers, M. Understanding responsibility under uncertainty: A critical and scoping review of autonomous driving systems. *J. Inf. Technol.* **2024**, *39*, 587–615. [CrossRef]
17. Korycki, Ł.; Krawczyk, B. Adversarial concept drift detection under poisoning attacks for robust data stream mining. *Mach. Learn.* **2023**, *112*, 4013–4048. [CrossRef] [PubMed]
18. Chen, L.; Wang, J.; Mortlock, T.; Khargonekar, P.; Al Faruque, M.A. Hyperdimensional uncertainty quantification for multimodal uncertainty fusion in autonomous vehicles perception. In *Proceedings of the 2025 IEEE/CVF Conference on Computer Vision and Pattern Recognition (CVPR), Nashville, TN, USA, 10–17 June 2025*; IEEE: New York, NY, USA, 2025; pp. 22306–22316.
19. Yang, K.; Tang, X.; Li, J.; Wang, H.; Zhong, G.; Chen, J.; Cao, D. Uncertainties in onboard algorithms for autonomous vehicles: Challenges, mitigation, and perspectives. *IEEE Trans. Intell. Transp. Syst.* **2023**, *24*, 8963–8987. [CrossRef]

https://doi.org/10.3390/e28020141

entropy

MDPI

Article

Bilateral Matching Method for Business Resources Based on Synergy Effects and Incomplete Data

Shuhai Wang [1,2,*], Linfu Sun [1,2] and Yang Yu [3]

1 School of Computing and Artificial Intelligence, Southwest Jiaotong University, Chengdu 611756, China
2 Manufacturing Industry Chain Collaboration and Information Support Technology Key Laboratory of Sichuan Province, Southwest Jiaotong University, Chengdu 610031, China
3 School of Computer Science and Software Engineering, Southwest Petroleum University, Chengdu 610500, China
* Correspondence: yw1688@my.swjtu.edu.cn

Abstract: On the third-party cloud platform, to help enterprises accurately obtain high-quality and valuable business resources from the massive information resources, a bilateral matching method for business resources, based on synergy effects and incomplete data, is proposed. The method first utilizes a k-nearest neighbor imputation algorithm, based on comprehensive similarity, to fill in missing values. Then, it constructs a satisfaction evaluation index system for business resource suppliers and demanders, and the weights of the satisfaction evaluation indices are determined, based on the fuzzy analytic hierarchy process (FAHP) and the entropy weighting method (EWM). On this basis, a bilateral matching model is constructed with the objectives of maximizing the satisfaction of both the supplier and the demander, as well as achieving the synergy effect. Finally, the model is solved using the linear weighting method to obtain the most satisfactory business resources for both supply and demand. The effectiveness of the method is verified through a practical application and comparative experiments.

Keywords: bilateral matching; synergy effect; business resources; fuzzy analytic hierarchy process; entropy weight method; data analytics

1. Introduction

The third-party cloud platform provides support for business collaboration for various enterprises, such as suppliers, distributors, service providers, 4S shops, and logistics providers. As the number of enterprises on the third-party cloud platform grows, so does their business collaboration, resulting in the accumulation of a large number of business resources [1,2]. These business resources include data resources, process resources, service resources, product resources, etc., which can help enterprises improve supply chain management efficiency, strengthen business collaboration, perform data analysis, provide decision support, and more. These bring greater competitive advantages and development opportunities to enterprises. However, with the continuous increase of business resources, it is difficult for enterprise users on the cloud platform to obtain high-quality and valuable resources that meet their own requirements. This leads to the problem of information overload. Therefore, on the third-party cloud platform, how to quickly and accurately obtain high-quality and valuable business resources from complex and massive information resources is one of the key problems in improving an enterprise's competitiveness and operational efficiency. To meet this challenge, we adopt a bilateral matching method. The method integrates the personalized business needs of both the supply and demand sides, selecting the most satisfying business resources for both parties from a vast array of information resources [2]. By optimizing the matching relationship between the supply and demand sides, it helps enterprises to efficiently identify the required resources, reduce information redundancy, and achieve an overall optimal collaboration effect between suppliers and demanders. In the field of cloud manufacturing, many scholars have conducted extensive studies on the matching problem, focusing on aspects such as research and development (R&D) tasks, quality of service (QoS), and business resources [1,2].

In terms of R&D tasks, Lu et al. [3] proposed a truthful double auction mechanism, to address the problem of matching users' task requirements and providers' resources in bilateral cloud markets. This mechanism uses Lyapunov optimization technology to minimize the cost for users, which is beneficial for both the cloud service provider and the user. Li et al. [4] proposed a novel two-sided matching model based on dual hesitant fuzzy preference information, to solve the fuzziness and uncertainty of preference information in the matching process of complex product manufacturing tasks on the cloud manufacturing platform. Liu et al. [5] proposed a task assignment method based on bilateral matching (TAMBM) between subtask and designer, to address the problem of collaborative design subtasks assignment in design teams. They constructed a multi-objective optimization model for collaborative design task allocation based on bilateral matching, and they used the improved sparrow search algorithm to solve the model. In terms of QoS, Hao et al. [6] proposed a QoS-based two-sided matching model of cloud services, in order to solve the problem of on-requirement mutual selection of service providers and tasks in a cloud manufacturing environment. For the manufacturer–dealer bilateral adaptation problem in the intelligent cloud manufacturing environment, Fang et al. [7] proposed a new bilateral adaptation algorithm based on Q-learning and an improved Gale–Shapley algorithm, to gain superior results. In order to evaluate and optimize the adaptability of service-matching strategies, Xue et al. [8] proposed a computational experiment-based evaluation framework for service-matching strategies, which can simulate all kinds of actual scenarios, to verify the performances of service-matching strategies. In terms of business resources, Yu et al. [2] proposed a business resource bilateral matching model (BRBMM), which can accurately obtain high-quality and valuable business resources from massive information resources. In order to improve the accuracy of matching decisions between manufacturing service resources and tasks in a cloud environment, Xiao et al. [9] proposed a matching decision method for manufacturing service resources, which considers multiple influencing factors in resource matching. In other applications, Wang et al. [10] proposed a two-sided matching model (TMM), to address the challenges of information asymmetry and low matching efficiency in the freight market by leveraging adverse user behaviors to enhance platform matching efficacy. To solve personnel–position matching issues, Yu et al. [11] introduced an intuitionistic fuzzy two-sided matching model (IFTMM), which employs novel intuitionistic fuzzy Choquet integral aggregation operators to describe correlations between evaluation attributes, and which effectively enhances accuracy in personnel–position matching.

The above methods studied the matching problem from different angles and achieved good results. However, they relied on matching the complete data. When the cloud platform cleans and organizes the received data, issues such as poor data quality and inconsistent data formats may lead to data loss [12]. This will impact the accuracy of the matching. Also, existing matching methods based on business resources rarely consider synergy effects. Therefore, the above methods cannot be perfectly applied to business resource matching on the third-party cloud platform, and there is a common problem of poor accuracy in the matching process. To solve these problems, this paper proposes the bilateral matching-method for business resources (BMBR) based on synergy effects and incomplete data. In order to solve the problem of missing data, the method firstly uses the comprehensive similarity-based k-nearest neighbor imputation algorithm (CSKI) to fill in the missing values. Then, a satisfaction evaluation index system is constructed, and the weights of the satisfaction evaluation indexes are determined based on the FAHP and the EWM. On this basis, a two-sided matching model is established based on synergy effects. Finally, the linear weighting method is applied to solving the model, in order to obtain the most satisfactory business resources for both the supply and demand sides.

The main contributions of this study are as follows: (1) Proposing CSKI for filling in missing values, which combines a business resource attributes-based similarity measure and a hybrid difference-based similarity measure. (2) Constructing a satisfaction evaluation index system based on the demander's requirements and the supplier's preferences. (3) The synergy effect is is determined by the the collaboration requirements between business resource demanders and suppliers. The two-sided matching model is established based on the synergy effects. (4) We conducted experiments on six different business resource datasets, and the results demonstrate that our proposed method can effectively improve matching accuracy compared to the state-of-the-art matching methods, and that it can enhance overall satisfaction for both parties.

The remaining sections of this paper are organized as follows: Section 2 introduces the proposed method. In Section 3, we present an example application and comparative analysis of this article. The paper is concluded in Section 4.

2. Methodology

The main structure of the proposed BMBR method is illustrated in Figure 1. It contains four components: (1) imputation of missing values; (2) constructing a satisfaction evaluation index system; (3) normalization of the satisfaction evaluation index values; (4) construction and solution of a multi-objective optimization model. In Figure 1, B is is a matrix formed by randomly extracting evaluation index-related data resources from the data space of the third-party cloud platform, and A is a matrix formed by extracting the attribute information of business resources from the data space of the third-party cloud platform.

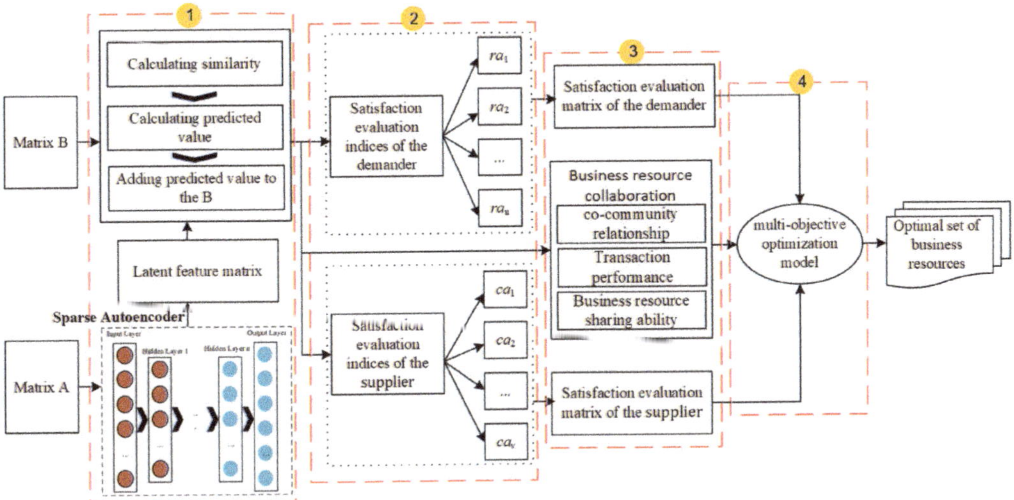

Figure 1. The structure of the proposed method.

2.1. Imputation of Missing Values

This section introduces CSKI, which aims to fill in missing values in B for accurate matching. The principle of CSKI is to find the k' data points that are most similar to the missing data based on the existing data points, and then, to use them to predict and fill in the missing values. To calculate the missing values, we need to evaluate the similarity values between each pair of business resources.

2.1.1. Quantification of the Textual Data

The original business resource dataset comprises text data that require conversion into numerical form for bilateral matching. To facilitate this conversion, a text convolutional neural network (TextCNN) is employed. Subsequently, the text data are classified into five categories: excellent (5 points), good (4 points), average (3 points), poor (2 points), and very poor (1 point).

TextCNN is a text classification model based on convolutional neural networks (CNN). It usually consists of the following four layers: input layer, convolution layer, pooling layer, and fully connected layer. The input layer converts B into a matrix of word embeddings with dimensions $n \times k$ through the word2vec model, where n represents the number of words in the textual data and k represents the dimension of the word embedding matrix. The convolutional layer is used to extract local features. In this layer, convolutional kernels of sizes 2, 3, and 4 are employed, to capture relationships between different character spans. The pooling layer extracts important information from the feature maps computed by the convolutional layer [13]. In this layer, we utilize 1-max pooling for all convolutional kernels and then cascade them, to obtain the final feature vector. The fully connected layer serves as the last layer in the TextCNN model construction. It is built based on the output of the pooling layer and the number of classification categories. The softmax function is employed to obtain the ultimate classification results. In this layer, dropout is used to avoid overfitting.

2.1.2. Business Resource Attributes-Based Similarity Measure

The similarity measure based on the business resource attributes is calculated by assessing the attribute information of the resources (e.g., type, quantity, volume, customer ID, etc.), to determine the similarity between business resources. This is called (SMBRA). The attribute information usually has large dimensions, which increases the computational complexity of the similarity calculation [14,15]. In this paper, we use a sparse autoencoder to reduce the dimensionality. The sparse autoencoder is a neural network model for unsupervised learning that can learn a set of meaningful feature representations from input data. It encodes the input data into a low-dimensional sparse representation by training a neural network with multiple hidden layers, and it then reconstructs the original input data, using a decoder. Compared to traditional autoencoders, sparse autoencoders incorporate sparsity constraints on the activation function of the hidden layers.

A sparse autoencoder consists of an encoder and a decoder. Suppose $A = \{X_1, X_2, \cdots, X_i, \cdots, X_n\}$ denotes the business resource attribute data; n denotes the number of training samples; $X_i = (x_{i1}, x_{i2}, \ldots, x_{ip})$ is a p-dimensional attribute vector. The encoder of the sparse autoencoder can be applied, to obtain the nonlinear representations of the input vectors [16]. The formulation of the encoder is shown as follows:

$$h = f(WA + b) \tag{1}$$

where h is the feature vector, W denotes the weight matrix for the encoder, f represents the activation function, and b represents the bias vector for the encoder. The formulation of the decoder is shown as follows:

$$Y = f'(W'h + b') \tag{2}$$

where W' represents the weight matrix for the decoder, f' is the activation function, b' denotes the bias vector for the decoder, and Y is the reconstruction of A. The objective of F_{cost} is to minimize the reconstruction error between input and output:

$$F_{\text{cost}} = \frac{1}{n} \sum_{i=1}^{n} \|Y_i - X_i\|^2 \tag{3}$$

We add an additional sparse penalty term, to optimize the objective function. The sparse penalty term $J_{\text{sparse}}(\rho)$ is shown as follows:

$$J_{\text{sparse}}(\rho) = \sum_{m=1}^{q} \left(\rho \log \frac{\rho}{\rho_m} + (1-\rho) \log \frac{1-\rho}{1-\rho_m} \right) \tag{4}$$

$$\rho_m = \frac{1}{n}\sum_{i=1}^{n} f(W_m X_i + b_m) \tag{5}$$

where ρ_m denotes the average activation of the hidden unit $m; \rho$ is the sparse parameter; and q is the number of hidden-layer neurons.

In addition, a regularization item that can penalize the weights of the network is added to the loss function, to avoid overfitting [16]. It is shown as follows:

$$J_{\text{weight}}\,(W) = \lambda_1(\|W\|_2 + \|W'\|_2) \tag{6}$$

where λ_1 is the weight attenuation coefficient and $J_{\text{weight}}\,(W)$ represents the sparse penalty term. Accordingly, the objective function of the sparse autoencoder is represented as follows:

$$J_{\text{loss}}\,(W,b) = F_{\text{cost}} + J_{\text{weight}}\,(W) + \mu J_{\text{sparse}}\,(\rho) \tag{7}$$

where $J_{\text{loss}}\,(W,b)$ is the overall objective loss function and μ is the weighting coefficient of the sparse penalty term.

The sparse autoencoder described above has just one hidden layer, so it has a limited ability to learn features from data. To improve its learning ability, it is important to build a deep sparse autoencoder that can effectively learn potential features from the business resource attribute data. Therefore, this paper utilizes the learning model proposed in the literature [17] to train a deep sparse autoencoder. In the training algorithm, the first hidden layer can be trained using the input data, and then the output obtained from the first hidden layer can be used to train the second hidden layer, and so on [18]. A is the input data of the deep sparse autoencoder. The latent features X' of A can be represented as follows:

$$X' = \begin{matrix} X'_1 \\ \vdots \\ X'_i \\ \vdots \\ X'_n \end{matrix} \begin{bmatrix} x'_{11} & \cdots & x'_{1k} & \cdots & x'_{1\breve{u}} \\ \vdots & \ddots & \vdots & \ddots & \vdots \\ x'_{i1} & \cdots & x'_{ik} & \cdots & x'_{i\breve{u}} \\ \vdots & \ddots & \vdots & \ddots & \vdots \\ x'_{n1} & \cdots & x'_{nk} & \cdots & x'_{n\breve{u}} \end{bmatrix} \tag{8}$$

where X'_i are the latent features for the ith business resource, x'_{ik} represents the kth latent feature of X'_i, and $\breve{u}$ implies the number of latent features where $\breve{u} \ll p$.

Based on the above, we use cosine similarity to calculate the similarity between the ith and jth business resources in X'. Cosine similarity measures the angle between the corresponding vectors of the ith and jth business resources in the vector space. The value of cosine similarity ranges from -1 to 1, where a value of 1 signifies complete similarity, 0 indicates no similarity, and -1 denotes complete opposition. The similarity is calculated as follows:

$$\text{sim}(i,j)^{SMBRA} = \frac{\sum_{k=1}^{\breve{u}} x'_{ik} \times x'_{jk}}{\sqrt{\sum_{k=1}^{\breve{u}} (x'_{ik})^2}\sqrt{\sum_{k=1}^{\breve{u}} \left(x'_{jk}\right)^2}} \tag{9}$$

where $\text{sim}(i,j)^{SMBRA}$ is the similarity between the ith business resource and the jth business resource.

2.1.3. Hybrid Difference-Based Similarity Measure

To improve the efficiency of the similarity measurement in B, we use the hybrid difference-based similarity measure (HDSM) proposed by reference [14]. Suppose $B = \{Y_1, Y_2, \cdots, Y_i,$

$\cdots, Y_j, \cdots, Y_n\}$, where $Y_i = (y'_{i1}, y'_{i2}, \ldots, y'_{iu})$ and $Y_j = \left(y'_{j1}, y'_{j2}, \ldots, y'_{ju}\right)$, respectively, in which some y'_{ik} may be missing. The HDSM can be formulated as follows:

$$\text{sim}(i,j)^{HDSM} = 1 - \frac{R_i R_j + 1}{G} \tag{10}$$

where $R_i(R_j)$ is the sum of the non-missing values $y'_{ik}\left(y'_{jk}\right)$ of $Y_i(Y_j)$, and the corresponding $y'_{jk}(y'_{ik})$ represent the missing values. G is the product of the two sums of the non-missing values for both Y_i and Y_j:

$$R_i = \sum_{\substack{y'_{ik}\ \text{non-missing} \\ y'_{jk}\ \text{missing}}} y'_{ik} = \sum_{k \in I_i \backslash I_j} y'_{ik} \tag{11}$$

$$R_j = \sum_{\substack{y'_{jk}\ \text{non-missing} \\ y'_{ik}\ \text{missing}}} y'_{jk} = \sum_{k \in I_j \backslash I_i} y'_{jk} \tag{12}$$

$$G = \left(\sum_{y'_{ik}\ \text{non-missing}} y'_{ik}\right)\left(\sum_{y'_{jk}\text{non-missing}} y'_{jk}\right) = \left(\sum_{k \in I_i} y'_{ik}\right)\left(\sum_{k \in I_j} y'_{jk}\right) \tag{13}$$

where $I_i(I_j)$ denotes the set of (non-missing) values for the ith business resource (the jth business resource), and '$\backslash$' is the complement operator in the set theory.

2.1.4. Comprehensive Similarity and the Predicted Value

When there are more missing values, we use the HDSM to calculate similarity; when there are fewer missing values, we integrate the SMBRA and the HDSM, to accurately calculate the similarity between business resources. In the case of a few missing values, the algorithm should smoothly transition to using the original data values for the similarity calculation. The sigmoid function is used to conduct the smoothing process, in order to calculate the final similarity. The final similarity calculation is as follows:

$$FS_{ij} = \sigma \cdot \text{sim}(i,j)^{SMBRA} + (1-\sigma) \cdot \text{sim}(i,j)^{HDSM} \tag{14}$$

$$\sigma = 2 \times \left(1 - \frac{1}{1 + \exp(-|I_i|)}\right) \tag{15}$$

where σ is the sigmoid function.

The final similarity is utilized to establish the nearest neighbor set of the target business resource by selecting the business resources with the highest similarity values. These nearest neighbors are used to predict the value of item k for the ith business resource by Equation (16):

$$IR_{ik} = \frac{\sum_{j \in N_i} FS_{ij} \times y'_{ik}}{\sum_{j \in N_i} FS_{ij}} \tag{16}$$

where N_i is the nearest neighbors set of the ith business resource and IR_{ik} denotes the predicted value of the ith business resource on item k. The predicted value IR_{ik} is used to fill in the missing value for the ith business resource on item k.

2.2. *Constructing a Satisfaction Evaluation Index System*

The evaluation indices of satisfaction are important for BMBR. We carefully analyze the demander's requirements and the supplier's preferences, and we then construct a satisfaction evaluation index system.

2.2.1. Matching Analysis Based on Business Resource Demanders

Business resource demander-based matching aims to find the optimal business resources that meet the business requirements of the demander from a huge amount of information resources [2]. On the third-party cloud platform, it is influenced by several factors [19]. These factors include the quality, price, and timeliness of the resources, as well as the service capability, fulfillment capability, and responsiveness of the supplier. In summary, the satisfaction evaluation indices of the demander are shown in Table 1.

Table 1. Satisfaction evaluation index system based on business resources demanders.

Index	Index Value	Index Description	Index Nature
Quality (ra_1)	rv_1	The quality of the business resources.	Quantitative Positive
Price (ra_2)	rv_2	The price of the business resources.	Quantitative Reverse
Timeliness (ra_3)	rv_3	The timeliness with which the suppliers provide the business resources.	Quantitative Reverse
Service capability (ra_4)	rv_4	The after-sales service capability of the suppliers.	Quantitative Positive
Fulfillment Capability (ra_5)	rv_5	The supplier's ability to perform the contract.	Qualitative Positive
Responsiveness (ra_6)	rv_6	The supplier's responsiveness to the business resource needs.	Qualitative Positive

In Table 1, $rv_1, rv_2, rv_3, rv_4, rv_5$, and rv_6 indicate the evaluation index values. They are as follows:

$$rv_1 = 1 - \frac{N_r}{N_s} \tag{17}$$

$$rv_2 = P_r + C_c \tag{18}$$

$$rv_3 = T_r + T_t \tag{19}$$

$$rv_4 = S_o + (1 - S_c) \tag{20}$$

In Equation (17), rv_1 represents the value of ra_1, N_s is the total sales volume of the business resources, and N_r is the return quantity. In Equation (18), rv_2 denotes the value of ra_2, P_r is the price of the business resources, and C_c is the collaboration cost. In Equation (19), rv_3 denotes the value of ra_3, T_r is the response time, and T_t is the delivery time. In Equation (20), rv_4 denotes the value of ra_4, S_o indicates an on-time delivery rate for the business resources, S_c indicates the complaint rate of the business resources, rv_5 denotes the value of ra_5, and rv_6 is the value of ra_6. They are determined qualitatively by the demanders.

2.2.2. Matching Analysis Based on Business Resource Suppliers

Business resource supplier-based matching aims to select the best demander that meets the supplier's preference from the demanders [2]. The satisfaction evaluation indices of the supplier are shown in Table 2:

Table 2. Satisfaction evaluation index system based on business resource suppliers.

Index	Index Value	Index Description	Index Nature
Reputation (ca_1)	cv_1	The corporate reputation of the demander.	Qualitative Positive
Payment speed (ca_2)	cv_2	The speed at which the demander pays.	Qualitative Positive
Collaboration potential (ca_3)	cv_3	The long-term cooperation capacity of the demander.	Qualitative Positive

In Table 2, cv_1, cv_2, and cv_3 indicate the evaluation index values. They are determined qualitatively by the suppliers.

2.3. Normalization of the Satisfaction Evaluation Index Values

In order to eliminate the dimensional and magnitude differences between different indicators, it is necessary to normalize the satisfaction evaluation indicator data [2]. We use the data from B to form the quantified satisfaction evaluation matrices RV and $CV.RV$ is a satisfaction evaluation matrix based on business resource suppliers. RV is shown below:

$$RV = \begin{bmatrix} rv_{11} & \cdots & rv_{1k} & \cdots & rv_{1u} \\ \vdots & \ddots & \vdots & \ddots & \vdots \\ rv_{i1} & \cdots & rv_{ik} & \cdots & rv_{iu} \\ \vdots & \ddots & \vdots & \ddots & \vdots \\ rv_{n1} & \cdots & rv_{nk} & \cdots & rv_{nu} \end{bmatrix} \tag{21}$$

where rv_{ik} represents the kth index value of the ith business resource in the RV matrix. Similarly, $CV \in R^{m\times n}$ is a satisfaction evaluation matrix based on business resource suppliers. Its elements are represented as cv_{ik}, where $1 \le i \le n$ and $1 \le k \le v$; cv_{ik} is the kth index value of the ith business resource in the CV matrix. Since the satisfaction evaluation indices all have different scales, it is necessary to normalize all the index values. Additionally, any contrary negative indicator values are converted to positive indicator values, to address the inconsistency of the index types:

$$dv'_{ik} = \begin{cases} \frac{dv_{ik}-dv_{\min}}{dv_{\max}-dv_{\min}}, & dv_{\max} - dv_{\min} \neq 0 \\ 1 & , dv_{\max} - dv_{\min} = 0 \end{cases} \tag{22}$$

$$dv'_{ik} = \begin{cases} \frac{dv_{\max}-dv_{ik}}{dv_{\max}-dv_{\min}}, & dv_{\max} - dv_{\min} \neq 0 \\ 1 & , dv_{\max} - dv_{\min} = 0 \end{cases} \tag{23}$$

where dv_{ik} is rv_{ik} or cv_{ik}, dv'_{ik} is the normalized value of dv_{ik}, which falls within the range [0, 1]; $dv_{\max}$ is the maximum value in the set $\{dv_{1k}, \ldots, dv_{ik}, \ldots, dv_{nk}\}$; and $dv_{\min}$ is the minimum value in the set $\{dv_{1k}, \ldots, dv_{ik}, \ldots, dv_{nk}\}$.

RV and CV are converted to the corresponding normalized satisfaction evaluation matrices RV' and CV' by Equations (22) and (23). RV' and CV' inherit the same dimensions, and their elements are denoted as rv'_{ik} and cv'_{ik}.

2.4. Determination of Weights

The determination of weights is a crucial step in bilateral matching. In business cooperation, the demands and suppliers of business resources have different preferences for the satisfaction evaluation indices, due to different perspectives of consideration. We use the FAHP to calculate the subjective weights of the evaluation indicators, in order to reflect the demands and preferences of both the demanders and the suppliers. However, using only subjective weights cannot reflect the objective differences in the evaluation indices. In order to more fully reflect the rationality of weighting, we use the EWM to calculate the objective weight of the evaluation indices.

2.4.1. FAHP

The FAHP is a decision analysis method that combines fuzzy theory and the analytic hierarchy process (AHP), which is mainly used to deal with complex decision factors with ambiguity and uncertainty. It is mainly used to evaluate the weight of multi-factor influences, especially when there are subjective judgments and ambiguities between factors. It determines the subjective weight through the following steps:

- Build Fuzzy Complementary Judgment Matrix

Assume that there is a set of relevant factors in the evaluation indicators ra_k $(k = 1,2,\ldots,u)$. Using the 0.1–0.9 scaling method shown in Table 3 for quantitative scaling, the fuzzy complementary judgment matrix $FI = [fi_{kk'}]_{u\times u}$ is obtained. The element of the FI denotes the importance of ra_k compared with $ra_{k'}$, $0 \leq fi_{kk'} \leq 1$ $(1 \leq k \leq k' \leq u)$, $fi_{kk'} + fi_{k'k} = 1$, $fi_{kk} = 0.5$. The FI serves as a crucial instrument for assessing the importance of the factor set. It is constructed by integrating the evaluation results of experts on the significance of each factor within the set of evaluation index factors.

Table 3. 0.1–0.9 scale method and its meaning.

Scale	Meaning of Scale
0.5	ra_k and $ra_{k'}$ are equally important
0.6	ra_k is slightly more important than $ra_{k'}$
0.7	ra_k is generally more important than $ra_{k'}$
0.8	ra_k is much more important than $ra_{k'}$
0.9	ra_k is more important than $ra_{k'}$
0.1, 0.2, 0.3, 0.4	y = 1 − x

- Weight Calculation

According to the opinions of k different experts, n' different fuzzy judgment matrices are constructed, denoted as $FI_1, FI_2, \ldots, FI_{l'}, \ldots, FI_{n'}$. The weight of the kth metric provided by the l'th expert opinion is calculated according to Equation (24):

$$w_k = \frac{\sum_{k'=1}^{u} fi_{kk'} + \frac{u}{2} - 1}{u(u-1)} \tag{24}$$

- Consistency Test

In order to determine whether the weights calculated according to Equation (24) are reasonable, it is necessary to perform a consistency test. The compatibility index between the judgment matrix and the weight matrix is as follows:

$$I(FI, W^*) = \frac{1}{u^2} \sum_{k=1}^{u} \sum_{k'=1}^{u} |fi_{kk'} + w_{k'k} - 1| \tag{25}$$

$$W^* = (w_{kk'})_{u \times u} \tag{26}$$

$$w_{kk'} = w_k / (w_k + w_{k'}) \tag{27}$$

If the value of the compatibility index is less than 0.1, the judgment matrix could be considered to have satisfactory consistency.

- Subjective Empowerment

The subjective weight vector $W^{s_1} = \left(w_1^{s_1}, w_2^{s_1}, \cdots, w_u^{s_1}\right)$ is obtained by combining the opinions of all experts through the maximum characteristic root method. The detailed steps of the maximum characteristic root method are described in the previous literature [20]. Similarly, the subjective weight vector $W^{s_2} = \left(w_1^{s_2}, w_2^{s_2}, \cdots, w_v^{s_2}\right)$ of the satisfaction evaluation indices based on the business resource suppliers is obtained.

2.4.2. EWM

The EWM is one of the classic algorithms for calculating the weight of the indicator [21]. It determines the weight by calculating the information entropy values of each indicator. For an indicator, the bigger the entropy value is, the smaller the degree of discreteness of the indicator is, the smaller the impact of the indicator [22]. The information entropy is calculated by its definition, as follows:

$$E_k = -\frac{1}{\ln n} \cdot \sum_{i=1}^{n} p_{ik} \cdot \log p_{ik} \tag{28}$$

where p_{ik} represents the index of the ith business resource under the kth indicator. And its formula is defined as follows:

$$p_{ik} = \frac{rv'_{ik}}{\sum_{i=1}^{n} rv'_{ik}} \tag{29}$$

The weight of the kth satisfaction evaluation index based on the business resource demanders is as follows:

$$w_k^{d_1} = \frac{1 - E_k}{\sum_{k=1}^{m}(1 - E_k)} \tag{30}$$

Similarly, the weight $w_k^{s_1}$ of the kth evaluation indicators based on the suppliers is obtained.

2.5. Construction and Solution of a Multi-Objective Optimization Model

The purpose of the bilateral matching for business resources is to ensure that both the demander and the provider participants achieve maximum satisfaction. Given the collaboration requirements between the demander and the provider, this paper integrates the synergy effect into a two-sided matching strategy.

2.5.1. Construction of Multi-Objective Optimization Model

Based on the RV' and CV', the supplier's maximum matching satisfaction and the demander's maximum matching satisfaction are as follows:

$$\max SF_1(sr_i) = 1 - \sqrt{\sum_{k=1}^{u}\left(w_k^{d_1} \times rv_k^{*'} - w_k^{s_1} \times rv'_{ik}\right)^2} \tag{31}$$

$$\max SF_2(sr_i) = 1 - \sqrt{\sum_{l=1}^{v}\left(w_l^{s_2} \times cv'_{il} - w_l^{d_2} \times cv_l^{*'}\right)^2} \tag{32}$$

$$\text{s.t. } w_k^{d_1} \geq 0, w_k^{s_1} \geq 0, \sum_{k=1}^{u} w_k^{d_1} = 1, \sum_{k=1}^{u} w_k^{s_1} = 1,$$

$$w_l^{s_2} \geq 0, w_l^{d_2} \geq 0, \sum_{l=1}^{v} w_l^{s_2} = 1, \sum_{l=1}^{v} w_l^{d_2} = 1$$

where sr_i is the ith business resource; $\max SF_1(sr_i)$ represents the maximization of demander satisfaction in business resource matching; $\max SF_2(sr_i)$ denotes the maximization of supplier satisfaction in business resource matching; $rv_k^{*'}$ refers to the normalized input value of the kth satisfaction evaluation index from the demander of business resources; $w_k^{d_1}$ is the subjective weight of $rv_k^{*'}$; $w_k^{s_1}$ is the objective weight of rv'_{ik}; $cv_l^{*'}$ is the normalized input value of the kth satisfaction evaluation index from the supplier of business resources; $w_l^{s_2}$ is the objective weight of cv'_{il}; $w_l^{d_2}$ is the subjective weight of $cv_l^{*'}$. We utilize the above FAHP to determine the subjective weight. Additionally, we employ the above EWM to calculate the objective weight.

In order to help enterprises accurately obtain high-quality and valuable business resources on the third-party cloud platform, it is necessary to consider the collaboration requirements between business resource demanders and suppliers [12,23]. The better the synergy between business resource demander u and supplier v, the higher the likelihood of u choosing the ith business resource provided by v. Therefore, in this study, the synergy satisfaction of u choosing i is measured by the degree of synergy effect between u and v. The synergy effect is mainly expressed in three aspects: co-community relationship, transaction performance, and business resource-sharing ability.

Communities include various cloud platforms, alliances, and online groups [24]. The strength of the common community relationship QS depends on the number of common communities in which both u and v participate:

$$QS = \frac{|NR_u \cap NR_v|}{|NR_u \cup NR_v|} \quad (33)$$

where $NS_u(NR_v)$ is a set of communities in which $u(v)$ participates.

Transaction performance can reduce transaction costs and increase service efficiency [25]. The interactive transaction strength CS is dependent on the total transaction volume TA in all periods and the cooperation activities CA in the current period. CS can be calculated as follows:

$$CS = \eta_1 \frac{\sum_{k=1}^{m} CT_{uv}^{k} \times N_{uv}^{k}}{\max_{f,v} \sum_{k=1}^{m} CT_{fv}^{k} \times N_{fv}^{k}} + \eta_2 \frac{CT_{uv}^{\text{now}}}{\max_{f,v}^{m} \sum_{k=1}^{m} CT_{uv}^{\text{now}}}, f = 1, 2, \ldots, n \quad (34)$$

where CT_{uv}^{k} and N_{uv}^{k} are the number and the single transaction volume of the transactions in the kth period, respectively; f denotes the supplier corresponding to the business resource; CT_{uv}^{now} is the transaction volume between u and v in the current period; and η_1 and η_2 indicate the relevant criteria weights.

Business resource sharing ability means the level of information sharing. It is shown as follows:

$$IS = \frac{Nt_{uv}}{Pt} \quad (35)$$

where IS denotes business resource sharing capacity; Nt_{uv} represents the number of times u uses the business resources provided by v. Pt is a fixed period.

In conclusion, the synergy satisfaction is shown below:

$$SF_3(sr_i) = \delta_1 QS'_{uv} + \delta_2 CS'_{uv} + \delta_3 IS'_u \quad (36)$$

where $QS'_{uv}, CS'_{uv}, IS'_u$ are normalized numbers using Equation (22), and $\delta_1, \delta_2, \delta_3$ denote the weights of $QS'_{uv}, CS'_{uv}, IS'_u$ respectively.

2.5.2. Solution of Multi-Objective Matching Model

For resolving this multi-objective optimization model, the linear weighting method is exploited, to convert the multi-objective model into a single-objective optimization model [25]. This is shown as Equation (37):

$$\begin{aligned} \max SF(sr_i) &= \theta_1 \times SF_1(sr_i) + \theta_2 \times SF_2(sr_i) + \theta_3 \times SF_3(sr_i) \\ \text{s.t. } &\theta_1 \geq 0, \theta_2 \geq 0, \theta_3 \geq 0, \\ &\theta_1 + \theta_2 + \theta_3 = 1 \end{aligned} \quad (37)$$

where θ_1, θ_2, θ_3 are the weights of $SF_1(sr_i)$, $SF_2(sr_i)$, $SF_3(sr_i)$, respectively. By default, $\theta_1 = \theta_2 = \theta_3 = 1/3$. However, in the actual business environment, the values of θ_1, θ_2, and θ_3 can be determined based on the specific requirements of both the demander and the supplier.

3. Example Application and Comparison Analysis

For this section, an example of bilateral matching on the "ASP/SaaS-based manufacturing value chain collaboration platform" was applied, to verify the effectiveness of the proposed method. Furthermore, to evaluate the performance, we compared it with other state-of-the-art matching methods.

To implement the proposed method, we utilized the Python 3.9 programming language in Anaconda software version 2021. We obtained 300,000 customer transaction data of parts agents from the ASP/SaaS-based manufacturing industry value chain collaboration platform for 2019–2021 [2,26]. We extracted data resources related to auto parts from the data space of the platform, to form six datasets [2]. The first dataset, consisting of "Engine Parts", was called dataset_1. The second dataset, consisting of "Clutch and Transmission Parts", was called dataset_2. The third dataset, consisting of "Hydraulic Lift

Parts", was called dataset_3. The fourth dataset, consisting of "Body and Interior / Exterior Parts", was called dataset_4. The fifth dataset, consisting of "Electrical Parts", was called dataset_5. The sixth dataset, consisting of "Brake Parts", was called dataset_6. We set the following core parameters for the TextCNN: the convolution sizes were 2, 3, and 4; the number of filters was 100; the dropout rate was 0.5; and the batch size was 128. The feature dimension of the word was 100, the window size was 5, and the minimum word frequency for truncation was 5.

3.1. Example Application

The paper employed the business resources of engine parts as a case study to validate the proposed method. Specifically, we randomly selected 12,000 data resources related to auto parts from dataset_1, which constituted matrix B, as presented in Table 4. To process the textual data in Table 4, we utilized the textCNN for quantifying the text information. Subsequently, we presented the resulting quantized data in the same table. For Table 4, we applied the CSKI approach to addressing missing values, which led to the generation of an updated Table 4 displaying the results obtained after filling in the missing values.

Table 4. Parts business resource.

Business Resource	Return Quantity	Return Quantity (after Filling)	Total Volume sales	Total Volume Sales (after Filling)	...	Response Speed	Response Speed (Quantified Value)	...
rs_1	599	599		19,484	...	Responded more promptly...	5	...
rs_2	192	192	15,500	15,500	...	The company responded quickly ...	4	...
...	...	...	...	...	...	...	...	...
rs_{1199}	525	525	10,014	10,014	...	Had a faster response time ...	4	...
rs_{1200}		328	16,561	16,561	...	The response speed was general...	3	...

The paper took the business data resource requirements of an automobile after-sales service enterprise ds_1 for a certain engine part as an example, to verify the feasibility and effectiveness of the proposed method. Through preliminary screening, eight business resources from different suppliers were identified: namely, $rs_1, rs_2, rs_3, rs_4, rs_5, rs_6, rs_7, rs_8$. Subsequently, bilateral matching of business resources was realized. The data from Table 4 was utilized to construct satisfaction evaluation matrices RV and CV in Table 5, based on the satisfaction evaluation index system. Subsequently, normalized satisfaction matrices, denoted as RV' and CV', were derived from Table 5, using Equations (22) and (23). These normalized matrices are presented in Table 6.

Table 5. Satisfaction matrices of business resources.

	RV						CV		
Business resource	rv_1	rv_2	rv_3	rv_4	rv_5	rv_6	cv_1	cv_2	cv_3
rs_1	0.9952	37.68	10.7	1.7	2	4	4	4	5
rs_2	0.9847	34.2	2.4	1.71	3	4	3	1	4
rs_3	0.9111	33.6	31.5	1.6	1	1	1	4	2
rs_4	0.9575	45.88	9.4	1.71	2	2	5	3	3
rs_5	0.9910	39.4	23.4	1.79	1	3	4	2	4
rs_6	0.9886	40.61	4.5	1.64	2	3	5	5	1
rs_7	0.9834	39.6	20.7	1.71	2	3	2	4	5
rs_8	0.9916	39.83	17.4	1.72	5	3	5	3	4
Matching request	rv_1^*	rv_2^*	rv_3^*	rv_4^*	rv_5^*	rv_6^*	cv_1^*	cv_2^*	cv_3^*
ds_1	0.98	35	10	1.8	4	5	4	5	3

Table 6. Normalized satisfaction matrices of business resources.

	RV						*CV*		
Business resource	rv'_1	rv'_2	rv'_3	rv'_4	rv'_5	rv'_6	cv'_1	cv'_2	cv'_3
rs_1	1	0.6393	0.7148	0.5	0.25	0.75	0.75	0.75	1
rs_2	0.8751	0.9111	1	0.55	0.5	0.75	0.5	0	0.75
rs_3	0	1	0	0	0	0	0	0.75	0.25
rs_4	0.5517	0	0.7595	0.55	0.25	0.25	1	0.5	0.5
rs_5	0.9501	0.5055	0.2784	0.95	0	0.5	0.75	0.25	0.75
rs_6	0.9215	0.4111	0.9278	0.2	0.25	0.5	1	1	0
rs_7	0.8597	0.4899	0.3711	0.55	0.25	0.5	0.25	0.75	1
rs_8	0.9572	0.4719	0.4845	0.6	1	0.5	1	0.5	0.75
Matching request	$rv_1^{*'}$	$rv_2^{*'}$	$rv_3^{*'}$	$rv_4^{*'}$	$rv_5^{*'}$	$rv_6^{*'}$	$cv_1^{*'}$	$cv_2^{*'}$	$cv_3^{*'}$
ds_1	0.8193	0.8487	0.7388	1	0.75	1	0.75	1	0.5

The data from Table 4 were used in Equations (33)–(35) to calculate QS', CS', IS'. The weight coefficients were set as $\delta_1 = \delta_2 = \delta_3 = 1/3$ for solving the mathematical optimization model [25]. These weights and data were then applied in Equation (36) to calculate SF_3. The corresponding results are presented in Table 7.

Table 7. Matching satisfaction in different dimensions.

Business Resource	QS'	CS'	IS'	SF_3	SF_1	SF_2	SF
rs_1	0.8649	0.8134	0.9418	0.8734	0.8614	0.8239	0.8529
rs_2	0.7268	0.7867	0.9101	0.8079	0.8693	0.6442	0.7738
rs_3	0.7839	0.6610	0.8466	0.7638	0.6761	0.7296	0.7232
rs_4	0.7162	0.9256	0.9524	0.8647	0.7716	0.8263	0.8209
rs_5	0.7379	0.8205	0.9312	0.8299	0.8085	0.7404	0.7929
rs_6	0.8400	0.7682	0.8677	0.8253	0.8003	0.8171	0.8143
rs_7	0.7519	0.8571	0.9471	0.8520	0.8267	0.7572	0.8120
rs_8	0.7745	0.7837	0.9418	0.8333	0.7453	0.8092	0.7959

The subjective weights of the evaluation indices $ra_1 - ra_6$ were calculated by the FAHP. They were $w_1^{d_1} = 0.1911, w_2^{d_1} = 0.1667, w_3^{d_1} = 0.1581, w_4^{d_1} = 0.1734, w_5^{d_1} = 0.1644$, and $w_6^{d_1} = 0.1463$. The objective weights of the evaluation indices $ra_1 - ra_6$ were calculated by the EWM. They were $w_1^{s_1} = 0.1011, w_2^{s_1} = 0.1312, w_3^{s_1} = 0.1472, w_4^{s_1} = 0.1534$, $w_5^{s_1} = 0.3249$, and $w_6^{s_1} = 0.1422$. The subjective weights of the evaluation indices $ca_1 - ca_3$ were calculated by the FAHP. They were $w_1^{d_2} = 0.3172, w_2^{d_2} = 0.3538$, and $w_3^{d_2} = 0.329$. The objective weights of the evaluation indices $ca_1 - ca_3$ were calculated by the EWM. They were $w_1^{s_2} = 0.3289, w_2^{s_2} = 0.3356$, and $w_3^{s_2} = 0.3355$. The weights mentioned above, along with the data from Tables 6 and 7, were used in Equations (31), (32) and (37) to calculate SF_1, SF_2, and SF. The detailed results can be found in Figure 2. After performing descending sorting on the satisfaction values corresponding to different dimensions, the sorting results of SF_1, SF_2, and SF were obtained. The sorting result of SF_1 was $rs_2 > rs_1 > rs_7 > rs_5 > rs_6 > rs_4 > rs_8 > rs_3$. The sorting result of SF_2 was $rs_4 > rs_1 > rs_6 > rs_8 > rs_7 > rs_5 > rs_3 > rs_2$. The sorting result of SF was $rs_1 > rs_4 > rs_6 > rs_7 > rs_8 > rs_5 > rs_2 > rs_3$.

In Figure 2, it can be observed that in the SF_1 ranking, rs_2 had the highest satisfaction, indicating that this resource was most suitable for meeting the demander's requirements. In the SF_2 ranking, rs_4 had the highest satisfaction, indicating that this resource best met the supplier's requirements. According to the SF ranking, it is evident that rs_1 had the highest satisfaction, ranking second in both SF_1 and SF_2. And rs_1's collaborative satisfaction value was significantly better than others. This indicates that BMBR not only meets the requirements of the supplier and demander very well, but also takes into account the synergy effects.

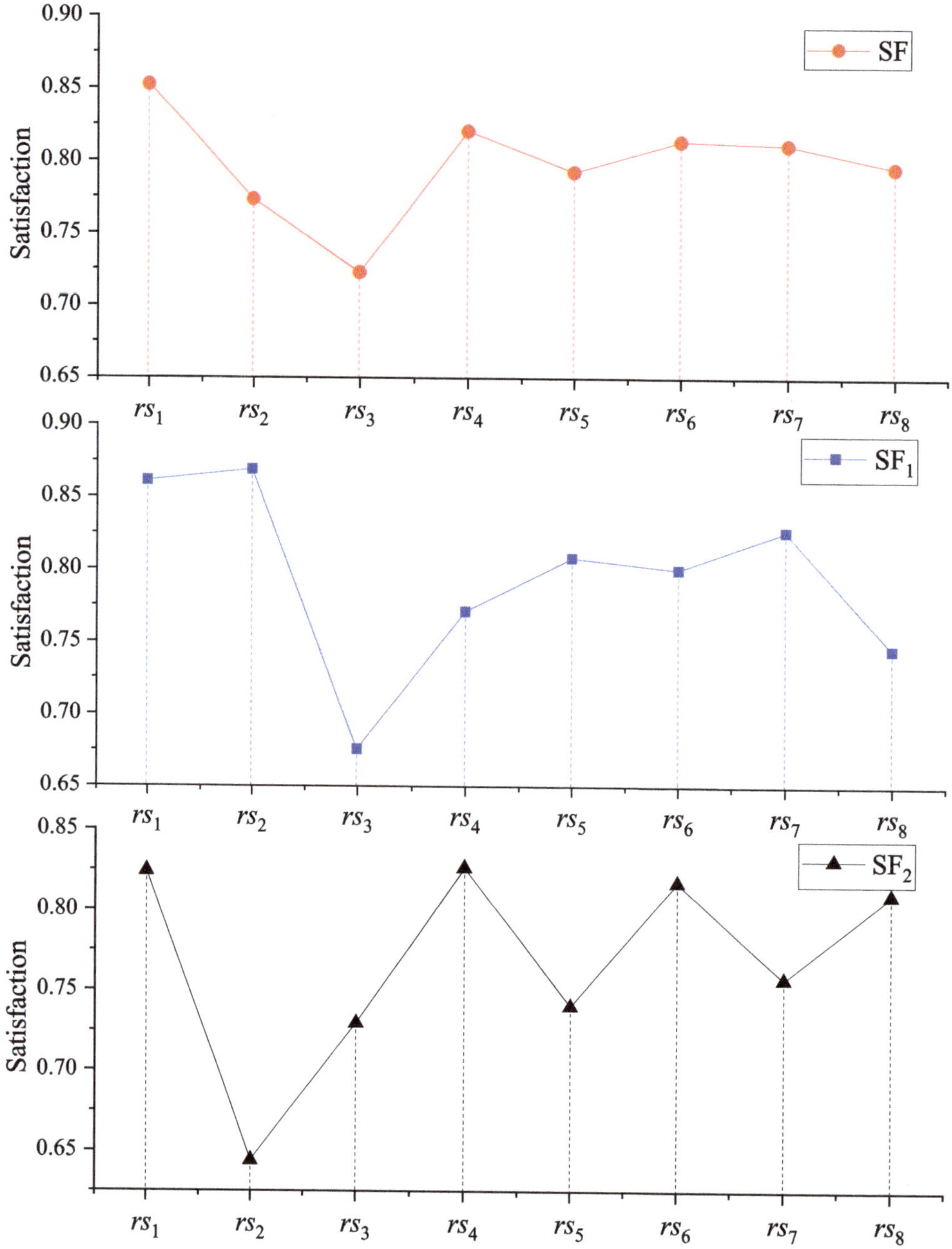

Figure 2. The results of SF_1, SF_2, and SF.

3.2. Evaluation Indicators and Comparison Analysis

3.2.1. Evaluation Indicators

To validate the effectiveness of BMBR, we evaluated the performance of the method with accuracy (ACC) and the F1 measure. Accuracy is the proportion of the number of samples that the method predicts correctly over the total number of samples. It can be calculated as

$$F_{ACC} = \frac{TP + TN}{TP + TN + FP + FN} \tag{38}$$

where F_{ACC} indicates the ACC value; TP is the number of positive samples judged as positive; TN is the number of negative samples judged as negative; FP is the number of negative samples judged as positive; and FN is the number of positive samples judged as negative [27]. Positive samples are business resources that are actually used by the demander. Negative samples are business resources that are not used by the demander. The larger the ACC value is, the better the performance of the match is.

The F_1 measure reflects the overall ability of bilateral matching. A higher F_1 value indicates better quality of matching. F_1 can be calculated as

$$F_1 = \frac{2PR}{P + R} = \frac{2TP}{2TP + FP + FN} \tag{39}$$

$$P = \frac{TP}{TP + FP}, \quad R = \frac{TP}{TP + FN} \tag{40}$$

where P represents Precision and R represents Recall.

3.2.2. Comparison Analysis

This paper conducted experiments on six datasets, to evaluate the performance of the proposed method compared with other matching methods. The abbreviations and full terms of the other matching methods are detailed in Table 8.

Table 8. Abbreviations and full terms.

Abbreviation	Full Term
TAMBM [5]	task assignment method based on bilateral matching
BRBMM [2]	business resource bilateral matching model
TMM [10]	two-sided matching model
IGARSM [28]	improved genetic algorithm for resource service matching
IFTMM [11]	intuitionistic fuzzy two-sided matching model
BMBR-SS	BMBR without synergy satisfaction
BMBR-SSC	BMBR without synergy satisfaction and CSKI
BMBR-SSCK	BMBR-SSC with k-nearest neighbor
BMBR-SSCE	BMBR-SSC with expectation maximization
BMBR-SSCM	BMBR-SSC with multiple imputation
BMBR-SSCR	BMBR-SSC with regression model

To validate the effectiveness of BMBR, we compared BMBR with BMBR-SS, BMBR-SSC, BMBR-SSCK, BMBR-SSCE, BMBR-SSCM, and BMBR-SSCR. The comparison result of the experiment is detailed in Figure 3. As shown in Figure 3, the ACC values of BMBR-SS were higher than BMBR-SSC, BMBR-SSCK, BMBR-SSCE, BMBR-SSCM, and BMBR-SSCR on all six datasets. This indicates that CSKI in BMBR effectively filled in missing values, thereby improving the matching accuracy of BMBR. Additionally, BMBR had a higher ACC value than BMBR-SS, indicating that incorporating synergy effects into the matching method improved the matching performance.

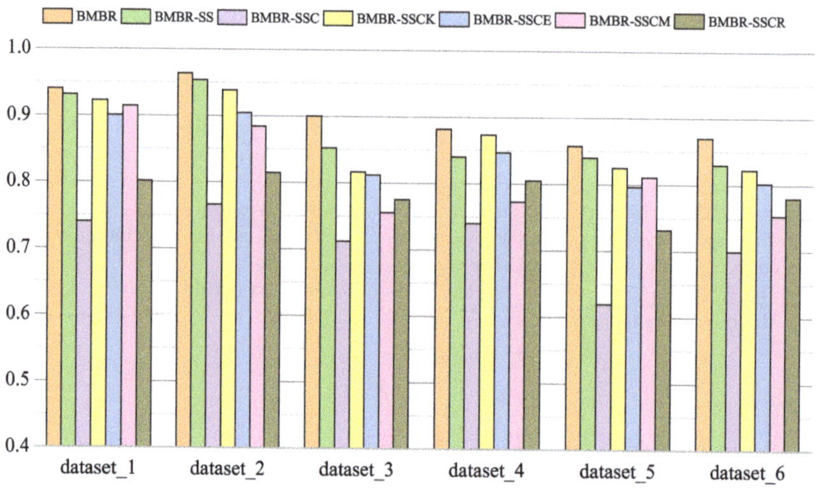

Figure 3. Comparison of different algorithms on different datasets.

To further validate the performance of the proposed method, we compared BMBR with TAMBM, BRBMM, TMM, IGARSM, and IFTMM on two datasets (dataset_2 and dataset_6). As shown in Figure 4, the F_1 value gradually decreased as the number of business resources increased. And it is easy to see that the F_1 value of BMBR was significantly higher than that of TAMBM, BRBMM, TMM, and IFTMM on two datasets. This indicates that the matching quality of BMBR is superior to the other five methods. And this indicates that BMBR plays a positive role in improving matching quality.

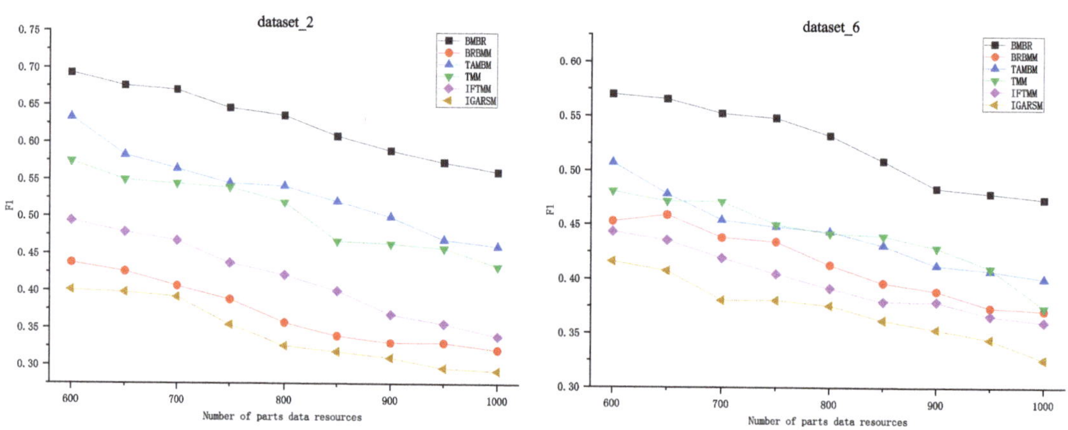

Figure 4. Comparative analysis of business resource matching quality.

4. Conclusions

On the third-party cloud platform, to help enterprises quickly and accurately obtain high-quality valuable business resources from the complex and massive information resources, we propose a bilateral matching method for business resources based on synergy effects and incomplete data. This method firstly applies CSKI, to address the issue of missing values. Then, it constructs a satisfaction evaluation index system for both supplier and demander, and the weights of the satisfaction evaluation indices are determined based on the FAHP and the EWM. Finally, a bilateral matching model of the business resources is constructed with the objectives of maximizing the matching satisfaction of both the supplier and the demander, as well as achieving the synergy effect. The rationality and effectiveness of the proposed model were validated through experimental analysis, using the engine parts data resource in the automobile after-sales service industry as an example. The superiority effectiveness proposed was verified by comparing with other methods.

Although this research work has some advantages in bilateral matching, there are still some limitations. For example, the proposed method lacks the ability to adjust in real time for dynamic changes of business resources on the third-party cloud platform. In our future work, we will introduce adaptive algorithms, to make the matching method dynamically adaptable, to respond to data changes and user demands in real time. In addition, we will apply this method to other fields, to verify the applicability of the proposed method.

Author Contributions: Conceptualization, S.W.; methodology, S.W. and Y.Y.; validation, S.W.; data curation, S.W. and L.S.; writing—original draft preparation, S.W.; writing—review and editing, S.W., L.S., and Y.Y. All authors have read and agreed to the published version of the manuscript.

Funding: This research received no external funding.

Institutional Review Board Statement: Not applicable.

Data Availability Statement: The data presented in this study are available upon request from the corresponding author. The data are not publicly available, due to copyright.

Acknowledgments: Our thanks to the editorial team and all the anonymous reviewers who helped us improve the quality of this paper.

Conflicts of Interest: The authors declare no conflicts of interest.

References

1. Yu, Y.; Sun, L.; Wang, S. Tenant-centric attribute semantic access control policy model for the cloud service platform. *J. Sens.* **2022**, *2022*, 3314881. [CrossRef]
2. Yu, Y.; Sun, L.F.; Ren, C.H.; Han, M. Bilateral matching model of business resources for multi-service value chain. *Comput. Integr. Manuf. Syst.* **2021**, *27*, 1397–1409.
3. Lu, L.; Yu, J.; Zhu, Y.; Li, M. A double auction mechanism to bridge users' task requirements and providers' resources in two-sided cloud markets. *IEEE Trans. Parallel Distrib. Syst.* **2017**, *29*, 720–733. [CrossRef]
4. Li, B.; Yang, Y.; Su, J.; Zhang, N.; Wang, S. Two-sided matching model for complex product manufacturing tasks based on dual hesitant fuzzy preference information. *Knowl.-Based Syst.* **2019**, *186*, 104989. [CrossRef]
5. Liu, D.T.; Wu, D.L.; Huang, K.Z. An intelligent optimal assignment method of collaborative design tasks. In Proceedings of the Eighth ASIA International Symposium on Mechatronics, Singapore, 13 July 2022; pp. 438–448.
6. Zhao, J.; Wang, X. Two-sided matching model of cloud service based on QoS in cloud manufacturing environment. *Comput. Integr. Manuf. Syst.* **2016**, *22*, 104–112.
7. Fang, Z.; Hu, Q.; Sun, H.; Chen, G.; Qi, J. Research on intelligent cloud manufacturing resource adaptation methodology based on reinforcement learning. In Proceedings of the International Conference on Artificial Intelligence and Security, Cham, Switzerland, 9 July 2021; pp. 155–166.
8. Xue, X.; Wang, S.; Zhang, L.J.; Feng, Z.Y. Evaluating of dynamic service matching strategy for social manufacturing in cloud environment. *Future Gener. Comput. Syst.* **2019**, *91*, 311–326. [CrossRef]
9. Xiao, Y.; Li, C.; Song, L.; Yang, J.; Su, J. A multidimensional information fusion-based matching decision method for manufacturing service resource. *IEEE Access* **2021**, *9*, 39839–39851. [CrossRef]
10. Wang, Z.; Li, Y.; Gu, F.; Guo, J.; Wu, X. Two-sided matching and strategic selection on freight resource sharing platforms. *Phys. A Stat. Mech. Its Appl.* **2020**, *559*, 1–18. [CrossRef]
11. Yu, D.; Xu, Z. Intuitionistic fuzzy two-sided matching model and its application to personnel-position matching problems. *J. Oper. Res. Soc.* **2020**, *71*, 312–321. [CrossRef]
12. Azevedo, E.M.; Leshno, J.D. A supply and demand framework for two-sided matching markets. *J. Political Econ.* **2016**, *124*, 1235–1268. [CrossRef]
13. Li, X.; Chen, P.; Yu, X.; Jiang, N. Analysis of the relationship between motor imagery and age-related fatigue for CNN classification of the EEG data. *Front. Aging Neurosci.* **2022**, *14*, 909571. [CrossRef] [PubMed]
14. Amer, A.A.; Abdalla, H.I.; Nguyen, L. Enhancing recommendation systems performance using highly-effective similarity measures. *Knowl.-Based Syst.* **2021**, *217*, 1–19. [CrossRef]
15. Moradi, P.; Ahmadian, S. A reliability-based recommendation method to improve trust-aware recommender systems. *Expert Syst. Appl.* **2015**, *42*, 7386–7398. [CrossRef]

16. Ahmadian, M.; Ahmadi, M.; Ahmadian, S. A reliable deep representation learning to improve trust-aware recommendation systems. *Expert Syst. Appl.* **2022**, *197*, 116697 . [CrossRef]
17. Hinton, G.E.; Salakhutdinov, R.R. Reducing the dimensionality of data with neural networks. *Science* **2006**, *313*, 504–507. [CrossRef]
18. Ahmadian, S.; Ahmadian, M.; Jalili, M. A deep learning based trust-and tag-aware recommender system. *Neurocomputing* **2022**, *488*, 557–571. [CrossRef]
19. Adjei, J.K.; Adams, S.; Mamattah, L. Cloud computing adoption in Ghana; accounting for institutional factors. *Technol. Soc.* **2021**, *65*, 101583. [CrossRef]
20. Zhou, B.; Sun, B.; Zang, T.; Cai, Y.; Wu, J.; Luo, H. Security risk assessment approach for distribution network cyber physical systems considering cyber attack vulnerabilities. *Entropy* **2022**, *25*, 47. [CrossRef]
21. Fang, Z. Improved KNN algorithm with information entropy for the diagnosis of Parkinson's disease. In Proceedings of the International Conference on Machine Learning and Knowledge Engineering, Guilin, China, 25–27 February 2022; pp. 98–101.
22. Isik, F. An entropy-based approach for measuring complexity in supply chains. *Int. J. Prod. Res.* **2010**, *485*, 3681–3696. [CrossRef]
23. Jiang, P.; Guo, S.; Du, B.; Guo, J. Two-sided matching decision-making model for complex product system based on life-cycle sustainability assessment. *Expert Syst. Appl.* **2022**, *208*, 118184. [CrossRef]
24. Ren, M.; Ren, L.; Jain, H. Manufacturing service composition model based on synergy effect: A social network analysis approach. *Appl. Soft Comput.* **2018**, *70*, 228–300. [CrossRef]
25. Liu, X.; Zhang, L.; Deng, Q.; Li, M.; Jiang, C. Bilateral matching for collaborative remanufacturing services based on multi-attribute preferences and mutual interactions. *J. Intell. Manuf.* **2024**, *35*, 1353–1372. [CrossRef]
26. ASP/SaaS-Based Manufacturing Industry Value Chain Collaboration Platform. Available online: http://www.autosaas.cn/ (accessed on 5 December 2023).
27. Zhao, H.; Zhang, X.; Xu, Y.; Gao, L.; Ma, Z.; Sun, Y.; Wang, W. Predicting the risk of hypertension based on several easy-to-collect risk factors: A machine learning method. *Front. Public Health* **2021**, *9*, 619429. [CrossRef] [PubMed]
28. Zhang, M.; Li, C.; Shang, Y.; Li, C. Research on resource service matching in cloud manufacturing. *Manuf. Lett.* **2018**, *15*, 50–54. [CrossRef]

entropy

Article

Urban Flood Resilience Evaluation Based on Heterogeneous Data and Group Decision-Making

Xiang He [1], Yanzhu Hu [1,*], Xiaojun Yang [2], Song Wang [1] and Yingjian Wang [1]

1 School of Intelligent Engineering and Automation, Beijing University of Posts and Telecommunications, Beijing 100876, China; hexiang6@bupt.edu.cn (X.H.); wongsangwongsang@163.com (S.W.); wangyingjian@bupt.edu.cn (Y.W.)
2 Unit 63892 of PLA, Luoyang 471000, China; yangxiaojun2007@gmail.com
* Correspondence: bupt_automation_safety_yzhu@bupt.edu.cn

Abstract: In recent years, urban floods have occurred frequently in China. Therefore, there is an urgent need to strengthen urban flood resilience. This paper proposed a hybrid multi-criteria group decision-making method to assess urban flood resilience based on heterogeneous data, group decision-making methodologies, the pressure-state–response model, and social–economic–natural complex ecosystem theory (PSR-SENCE model). A qualitative and quantitative indicator system is formulated using the PSR-SENCE model. Additionally, a new weighting method for indicators, called the synthesis weighting-group analytic hierarchy process (SW-GAHP), is proposed by considering both intrapersonal consistency and interpersonal consistency of decision-makers. Furthermore, an extensional group decision-making technology (EGDMT) based on heterogeneous data is proposed to evaluate qualitative indicators. The flexible parameterized mapping function (FPMF) is introduced for the evaluation of quantitative indicators. The normal cloud model is employed to handle various uncertainties associated with heterogeneous data. The evaluations for Beijing from 2017 to 2021 reveal a consistent annual improvement in urban flood resilience, with a 14.1% increase. Subsequently, optimization recommendations are presented not only for favorable indicators such as regional economic status, drainability, and public transportation service capacity but also for unfavorable indicators like flood risk and population density. This provides a theoretical foundation and a guide for making decisions about the improvement of urban flood resilience. Finally, our proposed method shows superiority and robustness through comparative and sensitivity analyses.

Keywords: urban flood resilience; group decision-making; heterogeneous data; indicator system; normal cloud model

1. Introduction

Since the onset of the Industrial Revolution, there has been a significant increase in humanity's impact on the natural environment. This has resulted in climate change and environmental degradation, posing a threat to the delicate global ecological balance and the survival of mankind. The UN Office for Disaster Risk Reduction (UNDRR) released the Global Assessment Report (GAR 2023), which emphasizes how critical it is to build resilience to face and overcome adversity. Almost 3000 natural disasters occurred worldwide between 2021 and 2023. Of these, meteorological disasters constituted the majority, accounting for over 60%. The relentless recurrence of events like heavy rains, floods, hurricanes, and tornadoes has resulted in significant loss of life, extensive property damage, and societal instability.

Scholars have given the idea of resilient cities much attention. In 2013, the Urban Resilience Framework was unveiled by the Rockefeller Foundation as part of the "100 Resilient Cities" initiative, which chose 100 communities globally for practical application and study [1]. As a result, the concept of "urban flood resilience" was created. Currently, urban flood resilience has become a subject of extensive research. Orense et al. [2] developed a coastal community resilience evaluation system from a risk perspective, applying the analytic hierarchy process (AHP) and Delphi technique for vulnerability assessment and management. Kotzee et al. [3] introduced a socioecological index and applied it to three flood-prone cities in South Africa, choosing 24 social and ecological factors to evaluate the regional distribution of flood impacts. Dong and his colleagues [4] analyzed flood control strategies for cattle farms in Heilongjiang Province using 15 factors to characterize the natural environment, culture, community, and economy.

Although previous studies have greatly advanced the assessment of urban flood resilience, these studies only considered the ability to withstand flood disasters in urban flood resilience. As a result, the identification of weak points in the resilience process and a greater comprehension of the theories and mechanisms behind urban resilience are overlooked. Additionally, many evaluation methods predominantly focus on qualitative discussions, with only a few combining both subjective and objective elements.

In light of these considerations, this research endeavors to analyze the resilience process and its characteristics. To identify relevant factors, a conceptual framework known as the PSR-SENCE model is first built. Subsequently, to determine the primary contributing factors, a thorough systematic review (SR) was performed. Finally, the ultimate influencing factors are determined through group decision-making involving experienced experts in relevant fields. This represents the paper's first major contribution.

In research on methods for evaluating urban flood resilience, some studies tend to construct specific indicators for evaluating disaster resilience [3,5,6]. However, urban flood resilience is a multidimensional, comprehensive cross-temporal capability, and the scope of consideration of a single indicator is too one-sided and difficult to fully express its characteristics. Multi-Criteria Decision-Making (MCDM) is an extension of decision theory. Hence, the MCDM method, which serves as a means to assess or rank objects based on a range of diverse criteria, has found extensive application in flood disaster assessment. However, in the research on calculating indicator weights via GAHP, most previous papers focused on aggregating individual preferences to group consensus [7–10] but ignored the importance of determining the weights of decision-makers. This paper proposes a synthesis weights GAHP (SW-GAHP) method, which comprehensively considers decision-makers' intrapersonal consistency and interpersonal consistency to determine the decision-makers' weights. This constitutes the second primary contribution of this paper.

In previous multi-criteria evaluation approaches [11–15], there has often been a focus on assessing quantitative indicators, with limited discussion on qualitative indicators. The integration of both quantitative and qualitative evaluation methods has been constrained, resulting in evaluation outcomes lacking a deeper understanding and failing to comprehensively capture the overall problem. This paper adopts an approach that combines both quantitative and qualitative evaluations. In terms of assessing quantitative indicators, traditional methods [11–15] typically employed the linear normalization method. However, some indicators do not adhere to linear patterns. Thus, this paper employs the flexible parameterized mapping function (FPMF) for the evaluation of quantitative indicators. The FPMF can accommodate both linear and nonlinear change patterns, making it more versatile. This forms the third primary contribution of this paper.

In terms of assessing qualitative indicators, group decision-making (GDM) technology is currently used extensively. However, previous expert empowerment methods for GDM treatment, such as direct customized allocation by a super decision-maker, are usually subjective. Yang et al. [16] adopted an objective weighting approach that combines the degree of uncertainty and the consistency of participants' evaluation results based on normal cloud models. However, their consistency calculation only considered the expected values of the evaluation results. The fourth primary contribution of this paper lies in describing the distance computation technique of the normal cloud model and introducing a novel technique for group decision-making known as the extensional group decision-making technology (EGDMT).

Numerous uncertainties exist in both quantitative and qualitative indicators, and researchers have employed various concepts to characterize these uncertainties. Li et al. [17,18] presented the idea of a cloud model that both represents randomness and fuzziness based on probability theory and type-2 fuzzy sets. Recently, Yang et al. [16] and numerous other scholars [19–22] have explored decision-making methodologies grounded in cloud models. NCMs stand out by being capable of jointly modeling fuzziness and randomness while offering more straightforward and intuitive operations. Consequently, the use of NCMs has grown significantly in recent years. The introduction of a heterogeneous decision-making information fusion method is the paper's fifth important contribution. This method can combine exact numbers, statistical data, interval numbers, linguistic terms, NCMs, and linguistic expressions.

To summarize, this paper's primary contributions are as follows:

(1). A conceptual framework for evaluating urban flood resilience was established by the PSR-SENCE model, and an extensive SR approach was integrated to produce an indicator system for thorough evaluation.
(2). A novel indicator weight determination method named SW-GAHP is proposed, which takes into account both intrapersonal and interpersonal consistency while considering the decision-making quality of different decision-makers.
(3). The use of the FPMF method for resilience calculation of quantitative indicators can handle both linear and nonlinear patterns for indicators with different meanings, thereby accurately reflecting their actual impact on urban flood resilience.
(4). An EGDMT method is proposed for evaluating qualitative indicators, where decision-maker weights are determined based on the uncertainty degree and group consensus bias of their decision-making information.
(5). A heterogeneous decision-making information fusion method is introduced for evaluating qualitative indicators.

The remainder of this paper is organized as follows: Section 2 provides the prerequisite knowledge needed for understanding the paper. Section 3 outlines the construction of the evaluation indicator system. Section 4 introduces the urban flood resilience evaluation methodology, including the SW-GAHP, FPMF, and EGDMT methods. In Section 5, the proposed method is applied to a case study of Beijing's flood resilience evaluation, and recommendations are made in light of the findings' analysis. Section 6 offers a comprehensive and detailed comparison with previous methods. Finally, Section 7 offers concluding thoughts.

2. Preliminaries

2.1. Cloud Model Theory

Let T be a qualitative term that is defined on the discourse universe $U = \{u\}$. Let $x \in U$ be a random instance of T, and $\mu_T(x) \in [0,1]$ represents the degree of certainty that x belongs to T, which corresponds to a stochastic variable exhibiting stable trends. The cloud model describes a concept through three numerical characteristics: expectation (Ex), entropy (En), and hyper-entropy (He).

Ex represents the mathematical average of the cloud droplet's position within the universe. It serves as the most representative point embodying the qualitative concept and acts as the sample that is most commonly used to quantify the concept.

En measures the degree of uncertainty, taking into account the concept's fuzziness and randomness. On one hand, En quantifies the randomness of the qualitative concept, reflecting the dispersion of cloud droplets representing the concept. On the other hand, En measures the ambivalence of the qualitative concept, indicating the range of acceptable cloud droplet values within the universe space.

He is the uncertainty degree of En.

2.1.1. Normal Cloud Model

The normal cloud model (NCM) is based on the normal distribution and Gauss membership function [17].

Definition 1 ([23]). *Let U be the universe of discourse, and let $\widetilde{A}$ be a qualitative concept in U. If $x \in U$ is a random instantiation of concept $\widetilde{A}$, which satisfies $x \sim N\left(Ex, En'^2\right)$, $En' \sim N(En, He^2)$, and the certainty degree of x belonging to concept $\widetilde{A}$ satisfies*

$$y = e^{-\frac{(x-Ex)^2}{2(En')^2}} \tag{1}$$

Therefore, a normal cloud is the distribution of x throughout the universe U.

2.1.2. Operation Rules

Within the same universe, the arithmetic operation rules [24–28] for NCMs $C_1 = (Ex_1, En_1, He_1)$ and $C_2 = (Ex_2, En_2, He_2)$ are defined as follows:

$$C_1 + C_2 = \left(Ex_1 + Ex_2, \sqrt{En_1^2 + En_2^2}, \sqrt{He_1^2 + He_2^2}\right) \tag{2}$$

$$C_1 - C_2 = \left(Ex_1 - Ex_2, \sqrt{En_1^2 + En_2^2}, \sqrt{He_1^2 + He_2^2}\right) \tag{3}$$

$$C_1 \times C_2 = \left(Ex_1 Ex_2, \sqrt{(En_1 Ex_2)^2 + (En_2 Ex_1)^2}, \sqrt{(He_1 Ex_2)^2 + (He_2 Ex_1)^2}\right) \tag{4}$$

$$T_1/T_2 = \left(\frac{Ex_1}{Ex_2}, \sqrt{\left(\frac{En_1}{Ex_2}\right)^2 + \left(\frac{Ex_1 En_2}{Ex_2^2}\right)^2}, \sqrt{\left(\frac{He_1}{Ex_2}\right)^2 + \left(\frac{Ex_1 He_2}{Ex_2^2}\right)^2}\right) \tag{5}$$

Definition 2. *Let $C_1 = (Ex_1, En_1, He_1)$ and $C_2 = (Ex_2, En_2, He_2)$ be two NCMs in U. The distance between C_1 and C_2 is defined as follows:*

$$\text{bias}(C^d, \overline{C}) = \sqrt{\varepsilon\left|Ex^d - \overline{E}x\right|^2 + \phi\left|En^d - \overline{E}n\right|^2 + \varphi\left|He^d - \overline{H}e\right|^2}. \tag{6}$$

where $\varepsilon, \phi, \varphi$ are three proportionality coefficients, $0 < \varepsilon < 1, 0 < \phi < 1, 0 < \varphi < 1$.

Definition 3 ([24]). *Let $C_i = (Ex_i, En_i, He_i)$ $(i = 1, 2, \ldots, n)$ be a set of NCMs in U. The synthetic operator is a mapping CS: $C^n \to C$.*

$$CS(C_1, C_2, \ldots, C_n) = \left(\frac{1}{n}\sum_{i=1}^{n} Ex_i, \frac{1}{6}\left(\max_i(Ex_i + 3En_i) - \min_j\left(Ex_j - 3En_j\right)\right), \sqrt{\sum_{i=1}^{n} He_i^2}\right) \tag{7}$$

The En and He of the synthetic NCM are both larger than or equivalent to those of each individual NCM. Consequently, the synthetic NCM includes a wider range of uncertainties, thereby providing a broader and more generalized coverage of information.

Definition 4 ([24,26]). *Let $C_i = (Ex_i, En_i, He_i)(i = 1, 2, \ldots, n)$ be a set of NCMs in U. A mapping CWA: $C^n \to C$, serves as the weighted average operator following*

$$CWA(C_1, C_2, \ldots, C_n) = \sum_{i=1}^{n} w_i C_i / \sum_{i=1}^{n} w_i \tag{8}$$

where w_i is the weight of C_i.

According to the inference [24,26], if $w_i \in [0,1]$, $i = 1,2,\ldots,n$ is a real number and $\sum_{i=1}^{n} w_i = 1$; then, Equation (8) is easy to understand as follows:

$$CWA(C_1, C_2, \ldots, C_n) = \left(\sum_{i=1}^{n} w_i Ex_i, \sqrt{\sum_{i=1}^{n} (w_i En_i)^2}, \sqrt{\sum_{i=1}^{n} (w_i He_i)^2} \right) \tag{9}$$

2.2. Conversion of Heterogeneous Data

Within the framework of group decision-making, participants frequently provide assessment outcomes as heterogeneous decision information (HDI). HDI mainly appears in two variants: numeric and linguistic. The numeric form encompasses precise numbers, interval numbers, and statistical data. Conversely, linguistic form consists of linguistic terms and linguistic expressions.

The conversion method for heterogeneous data, as combined from Yang et al. [29] and Yang et al. [16], is as follows:

2.2.1. Conversion of Numeric Type Data

For an exact number, both En and He values are set to 0.

$$v \to T(v,0,0) \tag{10}$$

Let an interval number be represented as $I = [I^L, I^U]$. The conversion formula is as follows:

$$I \to T\left(\frac{I^L + I^U}{2}, \frac{I^U - I^L}{6}, 0 \right) \tag{11}$$

If statistical numbers follow a normal distribution or closely approximate it, the first step is to compute the mean μ and standard deviation σ of the numbers. The statistical numbers can then be represented using an NCM as follows:

$$S_{\sim N(\mu,\sigma)} \to T(\mu,\sigma,0) \tag{12}$$

2.2.2. Conversion of Linguistic Type Data

When experts offer their evaluation opinions, they may tend to prefer selecting linguistic-type information because it aligns with human language conventions. Linguistic type information consists of two primary forms: linguistic terms and linguistic expressions.

With a dataset gathered from 175 individuals, ranging from 0 to 10 on a scale, Yang et al. converted 32 language terms into NCMs using membership function fitting and fuzzy statistics [30]. In a subsequent study [29], five of the original 32 models and two adaptive linguistic terms, along with two linguistic terms, were utilized for credibility evaluations. NCMs encoded nine linguistic terms, as shown in Figure 1 [16]. The nine linguistic terms, each associated with distinct grades as delineated in Figure 1, are also used in this study's context.

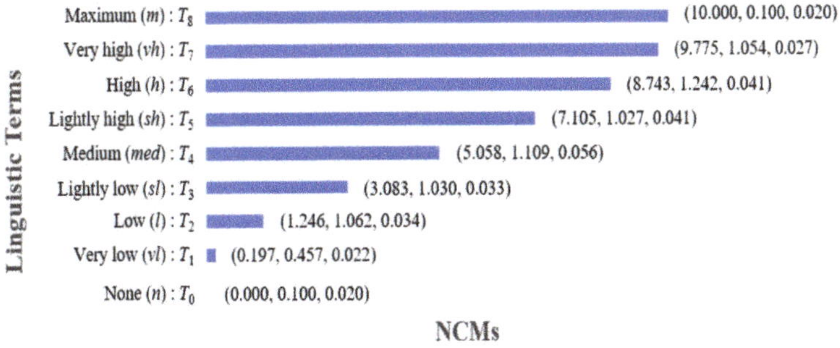

Figure 1. NCM-encoded nine linguistic terms.

When experts provide their evaluation opinions, they can directly choose appropriate linguistic terms from Figure 1.

Experts frequently turn to linguistic expressions to explain their opinions when faced with uncertainty while expressing hesitant opinions. However, it is important to note that linguistic expressions are not readily amenable to quantitative calculations and require conversion into hesitant linguistic term sets through specific conversion functions. Considering that Context-Free Grammar's (G_H) definition of the comparative linguistic approach closely resembles human expression, this paper adopts the rules outlined in Definition 5 for deriving linguistic expressions.

Definition 5 ([31])**.** *Let G_H be a context-free grammar, and $H = \{T_0, \ldots, T_n\}$ be a linguistic term set. The elements of $G_H = (V_N, V_T, I, P)$ are defined as follows:*

V_N = {*<primary term>, <composite term>, <unary relation>, <binary relation>, <conjunction >*};

V_T = {*lower than, greater than, at least, at most, between, and,* $T_0, T_1, \ldots, T_n$}; $I \in V_N$;

P = {*I ::=< primary term >|< composite term >,<primary term>::=* $T_0|T_1|\ldots|T_n$*, <composite term>::=<unary relation><primary term>|<binary relation ><primary term> <conjunction><primary term>, <unary relation>::= lower than|greater than|at least|at most, <binary relation>::=between, <conjunction>::=and*}.

Using the defined principles f_{G_H}, linguistic expressions are converted into hesitant cloud linguistic term sets (HCLTSs).

$$\begin{cases} f_{G_H}(T_i) = \{T_i | T_i \in H\} \\ f_{G_H}(\text{at most } T_i) = \{T_j | T_j \in H \text{ and } T_j \leq T_i\} \\ f_{G_H}(\text{lower than } T_i) = \{T_j | T_j \in H \text{ and } T_j < T_i\} \\ f_{G_H}(\text{at least } T_i) = \{T_j | T_j \in H \text{ and } T_j \geq T_i\} \\ f_{G_H}(\text{greater than } T_i) = \{T_j | T_j \in H \text{ and } T_j > T_i\} \\ f_{G_H}(\text{between } T_i \text{ and } T_j) = \{T_k | T_k \in H \text{ and } T_i \leq T_k \leq T_j\} \end{cases} \tag{13}$$

Finally, the synthetic operator given in Definition 3 is used to convert the HCLTS into an NCM.

3. Urban Flood Resilience Factors

3.1. Conceptual Framework

Rapport and Friend [32] first proposed the PSR model in 1979; subsequently, this model was altered by the United Nations Environment Programme (UNEP) and the Organization for Economic Cooperation and Development (OECD) and used to assess environmental concerns such as greenhouse gas impacts, pollution, and climate change (OECD, 2013) [33]. Three types of indicator layers make up the PSR model: pressure (P), state (S), and response (R).

The complex ecosystem of a city is thought to be represented by the social–economic–natural complex ecosystem (SENCE). On the basis of complex ecosystem theory, Wang and Ma (1984) [34] proposed the SENCE model in the 1980s. Three distinct systems are thought to comprise cities: society, economy, and nature [35]. In 2023, Zhu and Li established the PSR-SENCE model conceptual framework. Using this model as a conceptual framework for studying urban flood resilience's primary factors and how they interact, they identified 24 factors within three different dimensions [36].

Based on the PSR-SENCE model, in conjunction with the disaster system theory (DST), the framework for the concept of urban flood resilience is established within the following three dimensions: (1) Pressure Dimension: This dimension primarily quantifies the level of risk that the urban system faces in relation to urban flooding. It specifically addresses the inherent pressures placed on the composite urban ecosystem. It also includes factors contributing to flooding as outlined in DST. (2) State Dimension: This dimension primarily concerns the stable condition of the complex urban socio-economic and natural ecological system during flood disasters. It represents the environment's capacity to bear and endure floods in the DST. It embodies urban flood resilience attributes like robustness, redundancy, and timeliness, demonstrating the city system's ability to withstand and counteract the pressure exerted by flood disasters. Under the combined influence of flood disaster pressure and subsequent responses, the state also undergoes continuous changes. (3) Response Dimension: This dimension mainly focuses on the ability of urban entities, particularly those that bear the brunt of flood disasters, to implement response and recovery measures for urban social, economic, and natural systems post-flood disasters. It reflects the strategic, contemplative, and comprehensive qualities of urban flood resilience. Additionally, it highlights how urban institutions, such as businesses, social groups, governments, and citizens, are able to respond to flood disasters and draw lessons from both positive and negative experiences.

3.2. Identified Factors

Based on the aforementioned urban flood resilience conceptual framework, a comprehensive SR method is employed to identify the key factors that impact urban flood resilience. The following procedure outlines the factors that are needed to assess urban flood resilience.

(1). Screening: To begin, a search was carried out in the Web of Science Core Collection using keywords such as "urban flood resilience" or "city flood resilience" combined with "assessment" or "evaluation". This process yielded 1172 relevant papers. Subsequently, the titles and abstracts were screened, and 96 papers remained. Finally, a full-text review was conducted, papers that were less relevant to the scope of this study were eliminated, and a total of 87 papers were obtained.

(2). Expanding: After reviewing the selected papers, relevant and high-quality references were identified, leading to an expansion in the number of references to a total of 106.

(3). Extract: Key influencing factors were extracted from the papers, and those mentioned more than once were considered. In total, 48 factors were identified and categorized according to the urban flood resilience conceptual framework.

(4). Determine: Experts with over five years of experience in the fields of urban resilience, disaster risk reduction, and emergency management were consulted. Through expert discussions and deliberations, a final indicator system comprising 23 key influencing factors was established for the evaluation of urban flood resilience.

3.3. Urban Flood Resilience Evaluation Indicators

Following the outlined conceptual framework and factors identified, an urban flood resilience evaluation indicator system was developed, as depicted in Figure 2.

Each indicator's significance and assessment methodology are elaborately explained in Table 1, including a total of fifteen quantitative indicators and eight qualitative indicators.

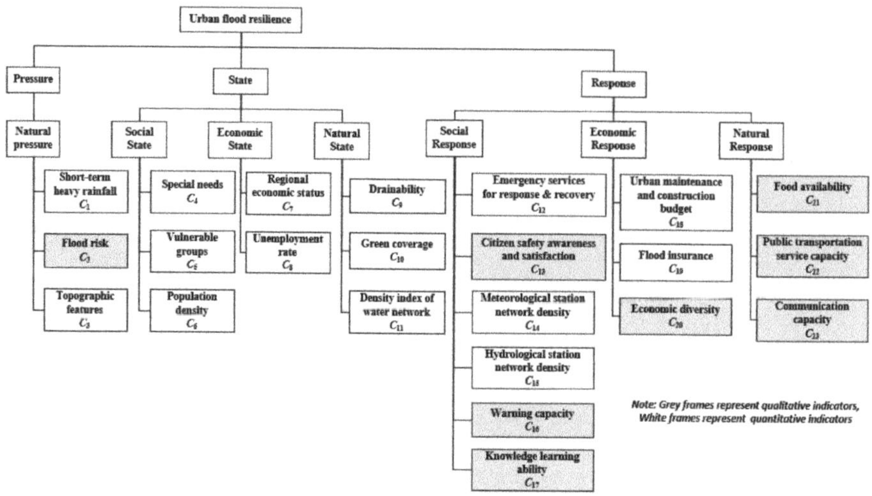

Figure 2. Urban flood resilience evaluation indicator system.

Table 1. The meaning and evaluation method of each indicator.

Dimensions	Indicators	Description	Expression	Justification
Pressure				
Natural pressure	Short-term heavy rainfall (C_1)	Daily rainfall statistics during the rainy season of the current year	$C_1 = \{r_d^1, r_d^2, \ldots, r_d^n\}$	[37–39]
	Flood risk (C_2)	The degree of flood risk faced by the city	Fuzzy	[40–42]
	Topographic feature (C_3)	Number between the highest and lowest points per area	$C_3 = h_h - h_l$	[43]
State				
Social state	Special needs (C_4)	Percentage of the population with disability	$C_4 = \frac{N_d}{N_{tp}}$	[44–46]
	Vulnerable groups (C_5)	Percentage of the population aged over 60 and under 15	$C_5 = \frac{N_{uf}+N_{os}}{N_{tp}}$	[44–46]
	Population density (C_6)	Population to area ratio	$C_6 = \frac{N_{tp}}{S}$	[47]
Economic state	Regional economic status (C_7)	Regional GDP data released by the National Bureau of Statistics	$C_7 = V_{ragdp}$	[48,49]
	Unemployment rate (C_8)	Proportion of urban unemployed population to total population	$C_8 = \frac{N_{jp}}{N_{wp}}$	[50]
Natural state	Drainability (C_9)	Density of urban drainage networks	$C_9 = \frac{L_{tdn}}{Area}$	[51–53]
	Green coverage (C_{10})	Proportion of the vertical projection area of vegetation on the ground per area	$C_{10} = \frac{S_g}{S}$	[51–53]
	Density index of water network (C_{11})	Average amount of river distribution per area	$C_{11} = \frac{\sum_{i=1}^{m} N_{ri}}{m}$	[51–53]
Response				
Social response	Emergency services for response and recovery (C_{12})	Number of police stations, fire stations, and emergency operation centers per 10,000 population	$C_{12} = \frac{\sum_{i=1}^{3} N_i}{N_{tp}}$	[54–56]
	Citizen safety awareness and satisfaction (C_{13})	Citizens' awareness of safety knowledge and their sense of safety attainment	Fuzzy	[57]

Table 1. *Cont.*

Dimensions	Indicators	Description	Expression	Justification
Social response	Meteorological station network density (C_{14})	The number of regional meteorological stations	$C_{14} = \frac{N_{ms}}{\text{Area}}$	[4,58,59]
	Hydrological station network density (C_{15})	The number of regional hydrological stations	$C_{15} = \frac{N_{hgs}}{\text{Area}}$	[4,58,60]
	Early warning capacity (C_{16})	Comprehensive prediction accuracy and warning efficiency	Fuzzy	[4,58,61]
	Knowledge learning ability (C_{17})	The ability to learn from and simulate past disaster experiences	Fuzzy	[62]
Economic response	Urban maintenance and construction budget (C_{18})	The proportion of financial expenditure dedicated to maintaining public safety in the city	$C_{18} = \frac{E_{psf}}{E_{clf}}$	[63]
	Flood insurance (C_{19})	Per capita insurance costs in the city	$C_{19} = \frac{E_{fir}}{N_{tp}}$	[64,65]
	Economic diversity (C_{20})	The richness or diversity of the city's economic forms	Fuzzy	[66]
Natural response	Food availability (C_{21})	The food supply capacity for the affected population in the city	Fuzzy	[67–69]
	Public transportation service capacity (C_{22})	The transportation capacity for personnel and materials	Fuzzy	[42,67,68]
	Communication capacity (C_{23})	The communication capability for emergency rescue operations	Fuzzy	[67,68,70]

4. Urban Flood Resilience Evaluation Methodology

4.1. Evaluation Framework

The proposed method has four primary steps, as described in Figure 3. First, an urban flood resilience evaluation indicator system is constructed (Section 3). Second, the weights of these indicators are determined using the SW-GAHP method (Section 4.2). Third, methods for evaluating quantitative and qualitative indicators are proposed (Section 4.3). Ultimately, all indicators' evaluation results are combined using the weighted average operator for NCMs, as described in Section 4.4.

4.2. Indicator Weight Calculation Using SW-GAHP

The AHP is recognized as one of the most prevalent methodologies for calculating indicator weights. Additionally, GAHP models are employed for issues involving multiple participants. This section introduces an enhanced GAHP method termed SW-GAHP for the weighting of indicators.

4.2.1. Synthesis Weighting Method (SWM) for DMs

Within GAHP research, the majority of previous studies have concentrated on the methods for aggregating individual preferences into group consensus [7–9]. However, the importance of ascertaining the weights of decision-makers (DMs) has not been adequately addressed.

This paper introduces a novel weighting approach of DMs termed SWM, which accounts for both intrapersonal and interpersonal consistencies in Pairwise Comparison Matrices (PCMs). Intrapersonal consistency pertains to the "inconsistency level" within a single PCM. A diminished "inconsistency level" indicates fewer internal contradictions within a PCM, suggesting superior decision-making quality. Conversely, interpersonal consistency is concerned with the divergence between individual preferences and the collective consensus. A smaller "deviation" reflects a greater alignment between an individual decision-maker and the rest of the DMs.

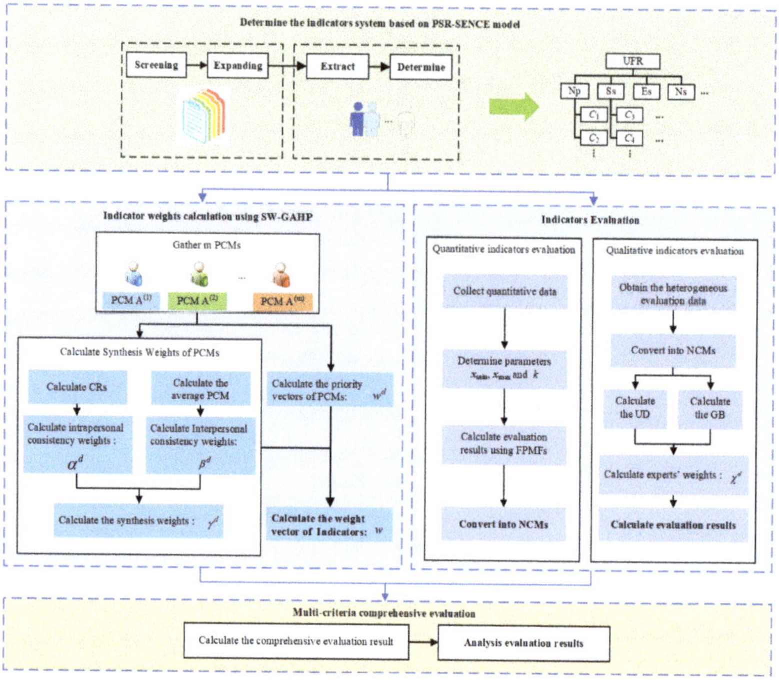

Figure 3. Flowchart of the methodology.

Intrapersonal Consistency

Let $C = \{c_1, c_2, \ldots, c_m\}$ represent a finite set of m indications, with the i-th indicator represented by c_i. A finite set of k DMs is denoted by $D = \{DM_1, DM_2, \ldots, DM_k\}$. The $m \times m$ matrix $A^d = \left[a_{ij}^d\right], d = 1, 2, \ldots, k$ represents the PCM^d of DM_d. if $\left(a_{ij}^d > 0\right.$ is positive for $\forall i$ and j) and reciprocal $\left(a_{ji}^d = 1/a_{ij}^d\right.$ for $\forall i$ and j). Its general element a_{ij} shows how many times item i is more important than element j. A PCM is said to be consistent if and only if $a_{ie} = a_{ij}a_{je}$ for $\forall i, j, e, 1 \leq i, j, e \leq n$. In practical decision-making problems, a PCM is likely to exhibit inconsistency. Nonetheless, the extent of consistency can vary significantly, quantifiable by the Consistency Ratio (CR).

$$CR = \frac{CI}{RI} \tag{14}$$

where RI represents the average CI value of randomly created PCMs of the same size and CI represents A's consistency index.

$$CI = \frac{\lambda_{\max} - m}{m - 1} \tag{15}$$

where $\lambda_{\max} \geq m$ is the largest eigenvalue of the PCM. In AHP, an acceptable degree of consistency is generally indicated by $CR < 0.1$.

The "inconsistency level" of PCM provided by an individual is measured using the CR.

$$\alpha^d = \frac{\max\left(0.1 - CR^d, 0\right)}{\sum\limits_{d=1}^{k} \max\left(0.1 - CR^d, 0\right)} \tag{16}$$

where CR^d is the CR of the d-th DM's PCM and α^d is the weight assigned to the d-th DM according to intrapersonal consistency.

Interpersonal Consistency

Interpersonal consistency is assessed by the variance of an individual DM's PCM from the mean of all DMs' PCMs. This variance is determined using the Euclidean distance.

Firstly, calculate the average matrix $\overline{A} = [\overline{a}_{ij}]_{m\times m}$ of all DMs as follows:

$$\overline{a}_{ij} = \frac{1}{k}(a_{ij}^1 + a_{ij}^2 + \ldots + a_{ij}^k) \tag{17}$$

Next, calculate the deviation of an individual DM's matrix A^d from the average matrix $\overline{A}$.

$$L_{A^d\overline{A}} = \sqrt{\sum_{i=1}^{m}\sum_{j=1}^{m}(a_{ij}^d - \overline{a}_{ij})^2} \tag{18}$$

Lastly, as the "deviation" measure is of a cost type, its normalization and standardization methods are defined as follows:

$$\begin{aligned} L^s_{A^d\overline{A}} &= 1 - \frac{L_{A^d\overline{A}}}{\sum\limits_{d=1}^{k} L_{A^d\overline{A}}}. \\ \beta^d &= \frac{L^s_{A^d\overline{A}}}{\sum\limits_{d=1}^{k} L^s_{A^d\overline{A}}} \end{aligned} \tag{19}$$

where β^d is the weight assigned to the d-th DM according to interpersonal consistency.

Synthesis Weights of DMs

By synthesizing interpersonal consistency and intrapersonal consistency, the synthesis weight of the d-th DM is calculated.

$$\gamma^d = \nu\alpha^d + (1-\nu)\beta^d \tag{20}$$

where ν is the adjustable parameter and $0 \leqslant \nu \leqslant 1$, γ^d is the synthesis weight assigned to the d-th DM.

4.2.2. Indicator Weighting

The weight vector DM_d, represented as $w^d = [w_1^d, w_2^d, \ldots, w_m^d]$, is the normalized eigenvector of the matrix A^d that corresponds to the biggest eigenvalue $\lambda_{\max}^d$. Subsequently, the weight of indicator C_i, denoted as w_i, is calculated using the arithmetic weighted average of the weight vectors from k DMs.

$$w_i = \sum_{d=1}^{k} \gamma^d w_i^d, i = 1, 2, \cdots, m. \tag{21}$$

Finally, the weight vector of m indicators using GAHP is $\boldsymbol{w} = [w_1, w_2 ..., w_m]$. Algorithm 1 describes the SW-GAHP algorithm.

Algorithm 1. SW-GAHP algorithm.

Input: PCMs $\{(A^d)_{m \times m}\}$ on m indicators from k DMs (d = 1, 2, . . ., k).
Output: $w = \{w_1, w_2, \ldots, w_m\}$.
Procedure:
1: ***for*** d = 1: k
2: Calculate the largest eigenvalue $\lambda^d_{\max}$ and its eigenvector w^d.
3: Calculate CR^d by Equations (14) and (15).
4: Calculate each DM's intrapersonal consistency weight α^d by Equation (16).
5: ***end***
6: Calculate the average matrix $\overline{A}$ of all DMs by arithmetic mean value.
7: ***for*** d = 1: k
8: Calculate the deviation $L_{A^d\overline{A}}$ of the d-th DM's PCM from $\overline{A}$ by Equation (18).
9: Calculate each DM's interpersonal consistency weight β^d by Equation (19).
10: Calculate each DM's synthesis weight γ^d by Equation (20).
11: ***end***
12: ***for*** i = 1: m
13: Calculate the weight w_i of indicator C_i by Equation (21).
14: ***end***

PCMs are used to determine the weight vectors of indications under the same parent indicator at each level, in line with the hierarchical structure of the indicator system. As a result, the weights of the indicators at lower levels are determined by multiplying the weight vectors in a sequential manner, starting at the highest level and working down to the lowest.

4.3. Indicator Evaluation

4.3.1. Quantitative Indicator Evaluation Using FPMF

The quantitative data include various dimensions and trends. Traditional normalization methods often utilize linear transformations, such as the 0–1 method. This paper adopts the FPMF [71] for normalizing all quantitative indicators. By integrating three adjustable pre-defined parameters: minimum value, maximum value, and exponent k, which cater to both linear and nonlinear function mappings with increasing or decreasing trends, this method demonstrates superior flexibility and adaptability.

In terms of directional trends, quantitative indicators are divided into benefit-type or cost-type categories. Benefit-type indicators, where higher values are more desirable, are mapped using increasing functions. Conversely, cost-type indicators, where lower values are preferred, are mapped using decreasing functions.

Within the category of benefit-type indicators, they are further classified into convex and concave increasing functions. In the case of cost-type indicators, decreasing functions are applied, which include both convex and concave decreasing functions.

The formula for the convex increasing function (CvIF) is as follows:

$$f(x) = \begin{cases} 0, \ x \le x_{\min} \\ 10 \cdot \left(\frac{x - x_{\min}}{x_{\max} - x_{\min}}\right)^k, \ x_{\min} < x < x_{\max} \\ 10, \ x \ge x_{\max} \end{cases} \tag{22}$$

The formula for the concave increasing function (CcIF) is as follows:

$$f(x) = \begin{cases} 10, \ x \le x_{\min} \\ 10 \cdot \left(1 - \left(\frac{x_{\max} - x}{x_{\max} - x_{\min}}\right)^k\right), \ x_{\min} < x < x_{\max} \\ 0, \ x \ge x_{\max} \end{cases} \tag{23}$$

The convex decreasing function (CvDF) is represented by the following formula:

$$f(x) = \begin{cases} 10,\ x \leq x_{\min} \\ 10 \cdot \left(\frac{x_{\max}-x}{x_{\max}-x_{\min}}\right)^k,\ x_{\min} < x < x_{\max} \\ 0,\ x \geq x_{\max} \end{cases} \quad (24)$$

The formula for the concave decreasing function (CcDF) is as follows:

$$f(x) = \begin{cases} 0,\ x \leq x_{\min} \\ 10 \cdot \left(1 - \left(\frac{x-x_{\min}}{x_{\max}-x_{\min}}\right)^k\right),\ x_{\min} < x < x_{\max} \\ 10,\ x \geq x_{\max} \end{cases} \quad (25)$$

In this context, $x_{\min}$ denotes the minimum value of the quantitative indicator, while $x_{\max}$ represents its maximum value, and k ($k \geq 1$) is an exponent that signifies varying rates of increase or decrease.

When $k = 1$, the mapping function $f(x)$ exhibits a linear increase/decrease within the range $[x_{\min}, x_{\max}]$. Conversely, for values of k other than 1, the mapping function $f(x)$ portrays a nonlinear increase/decrease within the same range $[x_{\min}, x_{\max}]$.

This paper includes fifteen quantitative indicators, of which eight are increasing and seven are decreasing; only C_1 is a statistical number, while the others are exact numbers. The extreme values of C_1, C_3, C_6, C_7, and C_8 are selected according to the relevant level classification standards. For example, if the daily rainfall is within the range of 0–10 mm, the rainfall level is categorized as light rain. A rainfall level greater than 250 mm is classified as exceptionally heavy. Therefore, the $x_{\min}$ for short-term heavy rainfall C_1 is set to 0 mm, and the $x_{\max}$ is set to 250 mm. If the elevation difference is between 0 and 200 m, it is a plain, and if it is greater than 2000 m, it is a mountain. Therefore, the $x_{\min}$ of topographic feature C_3 is set to 0, and the $x_{\max}$ is 2000. When the population density is less than 1 person/km^2, the area is an extremely sparsely populated area; when the population density is greater than 100 people/km^2, the area is a densely populated area. Therefore, $x_{\min}$ of population density C_6 is 0, $x_{\max}$ is 100, and so on. The determination of extreme values for the remaining indicators is achieved through expert consultation. Details regarding the FPMFs and associated parameters for various indicators are provided in Table 2.

Table 2. FPMFs and relevant parameters for different indicators.

Indicators	$x_{\min}$	$x_{\max}$	k	FPMF
C_1	0	250	2	CvDF
C_3	200	2000	1	CvDF
C_4	0	5%	3	CcDF
C_5	0	50%	3	CcDF
C_6	0	100	2	CcDF
C_7	0.6607	58.412	4	CcIF
C_8	2%	10%	2	CcDF
C_9	0	3.76	2	CcIF
C_{10}	25%	50%	2	CcIF
C_{11}	0	2269	3	CcDF
C_{12}	0	1	2	CcIF
C_{14}	0	500	2	CvIF
C_{15}	100	20,000	2	CcDF
C_{18}	0	10%	2	CcIF
C_{19}	0	10,000	2	CcIF

By employing the FPMFs and parameters outlined in Table 2, the evaluation result e_i of the quantitative indicator C_i is determined. Subsequently, this result is transformed into an NCM Ce_i according to the method described in Section 2.2.

4.3.2. Qualitative Indicator Evaluation Using Group Decision-Making Techniques with Heterogeneous Data

Experts may represent their evaluation opinions of qualitative indicators by exact numbers, interval numbers, linguistic terms, or linguistic expressions. An exact number or interval number can be converted into an NCM by (10) or (11) in Section 2.2.1. A linguistic term can be encoded by an NCM, as shown in Figure 1 in Section 2.2.2. A linguistic expression can be represented by the context-free grammar GH and then converted into an NCM as described in Section 2.2.2. Consequently, our qualitative indicator evaluation method is capable of managing heterogeneous data, and uncertainty is modeled and propagated by NCMs.

In order to more accurately determine the weight of DMs, this paper defined the distance between two NCMs by incorporating *En* and *He* in the calculation of consistency. Thus, an EGDMT method is proposed based on the uncertainty degree and group consensus bias, which is considered more comprehensively without increasing the burden on the DMs.

(1). Uncertainness degree

The uncertainty degree (UD) of an NCM is described as follows:

$$\begin{aligned} \eta^d &= En^d + 3He^d, d = 1, 2, \ldots, k. \\ UD^d &= \frac{1 - \eta^d \Big/ \sum_{d=1}^{k} \eta^d}{\sum_{d=1}^{k} \left(1 - \eta^d \Big/ \sum_{d=1}^{k} \eta^d\right)} \end{aligned} \tag{26}$$

where (Ex^d, En^d, He^d) represents the evaluation result of the d-th DM, and UD^d denotes the UD of the d-th DM.

(2). Group consensus bias

Group consensus bias (GB) is defined as the deviation of an individual's evaluation result from the collective outcome. In this study, the three parameters of NCM, specifically *Ex*, *En*, and *He*, are utilized to calculate GB.

Initially, the mean of all DMs' evaluation results is calculated as follows:

$$\overline{C} = (\overline{E}x, \overline{E}n, \overline{H}e) = \frac{1}{k}\sum_{d=1}^{k} C^d \tag{27}$$

where C^d represents the evaluation result given by the d-th DM.

Subsequently, the bias of the d-th DM is computed as follows:

$$\text{bias}(C^d, \overline{C}) = \sqrt{\varepsilon\left|Ex^d - \overline{E}x\right|^2 + \phi\left|En^d - \overline{E}n\right|^2 + \varphi\left|He^d - \overline{H}e\right|^2} \tag{28}$$

where $\varepsilon, \phi, \varphi$ are three adjustable parameters.

Finally, the metric termed "deviation degree" is categorized as a cost-type indicator. The standardization and normalization methods for this metric are described as follows:

$$\begin{aligned} \delta^d &= 1 - \frac{d(C^d, \overline{C})}{\sum_{d=1}^{k} d(C^d, \overline{C})}, d = 1, 2, \cdots, k. \\ GB^d &= \frac{\delta^d}{\sum_{d=1}^{k} \delta^d} \end{aligned} \tag{29}$$

where GB^d represents the weight assigned to the d-th DM based on the GB.

(3). Qualitative indicator evaluation

In the end, the relative weight of each DM is determined by combining the UD and GB.

$$\chi^d = \mu UD^d + (1-\mu)GB^d \tag{30}$$

where μ is the adjustable parameter and $0 < \mu < 1$, and χ^d is the relative weight of the d-th DM.

Using the weighted arithmetic mean method, the evaluation result of the qualitative indicator C_i, denoted as Ce_i, is calculated.

$$Ce_i = \sum_{d=1}^{k} \chi^d e_i^d, i = 1, 2, \cdots, m \tag{31}$$

where e_i^d ($d = 1, 2, \ldots, k$) is the evaluation result of C_i from DM_d.

Algorithm 2 describes the EDGMT algorithm for evaluating qualitative indicators.

Algorithm 2. EGDMT with heterogeneous data for the evaluation of qualitative indicators.

Input: heterogeneous data on a qualitative indicator from k DMs.
Output: the evaluation result Ce_i.
Procedure:
1: Covert heterogeneous data into NCMs (Ex^d, En^d, He^d), ($d = 1, 2, \ldots, k$).
2: ***for*** $d = 1$: k
3: Calculate each DM's UD^d by Equation (26).
4: ***end***
5: Calculate average NCM $\overline{C}$ of NCMs by Equation (27).
6: ***for*** $d = 1$: k
7: Calculate the bias $d(C^d, \overline{C})$ of an individual DM's NCM from the average NCM of DMs by Equation (28).
8: Calculate each DM's GB^d by Equation (29).
9: Calculate each DM's weight χ^d by Equation (30).
10: ***end***
11: Calculate the evaluation result of a qualitative indicator C_i represented as Ce_i by Equation (31).

4.4. Multi-Criteria Comprehensive Evaluation

The indicators' evaluation results, both quantitative and qualitative, are $Ce = [Ce_1, Ce_2, \ldots, Ce_m]$, and the weights of the indicators are $w = [w_1, w_2, \ldots, w_m]$. Then, the weighted average operator of the NCM (Section 2.1.2) is used to aggregate the evaluation results of multiple indicators.

$$Re = \sum_{i=1}^{m} w_i Ce_i \tag{32}$$

5. Case Study

In this section, to illustrate the implementation specifics and prove the viability of the suggested approach, a real-world example of an urban flood resilience evaluation of Beijing from 2017 to 2021 is provided.

5.1. Calculate the Weights of the Indicators

PCMs are required for three indications in the first level of the Beijing urban flood resilience indicator system: pressure, state, and response. As shown in Table 3, six 3×3 PCMs were collected from six DMs.

The six PCMs' weight vectors were computed as follows: [0.3889, 0.2778, 0.3333], [0.3810, 0.2857, 0.3333], [0.4836, 0.1677, 0.3487], [0.3889, 0.2778, 0.3333], [0.3636, 0.3030,

0.3333], and [0.3810, 0.2857, 0.3333]. The CRs were computed as follows: 0, 0, 0.0009, 0, 0, or 0. The $L_{A^d\overline{A}}$ values were calculated as 0.2408, 0, 0.3253, 1.6306, 0.2408, 0.5069, and 0.3253. Then, for $\lambda = 0.5$, the weights of the six DMs were calculated as 0.1761, 0.1735, 0.1329, 0.1761, 0.1679, and 0.1735. Lastly, using the weighted arithmetic mean of the six weight vectors, the weight vectors of the three indicators were calculated to be [0.3945, 0.2701, 0.3354].

Table 3. The first level indicators' six PCMs from six DMs.

1				1				1				1	2	1		1				1		
2	1			3	1	1		3	1	1			1			4	1	2		3	1	
4	2	1		3		1		3		1			2	1		2		1		3	2	1

Likewise, three 3 × 3 PCMs for the second-level indications in the "state" category were acquired from three DMs. It was determined that the weight vectors for the three indicators under "state" were [0.2790, 0.3208, 0.4001]. Additionally, five 3 × 3 PCMs were gathered from five DMs in order to support the "response" second-level indicators. The three indicators under "response" have been determined to have the following weight vector: [0.3922, 0.2760, 0.3318]. The weight vector for the sole indicator under 'pressure' was assigned a value of 1.

Furthermore, in the third-level indicator system, there are seven indicators. These seven indicators' weight vectors were computed as follows: [0.4965, 0.3086, 0.1949], [0.1595, 0.2426, 0.5979], [0.7073, 0.2927], [0.4129, 0.2133, 0.3738], [0.1210, 0.0986, 0.2878, 0.2959, 0.1081, 0.0886], [0.5086, 0.1868, 0.3047], and [0.2327, 0.3511, 0.4122].

Consequently, the 23 bottom-level indicators' weights were determined and are shown in Table 4. The indicator bearing the highest weight is C_7, whereas C_4 possesses the lowest weight. The calculated weights for the indicators were applied to all years from 2017 to 2021.

Table 4. The weight calculation results for the indicators from 2017 to 2021.

	C_1	C_2	C_3	C_4	C_5	C_6	C_7	C_8	C_9	C_{10}	C_{11}	C_{12}
Weight	0.0897	0.0546	0.0384	0.0150	0.0293	0.0599	0.1002	0.0323	0.0511	0.0444	0.0465	0.0367
Rank	2	6	11	23	19	5	1	16	7	10	9	13
	C_{13}	C_{14}	C_{15}	C_{16}	C_{17}	C_{18}	C_{19}	C_{20}	C_{21}	C_{22}	C_{23}	
Weight	0.0155	0.0297	0.0314	0.0330	0.0161	0.0612	0.0244	0.0340	0.0376	0.0510	0.0680	
Rank	22	18	17	15	21	4	20	14	12	8	3	

5.2. Obtain the Evaluation Data

The evaluation method is proposed in Section 4.3. We illustrate the process of calculating the evaluation results of indicators using data from 2021. The same process can be applied in other years.

Quantitative data from 2017 to 2021 were sourced from various authorities, including the National Statistical Yearbook, Beijing Statistical Yearbook, Chinese meteorological stations, China Water Resources News, and the Beijing Water Authority. These data include 15 indicators: C_1, C_3 to C_{12}, C_{14}, C_{15}, C_{18}, and C_{19}. Notably, C_1 represents the statistical data of daily rainfall during the rainy season in 2021. Conversely, qualitative indicators C_2, and C_{21} to C_{23} were evaluated by five experts in the natural domain using heterogeneous data. Indicator C_{20} was assessed by four experts in the economic domain, while C_{13}, C_{16}, and C_{17} were evaluated by three experts in the social domain. The evaluation of all 23 indicators in 2021 is depicted in Table 5.

These qualitative evaluation data were subsequently converted into NCMs using the method described in Section 2.2, as shown in Table 6.

Table 5. The evaluation of 23 indicators in 2021.

	C_1	C_3	C_4	C_5	C_6	C_7	C_8	C_9
2021	--	940.71	2.49%	26.34%	1334	18.398	3.20%	1.15
	C_{10}	C_{11}	C_{12}	C_{14}	C_{15}	C_{18}	C_{19}	
	49%	166	0.25	514	37.17	6.90%	3795.51	
	C_2	C_{21}	C_{22}	C_{23}				
	DM_1: *[1, 2]* DM_2: *low* DM_3: (1.5, 0.5, 0.033) DM_4: *lower than low* DM_5: 1.5	DM_1: *[8, 9]* DM_2: *high* DM_3: (8.5, 0.5, 0.033) DM_4: *greater than high* DM_5: 8.3	DM_1: *[7, 8]* DM_2: *sh* DM_3: (7.5, 0.5, 0.033) DM_4: *between sh and high* DM_5: 7.5	DM_1: *[8.5, 9.5]* DM_2: *vh* DM_3: (9.5, 0.5, 0.033) DM_4: *between high and vh* DM_5: 9.4				
	C_{13}	C_{16}	C_{17}	C_{20}				
	DM_6: 7 DM_7: *sh* DM_8: between *sh* and *high*	DM_6: *8.8* DM_7: *high* DM_8: between *high* and *vh*	DM_6: *8* DM_7: *sh* DM_8: between *sh* and *high*	DM_9: *8.2* DM_{10}: (8.3, 0.5, 0.023) DM_{11}: *[8, 8.6]* DM_{12}: *lower than high*				

Table 6. The NCMs for 5 years according to the 23 indicators.

	C_2	C_{21}	C_{22}	C_{23}
2021	DM_1: (1.5000, 0.1667, 0) DM_2: (1.2460, 1.0620, 0.0340) DM_3: (1.5000, 0.5000, 0.0330) DM_4: (0.0985, 0.4570, 0.0297) DM_5: (1.5000, 0, 0)	DM_1: (8.5000, 0.1667, 0) DM_2: (8.7430, 1.2420, 0.0410) DM_3: (8.5000, 0.5000, 0.3300) DM_4: (9.8875, 1.0540, 0.0336) DM_5: (8.3000, 0, 0)	DM_1: (7.5000, 0.1667, 0) DM_2: (7.1050, 1.0270, 0.0410) DM_3: (7.5000, 0.5000, 0.3300) DM_4: (7.9240, 1.4075, 0.0580) DM_5: (7.5000, 0, 0)	DM_1: (9.0000, 0.1667, 0) DM_2: (9.7750, 1.0540, 0.0270) DM_3: (9.5000, 0.5000, 0.3300) DM_4: (9.2590, 1.3200, 0.0491) DM_5: (9.4000, 0, 0)
	C_{13}	C_{16}	C_{17}	C_{20}
	DM_1: (7.0, 0, 0) DM_2: (7.1050, 1.0270, 0.0410) DM_3: (7.9240, 1.4075, 0.0580)	DM_1: (8.80, 0, 0) DM_2: (8.7430, 1.2420, 0.0410) DM_3: (9.2590, 1.3200, 0.0491)	DM_1: (8.0, 0, 0) DM_2: (7.1050, 1.0270, 0.0410) DM_3: (7.9240, 1.4075, 0.0580)	DM_1: (8.2, 0, 0) DM_2: (8.3, 0.5000, 0.0230) DM_3: (8.3, 0.1, 0) DM_4: (7.9240, 1.4075, 0.0580)

Finally, the 15 quantitative indicators were standardized and converted into NCMs through FPMF, as well as through the conversion of heterogeneous data. The eight qualitative indicators were transformed into NCMs using heterogeneous data conversion and the EGDMT, as illustrated in Table 7.

Table 7. The NCMs of 23 indicators in 2021.

	C_1	C_2	C_3	C_4	C_5
2021	(9.2698, 0.8889, 0)	(1.8401, 0.4911, 0.0172)	(5.8849, 0, 0)	(8.7649, 0, 0)	(8.5380, 0, 0)
	C_6	C_7	C_8	C_9	C_{10}
	(0, 0, 0)	(7.6954, 0, 0)	(9.7750, 0, 0)	(5.1816, 0, 0)	(9.9840, 0, 0)
	C_{11}	C_{12}	C_{13}	C_{14}	C_{15}
	(9.9961, 0, 0)	(4.8160, 0, 0)	(6.2672, 0.7222, 0.0328)	(10, 0, 0)	(9.9999, 0, 0)
	C_{16}	C_{17}	C_{18}	C_{19}	C_{20}
	(9.0809, 0.7731, 0.0272)	(9.1224, 0.7755, 0.0273)	(9.0390, 0, 0)	(10, 0, 0)	(9.0549, 0.5483, 0.0731)
	C_{21}	C_{22}	C_{23}		
	(9.0333, 0.6885, 0.1034)	(7.0694, 0.6756, 0.0959)	(9.3771, 0.6774, 0.1143)		

5.3. Comprehensive Evaluation and Analysis

In Sections 5.1 and 5.2, the weights and evaluation results for the indicators are derived. Then, the evaluation results for Beijing's flood resilience are computed using the weighted average cloud operator, as shown in Table 8.

Table 8. The evaluation results for Beijing's flood resilience from 2017 to 2021.

	2021	2020	2019	2018	2017
Result	(7.5733, 0.1111, 0.0104)	(7.0543, 0.0902, 0.0109)	(7.0090, 0.0962, 0.0118)	(6.7500, 0.1016, 0.0114)	(6.6388, 0.1021, 0.0121)

As the cloud model incorporates *Ex*, *En*, and *He*, the assessment results are analyzed using a multi-area graph, taking into full consideration the uncertainty contained in the evaluation results. In the multi-area graph, the expected value curve is depicted by the central dark green line, demonstrating the variation of expected values with the indicator values. The regions transitioning from dark green to light green denote the "basic values", "peripheral values", and "uncertain values" areas in that order.

Consideration is given to the score cloud parameters (*Ex*, *En*, *He*). The "basic value" region corresponds to the score interval $[Ex - En, Ex + En]$. According to the characteristics of the normal cloud model, this interval contributes 68.26% of the total contribution. The "peripheral value" region includes the intervals $[Ex - En, Ex - 3En]$ and $[Ex + En, Ex + 3En]$, collectively accounting for 31.48% of the total contribution. Together, the "basic value" and "peripheral value" regions constitute 99.74% of the total contribution, indicating the fuzzy range of the score.

The outermost region, known as the "uncertain value" region, includes $[Ex - 3En, Ex - 3(En + 3He)]$ and $[Ex + 3En, Ex + 3(En + 3He)]$. This area is subject to both subjective and objective uncertainty factors.

The evaluation results of Beijing's urban flood resilience and the top three ranked indicators, regional economic status (C_7), short-term heavy rainfall (C_1), and communication capability (C_{23}), from 2017 to 2021 are shown in Figure 4.

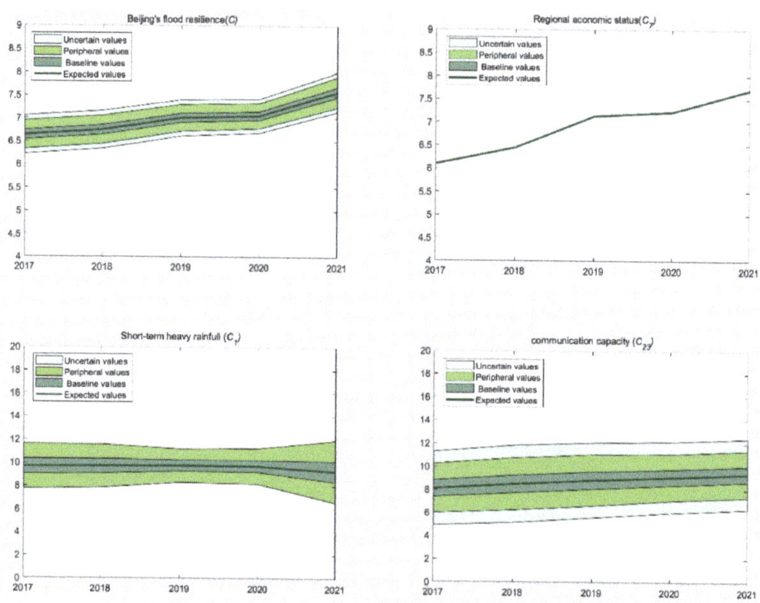

Figure 4. Changes in the evaluation results of Beijing's urban flood resilience from 2017 to 2021 and the top three ranked indicators.

It can be seen from Figure 4. The change pattern of Beijing's urban flood resilience can be summarized as a rapid increase during the periods of 2017–2019 and 2020–2021, with a slower increase between 2019 and 2020. The resilience score escalated from 6.6388 in

2017 to 7.5733 in 2021, reflecting a 14.1% enhancement. As shown in Figure 4 and Table 9, the rapid increase phase was primarily driven by significant improvements in the top ten indicators, including regional economic status (C_7), communication capacity (C_{23}), flood risk (C_2), and drainability (C_9). However, the slower increase phase occurred because the rate of improvement in these indicators decreased significantly, and the urban maintenance and construction budget (C_{18}), ranked fourth, actually declined.

Table 9. Evaluation results of key indicators of Beijing's urban flood resilience from 2017 to 2021.

	2017	2018	2019	2020	2021
C_{18}	(9.0140, 0, 0)	(9.0452, 0, 0)	(9.2710, 0, 0)	(9.1590, 0, 0)	(9.0390, 0, 0)
C_2	(1.6160, 0.6740, 0.0849)	(1.7054, 0.6730, 0.0686)	(1.7738, 0.6778, 0.1011)	(1.6671, 0.4989, 0.0613)	(1.8401, 0.4911, 0.0172)
C_9	(4.6896, 0, 0)	(4.8817, 0, 0)	(4.9575, 0, 0)	(4.9575, 0, 0)	(5.1816, 0, 0)

Figure 5 displays the weights of various indicators and their evaluation results for 2021. The angle of each sector illustrates the weight of the indicator. The green sector symbolizes the expected value of the indicator, while the light green region represents a portion of the "outer value" interval of the indicator, with a score range of $[Ex, Ex + 3En]$. The yellow sector signifies a segment of the "uncertain value" interval, characterized by a score range of $[Ex + 3En, Ex + 3(En + 3He)]$.

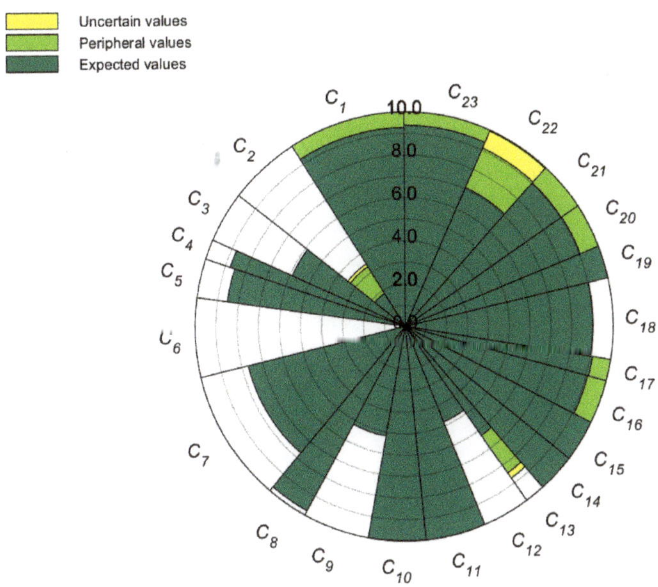

Figure 5. The evaluation results and weights of 23 indicators.

When Figure 5 is correlated with Table 4, it becomes evident that among the top ten indicators ranked by weight, the scores of positive indicators C_7, C_9, and C_{22} necessitate enhancement. Such improvements could be realized through the development of the regional economy, expansion of drainage pipelines, and optimization of road traffic, thereby augmenting urban flood resilience in Beijing. On the other hand, the scores of negative indicators C_6 and C_2 are relatively low, and increasing Beijing's urban flood resilience by reducing flood risk and population density is necessary. High scores, such as C_{23}, C_{18},

C_{11}, and C_{10}, pose greater challenges for improvement and can be maintained in their current state.

Moreover, the changes in uncertainty in the evaluation of Beijing's urban flood resilience and major indicators are shown in Figure 5. Using the 2021 data as a reference, Table 10 illustrates the representative indicators *En*, 2*En*, and *He* for uncertainty values, outer values, and basic values, which are integral to the uncertainty representation of Beijing's urban flood resilience. Figure 5 and Table 10 reveal that the uncertainty in Beijing's urban flood resilience has significantly decreased compared to the uncertainty in major indicators. The decrease rate (DR) of Beijing's urban flood resilience (C) is as high as 73.0% compared to that of the statistical indicator C_1, and it is 64.6% compared to that of the qualitative indicator C_{23}.

Table 10. The uncertainty of the evaluation of urban flood resilience and major indicators.

	En	*2En*	*He*	DR/%
C	0.2399	0.4798	0.0104	-
C_7	0	0	0	-
C_1	0.8889	1.7778	0	-
C_{23}	0.6774	1.3548	0.1143	-
$C–C_1$	-	-	-	73.0
$C–C_{23}$	-	-	-	64.6

$C–C_1$ represents the change in evaluation result C compared to the indicator C_1 score, while $C–C_{23}$ represents the change in evaluation result C compared to the indicator C_{23} score.

5.4. Sensitivity Analysis

λ denotes the adjustable parameter in the computation of indicator weights for the DM comprehensive weight, while μ is the adjustable parameter in the calculation of expert relative weights for indicator evaluation. Sensitivity analysis involves altering λ and μ from 0 to 1 to investigate the impacts of these adjustable parameters λ and μ on the final evaluation outcomes.

The impact of the variation in the urban flood resilience indicator weights with respect to λ is shown in Figure 6. As depicted in this figure, with increasing λ, only slight variation occurs in the indicator weights. This outcome suggests that the weights of indicators are not sensitive to variations in λ, indicating a strong correlation between intrapersonal and interpersonal consistency in the computation of indicator weights. The employed method for calculating indicator weights, SW-GAHP, exhibits high robustness.

The influence of varying μ on the qualitative evaluation outcomes of urban flood resilience indicators in 2021 is shown in Figure 7. During the evaluation of indicators, eight qualitative indicators were considered, originating from the social, economic, and natural domains. Table 11 displays the effect of μ on the DMs' weights of three social domain indicators (C_{13}, C_{16}, and C_{17}). This table indicates that the weights assigned by different experts to the same indicator exhibit notable variation with changes in μ values. However, as observed in Figure 7, the adjustable parameter μ exerts minimal influence on the evaluation results of the eight qualitative indicators, which remain largely constant. These findings suggest that the evaluation outcomes of qualitative indicators are not sensitive to μ, highlighting significant individual differences among experts but a negligible effect on collective results. This outcome also affirms the robustness of the EGDMT in indicator evaluation.

Figures 8 and 9 display the variations in the urban flood resilience evaluation results from 2017 to 2021. The analysis reveals that, on one hand, with μ = 0.5, irrespective of the λ value, the evaluation results from 2017 to 2021 exhibit only minor changes, while maintaining a consistent upward trend. On the other hand, with λ = 0.5, regardless of the μ value, the evaluation results for the same period remain nearly constant, with the overall upward trend continuing. These findings suggest that the urban flood resilience evaluation is not sensitive to either λ or μ, thus affirming the high robustness of the urban flood resilience assessment method proposed in this study.

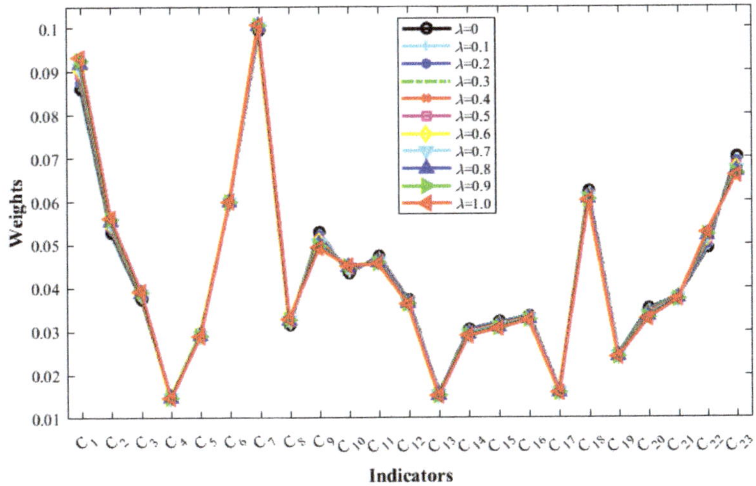

Figure 6. Changes in the indicator weight with λ.

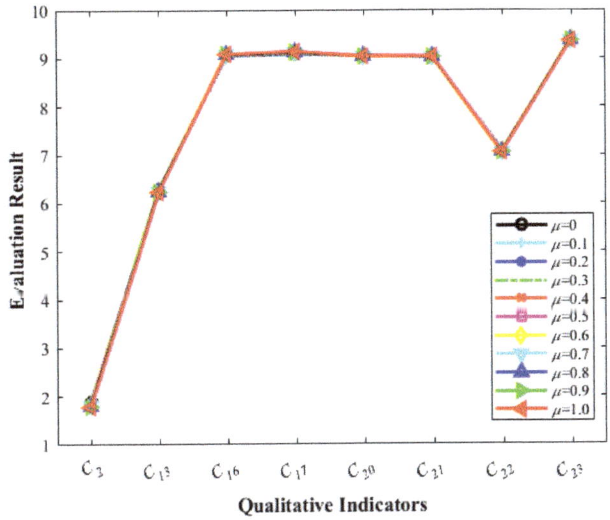

Figure 7. The indicator evaluation changes with μ.

Table 11. Variation in the weights assigned by DM in the social domain with respect to μ.

μ	C_{13}			C_{16}			C_{17}		
	χ^1	χ^2	χ^3	χ^1	χ^2	χ^3	χ^1	χ^2	χ^3
0.0	0.3157	0.2951	0.3893	0.2933	0.3405	0.3663	0.2899	0.3334	0.3767
0.5	0.4078	0.2936	0.2985	0.3966	0.2998	0.3036	0.395	0.2962	0.3088
1.0	0.5	0.2922	0.2078	0.5	0.259	0.241	0.5	0.259	0.241

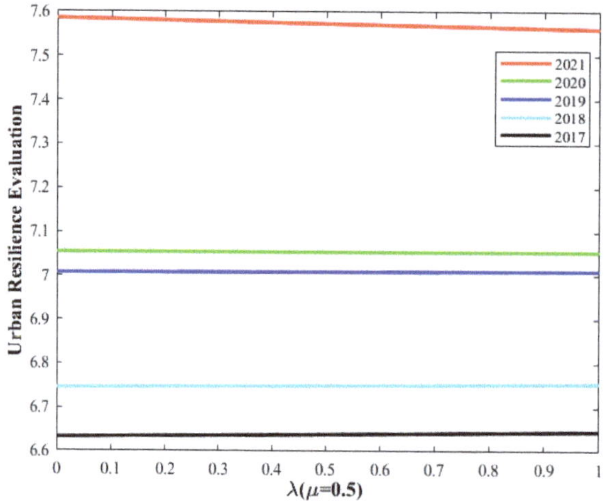

Figure 8. The urban flood resilience evaluation changes with λ.

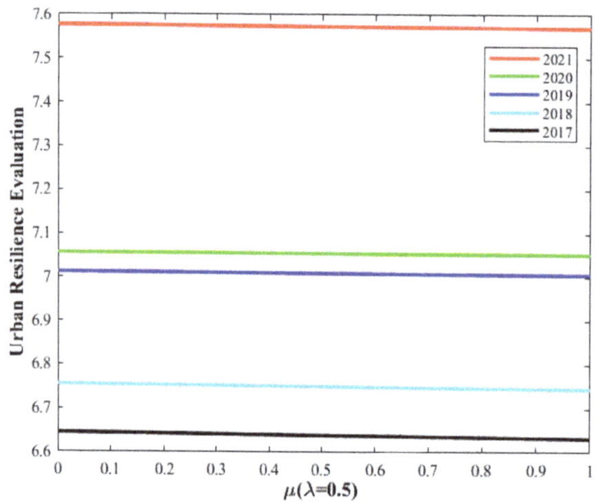

Figure 9. The urban flood resilience evaluation changes with μ.

6. Discussion

A comprehensive evaluation model is proposed in this paper, including both quantitative and qualitative indicators. The SW-GAHP method effectively integrates the inputs of multiple decision-makers, assigning relevance to decision-makers based on their intrapersonal and interpersonal consistency. This approach aligns more closely with real-world scenarios, yielding more precise indicator weights. For the appraisal of qualitative indicators, the EGDMT, capable of handling heterogeneous data with various uncertainties, is proposed. The evaluation of quantitative indicators is facilitated through the use of FPMF.

As far as we are aware, no research has been conducted that simultaneously takes into account heterogeneous data, qualitative and quantitative indicators, and an all-encompassing evaluation of urban flood resilience in the body of current literature. Since previous methods do not exhibit similar capabilities, direct computational comparisons are not feasible. Thus, this paper refrains from a direct methodological comparison. Instead, a comparative analysis is conducted to highlight the distinctive attributes of our proposed method. The comparison of our approach with several recent methodologies is detailed in Table 12.

Table 12. Analytical comparison using recent methods.

Methods	Indicator Selection	Indicator Evaluations	Data Types	Indicator Weights	Expert Weights	Result
Zhang, Shang. [11]	PSR-SEEI	Linear normalization	Exact numbers	EWM+AHP	--	a crisp number
Zhang et al. [15]	SEIE	Linear normalization	Exact numbers	AHP	--	a crisp number
Li, Zhang, et al. [61]	RCRA	Quantitative indicators: linear normalization Qualitative indicators: Group decision-making	Exact numbers Hesitant fuzzy set	weighted averaging operator	minimum divergence model	a crisp number
Proposed method	PSR-SENCE+SR	Quantitative indicators: FPMF Qualitative indicators: Group decision-making	Exact numbers Interval numbers Statistical numbers Linguistic terms Linguistic expressions	SW-GAHP	SWM UD+GB	an NCM

Given the multitude of factors that must be considered in evaluating urban flood resilience, it is essential to devise a MCDM method that can effectively include both qualitative and quantitative indicators. Initially, in constructing the indicator systems, prior methodologies [11,15,61] employed their respective frameworks to thoroughly examine the disturbance process of urban floods. This analysis includes the "pressure" prior to the disturbance, the "state" during the disturbance, and the "adaptation" subsequent to the disturbance. However, there is a lack of comprehensive and systematic indicator screening methods. This paper uses a comprehensive SR indicator screening method and describes in detail the process of selecting 23 key indicators from 1172 related studies. This approach is more universal than the other methods and has certain guiding significance in this research field. Secondly, the resilience of quantitative indicators, when calculated using the linear normalization method, often fails to accurately represent the actual degree of resilience. In this paper, the resilience of quantitative indicators is determined through the FPMF method. This method is adept at adapting to both linear and nonlinear change rules of indicators with varying meanings, thus accurately reflecting their real impact on urban flood resilience. Thirdly, group decision-making technology is used to evaluate the resilience of qualitative indicators in the face of uncertainty. As indicated in Table 12, prior methods [11,15] are limited to handling exact numbers, and Li, Zhang, et al. [61] can also accommodate hesitant fuzzy information containing uncertainty. In contrast, the methodology proposed in this paper is capable of managing heterogeneous data, including exact numbers, statistical data, interval numbers, linguistic terms, and linguistic expressions. Regarding the allocation of indicator weights, previous methods [11,15,61] did not utilize group decision-making technology. While Zhang and Shang [61] involved five decision-makers in the evaluation of qualitative indicators, they only considered the group consensus among DMs for the weight of DMs. The SW-GAHP method allows multiple DMs to participate and assign the weight of indicators by combining the intrapersonal and interpersonal consistency of the DMs, effectively using collective intelligence. Finally, a novel qualitative indicators evaluation method, the EGDMT, is proposed. This method can handle and convey uncertain information during the evaluation process, and the final results incorporate both numerical values and uncertainties, a feature not found in previous methods [11,15,61], which lack the capability to manage uncertainty, yielding only deterministic results.

The application case and the comparative analysis herein demonstrate that this paper offers a more rational and effective approach for urban flood resilience evaluation. It utilizes a hybrid multi-indicator group decision-making method based on the PSR-SENCE model, heterogeneous data, and group decision-making techniques. The advantages of the methodology presented in this paper with regard to earlier approaches are clearly articulated.

(1). A comprehensive SR method was utilized to identify 23 critical influencing factors.
(2). A thorough qualitative and quantitative evaluation of urban flood resilience was conducted.
(3). The resilience evaluation of quantitative indicators accounted for both linearity and nonlinearity, in accordance with their respective meanings, employing the FPMF method for evaluation.
(4). Group decision-making technology is used to evaluate qualitative indicators, allowing multiple decision-makers in the field to participate while weighting based on the decision-maker's contribution, considering intrapersonal consistency and interpersonal consistency.
(5). Heterogeneous data, including various uncertainties, such as exact numbers, statistical data, interval numbers, linguistic terms, NCMs, and linguistic expressions, are utilized to articulate evaluation results. This approach significantly increases the flexibility and applicability of knowledge representation across different stakeholders.
(6). A new method for determining indicator weights, designated SW-GAHP, is proposed. This method comprehensively assesses the decision-making quality in a rational manner. It ensures a more objective and precise determination of weights for each evaluation indicator.
(7). Cloud model theory is applied to manage the uncertainty inherent in heterogeneous data. The final result, represented by an NCM, incorporates not only numerical information but retains uncertainty information as well.
(8). A new evaluation method, EGDMT, is proposed to evaluate the qualitative indicators. This method facilitates a comprehensive and accurate evaluation of urban flood resilience without imposing additional burden on decision-makers, proving to be more reasonable and effective compared to previous methods.
(9). The hybrid MCGDM method is characterized by a clear problem description and a transparent implementation process. All calculations can be executed automatically through programming.

7. Conclusions

Extreme flooding is a significant challenge for urban development and building in an era of rapidly increasing population expansion and urbanization. This paper proposes a hybrid MCDM method based on the PSR-SENCE model, heterogeneous data, and group decision-making technology (GDMT). Based on the PSR-SENCE model, a combined indicator system including both quantitative and qualitative measures is constructed. Additionally, a new indicator weight calculation method called SW-GAHP is proposed. This method thoroughly considers both the intrapersonal consistency and interpersonal consistency of different DMs, increasing the rationality and accuracy of the weights of the indicators. An EGDMT method based on heterogeneous data is proposed for the evaluation of qualitative indicators. This method accounts for the uncertain degree and group consensus bias of DMs. It not only eases the burden on the super-decision-maker but also uses collective wisdom for decision-making, thereby minimizing the influence of individual biases on the overall evaluation. For the assessment of quantitative indicators, the more pragmatic FPMF method is utilized to enhance the rationality of quantitative indicator evaluation. Subsequently, the evaluation of both quantitative and qualitative indicators is converted into NCMs, enabling a consistent consideration of the uncertainty inherent in various heterogeneous data. The urban flood resilience evaluation not only includes numerical information but also retains uncertainty information, aligning more closely with human cognition and facilitating ease of understanding and acceptance. The evaluation of urban flood resilience in Beijing shows a year-on-year improvement from 2017 to 2021 with an overall increase of 14.1%. Moreover, based on the 2021 data, the uncertainty in the urban flood resilience evaluation of Beijing is significantly reduced, particularly when compared to the top three ranked indicators of short-term heavy rainfall and communication capacity. This underscores the effectiveness of the method that integrates qualitative and quantitative aspects, thereby enhancing the precision of urban flood resilience evaluation. Recommendations for positive indicators such as regional economic status, drainage capability, and public transportation service capacity include the vigorous development of regional economies, enhancement of urban drainage capacity, and optimization of urban road traffic management. For negative indicators like flood risk and population density, strategies involve reducing land population density through relevant diversion policies, enhancing residential environments, and decreasing the faced flood risk. These recommendations offer a theoretical foundation and decision-making guidance for improving urban flood resilience. Finally, through comparative and sensitivity analyses, the superiority and robustness of the method have been substantiated.

Author Contributions: Conceptualization, X.H. and Y.H.; Methodology, X.H. and Y.H.; Software, X.H.; Validation, X.H.; Formal analysis, X.Y.; Writing—original draft, X.H.; Writing—review & editing, X.H. and X.Y.; Visualization, X.H.; Supervision, Y.W.; Funding acquisition, S.W. All authors have read and agreed to the published version of the manuscript.

Funding: This work was supported by Beijing Municipal Science and Technology Plan Project under Grant Z221100005222020.

Data Availability Statement: The datasets generated during and/or analyzed during the current study are available from the corresponding author on reasonable request.

Conflicts of Interest: The authors declare that the work described has not been published before, that it is not under consideration for publication anywhere else, and that its publication has been approved by all co-authors, if any, as well as by the responsible authorities—tacitly or explicitly—at the institute where the work has been carried out. The publisher will not be held legally responsible should there be any claims for compensation. The authors have no relevant financial or non-financial interests to disclose.

References

1. Aijun, Q.; Wei, B.; Jing, G. Exploration and Innovation of Strategy Formulation Method of 100 Resilient Cities Project: A Case study of Deyang City, Sichuan Province. *Urban Dev. Stud.* **2019**, *26*, 38–44.
2. Orencio, P.M.; Fujii, M. A localized disaster-resilience index to assess coastal communities based on an analytic hierarchy process (AHP). *Int. J. Disaster Risk Reduct.* **2013**, *3*, 62–75. [CrossRef]
3. Kotzee, I.; Reyers, B. Piloting a social-ecological index for measuring flood resilience: A composite index approach. *Ecol. Indic.* **2016**, *60*, 45–53. [CrossRef]
4. Liu, D.; Feng, J.; Li, H.; Fu, Q.; Li, M.; Faiz, M.A.; Ali, S.; Li, T.; Khan, M.I. Spatiotemporal variation analysis of regional flood disaster resilience capability using an improved projection pursuit model based on the wind-driven optimization algorithm. *J. Clean. Prod.* **2019**, *241*, 118406. [CrossRef]
5. Bergstrand, K.; Mayer, B.; Brumback, B.; Zhang, Y. Assessing the relationship between social vulnerability and community resilience to hazards. *Soc. Indic. Res.* **2015**, *122*, 391–409. [CrossRef] [PubMed]
6. Bertilsson, L.; Wiklund, K.; de Moura Tebaldi, I.; Veról, A.P.; Miguez, M.G. Urban flood resilience–A multi-criteria index to integrate flood resilience into urban planning. *J. Hydrol.* **2019**, *573*, 970–982. [CrossRef]
7. Duleba, S.; Szádoczki, Z. Comparing aggregation methods in large-scale group AHP: Time for the shift to distance-based aggregation. *Expert Syst. Appl.* **2022**, *196*, 116667. [CrossRef]
8. Grošelj, P.; Stirn, L.Z.; Ayrilmis, N.; Kuzman, M.K. Comparison of some aggregation techniques using group analytic hierarchy process. *Expert Syst. Appl.* **2015**, *42*, 2198–2204. [CrossRef]
9. Grošelj, P.; Dolinar, G. Group AHP framework based on geometric standard deviation and interval group pairwise comparisons. *Inf. Sci.* **2023**, *626*, 370–389. [CrossRef]
10. Dong, Q.; Cooper, O. A peer-to-peer dynamic adaptive consensus reaching model for the group AHP decision making. *Eur. J. Oper. Res.* **2016**, *250*, 521–530. [CrossRef]
11. Zhang, Y.; Shang, K. Cloud model assessment of urban flood resilience based on PSR model and game theory. *Int. J. Disaster Risk Reduct.* **2023**, *97*, 104050. [CrossRef]
12. Cao, F.; Xu, X.; Zhang, C.; Kong, W. Evaluation of urban flood resilience and its Space-Time Evolution: A case study of Zhejiang Province, China. *Ecol. Indic.* **2023**, *154*, 110643. [CrossRef]
13. Ji, J.; Wang, D. Evaluation analysis and strategy selection in urban flood resilience based on EWM-TOPSIS method and graph model. *J. Clean. Prod.* **2023**, *425*, 138955. [CrossRef]
14. Jiang, F.; Xie, Z.; Xu, J.; Yang, S.; Zheng, D.; Liang, Y.; Hou, Z.; Wang, J. Spatial and component analysis of urban flood Resiliency of kunming city in China. *Int. J. Disaster Risk Reduct.* **2023**, *93*, 103759. [CrossRef]

15. Zhang, Z.; Zhang, J.; Zhang, Y.; Chen, Y.; Yan, J. Urban Flood Resilience Evaluation Based on GIS and Multi-Source Data: A Case Study of Changchun City. *Remote Sens.* **2023**, *15*, 1872. [CrossRef]
16. Yang, X.; Xu, Z.; Xu, J. Large-scale group Delphi method with heterogeneous decision information and dynamic weights. *Expert Syst. Appl.* **2023**, *213*, 118782. [CrossRef]
17. Li, D. Membership clouds and membership cloud generators. *Comput. Res. Dev.* **1995**, *32*, 15–20.
18. Li, D.; Han, J.; Shi, X.; Chan, M.C. Knowledge representation and discovery based on linguistic atoms. *Knowl.-Based Syst.* **1998**, *10*, 431–440. [CrossRef]
19. Wang, J.; Peng, L.; Zhang, H.; Chen, X. Method of multi-criteria group decision-making based on cloud aggregation operators with linguistic information. *Inf. Sci.* **2014**, *274*, 177–191. [CrossRef]
20. Peng, H.G.; Wang, J.Q. A multicriteria group decision-making method based on the normal cloud model with Zadeh's Z-numbers. *IEEE Trans. Fuzzy Syst.* **2018**, *26*, 3246–3260. [CrossRef]
21. Wang, P.; Xu, X.; Huang, S.; Cai, C. A linguistic large group decision making method based on the cloud model. *IEEE Trans. Fuzzy Syst.* **2018**, *26*, 3314–3326. [CrossRef]
22. Liu, H.C.; Wang, L.E.; Li, Z.W.; Hu, Y.P. Improving risk evaluation in FMEA with cloud model and hierarchical TOPSIS method. *IEEE Trans. Fuzzy Syst.* **2018**, *27*, 84–95. [CrossRef]
23. Li, D.; Liu, C.; Gan, W. A new cognitive model: Cloud model. *Int. J. Intell. Syst.* **2009**, *24*, 357–375. [CrossRef]
24. Yang, X.J.; Zeng, L.; Zhang, R. Cloud Delphi method. *Int. J. Uncertain. Fuzziness Knowl.-Based Syst.* **2012**, *20*, 77–97. [CrossRef]
25. Yang, X.J.; Zeng, L.; Luo, F.; Wang, S.X. Cloud hierarchical analysis. *J. Inf. Comput. Sci.* **2010**, *7*, 2468–2477.
26. Yang, X.J.; Yan, L.L.; Zeng, L. How to handle uncertainties in AHP: The Cloud Delphi hierarchical analysis. *Inf. Sci.* **2013**, *222*, 384–404. [CrossRef]
27. Li, D.; Du, Y. *Artificial Intelligence with Uncertainty*; CRC Press: Boca Raton, FL, USA, 2017.
28. Li, C.B.; Qi, Z.Q.; Feng, X. A multi-risks group evaluation method for the informatization project under linguistic environment. *J. Intell. Fuzzy Syst.* **2014**, *26*, 1581–1592. [CrossRef]
29. Yang, X.; Xu, Z.; He, R.; Xue, F. Credibility assessment of complex simulation models using cloud models to represent and aggregate diverse evaluation results. In *International Conference on Intelligent Computing*; Springer International Publishing: Cham, Switzerland, 2019; pp. 306–317.
30. Yang, X.; Yan, L.; Peng, H.; Gao, X. Encoding words into Cloud models from interval-valued data via fuzzy statistics and membership function fitting. *Knowl.-Based Syst.* **2014**, *55*, 114–124. [CrossRef]
31. Rodríguez, R.M.; Martínez, L.; Herrera, F. A group decision making model dealing with comparative linguistic expressions based on hesitant fuzzy linguistic term sets. *Inf. Sci.* **2013**, *241*, 28–42. [CrossRef]
32. Rapport, D.J.; Friend, A. *Towards a Comprehensive Framework for Environmental Statistics: A Stress-Response Approach*; Statistics Canada: Ottawa, Canada, 1979.
33. OECD 2013. Framework of OECD work on environmental data and indicators. In *Environment at a Glance 2013*; OECD iLibrary: Paris, France, 2013. [CrossRef]
34. Ma, S.J.; Wang, R.S. The social-economic-natural complex ecosystem. *Acta Ecol. Sin.* **1984**, *4*, 1–9.
35. Wang, R.; Li, F.; Hu, D.; Li, B.L. Understanding eco-complexity: Social-economic-natural complex ecosystem approach. *Ecol. Complex.* **2011**, *8*, 15–29. [CrossRef]
36. Zhu, S.; Li, D.; Feng, H.; Zhang, N. The influencing factors and mechanisms for urban flood resilience in China: From the perspective of social-economic-natural complex ecosystem. *Ecol. Indic.* **2023**, *147*, 109959. [CrossRef]
37. Porio, E. Vulnerability, adaptation, and resilience to floods and climate change-related risks among marginal, riverine communities in Metro Manila. *Asian J. Soc. Sci.* **2011**, *39*, 425–445. [CrossRef]
38. Qi, W.; Ma, C.; Xu, H.; Zhao, K. Urban flood response analysis for designed rainstorms with different characteristics based on a tracer-aided modeling simulation. *J. Clean. Prod.* **2022**, *355*, 131797. [CrossRef]
39. Forrest, S.A.; Trell, E.M.; Woltjer, J. Socio-spatial inequalities in flood resilience: Rainfall flooding in the city of Arnhem. *Cities* **2020**, *105*, 102843. [CrossRef]
40. Disse, M.; Johnson, T.G.; Leandro, J.; Hartmann, T. Exploring the relation between flood risk management and flood resilience. *Water Secur.* **2020**, *9*, 100059. [CrossRef]
41. Gersonius, B.; Nasruddin, F.; Ashley, R.; Jeuken, A.; Pathirana, A.; Zevenbergen, C. Developing the evidence base for mainstreaming adaptation of stormwater systems to climate change. *Water Res.* **2012**, *46*, 6824–6835. [CrossRef]
42. Lu, X.; Liao, W.; Fang, D.; Lin, K.; Tian, Y.; Zhang, C.; Zheng, Z.; Zhao, P. Quantification of disaster resilience in civil engineering: A review. *J. Saf. Sci. Resil.* **2020**, *1*, 19–30. [CrossRef]
43. Percival, S.; Teeuw, R. A methodology for urban micro-scale coastal flood vulnerability and risk assessment and mapping. *Nat. Hazards* **2019**, *97*, 355–377. [CrossRef]
44. Braun, B.; Aßheuer, T. Floods in megacity environments: Vulnerability and coping strategies of slum dwellers in Dhaka/Bangladesh. *Nat. Hazards* **2011**, *58*, 771–787. [CrossRef]
45. Chakraborty, L.; Rus, H.; Henstra, D.; Thistlethwaite, J.; Minano, A.; Scott, D. Exploring spatial heterogeneity and environmental injustices in exposure to flood hazards using geographically weighted regression. *Environ. Res.* **2022**, *210*, 112982. [CrossRef] [PubMed]

46. Lee, H.K.; Hong, W.H.; Lee, Y.H. Experimental study on the influence of water depth on the evacuation speed of elderly people in flood conditions. *Int. J. Disaster Risk Reduct.* **2019**, *39*, 101198. [CrossRef]
47. Damm, M. Mapping Social-Ecological Vulnerability to Flooding. A Sub-National Approach for Germany. Ph.D. Thesis, Rheinische Friedrich-Wilhelms-Universität Bonn, Bonn, Germany, 2010.
48. Zhang, H.; Yang, J.; Li, L.; Shen, D.; Wei, G.; Dong, S. Measuring the resilience to floods: A comparative analysis of key flood control cities in China. *Int. J. Disaster Risk Reduct.* **2021**, *59*, 102248. [CrossRef]
49. Zhu, S.; Li, D.; Huang, G.; Chhipi-Shrestha, G.; Nahiduzzaman, K.M.; Hewage, K.; Sadiq, R. Enhancing urban flood resilience: A holistic framework incorporating historic worst flood to Yangtze River Delta, China. *Int. J. Disaster Risk Reduct.* **2021**, *61*, 102355. [CrossRef]
50. Li, G.; Kou, C.; Wang, Y.; Yang, H. System dynamics modelling for improving urban resilience in Beijing, China. *Resour. Conserv. Recycl.* **2020**, *161*, 104954. [CrossRef]
51. Alexandre, K. When it rains: Stormwater management, redevelopment, and chronologies of infrastructure. *Geoforum* **2018**, *97*, 66–72. [CrossRef]
52. Fenner, R.; O'Donnell, E.; Ahilan, S.; Dawson, D.; Vercruysse, K. Achieving urban flood resilience in an uncertain future. *Water* **2019**, *11*, 1082. [CrossRef]
53. Hsieh, C.H.; Feng, C.M. The highway resilience and vulnerability in Taiwan. *Transp. Policy* **2020**, *87*, 1–9. [CrossRef]
54. Sen, M.K.; Dutta, S.; Kabir, G.; Pujari, N.N.; Laskar, S.A. An integrated approach for modelling and quantifying housing infrastructure resilience against flood hazard. *J. Clean. Prod.* **2021**, *288*, 125526. [CrossRef]
55. Huang, G.; Li, D.; Zhu, X.; Zhu, J. Influencing factors and their influencing mechanisms on urban resilience in China. *Sustain. Cities Soc.* **2021**, *74*, 103210. [CrossRef]
56. Khalili, S.; Harre, M.; Morley, P. A temporal framework of social resilience indicators of communities to flood, case studies: Wagga wagga and Kempsey, NSW, Australia. *Int. J. Disaster Risk Reduct.* **2015**, *13*, 248–254. [CrossRef]
57. *GB/T 40947-2021*; Guide for Safety Resilient City Evaluation. Standardization Administration of China: Beijing, China, 2021.
58. Gawith, D.; Daigneault, A.; Brown, P. Does community resilience mitigate loss and damage from climaterelated disasters? Evidence based on survey data. *J. Environ. Plan. Manag.* **2016**, *59*, 2102–2123. [CrossRef]
59. Chandra, A.; Williams, M.; Plough, A.; Stayton, A.; Wells, K.B.; Horta, M.; Tang, J. Getting Actionable About Community Resilience: The Los Angeles County Community Disaster Resilience Project. *Am. J. Public Health* **2013**, *103*, 1181–1189. [CrossRef]
60. Ha'apio, M.O.; Gonzalez, R.; Wairiu, M. Is there any chance for the poor to cope with extreme environmental events? Two case studies in the Solomon Islands. *World Dev.* **2019**, *122*, 514–524. [CrossRef]
61. Li, Z.; Zhang, X.; Ma, Y.; Feng, C.; Hajiyev, A. A multi-criteria decision making method for urban flood resilience evaluation with hybrid uncertainties. *Int. J. Disaster Risk Reduct.* **2019**, *36*, 101140. [CrossRef]
62. Folke, C. Resilience: The emergence of a perspective for social–ecological systems analyses. *Glob. Environ. Change* **2006**, *16*, 253–267. [CrossRef]
63. Luthar, S.S.; Cicchetti, D.; Becker, B. The construct of resilience: A critical evaluation and guidelines for future work. *Child Dev.* **2000**, *71*, 543–562. [CrossRef]
64. Douglas, I.; Garvin, S.; Lawson, N.; Richards, J.; Tippett, J.; White, I. Urban pluvial flooding: A qualitative case study of cause, effect and nonstructural mitigation. *J. Flood Risk Manag.* **2010**, *3*, 112–125. [CrossRef]
65. Gall, M.; Borden, K.A.; Emrich, C.T.; Cutter, S.L. The unsustainable trend of natural hazard losses in the United States. *Sustainability* **2011**, *3*, 2157–2181. [CrossRef]
66. Xiao, Y.; Drucker, J. Does economic diversity enhance regional disaster resilience? *J. Am. Plan. Assoc.* **2013**, *79*, 148–160. [CrossRef]
67. Bukvic, A.; Smith, A.; Zhang, A. Evaluating drivers of coastal relocation in Hurricane Sandy affected communities. *Int. J. Disaster Risk Reduct.* **2015**, *13*, 215–228. [CrossRef]
68. Orabi, W.; Senouci, A.B.; El-Rayes, K.; Al-Derham, H. Optimizing resource utilization during the recovery of civil infrastructure systems. *J. Manag. Eng.* **2010**, *26*, 237–246. [CrossRef]
69. Kittipongvises, S.; Phetrak, A.; Rattanapun, P.; Brundiers, K.; Buizer, J.L.; Melnick, R. AHP-GIS analysis for flood hazard assessment of the communities nearby the world heritage site on Ayutthaya Island, Thailand. *Int. J. Disaster Risk Reduct.* **2020**, *48*, 101612. [CrossRef]
70. Makhoul, N. From sustainable to resilient and smart cities[C]//IABSE Symposium Report. *Int. Assoc. Bridge Struct. Eng.* **2015**, *105*, 1–6.
71. Yang, X.; Xu, Z.; Ouyang, H.; Wang, L. Credibility assessment of simulation models using flexible mapping functions. In Proceedings of the 2019 IEEE 8th Joint International Information Technology and Artificial Intelligence Conference, Chongqing, China, 24–26 May 2019; pp. 487–492.

entropy

MDPI

Article

Unique Method for Prognosis of Risk of Depressive Episodes Using Novel Measures to Model Uncertainty Under Data Privacy

Barbara Pękala [1,2,*], Dawid Kosior [1], Wojciech Rząsa [1], Katarzyna Garwol [1] and Janusz Czuma [3]

[1] Institute of Computer Science, University of Rzeszów, 35-310 Rzeszów, Poland; dkosior@ur.edu.pl (D.K.); wrzasa@ur.edu.pl (W.R.); kgarwol@ur.edu.pl (K.G.)
[2] Department of Artificial Intelligence, University of Information Technology and Management, 35-225 Rzeszów, Poland
[3] LUX MED—PROFEMED Medical Center, 35-315 Rzeszów, Poland; ddcad55@gmail.com
* Correspondence: bpekala@ur.edu.pl

Abstract

The research described in this paper focuses on key aspects of learning from data concerning the symptoms of depression and how to prevent it. The computer support system designed for that purpose combines data privacy protection from various sources and uncertainty modeling, especially for incomplete data. The mentioned aspects are key to real-life medical diagnostic problems. From among the different paradigms of machine learning, a federated learning-based approach was chosen as the most suitable to take up the challenge. Importantly, computer support in medical diagnostics often requires algorithms that are appropriate for processing data expressing uncertainty and that can ensure high-quality diagnostics. To achieve this goal, a novel decision-making algorithm is used that employs interval entropy measures based on the theory of interval-valued fuzzy sets. Such an approach enables one to take into account diagnostic uncertainty, express it exactly, and interpret it easily. Furthermore, the applied classification technique offers the possibility of a straightforward explanation of the diagnosis, which is a situation required by many physicians. The presented solution combines innovative technological approaches with practical user needs, fostering the development of more effective tools in mental health prevention.

Keywords: interval-valued fuzzy set theory; interval-valued entropy; data uncertainty; federated decision-making; depression risk detection

1. Introduction

This article presents some important results regarding work on a computer system designed to support the analysis of screening tests for identifying the risk of depressive episode occurrence and preventing depression. The use of machine learning algorithms will optimize systemic screening support for depression prevention, making the proposed solution a practical and efficient tool in public health. The proposed system will be available to researchers as a platform for knowledge and experience exchange, as well as to medical practitioners, particularly primary care physicians, to support them in identifying their patients' depression risk. It is worth emphasizing that detecting the initial symptoms of depression and implementing the appropriate therapy often prevent the development of the disease. Depression is an increasingly common disease in modern societies. Computer-aided diagnosis of depression is the subject of various studies. For example, applying deep learning to natural language processing and using it to analyze social media posts for the diagnosis of depression has great potential [1,2]. However, more can and should still be done not only to diagnose the existing disease but also to identify the risk of its future occurrence, which, as mentioned, allows for its prevention in many situations. In [3], a methodology for diagnosing the risk of depression was proposed. However, the issue of data privacy still was a problem, i.e., how to learn to indicate the risk of depression effectively with small datasets. The answer is an implementation of algorithms reaping the benefits of limited cooperation, i.e., from exchanging only information about certain parameters of classification/models. This aspect is addressed in this work. One of the main priorities of the system is the protection of the privacy of data taken from various sources through the use of federated learning techniques [4,5]. The occurrence of this need is common, especially in smaller medical centers where the collected data are not sufficient to successfully use AI techniques to support diagnosis (in this case, depression) due to their small sizes and various internal defects. Some medical data are survey-based, and thus burdened with uncertainty resulting from the specificity of the human mind. For example, individuals may interpret and describe the same situation differently depending on their mood or well-being at various points in time. As a result, the decision-making process based on them is also subject to uncertainty. That is why using advanced methods to present and handle uncertainty is a key element of the methodology adopted in this work. A distinctive feature of the described research is the implementation of a nonstandard decision-making algorithm that integrates interval entropy measures from an epistemic and ontic perspective, based on the theory of interval-valued fuzzy sets (IVFSs) [6,7].

Thus, this paper focuses on two key aspects of modern decision support systems: learning from distributed but federated data sources and modeling various forms of uncertainty. We discuss the following:

1. A federated technique for generating a global decision as a method that can respect uncertainty and provide support in cases with the problem of incomplete data (in the form of interval-valued fuzzy sets) and different local models;
2. Collective decision-making enhanced the effectiveness of local models in early diagnostic systems for depression. These models were developed using a new method that incorporates entropy measures from an epistemic perspective. In this work, we broaden the concept of entropy by introducing new definitions of interval entropy, viewed through an epistemic lens. We also investigate their potential applications, particularly highlighting their usefulness in different areas of data analysis.

2. Related Works

Depression is an increasingly prevalent condition in modern societies. According to data from the World Health Organization (WHO), an estimated 3.8% of the adult population is affected by depression, which translates to approximately 280 million people worldwide. In cases of moderate or severe depressive episodes, life-threatening situations may arise. In the most severe cases, depression can lead to suicide, with over 700,000 people dying by suicide globally each year. Suicide is the fourth leading cause of death among individuals aged 15–29 [8]. Current methods for diagnosing early-stage depression often rely on diagnostic tools that serve as support for psychiatrists. These include various assessment scales and tests such as the Beck Depression Inventory, Hamilton Depression Rating Scale, PHQ-9, QIDS-SR, HDRS, GDS, CES-D, and CESD-R [9,10]. One of the most recent tools, the CESD-R, was developed in 2004 by William Eaton et al. as an updated version of the CES-D scale [11]. This scale is among the most widely used instruments in psychiatric epidemiology. The CESD-R is a self-report tool in which individuals respond to 20 statements describing their potential well-being or behaviors. Respondents choose from five possible answers, ranging from 0 (not at all or less than one day) to 4 (nearly every day for two weeks). The total score ranges from 0 to 80 points. According to the authors, a score of 16 points or higher may indicate a concerning result, suggesting the need for psychiatric or psychological consultation [9].

The 16-point threshold is a topic of debate in the medical community. Therefore, in this article, we utilize the recently proposed and more sensitive test SenDD [3] for machine learning, which evaluates the risk of depressive episodes more rigorously than existing methods in the literature. Moreover, the presented approach prioritizes data privacy (using diverse datasets) and is designed to accommodate imprecise data sources, including those with missing values. Federated learning addresses privacy concerns by enabling collaborative algorithm training without the necessity of exchanging sensitive data, thus tackling key challenges in data governance and privacy [4,12,13]. Unlike distributed learning within data center environments or traditional methods of processing private data, federated learning presents unique challenges, including communication efficiency, heterogeneity, and privacy. This paradigm has been extensively studied in works such as [4,5,14], and we investigate its potential application in diagnosing depression. The second key issue addressed in this work is the problem of missing data. To tackle this, the theory of interval-valued fuzzy sets demonstrates itself as an effective tool for classifying data with uncertainty. Interval-valued fuzzy sets [6,7] offer flexibility in defining the degree to which elements belong to a given set concept [15]. Researchers have introduced a variety of operators and measures for interval-valued fuzzy sets. These include aggregation measures such as implication, entropy, or similarity, as well as containment measures (precedence index). These have been applied in decision-support processes [16–20]. Representing uncertainty is crucial for decision-making in the case of incomplete information or imprecise data. The selection of an appropriate representation method depends on the problem's context and the characteristics of the available data. In interval-valued fuzzy sets, uncertainty is managed by representing attribute values as intervals. This paper adopts an epistemic approach, where attribute or measurement values for individual objects are defined within the bounds of intervals. The literature contains several approaches for modeling uncertainty and imprecision to enable learning from incomplete or ambiguous data and classifying them, as explored in studies such as [21–23]. However, there is still a need for more effective methods to represent uncertainty. In this work, we propose interval entropy measures based on the concepts of possibility and necessity. To this end, we introduce various comparability measures to construct interval entropy measures that are either more restrictive or general compared to classical approaches. The proposed system integrates a federated machine learning algorithm with a novel diagnostic test to support preventive diagnostics particularly when the input data are incomplete.

3. Representation of Uncertainty by Interval-Valued Fuzzy Set Theory

The prevalent presence of uncertainty in real-life datasets constitutes the primary motivation for the research described in this paper. The direction and methods of the research, apart from enhancing federated learning, stem from many challenges of decision-making support, particularly in medical practice. Uncertainty or imprecision finds an effective representation through interval-valued fuzzy sets, as evidenced by numerous practical applications. The concept of interval-valued fuzzy sets is based on the understanding that uncertainty can arise from two distinct sources: epistemic and ontic. In the epistemic sense, which is exploited in this paper, uncertainty is attributed to the lack of precise knowledge, where the interval represents limit values encompassing a single desired value.

Application of IVFS to various real-world problems, such as pattern recognition, medical diagnosis, decision-making, and image thresholding, often involves leveraging critical measures like distances, inclusion, equivalence, similarity, or entropy within interval-valued fuzzy sets, as discussed in works such as [24–27].

Entropy measures, in particular, are a focal point of our research. We introduce a novel approach to defining these measures, specifically aimed at modeling uncertainty. Furthermore, these newly proposed entropy measures play a pivotal role as a core component of the innovative diagnostic system we have developed.

3.1. *Orders in the Interval Setting*

A crucial object in the interval-valued fuzzy set theory is a set $L^I = \{[\underline{\zeta},\overline{\zeta}] : \underline{\zeta},\overline{\zeta} \in [0,1], \underline{\zeta} \leqslant \overline{\zeta}\}$ which denotes a family of all subintervals of the unit interval. In the articles by Zadeh [7], Sambuc [6], Turksen [28], and Gorzalczany [29], an **interval-valued fuzzy set** (IVFS) Z in X ($X \neq \emptyset$) is defined as a mapping $Z : X \to L^I$ such that for each $x \in X$, the interval $Z(x) = [\underline{Z}(x), \overline{Z}(x)]$ expresses the degree of membership of an element x to Z. We assume that the considered universe of discourse will be finite—that is, $X = \{x_1, \ldots, x_n\}$. Further, the family of all interval-valued fuzzy sets in X will be denoted by IVFS(X). All elements $[\underline{\zeta},\overline{\zeta}]$ of L^I such that $\underline{\zeta} = \overline{\zeta}$ are called crisp.

What is more, we may denote $Z \in \text{IVFS}(X)$ as $Z = \{\langle x, Z(x)\rangle : x \in X,\ Z : X \to L^I\}$. The interval-valued fuzzy set is a straightforward generalization of a classical fuzzy set described by $\{\langle x, Z(x)\rangle : x \in X,\ Z : X \to [0,1]\}$. Indeed, for fuzzy sets, the membership of each element x is always a precisely given real number. On the other hand, the degree of membership of an element x to the interval-valued fuzzy set (perceived from the epistemic point of view—see [30]) is not precise: we know only its upper and lower bounds. This is why interval-valued fuzzy sets appear to be very useful for our considerations.

3.1.1. Partial and Linear Orders

The best-known partial order in L^I is defined as follows:

$$[\underline{\zeta},\overline{\zeta}] \leq_2 [\underline{\eta},\overline{\eta}] \quad \Leftrightarrow \quad \underline{\zeta} \leq \underline{\eta}, \quad \overline{\zeta} \leq \overline{\eta}. \tag{1}$$

with the joint and meet operations defined in L^I, respectively, as

$$[\underline{\zeta},\overline{\zeta}] \vee [\underline{\eta},\overline{\eta}] = [\max(\underline{\zeta},\underline{\eta}), \max(\overline{\zeta},\overline{\eta})], \quad [\underline{\zeta},\overline{\zeta}] \wedge [\underline{\eta},\overline{\eta}] = [\min(\underline{\zeta},\underline{\eta}), \min(\overline{\zeta},\overline{\eta})].$$

These create the structure $(L^I, \vee, \wedge)$, which is a complete lattice, where $1_{L^I} = [1,1]$ and $0_{L^I} = [0,0]$ are the greatest and the smallest element of $(L^I, \leqslant_2)$, respectively.

In many real-life problems, we need a linear order to compare any two intervals, so we are interested in extending the partial order $\leqslant_2$ to a linear one. We call this relation an admissible order as in the source paper [31], from which Definition 1 and Proposition 1 come.

Definition 1. *An order $\leq_{Adm}$ in L^I is called **admissible linear** if*

1. *$\leq_{Adm}$ is linear in L^I;*
2. *For all $\zeta, \eta \in L^I$ $\zeta \leq_{Adm} \eta$ whenever $\zeta \leqslant_2 \eta$.*

Proposition 1. *Let $\Psi, \Upsilon : [0,1]^2 \to [0,1]$ be two continuous aggregation functions such that for all $\zeta = [\underline{\zeta},\overline{\zeta}], \eta = [\underline{\eta},\overline{\eta}] \in L^I$, the equalities $\Psi(\underline{\zeta},\overline{\zeta}) = \Psi(\underline{\eta},\overline{\eta})$ and $\Upsilon(\underline{\zeta},\overline{\zeta}) = \Upsilon(\underline{\eta},\overline{\eta})$ hold if and only if $\zeta = \eta$. If the order $\leqslant_{\Psi,\Upsilon}$ on L^I is defined by*

$$\zeta \leqslant_{\Psi,\Upsilon} \eta \Leftrightarrow \Psi(\underline{\zeta},\overline{\zeta}) < \Psi(\underline{\eta},\overline{\eta}) \text{ or } (\Psi(\underline{\zeta},\overline{\zeta}) = \Psi(\underline{\eta},\overline{\eta}) \text{ and } \Upsilon(\underline{\zeta},\overline{\zeta}) \leqslant \Upsilon(\underline{\eta},\overline{\eta})), \tag{2}$$

then $\leqslant_{\Psi,\Upsilon}$ is admissible.

Admissible orders were studied, e.g., in [32,33]. A construction of admissible linear orders based on aggregation functions was explored (increasing operation $A : [0,1]^2 \to [0,1]$ such that $A(0,0) = 0$ and $A(1,1) = 1$ [34]).

3.1.2. Possibility and Necessity Issue

We will now discuss alternative definitions of orders on L^I. We observe structures with possible and necessary comparability relations (called "interval orders" in the sense used in the papers of Fishburn in 1970–1985 or Fodor and Roubens (1994)) suitable to the epistemic issue, which follow an intuitive approach to many real-life problems. Properties of the presented below comparability relations were also considered and partially described in [35] or [36].

Necessary Relation

We define the following case of comparability of intervals restricted to the partial or linear order, i.e., necessary relation, which we may interpret as conjunctive (ontic) relation. We say that one interval contains a collection of true values of each variable smaller than or equal to all true values from the second interval.

$$\zeta \leq_{nec} \eta \Leftrightarrow \overline{\zeta} \leq \underline{\eta}, \tag{3}$$

where $\zeta, \eta \in L^I$. It can be interpreted as a satisfied relation for disjoint collections of values. We observe that in L^I, the relation $\leq_{nec}$ is antisymmetric, is transitive, and has the Ferrers property [35].

Possible Relation

This relation describes a more general situation, which we may write as follows:

$$\zeta \leq_{pos} \eta \Leftrightarrow \underline{\zeta} \leq \overline{\eta}, \tag{4}$$

where $\zeta, \eta \in L^I$.

Notice that the relation $\leq_{pos}$ is more appropriate for the epistemic (disjunctive) setting of the intervals. So, if $[\underline{\zeta}, \overline{\zeta}]$ is an imprecise description of variable ζ and $[\underline{\eta}, \overline{\eta}]$ is an imprecise description of variable η, then $[\underline{\zeta}, \overline{\zeta}] \leq_{pos} [\underline{\eta}, \overline{\eta}]$ means that it is possible that the true value of ζ is smaller than or equal to the true value of η. Thus, the relation $\leq_{pos}$ can be interpreted straightforwardly [37].

3.2. *Aggregation Functions*

Now, we recall the concept of an aggregation function in L^I. We consider aggregation with respect to both relations $\leqslant_2$ and $\leqslant_{Adm}$. Later, we use the notation $\leq$ both for the partial or admissible linear order, with $0_{L^I} = [0,0]$ and $1_{L^I} = [1,1]$ as a minimal and maximal element of L^I, respectively. By replacing the monotonicity condition, the natural order $\leq$, with the admissible linear orders or relations $\leq_{pos}$ and $\leq_{nec}$, new types of aggregation functions are obtained [20] and denoted by $\mathcal{A}_{pos}$, $\mathcal{A}_{nec}$, respectively. Therefore, we use the concepts of aggregation consistent with the mentioned orders (similar to [20,33,38,39]) as follows:

Definition 2. *An operation $\mathcal{A} : (L^I)^n \to L^I$, where $n \geqslant 2$, is called an* ***interval-valued aggregation function*** *if it is increasing with respect to the order $\leq$ (partial or admissible linear or possible or necessary), i.e., for all $\zeta_i, \eta_i \in L^I$:*

$$\zeta_i \leq \eta_i \Rightarrow \mathcal{A}(\zeta_1, \ldots, \zeta_n) \leq \mathcal{A}(\eta_1, \ldots, \eta_n) \tag{5}$$

$$\text{and} \quad \mathcal{A}(\underbrace{0_{L^I},\ldots,0_{L^I}}_{n\times}) = 0_{L^I}, \quad \mathcal{A}(\underbrace{1_{L^I},\ldots,1_{L^I}}_{n\times}) = 1_{L^I}.$$

Sometimes, to shorten the notation, we write $\mathcal{A}_{i=1}^{n}(\zeta_i)$ instead of $\mathcal{A}(\zeta_1,\ldots,\zeta_n)$. This is especially useful when the aggregated objects cannot be denoted concisely.

Example 1. *The following operations represent classic, possible (belonging to the set of pos-aggregation functions—$\mathcal{A}_{pos}$), or necessary (belonging to the set of nec-aggregation functions—$\mathcal{A}_{nec}$) aggregation functions:*

$$\mathcal{A}_{mean}([\underline{\zeta},\overline{\zeta}],[\underline{\eta},\overline{\eta}]) = \left[\frac{\underline{\zeta}+\underline{\eta}}{2}, \frac{\overline{\zeta}+\overline{\eta}}{2}\right],$$

$$\mathcal{A}_{pos}([\underline{\zeta},\overline{\zeta}],[\underline{\eta},\overline{\eta}]) = \begin{cases} 0_{L^I} & \zeta = \eta = 0_{L^I} \\ [A(\underline{\zeta},\underline{\eta}),1], & \text{otherwise}, \end{cases}$$

$$\mathcal{A}_{nec}([\underline{\zeta},\overline{\zeta}],[\underline{\eta},\overline{\eta}]) = \left[\frac{\underline{\zeta}+\underline{\eta}}{2}, \max\left(\frac{\underline{\zeta}+\overline{\eta}}{2}, \frac{\overline{\zeta}+\underline{\eta}}{2}\right)\right],$$

where A is an aggregation function.

3.3. Interval Entropy

We can now proceed to the concept of interval entropy. We propose various comparability measures used to define entropy, which may be more restrictive or general compared to the classical approach. Whatever kind of uncertainty there is (imprecision, vagueness, partial truth, measurement errors, uncertainty of interpretation/evaluation of features, and the like), one may be interested in measuring its extent. In probability theory, Shannon's entropy [40] is commonly applied to quantify the average uncertainty of prediction in a random experiment. There exist also entropy-like measures in evidence theory (cf. [41]). De Luca and Termini [42] utilized entropy to evaluate the degree of fuzziness. Yager [43] proposed expressing the measure of uncertainty related to a fuzzy set by the distance between this fuzzy set and its complement. Later on, papers appeared in which generalizations of the entropy were defined for fuzzy sets, interval-valued fuzzy sets, and intuitionistic fuzzy sets (cf. [25,44,45]). Unfortunately, the proposed entropies still assumed scalar real values (from the unit interval), similar to fuzzy sets, and disregarding completely the fact that interval-valued fuzzy sets contain additional uncertainty connected with the inability or hesitance in the unambiguous determination of the membership function.

We are inspired by [46–48], which propose a definition of entropy based on partial or linear orders. In comparison with [47], we extend in this paper the definition of entropy by adding a fourth axiom, which is essential from the application point of view. It is an axiom of the stability of entropy with respect to negation N ($N : L^I \to L^I$ that is decreasing with respect to $\leq$ with $N(1_{L^I}) = 0_{L^I}$ and $N(0_{L^I}) = 1_{L^I}$ [49]). The presented definition proposed and studied in [50] also extends the definition of [48] by using the width of intervals (axiom e2), so uncertainty information is reflected more. But before that, we will introduce the following notation: for $e \in L^I$, such that $N(e) = e$, i.e., e is the equilibrium point, we denote by $\mathbf{E} \in \text{IVFS}(X)$ a mapping such that $\mathbf{E}(x) = e$ for all $x \in X$. Moreover, in this article, we develop the concept of entropy by introducing yet other (in the epistemic and ontic sense) definitions of interval entropy, and in the following sections, we examine their application potential, with particular emphasis on applications in broadly perceived data analysis.

Definition 3. *Let N be a strong (i.e., involutive and decreasing) interval negation with equilibrium point $e \in L^I$ closest to the point $[0.5, 0.5]$. A function $E_I : \mathrm{IVFS}(X) \to L^I$ is an* ***interval entropy*** *on $\mathrm{IVFS}(X)$ with respect to the negation N and order $\leq$ if for $A, B \in \mathrm{IVFS}(X)$, the following hold:*

(e1) $E_I(S) = 0_{L^I}$ *iff S is crisp;*
(e2) $E_I(\mathbf{E}) = [1 - w(e), 1]$*, where $w(e)$ is a width of interval e;*
(e3) $E_I(A) \leq E_I(B)$*, if $A(x) \leq B(x) \leq e$ or $A(x) \geq B(x) \geq e$ for all $x \in X$;*
(e4) $E_I(A) = E_I(A_N)$*, where $A_N(x) = N(A(x))$ for all $x \in X$.*

The next theorems show how to apply a similarity measure and adequate negation function from each class (standard, as well as possible and necessary as in [3]) for constructing an interval entropy. In the classic case, we have the following method of interval entropy construction [50]:

Proposition 2. *Let S_{std} be a similarity measure that satisfies conditions given in [50], where A_1 is an idempotent aggregation function. Then, a function $E_I : \mathrm{IVFS}(X) \to L^I$ defined as*

$$E_I(A) = S_{std}(A, A_N) \tag{6}$$

is the interval entropy with respect to an involutive interval negation N with equilibrium point e.

Example 2. *If we use a similarity measure given in [50] with any precedence indicator considered there, we obtain the interval entropy measures that fulfill condition (e4) in Definition 3 for the standard interval negation $N(x) = [1 - \overline{x}, 1 - \underline{x}]$, where $x = [\underline{x}, \overline{x}]$.*

Let us consider a new measure of possible entropy, also called an optimistic entropy measure that takes into account the comparability relation of intervals.

Definition 4. *Let N_{pos} be a strong involutive negation of the possibility of the equilibrium point $e \in L^I$ ($N_{pos}(e) = e$). Function $E_{pos} : IVFS(X) \to L^I$ is the interval possible entropy on IVFS(X) with respect to the negation N if for $A, B \in IVFS(X)$, the following hold:*

(EP1) $E_{pos}(A) = 0_{L^I}$*, if A is a crisp set;*
(EP2) $E_{pos}(\mathbf{E}) = [1 - w(e), 1]$*, where $w(e)$ is the width of interval e;*
(EP3) $E_{pos}(A) \leq_{pos} E_{pos}(B)$*, if $A(x) \leq_{pos} B(x) \leq_{pos} e$ or $A(x) \geq_{pos} B(x) \geq_{pos} e$ for all $x \in X$.*

The method of constructing the interval optimistic (possible) entropy based on the possible similarity measure is as follows:

Proposition 3. *Let S_{pos} be a possible similarity measure. Then, the function $E : IVFS(X) \to L^I$*

$$E_{pos}(A) = S_{pos}(A, A_{N_{pos}}) \tag{7}$$

is the interval possible entropy with respect to N_{pos} (involute interval possible negation with equilibrium point e).

Proof. If A is a crisp set, then we directly obtain $E_{pos}(A) = 0_{L^I}$. We can obtain (EP2) directly by the idempotency of the similarity measure and the idempotency of the aggregation function $\mathcal{A}$.
If $A \leq_{pos} B \leq_{pos} \mathbf{E}$, then $A \leq_{pos} B \leq_{pos} \mathbf{E} \leq_{pos} B_{N_{pos}} \leq_{pos} A_{N_{pos}}$ and, consequently, from the monotonicity of the similarity measure, we have

$$E_{pos}(A) = S_{pos}(A, A_{N_{pos}}) \leq_{pos} S_{pos}(A, B_{N_{pos}}) \leq_{pos} S_{pos}(B, B_{N_{pos}}) = E_{pos}(B).$$

In a similar way and by the symmetry of the similarity measure, we can prove the case $A \geq_{pos} B \geq_{pos} \mathbf{E}$, which ends the proof of (EP3) and Proposition 3. □

Example 3. *If we use the possibility similarity measure from [3], we then obtain an entropy measure that satisfies Equation (7) with respect to* $N(x) = [1-\overline{x}, 1-\underline{x}]$ *for*

$$S_{pos}(A,B) = \mathcal{A}_{i=1}^{n}\mathcal{B}(\mathrm{Prec}_{pos}(A(x_i), B(x_i)), \mathrm{Prec}_{pos}(B(x_i), A(x_i))),$$

where $\mathcal{A} = \mathcal{A}_{mean}$, $\mathcal{B} = \wedge$ *and* Prec_{pos} *fulfills*

$$\mathrm{Prec}_{\mathcal{A}}(a,b) = \begin{cases} [1-w(a), 1], & \text{if } a = b, \\ 1_{L^I}, & \text{if } a <_{pos} b, \\ \mathcal{A}_{pos}(N_{pos}(a), b), & \text{else.} \end{cases}$$

Another class of entropy is the necessary entropy measure, which uses the necessary relation when comparing intervals.

Definition 5. *Let N_{nec} be a strong (involute) interval necessary negation with an equilibrium point $e \in L^I$. The function $E_{nec} : IVFS(X) \to L^I$ is the interval necessary entropy on $IVFS(X)$ with respect to the negation of N_{nec} if for $A, B \in IVFS(X)$,*

(EN1) $E_{nec}(A) = 0_{L^I}$, *if A is a crisp set;*
(EN2) $E_{nec}(\mathbf{E}) = [1-w(e), 1]$;
(EN3) $E_{nec}(A) \leq E_{nec}(B)$, *if* $A(x) \leq_{nec} B(x) \leq_{nec} e$ *or* $A(x) \geq_{nec} B(x) \geq_{nec} e$ *for all* $x \in X$.

Analogously to possible entropy, based on the necessary similarity measure, we can obtain the necessary entropy:

Proposition 4. *Let S_{nec} be the necessary similarity measure. Then, the function $E_{nec} : IVFS(X) \to L^I$*

$$E_{nec}(A) = S_{nec}(A, A_{N_{nec}}) \tag{8}$$

is the interval necessary entropy with respect to N_{nec} (involutional interval necessary negation with equilibrium point e).

Proof. If A is a crisp set, then (cf. Example 3)

$$\{\mathrm{Prec}_{nec}(A(x_i), B(x_i)), \mathrm{Prec}_{nec}(B(x_i), A(x_i))\} \in \{0_{L^I}, 1_{L^I}\}$$

and because $\mathcal{B}_{nec}$ has a neutral element 1_{L^I}, we obtain $E_{nec}(A) = 0_{L^I}$.
(EN2) can be directly obtained from the idempotency similarity measure.
If $A \leq_{nec} B \leq_{nec} \mathbf{E}$, then $A \leq_{nec} B \leq_{nec} \mathbf{E} \leq_{nec} B_{N_{nec}} \leq_{nec} A_{N_{nec}}$ and by the isotonicity of the necessary similarity measure we have

$$E_{nec}(A) = S_{nec}(A, A_{N_{nec}}) \leq_{nec} S_{nec}(A, B_{N_{nec}}) \leq_{nec} S_{nec}(B, B_{N_{nec}}) = E_{nec}(B).$$

In a similar way, by the symmetry of the similarity measure, we can prove the following case: $A \geq_{nec} B \geq_{nec} \mathbf{E}$. This ends the proof of (EN3) and this proposition. □

Example 4. *If we use the necessary similarity measures from [3], then we obtain an entropy measure that satisfies Equation (8) with respect to* $N(x) = [1-\overline{x}, 1-\underline{x}]$.

4. Problem and Idea of Solution and Methodology

In this work, we support the problem of early diagnosis/prevention of depression, especially when a given medical center has few or incomplete data.

We investigate such situations when different data sources (medical centers supporting the diagnosis of depression prevention) have different datasets, not excluding imbalanced data (NON-IID data, i.e., Non-Independently and Non-Identically Distributed Data), and for privacy protection reasons (restrictive privacy regulations applicable to the creation of datasets) cannot make their data available to other centers. Alone, they have low diagnostic effectiveness. For such situations, we propose incorporating the idea of federated decision-making based on models obtained independently from separated data sources.

4.1. Dataset Description

The database on which the research was carried out in this work consists of answers to two diagnostic tests, (CESD-R (The Center for Epidemiologic Studies Depression Revised Scale) and SenDD (Sensitive Depression Diagnosis)), received by the CAWI technique. The same 750 students were respondents to each test. This collection will be expanded in the future, but as a cross-section of the student environment, it was a good basis for research.

The SenDD test includes 22 questions (condition attributes) plus a binary diagnosis (decision attribute). Condition attributes consist of 20 basic questions (attributes 1–20) and 2 verification questions (attributes 21–22) [3]. The answers to each question are as follows:

- Definitely yes: 4 points;
- Rather like this: 3 points;
- It's hard to say: 2 points;
- Probably not: 1 point;
- Definitely not: 0 points.

All twenty basic questions follow the pattern "the more, the worse", while two verification questions follow the pattern "the more, the better".

The dataset was constructed in two steps:

1. Answers to questions from the SenDD test (questions 1–22)
2. Decisions created in the following way:
   - For answers to questions 1–20, decisions obtained by the same respondent in the CESD-R test were assigned, a so-called initial (assuming a two-class representation of the decision): depression or no depression.
   - Then, using the SENSDEPR [3] algorithm, decisions that were on the borderline of decisions between classes were evaluated using verification questions and modified to classes: depression threat (includes cases of depression) and no depression.

The dataset used in the experiments described in this paper consists of 750 records (objects) with 501 "0" (no depression) values and 249 "1" (depression or subliminal depression) values as decision values. Moreover, it includes missing values on the level of approximately 5%. The dataset is described in more detail in [3].

The effectiveness in terms of obtaining greater sensitivity of the SenDD test compared to other datasets, as well as the method presented in Algorithm 1, was confirmed by using the CESD-R test after the initial calculation of the diagnosis (modified to binary: sick "1" or healthy "0"). Verification was realized in two-stage studies (repeated every 4 weeks on the same group of subjects for both tests) and we verified the SenDD test for its more sensitive diagnostics—i.e., earlier (by 4 weeks) indication of depression. This is an important piece of information regarding more sensitive tests (20% of respondents confirmed depression 4 weeks later with the CESD-R test) [3].

Algorithm 1: Diagnosing danger of depression

input : dataset P—collection of objects described by 20-element vectors of values of condition attributes $i \in C$, two verification attributes (numbered by 21, 22), and scalar value of decision attribute;
k—number of nearest neighbors;
y—object under classification.

output: Decision class for the tested object y

▷ Two-stage data fuzzification
for *each* $i \in C$ **do**
  for *each* $x \in P$ **do**
    normalize value $x[i]$ to unit interval [0, 1], namely,
    $x[i] \leftarrow \frac{x[i]-m_i}{M_i-m_i}$, where M_i, m_i maximal and minimal values of i, respectively (FS)
  end
end
for *each* $x \in P$ **do**
  for *each* $i \in C$ **do**
    if $x[i]$ is missing **then** $x[i] \leftarrow [0,1]$ (IFVS)
    else $x[i] \leftarrow [x[i], x[i]]$ (IFVS)
    end
  end
end
▷ Finding k nearest neighbors of y
for *all* $x \in P$ **do**
  $sim(x) \leftarrow S(x,y)$
end
Find $sim[x_1, \ldots, x_k]$, i.e., k most similar objects to y.
if *only decision class = 1 is represented in* $sim[x_1, \ldots, x_k]$ **then**
  return 1
end
if *all k nearest neighbors represent decision class = 0* **then**
  replace k-th neighbour with nearest neighbour from decision class = 1
end
▷ Aggregation
for *each decision class* $dec \in \{0,1\}$ **do**
  Select from $sim[x_1, \ldots, x_k]$ its representative x^{dec} with the lowest values of entropy
end
$E^0 \leftarrow E(x^0), E^1 \leftarrow E(x^1)$
$S^0 \leftarrow sim(x^0), S^1 \leftarrow sim(x^1)$
$y[dec] \leftarrow Classify(S_0, S_1)$ (Algorithm 2)
▷ Sensitivity of diagnosis—modification of decision assignment:
$y[dec] \leftarrow Verify\_Decision(y[21], y[22], y[dec])$ (Algorithm 3)
return $y[dec]$

4.2. The Procedure of Depression Prediction

The procedure proposed below takes into account all the research challenges we set: i.e., maintaining privacy and handling imperfections in data, such as uncertainty or non-balanced data. The procedure consists of the following three stages:

1. Algorithm 1 (included also Algorithms 2 and 3)—which learns depression prediction in the local mode, i.e., individually for each local data in the form of SenDD test answers. The algorithm utilizes interval entropy and similarity measures. Its role is analogous to learning individual classifiers of ensemble classifiers;
2. Algorithm 4—which generates collective and optimal decisions for several NON-IID data. It is a kind of classification conflict resolution;
3. Algorithm 5 ("Decision Rule")—which accepts or rejects changes in the decision value suggested by Algorithm 4.

We will discuss all three stages below.

Algorithm 2: Procedure Classify (interval dec_0, interval dec_1)

▷ Attention! The order of ifs is important.
if $\mathbf{w(dec_1) < w(dec_0)}$ **then**
    if $\underline{dec_1} \geq 0.5$ **then return** 1 (class "1" wins)
    if $\underline{dec_0} \geq 0.5$ **then return** 0 (class "0" wins)
    if $\overline{dec_1} \geq 0.5$ **then return** 1
    if $\overline{dec_0} \geq 0.5$ **then return** 0
    return"No Decision"
end
if $\mathbf{w(dec_1) > w(dec_0)}$ **then**
    if $\underline{dec_0} \geq 0.5$ **then return** 0
    if $\underline{dec_1} \geq 0.5$ **then return** 1
    if $\overline{dec_0} \geq 0.5$ **then return** 0
    if $\overline{dec_1} \geq 0.5$ **then return** 1
    return "No Decision"
end
if $\mathbf{w(dec_1) = w(dec_0)}$ **then**
    if $dec_1 \leq dec_0$ **then**
        if $\underline{dec_0} \geq 0.5$ **then return** 0
        if $\underline{dec_1} \geq 0.5$ **then return** 1
        if $\overline{dec_0} \geq 0.5$ **then return** 0
        if $\overline{dec_1} \geq 0.5$ **then return** 1
        return "No Decision"
    end
    if $dec_0 < dec_1$ **then**
        if $\underline{dec_1} \geq 0.5$ **then return** 1
        if $\underline{dec_0} \geq 0.5$ **then return** 0
        if $\overline{dec_1} \geq 0.5$ **then return** 1
        if $\overline{dec_0} \geq 0.5$ **then return** 0
        return" No Decision"
    end
end

Algorithm 3: Procedure Verify_Decision (interval val_1, interval val_2, interval dec)

if $val_1 < 2$ *and* $val_2 < 2$ *and* $dec = 0$ **then**
    if $D(S(y, o_x), S(y, o_z)) < 0.5$ **then**
        return $dec = 1$
    else
        return $dec = 0$
    end
end

Algorithm 4: Federated system for diagnosing risk of depression

```
input  : Z = set of local models of data;
         y—object under classification;
output: Decision class for the classified object y
▷ Step 1. Find the decision of y on the basis of each local model by using Algorithm 1
y0 ← 0
y1 ← 0
▷ Local models "vote" for the decision of y: 0 or 1
for all z ∈ Z do
    if y[dec]^z = 0 then
        y0 ++
    end
    if y[dec]^z = 1 then
        y1 ++
    end
end
▷ Step 2. Establish collective decision based on federation
if y0 = y1 then
    if y0 = 0 then
        return "No Decision"
    else
        if Aggregation (Entropies of class [dec] = 1) > Aggregation (Entropies of class [dec] = 0)
         then
            return y[dec] = 0
        else
            return y[dec] = 1
        end
    end
else
    if y0 > y1 then
        return y[dec] = 0
    else
        return y[dec] = 1
    end
end
```

Algorithm 5: Procedure Decision_Rule (measure $EF \in \{ACC, SENS, SPEC, PREC\}$, table of EF values for all datasets z_i and federated model with final decision (FD))

```
z_max ← arg max_i(EF(z_i)) for z_i ∈ Z
if EF(FD) ≥ EF(z_max) then
    return [dec]_FD
else
    return [dec]_{z_max}
end
```

4.2.1. New Algorithms for Diagnosis of Depression

Algorithm 1 for depression detection is based on the answers to the SenDD questionnaire. The proposed algorithm is an epistemic extension of the SENSDEPR algorithm [3]. Unlike the previous algorithm, we propose the use of entropy as a measure of assessing data uncertainty.

In the initial phase of the algorithm, we perform a two-stage fuzzification procedure on the input data values. This reduces each value to an interval from the L^I family. In particular, each certain value a is normalized to the value $b \in [0,1]$ and replaced by the interval $[b,b]$. Missing values are replaced by the interval $[0,1]$.

The kNN algorithm is the basis of the approach proposed in Algorithm 1. The choice of kNN as the classification method used in the system was dictated, first of all, by the research conducted in [3,9,51,52], where kNN turned out to be one of the most effective methods in the problem of diagnosing depression. As a well-explained tool, it is the best choice for our system. By good explainability, we mean a process of searching for a diagnosis and its interpretation that is understandable by domain specialists. The technique we propose for searching for a diagnosis among objects with a similar distribution of features (similar answers) is analogous to the procedure used in medicine called "case study" and is accepted by medical communities. Additionally, taking into account imprecision through the use of IVFS provides a natural combination of machine learning and human thinking often associated with uncertainty. In the mentioned articles, we may observe comparing methods of classification with results obtained using other methods of machine learning and different psychiatric tests with new tests used in the diagnosis of depression. For example, in [51], one can observe an application of the kNN and Random Forest algorithms for diagnosing depression based on CESD-R test answers. In this application, the kNN algorithm classified better than Random Forest. The choice of test CESD-R as a source of decision values assigned to objects from the SenDD dataset was dictated by its efficiency in comparison with the following depression diagnosing tests: Beck, Hamilton Depression Rating Scale, PHQ-9, QIDS-SR, HDRS, GDS, and CES-D [3,9,10]. The obtained dataset in our research was used for testing a new, more effective, and sensitive diagnostic model based on the following:

- SenDD;
- Algorithms 1–4;
- Algorithm 5 (Decision Rule), which is explained in the next part of this paper.

The selection of nearest neighbors of a classified object is realized first by choosing k most similar (according to used similarity measure) objects from input data and next by taking the most similar representatives of each decision class present among k nearest neighbors. Interval values of similarity measures are the basis of the choice of the decision value for the object under classification. In particular, in the presented Algorithm 1, we apply the "selection method" based on the width of intervals, a critical point 0.5, and four types of order, namely, $\leq \in \{\leq_2, \leq_{Adm}, \leq_{pos}, \leq_{nec}\}$.

Then, among the k most similar objects to y in each decision class (lines 16–19), we use the object entropy measure and select the one with the lowest uncertainty, i.e., the lowest entropy (lines 21–22 of the algorithm code). Thus, in the next step of the algorithm, for the two intervals obtained corresponding to each class, we use the following method leading to the decision-making, where for the classes "0" (no depression) and "1" (depression or subliminal depression), intervals are denoted as d_0 and d_1, respectively, in accordance with their connection with the neutral value $[0.5, 0.5]$. In addition, the algorithm may refrain from making decisions "No Decision" (procedure Classify (Algorithm 2) in line 24). This, in turn, is subject to possible correction in the last part of the algorithm depending on the patient's answers to the last two so-called verifying questions (attributes 21 and 22 with values less than 2 on a scale [0–4], which means a negative psychological situation for the respondent, according to expert assessment). In such a situation, for a primary diagnosis that does not indicate depression, a change is made (procedure Verify_Decision (Algorithm 3) on line 26).

The following symbols are used in Algorithms 1–3:

- x—element of input dataset P;
- x[i]—i-th coordinate of vector x;
- w(r)—width of interval r;
- $\underline{r}, \overline{r}$—left and right end of interval r;
- o_x—object which is the most similar to y;
- o_z—object which is the most similar to y with decision value "1", i.e., $o_z[dec] = 1$;
- $o_x[21]$, $o_x[22]$—values of attributes 21, 22
  (the answers for verification questions 21 and 22) of object o_x;
- D—distance measure,
$$D([\underline{\zeta}, \overline{\zeta}], [\underline{\eta}, \overline{\eta}]) = \max(|\underline{\zeta} - \underline{\eta}|, |\overline{\zeta} - \overline{\eta}|);$$
- E—entropy measure constructed by methods of Propositions 6, 9, and 12, respectively, for classes standard, possible, and necessary ($E \in \{E_{std}, E_{pos}, E_{nec}\}$);

- S—similarity measure constructed by methods from [3,50]: $S \in \{S_{std}, S_{pos}, S_{nec}\}$ (S_{pos} cf. Example 10).

4.2.2. Federated Decision-Making

In Algorithm 4, which is the second step of the procedure for depression prediction, we present a method for generating the final decision—a global decision. It uses decisions obtained in Algorithm 1 based on data in each local set participating in the federation for a given object. The federated decision (final decision, Algorithm 5) is based on the idea of federated learning [4,5], where decisions obtained on local data have an impact on the final decision (provided that they do not spoil the effectiveness of the local model) based on the plurality voting technique. The proposed method additionally takes into account the use of the entropy measure in the case of an equal number of obtained local decisions for each class.

The **Decision Rule** procedure (Algorithm 5) suggests federated decision-making $[dec]_{FD}$ (Algorithm 4) only for local sets with local model efficiency lower than the collective decision designation in order to make a final decision (FD). The goal is to not worsen the quality of classification for all local datasets.

Let us recall the definitions of some of the coefficients used in Algorithm 5 and experiments:

- Accuracy: $ACC = \frac{TP+TN}{TP+TN+FP+FN}$;
- Specificity: $SPEC = \frac{TN}{TN+FP}$;
- Precision: $PREC = \frac{TP}{TP+FP}$;
- Sensitivity: $SENS = \frac{TP}{TP+FN}$.

Here, TP stands for the number of correctly classified positive cases, TN is the number of correctly classified negative cases, FP is the number of incorrectly classified negative cases, and FN is the number of incorrectly classified positive cases.

Proposing the use of the new entropy in the epistemic aspect in both of the new proposed algorithms (generating an individual decision in individual local sets and generating a federated decision) is a novelty presented in this paper and the effectiveness of this will be presented in the next section.

5. Experimental Results of Different Aspects of Real Problems

We demonstrate the effectiveness of the proposed algorithms using widely used measures of accuracy (ACC), sensitivity (SENS), specificity (SPEC), and precision (PREC).
We investigate the mentioned values of effectiveness obtained in the following scenarios:

1. Scenario 1: centralized model. The model was trained on a 70% input dataset and tested on a 30% input dataset. We compared the SENSDEPR algorithm [3] and Algorithm 1.
2. Scenario 2: local models. Due to biased data division (NON-IID data), the distribution of classes among clients was uneven. We created three local models from the input dataset. Client 1 received a balanced division of classes with a 50–50% split of decision classes. However, Clients 2 and 3 received an unbalanced distribution, with one having 80% cases of class 0 and the other having 80% cases of class 1. Local models were tested on a balanced 15% test set separated from the dataset before splitting into local sets.
3. Scenario 3: federated decision-making based on Algorithm 4. The method was used only for local models with lower effectiveness than the federation's effectiveness (Algorithm 5).

It is worth noting that during the experiments (in Figure 1), only one effectiveness measure was applied in the Decision Rule procedure (Algorithm 5). Namely, it was the accuracy measure. Despite this, values of other efficiency parameters (SENS, SPEC, PREC) were also recorded.

In each scenario, 10-fold cross-validation was used. In addition, various model parameters were considered:

- $k \in \{1, 3, 5, 7\}$;
- Operator aggregation functions, orders, and similarity were used to build adequate classes (standard/classic, possible, and necessary for different entropy measures).

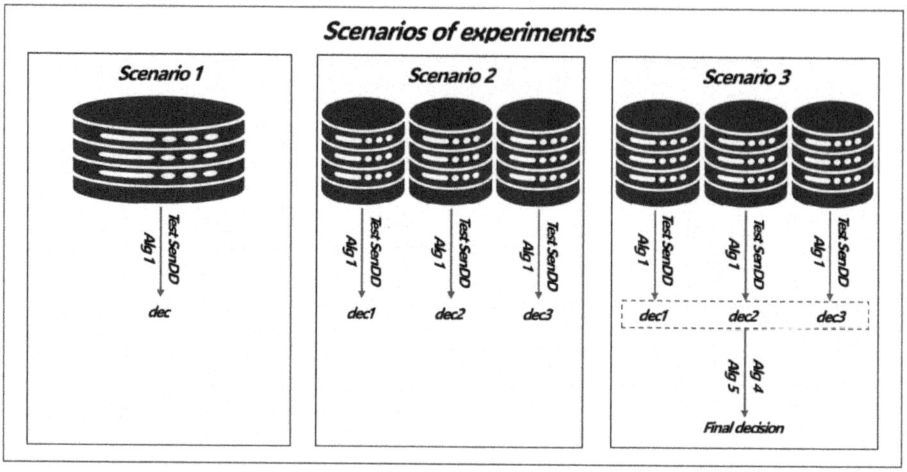

Figure 1. Experimental scenarios.

We present the best results in Tables 1–4.

Firstly, in Scenario 1, i.e., in the Baseline Model, where the dataset was complete and lacked any uncertainty (due to removing cases with missing values), the SENSDEPR algorithm described in [3] (which has also been compared with other methods of diagnosis given in the literature) is compared with Algorithm 1. The outputs are presented in Table 1 for optimal results obtained in the considered possible cases (possible similarity, entropy, and aggregation were used).

Table 1. Performance of algorithms with full data.

Scenarios	Dataset	ACC	SENS	SPEC	PREC
Scenario 1—Baseline—Algorithm SENSDEPR	All Data	0.97	**0.81**	0.984	**0.981**
Scenario 1—Baseline—Algorithm 1	All Data	**0.988**	0.785	**0.989**	0.865

Experiments conducted according to scenarios 2 and 3 are presented separately for the three discussed classes of entropy measures: classic, possible, and necessary aspects. The results demonstrate that the federated model, corresponding to scenario 3, achieved higher efficiency compared to the other scenarios. We observed enhanced performance in key metrics such as accuracy, sensitivity, specificity, and precision. Improving sensitivity and specificity is particularly important for NON-IID data, especially for possible entropy measures used in Algorithm 1. A similar dependency arose for the centralized model when compared with the most effective similarity measure used in the SENSDEPR algorithm [3]. This observation is significant as it underscores the potential of the proposed algorithm in future studies of other real problems by using **possible measure similarity or entropy**, i.e., optimal measures from the point of view of representation uncertainty. We also present the best results of classification efficiency in the tables below when using accuracy as efficiency in the Decision Rule algorithm (Algorithm 5) (EF = ACC).

Firstly, in Table 2, we can see the performance of the model on NON-IID data in the classic case:

Table 2. Performance on NON-IID data in classic case.

Scenarios	Dataset	ACC	SENS	SPEC	PREC
Scenario 2 –Local Models	Client 1	**0.764**	0.781	0.685	0.744
	Client 2	0.653	0.58	0.904	0.599
	Client 3	0.616	0.973	0.646	0.616
Scenario 3—Federated Decision-Making (Algorithm 4)		0.723	0.715	0.735	0.732
Decision Rule (Algorithm 5)		**0.764**	0.781	0.685	0.744

Now, in Table 3, we present the performance of the model on NON-IID data in the possible case: Finally, we compare in Table 4 the above results with the performance of the model on NON-IID data in the necessary case:

Table 3. Performance on NON-IID data in possible case.

Scenarios	Dataset	ACC	SENS	SPEC	PREC
Scenario 2 –Local Models	Client 1	**0.887**	0.887	0.667	0.854
	Client 2	0.871	0.488	0.959	0.654
	Client 3	0.642	0.987	0.354	0.642
Scenario 3—Federated Decision-Making (Algorithm 4)		0.7125	0.635	0.79	0.769
Decision Rule (Algorithm 5)		**0.887**	0.887	0.667	0.854

Table 4. Performance on NON-IID data in necessary case.

Scenarios	Dataset	ACC	SENS	SPEC	PREC
Scenario 2 –Local Models	Client 1	0.695	0.67	0.72	0.717
	Client 2	**0.746**	0.467	0.895	0.653
	Client 3	0.597	0.895	0.573	0.572
Scenario 3—Federated Decision-Making (Algorithm 4)		0.701	0.685	0.7175	0.716
Decision Rule (Algorithm 5)		**0.746**	0.467	0.895	0.653

In Tables 1–4, we present the best results for each class for different parameters such as aggregations, order, and number of k ($k = 5$) for similarities of objects and, finally, entropy measures. The best results were observed for **possible measures**, especially for S_{pos} (from Example 3), which was also used in the construction of **possible entropy measures**. We see the greatest progress (we improved the efficiency of the classification of weak clients while not worsening the efficiency of strong partners (clients) of the federation) for key measures such as ACC and PREC, which is a priority for equally important problems such as people's health and safety.

6. Summary and Future Plans

In this article, we demonstrated an actual application and the use of new definitions of entropy in the necessary, possible, and standard aspects of a modification of the diagnostic model based on a generalized kNN algorithm. We introduced entropies in the optimistic and pessimistic aspects of interval-valued fuzzy relations. The new algorithm creates a more sensitive diagnosis. We also proposed an ensemble decision-making method for small and NON-IID datasets.

The interval calculus approach proposed in the article turned out to be very effective. Intervals were used to represent the uncertainty of data, and the comparability measures related to the interval calculus take into account different epistemic, more or less restrictive (possible or necessary) approaches, as illustrated with the comparability measures considered—i.e., entropy measures tend to be more flexible due to uncertainty.

In particular, the new entropy measure proposed in this paper proved to be useful for improving the efficiency of the proposed algorithm for proposing decisions under conditions of small or faulty datasets and in cases dealing with data privacy problems.

Proposing the use of entropy in both algorithms (generating an individual decision in individual local sets and generating a federated decision) is a novel aspect in this paper.

The research we present is preliminary research. In the next stages, we plan to obtain consent for clinical trials from a relevant bioethics committee and expand the research in the following areas:

- Consideration of different screening periods to determine the sensitivity threshold of the test;
- Use of different methods of the imputation of missing data;
- Taking into account the influence of membership in different social groups on decisions (examination of the influence of social–psychological characteristics on decisions), different types of data, etc.

Moreover, in the future, we will continue tests on the correctness of the process of decision-making to tune algorithms to work in an online system for producing fast diagnoses. The created system will be used in screening selected risk groups, including school-age children, who increasingly exhibit mood disorders. The system for diagnosing risk of depression will be widely used among people of different age groups. Thus, the database will be expanded.

Realizing that the proposed system, especially the local classification of threats, is strongly related to the specificity of a given problem/disease entity, the problem of developing the indicated federated decision-making technique will be associated with the modification of the classification algorithm in relation to the new research problem.

The development of the methodology will take the following into account:

- Various data types, including categorical data. The database will be expanded with additional information about living conditions collected in interviews to propose a relationship between the diagnosis and the socioeconomic situation of respondents.
- Comparison with other methods used in the diagnosis of depression, as well as analysis of the potential use of other methods taking into account data noise.

Author Contributions: Conceptualization, B.P. and D.K.; methodology, W.R. and B.P.; software, D.K.; validation, W.R., D.K., B.P. and J.C.; formal analysis and investigation, W.R., D.K., B.P. and J.C.; data curation, K.G.; visualization and writing—review and editing, W.R., B.P. and K.G. All authors have read and agreed to the published version of the manuscript.

Funding: This research received no external funding.

Institutional Review Board Statement: Not applicable.

Informed Consent Statement: Informed consent was obtained from all subjects involved in the study despite full anonymization.

Data Availability Statement: Anonymized data are available at the following link: https://tiny.pl/92s9g (accessed on 25 January 2025).

Conflicts of Interest: The authors declare no conflicts of interest.

References

1. Wani, M.; Elaffendi, M.; Shakil, K.; Imran, A.; Abd El-Latif, A. Depression Screening in Humans with AI and Deep Learning Techniques. *IEEE Trans. Comput. Soc. Syst.* **2022**, *10*, 2074–2089. [CrossRef]
2. Szkoła, J.; Pancerz, K. Pattern Recognition in Sequences Using Multistate Sequence Autoencoding Neural Networks. In Proceedings of the 2019 International Conference on Information and Digital Technologies (IDT), Zilina, Slovakia, 25–27 June 2019; pp. 443–448. [CrossRef]
3. Pękala, B.; Garwol, K.; Czuma, J.; Kosior, D.; Zaręba, L.; Chyła, M. Early detection of the risk of depressive episodes using a proprietary diagnostic test by new epistemic similarity measures. *Appl. Soft Comput.* **2023**, *148*, 110910. [CrossRef]
4. Yang, Q.; Liu, Y.; Chen, T.; Tong, Y. Federated Machine Learning: Concept and Applications. *ACM Trans. Intell. Syst. Technol.* **2019**, *10*, 1–19. [CrossRef]
5. Wilbik, A.; Grefen, P. Towards a Federated Fuzzy Learning System. In Proceedings of the IEEE International Conference on Fuzzy Systems (FUZZ-IEEE), Luxembourg, 11–14 July 2021; pp. 1–6.
6. Sambuc, R. Fonctions ϕ-Floues: Application á l'aide au Diagnostic en Pathologie Thyroidienne. Ph.D. Thesis, Faculté de Médecine de Marseille, Marseille, France, 1975. (In French)
7. Zadeh, L. The concept of a linguistic variable and its application to approximate reasoning–I. *Inf. Sci.* **1975**, *8*, 199–249. [CrossRef]
8. World Health Organization. *Depression*; World Health Organization: Geneva, Switzerland, 2021.
9. Koziara, K. Assessment of depressiveness in population. Psychometric evaluation of the Polish version of the CESD-R. *Psychiatr. Pol.* **2016**, *50*, 1109–1117. [CrossRef]
10. Zezhi, L.; Meihua, R.; Jun, C.; Yiru, F. Major Depressive Disorder: Advances in Neuroscience Research and Translational Applications. *Neurosci. Bull. Vol.* **2021**, *37*, 863–880.
11. Eaton, W.W.; Smith, C.; Ybarra, M.; Muntaner, C.; Tien, A. Center for Epidemiologic Studies Depression Scale: Review and Revision (CESD and CESD-R). *Use Psychol. Test. Treat. Plan. Outcomes Assess.* **2004**, *3*, 363–377. [CrossRef]
12. Li, T.; Sahu, A.K.; Talwalkar, A.; Smith, V. Federated Learning: Challenges, Methods, and Future Directions. *IEEE Signal Process. Mag.* **2020**, *37*, 50–60. [CrossRef]

13. Kairouz, P.; McMahan, B.; Avent, B.; Bellet, A.; Bennis, M.; Bhagoji, A.N.; Bonawitz, K.; Charles, Z.; Cormode, G.; Zhao, S.; et al. Advances and Open Problems in Federated Learning. *Found. Trends® Mach. Learn.* **2021**, *14*, 1–210. [CrossRef]
14. Yan, H.; Hu, L.; Xiang, X.; Liu, Z.; Yuan, X. Privacy-preserving collaborative learning for mitigating indirect information leakage. *Inf. Sci.* **2021**, *548*, 423–437. [CrossRef]
15. Bustince, H.; Barrenechea, E.; Pagola, M.; Fernandez, J.; Xu, Z.; Bedregal, B.; Montero, J.; Hagras, H.; Herrera, F.; Baets, B.D. A Historical Account of Types of Fuzzy Sets and Their Relationships. *IEEE Trans. Fuzzy Syst.* **2016**, *24*, 179–194. [CrossRef]
16. Sanz, J.A.; Bustince, H.; Fernández, A.; Herrera, F. IIVFDT: Ignorance functions based interval-valued fuzzy decision tree with genetic tuning. *Int. J. Uncertain. Fuzziness Knowl. Based Syst.* **2012**, *20*, 1–30. [CrossRef]
17. Xu, G.; Liu, F. An approach to group decision making based on interval multiplicative and fuzzy preference relations by using projection. *Appl. Math. Model.* **2013**, *37*, 3929–3943. [CrossRef]
18. Liu, F.; Zhang, W.G.; Zhang, L.H. A group decision making model based on a generalized ordered weighted geometric average operator with interval preference matrices. *Fuzzy Sets Syst.* **2014**, *246*, 1–18. [CrossRef]
19. Dyczkowski, K. *Intelligent Medical Decision Support System Based on Imperfect Information. The Case of Ovarian Tumor Diagnosis*; Springer: Berlin/Heidelberg, Germany, 2018; Volume 735. [CrossRef]
20. Bentkowska, U. New types of aggregation functions for interval-valued fuzzy setting and preservation of pos-B and nec-B-transitivity in decision making problems. *Inf. Sci.* **2018**, *424*, 385–399. [CrossRef]
21. Zeraatkar, S.; Afsari, F. Interval–valued fuzzy and intuitionistic fuzzy–KNN for imbalanced data classification. *Expert Syst. Appl.* **2021**, *184*, 115510. [CrossRef]
22. Shu, W.; Qian, W.; Xie, Y.; Tang, Z. An efficient uncertainty measure-based attribute reduction approach for interval-valued data with missing values. *Int. J. Uncertain. Fuzziness Knowl. Based Syst.* **2019**, *27*, 931–947. [CrossRef]
23. Dai, J.; Wang, Z.; Huang, W. Interval-valued fuzzy discernibility pair approach for attribute reduction in incomplete interval-valued information systems. *Inf. Sci.* **2023**, *642*, 119215. [CrossRef]
24. Palmeira, E.S.; Bedregal, B.; Bustince, H.; Paternain, D.; Miguel, L.D. Application of two different methods for extending lattice-valued restricted equivalence functions used for constructing similarity measures on L-fuzzy sets. *Inf. Sci.* **2018**, *441*, 95–112. [CrossRef]
25. Takáč, Z.; Minárová, M.; Montero, J.; Barrenechea, E.; Fernandez, J.; Bustince, H. Interval-valued fuzzy strong S-subsethood measures, interval-entropy and P-interval-entropy. *Inf. Sci.* **2018**, *432*, 97–115. [CrossRef]
26. Żywica, P. Modelling Medical Uncertainties with Use of Fuzzy Sets and Their Extensions. In *Proceedings of the Information Processing and Management of Uncertainty in Knowledge-Based Systems. Applications*; Medina, J., Ojeda-Aciego, M., Verdegay, J.L., Perfilieva, I., Bouchon-Meunier, B., Yager, R.R., Eds.; Springer: Cham, Switzerland, 2018; pp. 369–380. [CrossRef]
27. Pękala, B.; Bentkowska, U.; Sesma-Sara, M.; Fernandez, J.; Lafuente, J.; Altalhi, A.; Knap, M.; Bustince, H.; Pintor, J.M. Interval Subsethood Measures with Respect to Uncertainty for the Interval-Valued Fuzzy Setting. *Int. J. Comput. Intell. Syst.* **2020**, *13*, 167–177. [CrossRef]
28. Turksen, I.B. Interval valued fuzzy sets based on normal forms. *Fuzzy Sets Syst.* **1986**, *20*, 191–210. [CrossRef]
29. Gorzałczany, M.B. A method of inference in approximate reasoning based on interval-valued fuzzy sets. *Fuzzy Sets Syst.* **1987**, *21*, 1–17. [CrossRef]
30. Couso, I.; Dubois, D. Statistical reasoning with set-valued information: Ontic vs. epistemic views. *Int. J. Approx. Reason.* **2014**, *55*, 1502–1518. [CrossRef]
31. Bustince, H.; Fernandez, J.; Kolesárová, A.; Mesiar, R. Generation of linear orders for intervals by means of aggregation functions. *Fuzzy Sets Syst.* **2013**, *220*, 69–77. [CrossRef]
32. Asiain, M.J.; Bustince, H.; Bedregal, B.; Takáč, Z.; Baczyński, M.; Paternain, D.; Dimuro, G. About the Use of Admissible Order for Defining Implication Operators. In Proceedings of the Information Processing and Management of Uncertainty in Knowledge-Based Systems, IPMU 2016, Eindhoven, The Netherlands, 20–24 June 2016; Springer: Cham, Switzerland, 2016; pp. 353–362.
33. Zapata, H.; Bustince, H.; Montes, S.; Bedregal, B.; Dimuro, G.; Takáč, Z.; Baczyński, M.; Fernandez, J. Interval-valued implications and interval-valued strong equality index with admissible orders. *Int. J. Approx. Reason.* **2017**, *88*, 91–109. [CrossRef]
34. Beliakov, G.; Pradera, A.; Calvo, T. Aggregation Functions: A Guide for Practitioners. In *Studies in Fuzziness and Soft Computing*; Springer: Berlin/Heidelberg, Germany, 2007.
35. Pękala, B.; Bentkowska, U.; Bustince, H. On comparability relations in the class of interval-valued fuzzy relations. *Tatra Mt. Math. Publ.* **2016**, *66*, 91–101. [CrossRef]
36. Pękala, B. Uncertainty Data in Interval-Valued Fuzzy Set Theory: Properties, Algorithms and Applications. In *Studies in Fuzziness and Soft Computing*; Springer: Berlin/Heidelberg, Germany, 2019; Volume 367.
37. Dubois, D.; Prade, H. Gradualness, uncertainty and bipolarity: Making sense of fuzzy sets. *Fuzzy Sets Syst.* **2012**, *192*, 3–24. [CrossRef]

38. Beliakov, G.; Sola, H.B.; Sánchez, T.C. A Practical Guide to Averaging Functions. In *Studies in Fuzziness and Soft Computing;* Springer: Berlin/Heidelberg, Germany, 2016; Volume 329.
39. Komorníková, M.; Mesiar, R. Aggregation functions on bounded partially ordered sets and their classification. *Fuzzy Sets Syst.* **2011**, *175*, 48–56. [CrossRef]
40. Shannon, C. The mathematical theory of communication. *Bell Syst. Tech. J.* **1948**, *27*, 379–423+623–656. [CrossRef]
41. Klir, G.J.; Harmanec, D. On modal logic interpretation of possibility theory. *Int. J. Uncertain. Fuzziness Knowl.-Based Syst.* **1994**, *2*, 237–245. [CrossRef]
42. De Luca, A.; Termini, S. A definition of nonprobabilistic entropy in the setting of fuzzy theory. *Inf. Control* **1972**, *20*, 301–312. [CrossRef]
43. Yager, R. On measure of fuzziness and negation, Part 1: Membership in the unite interval. *J. Gen. Syst.* **1979**, *5*, 189–200. [CrossRef]
44. Burillo, P.; Bustince, H. Entropy on intuitionistic fuzzy sets and on interval-valued fuzzy sets. *Fuzzy Sets Syst.* **1996**, *78*, 305–316. [CrossRef]
45. Szmidt, E.; Kacprzyk, J. Entropy for intuitionistic fuzzy sets. *Fuzzy Sets Syst.* **2001**, *118*, 467–477. [CrossRef]
46. Takáč, Z.; Bustince, H.; Pintor, J.M.; Marco-Detchart, C.; Couso, I. Width-Based Interval-Valued Distances and Fuzzy Entropies. *IEEE Access* **2019**, *7*, 14044–14057. [CrossRef]
47. Pękala, B.; Kosior, D.; Dyczkowski, K.; Szkoła, J. Application of entropy measures with uncertainty in classification methods with missing data problem. In Proceedings of the IEEE International Conference on Fuzzy Systems (FUZZ-IEEE), Luxembourg, 11–14 July 2021; pp. 1–8.
48. Zeng, W.; Guo, P. Normalized distance, similarity measure, inclusion measure and entropy of interval-valued fuzzy sets and their relationship. *Inf. Sci.* **2008**, *178*, 1334–1342. [CrossRef]
49. Asiain, M.J.; Bustince, H.; Mesiar, R.; Kolesárová, A.; Takáč, Z. Negations with Respect to Admissible Orders in the Interval-Valued Fuzzy Set Theory. *IEEE Trans. Fuzzy Syst.* **2018**, *26*, 556–568. [CrossRef]
50. Pękala, B.; Dyczkowski, K.; Grzegorzewski, P.; Bentkowska, U. Inclusion and similarity measures for interval-valued fuzzy sets based on aggregation and uncertainty assessment. *Inf. Sci.* **2021**, *547*, 1182–1200. [CrossRef]
51. Hong, J.; Kim, J.; Kim, S.; Oh, J.; Lee, D.; Lee, S.; Uh, J.; Yoon, J.; Choi, Y. Depressive Symptoms Feature-Based Machine Learning Approach to Predicting Depression Using Smartphone. *Healthcare* **2022**, *10*, 1189. [CrossRef]
52. Cahutay, C.R.; Vicente, A.J. #ActuallyDepressed: Characterization of Depressed Tumblr Users' Online Behavior from Rules Generation Machine Learning Technique. In Proceedings of the 31st Pacific Asia Conference on Language, Information and Computation, Cebu City, Philippines, 16–18 November 2017; pp. 132–139.

entropy

MDPI

Article

Improving the CRCC-DHR Reliability: An Entropy-Based Mimic-Defense-Resource Scheduling Algorithm

Xinghua Wu [1,2], Mingzhe Wang [2,*], Yun Cai [3], Xiaolin Chang [1,*] and Yong Liu [2]

1 School of Cyberspace Science and Technology, Beijing Jiaotong University, Beijing 100044, China; 22115141@bjtu.edu.cn
2 Institute of Computing Technology, China Academy of Railway Sciences, Beijing 100081, China; liuyong1@rails.cn
3 School of Information Science and Technology, Southwest Jiaotong University, Chengdu 610031, China; zhouxiaoxia@swjtu.edu.cn
* Correspondence: wangmingzhe@rails.cn (M.W.); xlchang@bjtu.edu.cn (X.C.)

Abstract

With more China railway business information systems migrating to the China Railway Cloud Center (CRCC), the attack surface is expanding and there are increasing security threats for the CRCC to deal with. Cyber Mimic Defense (CMD) technology, as an active defense strategy, can counter these threats by constructing a Dynamic Heterogeneous Redundancy (DHR) architecture. However, there are at least two challenges posed to the DHR deployment, namely, the limited number of available schedulable heterogeneous resources and memorization-based attacks. This paper aims to address these two challenges to improve the CRCC-DHR reliability and then facilitate the DHR deployment. By reliability, we mean that the CRCC-DHR with the limited number of available heterogeneous resources can effectively resist memorization-based attacks. We first propose three metrics for assessing the reliability of the CRCC-DHR architecture. Then, we propose an incomplete-information-based game model to capture the relationships between attackers and defenders. Finally, based on the proposed metrics and the captured relationship, we propose a redundant-heterogeneous-resources scheduling algorithm, called the Entropy Weight Scheduling Algorithm (REWS). We evaluate the capability of REWS with the three existing algorithms through simulations. The results show that REWS can achieve a better reliability than the other algorithms. In addition, REWS demonstrates a lower time complexity compared with the existing algorithms.

Keywords: China Railway Cloud Center; DHR architecture; entropy; game theory; mimic defense; scheduling

1. Introduction

The China Railway Cloud Center (CRCC) is primarily responsible for the construction and deployment of various business information systems supporting China Railway internal services, production, management, and office functions to various end nodes [1]. These nodes may be the China Railway Corporation nodes, regional center nodes, or station-segment nodes [1]. Figure 1 illustrates the CRCC architecture, characterized by the deployment of unified computing resources and unified security protection resources at the central nodes of the corporation. The CRCC should meet the security requirements of the regional center nodes and station-segment nodes when these nodes access various business systems deployed in the CRCC. This is achieved by implementing unified security protection and access aggregation measures at the network edges of these nodes. These protection measures ensure secure data access across different application domains.

Figure 1. The architecture of the CRCC.

The past years have witnessed a surge in the number and sophistication of zero-day vulnerabilities, which pose a critical threat to organizations of all sizes [2], and an increase in APT attacks on the critical infrastructures, such as public transportation and electricity [3–5]. As the scale of information system construction in the CRCC has continuously expanded, the risk of various attacks is becoming even more severe. There are the following two main reasons.

(1) The attack surface of various application systems is growing [6]. As various production, offices, and service systems of the railway rapidly expand, the types of intelligent terminals at regional center nodes and station-segment nodes keep being diversified. Additionally, the stations accommodate many more individuals, through which attacks may be carried out on the CRCC if these individuals are not protected well. This leads to a gradual increase in the overall attack surface of the CRCC systems. As a result, the probability of attack occurrence is continuously rising.

(2) Artificial Intelligence (AI) technologies and advancements are being used in cyber attacks [7,8]. The attacks can apply the knowledge memorization of previous attacks to make adaptive adjustment to the defense strategy, thus making the attack more persistent, covert, and not easy to counter.

Techniques of addressing security and reliability issues include Moving Target Defense (MTD) [9–11], Cyber Mimic Defense (CMD) [12,13], Byzantine Fault Tolerance [14–16], and Redundancy Fault Tolerance [17,18] technologies. The characteristics of these technologies are summarized in Table 1.

Table 1. Comparison of different technical characteristics ("$\surd$" indicates that the condition is satisfied).

Approach	Primary Model	Features			Fault Tolerance
		Dynamic	Heterogeneity	Redundancy	
BFT	Master-slave			$\surd$	$3f-1$
FTR	Master-slave			$\surd$	$f+1, 2f, 3f\ldots$
MTD	Master-slave	$\surd$		$\surd$	$f+1, 2f, 3f\ldots$ or time redundancy
CMD	customizable	$\surd$	$\surd$	$\surd$	customizable

Among the techniques mentioned, Cyber Mimic Defense (CMD) technology is one of the prevailing methods. It aims to make the targeted system uncertain and dynamic in time and space so as to effectively counter potential attacks. CMD technology constructs a Dynamic Heterogeneous Redundancy (DHR) architecture. This architecture introduces the fault-tolerant features of dynamism, heterogeneity, and redundancy into the system. It also introduces closed-loop feedback features into the system. These introduced features enhance the system's robustness and intrinsic security [19–21]. Compared with other technologies, CMD offers more flexibility in the architectural pattern and fault-tolerant form. As a result, CMD technology significantly enhances the security and reliability of systems in various complex scenarios.

Studies and the application of CMD technology have demonstrated its effectiveness in addressing endogenous security problems. However, there are at least two weaknesses in applying this technology within the CRCC.

Weakness 1: The existing research assumes that there are infinite schedulable heterogeneous resources in the cloud environment.

Weakness 2: They assume that there is no information entropy decay in the redundancy scheduling process. This decay makes the entire CMD system unable to guarantee its reliability when there exist memorization-based attacks. By memorization, we mean that the adversary can apply the information, which the adversary obtains in the previous attacks, to the later attacks. But this decay exists when there is a finite number of schedulable resources and there exists memorization-based attacks.

This paper aims to deal with these two weaknesses. The main contributions are listed as follows.

(**Contribution 1**) We propose three reliability assessment metrics for the CRCC-DHR architecture under the conditions of limited schedulable heterogeneous resources and memorization-based attacks. The metrics are detailed in Section 3, including the number of scheduling states of the redundancy resources (executors), the information entropy value, and the decay rate of the information entropy value. These metrics are based on the information, which can be obtained by the adversary after a successful attack and will be applied to the subsequent attacks.

(**Contribution 2**) We propose an incomplete-information-based game model to capture the relationships between attackers and defenders for the DHR architecture under the conditions of limited schedulable resources and memorization-based attacks. We also apply information entropy to solve the model and then derive the condition that should be satisfied in order to guarantee the maximum attacker–defender equilibrium gain.

(**Contribution 3**) We propose an information-entropy-weight-based redundant executor scheduling algorithm. We firstly define the reliability maximization model, where we define the objective function based on the metrics in **Contribution 1**, and we construct the constraints based on both the metrics in **Contribution 1** and the game model developed in **Contribution 2**.

We perform simulations to evaluate the proposed algorithm's capability by comparing it with three existing algorithms, with respect to the traditional scheduling cycle metrics as well as the metrics proposed in this paper.

The subsequent parts of this paper are organized as follows. Related work is presented in Section 2. The reliability index model under the conditions of limited schedulable resources and with a memorization-based attack is introduced in Section 3. The game theory modelling method and the scheduling algorithm are introduced in Section 4. Experimental simulations are carried out in Section 5, and the conclusions of this paper and outlooks of the future work are presented in Section 6.

The variables in the article and the symbols of the formulas are shown in Table 2.

Table 2. Symbol definition.

Symbol	Definition
A	A mimic defense system
a_i	The i-th redundant resources/executors in A
n	The number of redundant resources/executors in redundant resource pools
m	The number of redundant executors in a scheduling process
k	The number of failed redundancies in system A
$p(a_i)$	Probability that the redundant executor a_i is disabled by an attack
$p(a_i \ldots a_l)_{l-i}$	Jointly distributed probability of the failure of l-i redundancies together
$p(A)_m$	The failure probability of system A with a scheduling redundancy of m
p_{xt}	The probability that x_t pieces of information are available
$F(p_{xt})$	The uncertain function of the probability of the occurrence of x_t
t	The t-th scheduling state, $1 \leq t \leq T$
T	The number of (scheduling) states
$F_{PA}(t)$	The information entropy metric of system A
$F_{PA}(\Delta t)$	The decay rate of the information entropy value
b	Attack cost for an adversary $b > 0$
c	Defender's base gain when the system is functioning normally, $c > 0$
e	Attacker's base gain when undetected, $e > 0$
d	Cost to the defender when scheduling 1 redundant executor, $0 < nd \leq c$
B	Total gain from a successful attack by an attacker, $0 < nb \leq B$
λ	Proportionality parameter of return expectations for different ranges of values of k, $0 < \lambda < 1$
$\{\alpha, \beta\}$	Equilibrium solution of the game model
$t(a_i)$	Attacked state of the redundant executor a_i
$w(F_{Pai}(t))$	Information entropy weight function of the redundant executor a_i in state t
$w(F_{Pai}(\Delta t))$	The rate of change of the information entropy weights when the redundant executor a_i changes from state t_i to state $t_i + 1$
$e_{ai}(t_0)$	Decay rate threshold for information entropy values
d_i	Classification of computational results for redundant executor a_i
ε_{ai}	Randomized offset values for redundant executor a_i weights
V	Mimetic adjudication results

2. Related Work

The DHR architecture [12,13] is the core architecture of the CMD, including the components of input agents, executors, voters, policy schedulers, and a pool of heterogeneous redundant executors, as illustrated in Figure 2. The fundamental processing flow of the system is as follows:

(i) Dynamically Allocating Redundant Executors: The scheduling module dynamically assigns redundant executors from the pool to the processing module using a dynamic selection algorithm.

(ii) Forwarding User-Sent Message Status: The input agent forwards the status of the messages sent by the user to different redundant executors within the processing module.

(iii) Processing and Making a Consistent Decision: The redundant executors process the received requests and send them to the voting unit. The voting unit then makes a consistent decision and produces the output result.

(iv) Negative Feedback and Redundant Executors Rescheduling: If any inconsistent rulings are detected during the decision-making process, the redundant resources/executors that are responsible receive negative feedback. This feedback is sent back to the scheduling module, which triggers the rescheduling of the redundant executors.

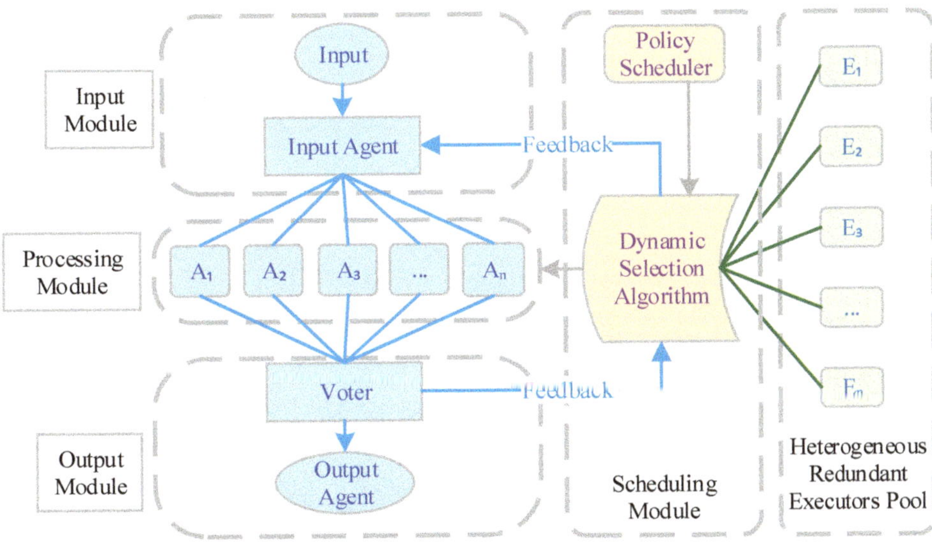

Figure 2. Dynamic Heterogeneous Redundancy model structures.

There exists research on mimic defense architectures for public and private cloud networks. Li et al. [22] proposed a mimic cloud security architecture called Mimi-cloud for 5G core networks. This architecture enhances the security of 5G core networks by uniformly computing the heterogeneous vector metrics of container cloud environments. It also improves security through unified Kubernetes scheduling and the cross-checking of container cloud executables. Wu et al. [23] introduced an active defense development framework for cloud-native environments. They used technologies such as multi-version assembly, multi-instance deployment, and diversified compilation to increase the system complexity and then improve its ability to resist attacks. Wang et al. [24] proposed an IoT DHR architecture based on the double deep reinforcement learning network (DDQN).

They used the DDQN network to train and optimize scheduling and decision strategies. This enables dynamic scheduling in container cloud environments driven by Kubernetes. Sepczuk [25] developed a defense model that combines the DHR architecture with a WAF firewall in a cloud environment. The WAF firewall establishes temporary redundant execution rules when potential HTTP attacks are detected, thereby enhancing the security of the system.

Regarding the optimization of mimic defense strategies, the relevant research primarily uses various modelling techniques, which mathematically model and simulate the dynamic scheduling strategies of redundant executors. These modelling techniques include probability models, game models, and information entropy models, which are detailed in the following.

(i) Studies based on probabilistic modeling.

This type of study is a classical approach. Through the probabilistic model, researchers optimize the probability of a successful attack on a redundant executor. They use the heterogeneity of the executor as a metric to assess the likelihood of an attack. Based on this assessment, they develop relevant scheduling strategies.

Chen et al. [26] addressed the nonlinear problem of component heterogeneity superposition. They introduced a heterogeneous evaluation model based on the minimum L-order error probability. Li et al. [27] proposed several scheduling algorithms, including a time threshold-based TIRTS scheduling algorithm, a task-based threshold TARTS scheduling algorithm, and the MQS multi-level queue scheduling algorithm. Zhu et al. [28] developed a comprehensive scheduling algorithm called HHAC. This algorithm is based on high-order heterogeneity and adaptive historical confidence. It aims to optimize the dynamic strategy of the DHR architecture. They also analyzed the dynamic indicators of the CRS, TIRTS, RSMS, and HHAC algorithms. Shao et al. [29] proposed a dynamic scheduling algorithm called HCDC. This algorithm is based on historical credibility and K-Means heterogeneous clustering. Through simulation experiments, they compared the HCDC algorithm with the RS, MD, and OMD algorithms in terms of attack rates and other indicators.

(ii) Studies based on game model and information entropy model.

Research based on the game model focus on analyzing the gain indicators for both attacking and defending parties within the DHR architecture. This involves examining the system's response to operational events. The goal is to improve the system reliability by optimizing the game strategies of both the attackers and defenders. Research using the information entropy model, on the other hand, assesses system reliability by monitoring changes in information entropy during the operation of the mimic defense system.

Hu et al. [30] analyzed the heterogeneity of redundant executors and the probability of being attacked based on the information entropy theory. They proposed a defense chain model incorporating information entropy and heterogeneity. The numerical analysis of the attack success rate was conducted using the successive Markov model to verify the effectiveness of the DHR architecture. Chen et al. [31] proposed a dynamic architecture evaluation method based on incomplete information game strategies. They used the Markov chain model to calculate and evaluate the benefits for both offense and defense. This approach was used to verify the security of the architecture. Shi et al. [32] developed an evolutionary DHR system. They addressed the issue of a limited number of heterogeneous executors by introducing evolutionary sub-strategies for the executors. The effectiveness of their proposed scheme was verified through the construction of a game model. Hu et al. [33] used the static game theory to explore the unique Nash equilibrium within the DHR architecture. They applied the Adam algorithm to analyze and validate the dynamics, heterogeneity, and failure rates affecting the DHR architecture in detail. Shao et al. [34]

proposed an active defense method, which exploited adaptive anomaly sensing for the mimic IoT. This method aimed to deal with uncertain threats, such as known vulnerabilities and backdoors existing within the IoT, which were difficult for traditional passive network security technologies to effectively counter.

In summary, there has been extensive research on the application of mimic defense architectures in cloud environments and the optimization of defense strategies. However, issues remain in two key areas of related research:

(i) Research on the mimic defense architecture in cloud-centric environments often assumes that there are sufficient schedulable heterogeneous resources. Currently, relevant studies mainly focus on leveraging Kubernetes as the management and scheduling center within the cloud center system architecture. Kubernetes is used for the unified and rapid deployment of container cloud environments and integrates with the DHR architecture to enhance system reliability. However, there is limited research on the reliability of private cloud centers as unified carriers for multi-system multiplexing. These centers typically have more uniform resources to be allocated and insufficient scheduling heterogeneity.

(ii) There is less research on the reliability of mimetic scheduling strategies against memorization-based attacks. Currently, research on mimic defense scheduling strategies mainly addresses none-memorization-based attacks. These attackers do not focus on specific targets or analyze the attack environment after the attack. In such cases, the system's long-term reliability can be maintained through scheduling and cleaning strategies for the redundant executors. However, the situation is different for those cases where there exist attacks with clear targets and 0-day vulnerability attacks. Traditional scheduling methods cannot fully clarify these threats in the short term. That is, there is a lack of research on the reliability of mimetic scheduling strategies under these conditions.

In our previous research [35], we modeled and analyzed the reliability-related metrics of the DHR architecture for application-oriented systems based on failure probability modeling in the CRCC. The process is as follows:

(i) We consider a mimic defense system A with a total redundancy of n and m heterogeneous redundant executors that can be dispatched at a time, denoted as $\{a_1 \ldots a_m\}_n$, and make the following assumptions:

Assumption 1. *The reliability factors affecting system A include only system failures due to attacks on the redundant executors and do not include other failure factors.*

Assumption 2. *When an adversary launches an attack, there is at most only a single redundant executor to fail, and the attack is an independent event.*

The system reliability $R(A)_m$ can be expressed by its failure probability function p. That is, as shown in Equation (1), where $p(A)_m$ denotes the failure probability of the proposed defense system A and $p(a_i \ldots a_j)_{j-i}$ denotes the joint distribution probability of l-i redundant executors failing together.

$$R(A)_m = 1 - p(A)_m = 1 - \sum_{l-i=[(m+1)/2]}^{m} p(a_i \ldots a_l)_{l-i} \quad (1)$$

(ii) We further set n redundant executors, each of which consists of some different components. For any two redundant executors, there is often a certain degree of homomorphic similarity between the different components. The higher the degree of similarity of the components or the higher the number of similar components, the higher the probability that a common-mode vulnerability will lead to the failure of the two redundant executors. The system failure probability can be further expressed in Equation (2):

$$p(A)_m = \sum_{l-i=[(m+1)/2]}^{m} p(a_i \ldots a_l)_{l-i} = \sum_{l-i=[(m+1)/2]}^{m} p(a_i)p\left(a_{i+1} \ldots a_l | a_i\right)_{l-i-1} \tag{2}$$

Also, noting that s_{ij} denotes the similarity of any two redundant executors a_i, a_j, the system A similarity can be represented by the matrix S as follows:

$$S = \begin{pmatrix} 1 & \cdots & s_{1n} \\ \vdots & \ddots & \vdots \\ s_{n1} & \cdots & 1 \end{pmatrix} \tag{3}$$

If the relationship between the similarity and the probability of an attack on a redundant executor is expressed as $f(s_{ij})$, then the probability $p(a_j|a_i)$ of the redundant executor a_i being successfully attacked can be expressed by Equation (4).

$$p(a_j|a_i) = p(a_j) \cdot f(s_{ij}) \tag{4}$$

Then, for system A, the failure probability $p(A)$ under the majority consensus decision condition, i.e., the number of failed redundancies k satisfies $k \geq [(m+1)/2]$, can be expressed by Equation (5).

$$p(A)_m = \sum_{k=[\frac{m+1}{2}]}^{m} \prod_{i=1, j \neq i}^{k} p(a_i)p(a_j)f(s_{ij}) \tag{5}$$

Through the above analysis, it can be concluded that there are two key factors affecting the failure probability of the DHR architecture, i.e., the probability $p(a_i)$ of redundant executors being attacked, and the similarity mapping function $f(s_{ij})$ between the redundant executors. $p(a_i)$ is related to the security of each component of the system, which is a relatively fixed attribute. $f(s_{ij})$ is related to the size of the entire resource pool of the cloud center, and the type and number of heterogeneous components. Since cloud environments are often built uniformly in practice, the number of heterogeneous resources that can be scheduled is very limited, and thus the range in the variation of the two attributes $p(a_i)$ and $f(s_{ij})$ is also limited, which does not allow for an effective assessment of the reliability of the CRCC-DHR architecture under the condition of limited schedulable resources.

This paper considers the CRCC-DHR where there are limited schedulable heterogeneous resources and various targeted memorization-based attacks from external networks. We use the information entropy model to perform the modeling and analysis. Additionally, we propose a redundancy scheduling algorithm based on random entropy weights and the game model. This algorithm aims to improve the reliability of the mimic defense architecture in environments with limited scheduling resources and memorization-based attacks.

3. Three Metrics for Assessing the Reliability of the CRCC-DHR Architecture

The discussions in Section 2 indicate that it is hard to assess the reliability of CRCC-DHR architectures well under the conditions of limited heterogeneous resources and memorization-based attacks using the failure probability approach [35]. Therefore, this section proposes information-entropy-based metrics to analyze the reliability of the CRCC-DHR architecture.

We consider the common attack chain for a system attack, including four stages: scanning, vulnerability detection, attack implantation, and attack maintenance, as shown in Figure 3.

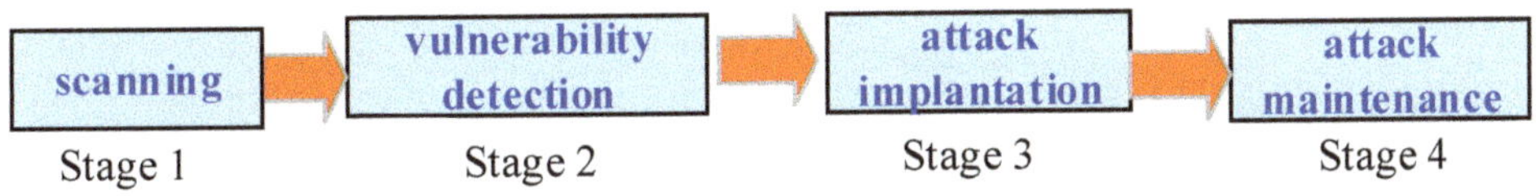

Figure 3. Attack chain.

For memorization-based attacks, the adversary often first scans and sniffs the target host and then implants an attack agent on the system through 0-day vulnerabilities. When the attack is blocked at any stage, the attacker will record the blocked state and then resume scanning and sniffing in the subsequent attacks.

It is known that the reliability of the redundant system A stems from the uncertainty of being attacked [30]. The greater the uncertainty, the more effort an attacker must employ, resulting in a higher system reliability. This uncertainty can be measured by the system's information entropy H, which is the expected value of the uncertainty probability for each redundant executor within the system. That is, for a system $X = \{x_t|x_1 \ldots x_l\}$ containing l executors, its total information entropy can be expressed by Equation (6).

$$H(X) = E(F(p_{xt})) = -\sum_{t=1}^{l} p_{xt} \log p_{xt} \quad (6)$$

where p_{xt} denotes the probability that x_t pieces of information are available, and $F(p_{xt})$ denotes an uncertain function of the probability of the occurrence of x_t.

We use $H(A)$ to denote the initial total entropy of the mimetic defense system A. Suppose there exists a 0-day vulnerability in A, which cannot be eliminated through offline cleaning for the time being. Then, under the condition of infinite redundant executor resources, the defender can force the attacker to repeat between states 1 and 2 by continuously performing new redundant executors' scheduling. That is, in the information entropy model, a single redundant executor can be attacked to make the entropy decrease. But when n tends towards infinity, the total information entropy of the system still remains undiminished. In addition, under the condition of finite redundant resources/executors, although the defender can conduct repeated scheduling by scheduling the complete redundant executors, the adversary has memory (that is, the adversary can conduct memorization-based attacks) and then can continuously increase the attack success probability. That is, in the information entropy model, the attacker's attack success probability increases with repeated scheduling, and the overall information entropy of the system decreases. The trend graph of the system information entropy in two cases is shown in Figure 4.

Before we present the information entropy-based metrics, we first give the following two assumptions:

Assumption 3. *The heterogeneous redundant system A adopts the classical majority-consistent strategy for output adjudication.*

Assumption 4. *There exists a state indicator T for a redundant executor a_i, which represents the adjustable interval of that redundant executor from completely risk-free to completely failed under the condition of having memorization-based attacks.* $p_{xt}(a_i)$ *denotes the failure probability of the* *system in the t-th state of a_i, $t \in (1, T)$, and $p_{xt}(a_i)$ is a monotonically increasing function of the state variable t.*

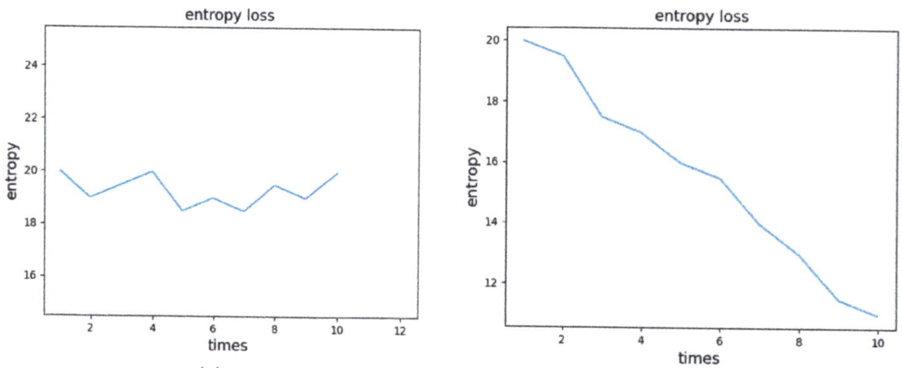

(a) (b)

Figure 4. (**a**) Trend of information entropy loss during the scheduling of redundant systems under infinite resources. (**b**) Trend of information entropy loss during the scheduling of redundant systems under finite resources.

Then, we assessed the total information entropy of the heterogeneous redundant system *A* being attacked by any redundant executor. That is, the total information entropy of the system is the sum of the information entropy of each redundant executor being attacked successfully, which can be expressed according to Equation (7).

$$\begin{aligned} H(A) &= H(a_1, \ldots, a_m) \\ &= -\Big(\sum_{t=1}^{T} p_{xt}(a_i) \log p_{xt}(a_i) + \sum_{t=1}^{T} p_{xt}(a_j|a_i) \log p_{xt}(a_j|a_i) + \ldots\Big) \\ &= -\sum_{i=1}^{m} \sum_{j=1}^{i} \sum_{t=1}^{k} \big(p_{xt}(a_i) f(s_{ij}) \log(p_{xt}(a_i) f(s_{ij}))\big) \end{aligned} \tag{7}$$

$$s.t.[(n+1)/2] \le m \le n$$
$$0 \le f(s_{ij}) \le 1$$

In Equation (7), when any redundant executor a_i fails due to an attack, $H(a_i)$ is reduced to 0, and the information entropy of the system decreases. However, the entropy of a single redundant executor a_i is not monotonically decreasing. With these discussions, we now present the three metrics:

(Metric 1) The number of scheduling states of the redundancy resources/executors

We choose **the number of scheduling states** T as the first metric, which can be used as a basis for the information entropy and the trend of the information entropy change. In addition, it can be used as a basis for analyzing metric normalization in comparison with other scheduling algorithms. See Section 5.

(Metric 2) The information entropy value

Equation (8) defines the uncertainty function $F_{PA}(t)$, which is a monotonically decreasing function in the range of $t \in [1, T]$ and is positively correlated with $H(A)$. $F_{PA}(t)$ is the **information entropy** metric of the system. By removing $p_{xt}(a_i)$ from Equation (7), we obtain the computing formula of $F_{PA}(t)$, as shown in Equation (8).

$$\begin{aligned} F_{PA}(t) &= -(\sum_{t=1}^{T} \log p_{xt}(a_i) + \sum_{t=1}^{T} \log p_{xt}(a_j|a_i) + \ldots) \\ &= -\sum_{i=1}^{m} \sum_{j=1}^{i} (f(s_{ij}) \cdot \sum_{t=1}^{T} \log(p_{xt}(a_i) f(s_{ij})) \end{aligned} \quad (8)$$

$$\begin{aligned} s.t.[(n+1)/2] \leq m \leq n \\ 0 \leq f(s_{ij}) \leq 1 \end{aligned}$$

(Metric 3) The decay rate of the information entropy value

In Equation (8), $F_{PA}(t)$ can denote the information entropy value of the CMD system A at the moment of state t. The smaller $F_{PA}(t)$, the less reliable the system. Additionally, when $F_{PA}(t)$ is 0, the system becomes completely unreliable. In addition, we propose the **decay rate of the information entropy value** $F_{PA}(\Delta t)$ as the third evaluation metric for assessing the system's reliability. $F_{PA}(\Delta t)$ can be expressed as in Equation (9).

$$F_{PA}(\Delta t) = -\sum_{i=1}^{m} \sum_{j=1}^{i} (f(s_{ij}) \cdot \log(\frac{p_{xt} + \Delta p_{x\Delta t}}{p_{xt}})) \quad (9)$$

A larger $F_{PA}(\Delta t)$ value indicates a larger decay rate in the system entropy information entropy value, i.e., the fewer times the system can cope with memorization-based attacks, and the lower the system's resistance to memorized attacks.

4. Scheduling Algorithm Based on the Information Entropy and Game Model

This section first presents a game model to capture the relationships between attackers and defenders, then the algorithm for scheduling redundant executors is given.

4.1. Game Model

Consider the game state of the mimic defense system for both attackers and defenders, each aiming for benefits. The adversary wishes to destroy the system by attacking the redundant executors to gain benefits, while the defender wishes to analyze the adversary's attack strategy to make corresponding defense scheduling and reduce the benefits gained by the attacker. The benefits of both sides are negatively correlated. In the process of strategy adjustment, when both the adversary and the defender cannot gain more benefits by adjusting the strategy, the game reaches equilibrium, at which time the adversary will give up the attack due to the inability to obtain the desired attack benefits.

In this model, whether the adversary launches a subsequent attack in any attack state t mainly depends on whether the probability of the adversary obtaining a gain satisfies its expectation when the state moves from t to $t+1$. Therefore, we first present the game model based on the complete information, i.e., the benefit matrix under the full information. Then, by pointing out its weakness, we give the game model based on incomplete information, and based on this, the equilibrium point is solved.

4.1.1. Game Model Based on Complete Information Conditions

Consider a game model $G = \{\Omega, T, P, U\}$.

(1) $\Omega = \{\Omega_A, \Omega_D\}$ denotes the game participants: attacker Ω_A and defender Ω_D.

(2) $T = \{T_A, T_D\}$ denotes the game strategy space, the attacker strategy $T_A = \{T_{A1}, T_{A2}\}$, and the defender strategy $T_D = \{T_{D1}, T_{D2}\}$. T_{A1} means that the attacker performs an attack strategy, T_{A2} means that the attacker performs a no-attack strategy, T_{D1}

means that the defender performs an active scheduling defense, and T_{D2} means that the defender shuts down the system.

(3) $P = \{\alpha_A, \beta_D\}$ denotes the game strategy execution probability space. The probability that the adversary attacks to execute the strategy is denoted as α_A and the probability that the defender executes the strategy is denoted as β_D. Thus, $\alpha_A = \{\alpha, 1-\alpha\}$ and $\beta_D = \{\beta, 1-\beta\}$.

(4) $U = \{U_A, U_D\}$ denotes the payoff space of the game participants. U_A is the attacker's payoff and U_D is the defender's payoff.

At the same time, we make the following assumptions:

Assumption 5. *Both players of the game will execute the strategy only if they are sure that the payoff of the strategy is positive.*

The gain parameter symbols of the adversary and the defender in system G are shown in Table 1. For the heterogeneous redundant system A with m redundancy, consider the offensive and defensive game strategies when the number of failed redundancies k satisfies $k < \left[\frac{m+1}{2}\right]$ and $k \geq \left[\frac{m+1}{2}\right]$, respectively, and construct the payoff matrix under the full information condition, as shown in Table 3.

Table 3. Payoff matrix under full information.

	$k < [(n+1)/2]$		**$k \geq [(n+1)/2]$**	
	T_{D1}	T_{D2}	T_{D1}	T_{D2}
T_{A1}	$(-kb, c-kd)$	$(e-kb, 0)$	$(B-kb, -kd)$	$(e-kb, 0)$
T_{A2}	$(e, c-kd)$	$(e, 0)$	$(e, c-kd)$	$(e, 0)$

From the results of the payoff matrix in Table 3, it is evident that under the conditions of complete information, the adversary can achieve the maximum gain regardless of the strategy adopted by the defender. There is no equilibrium point. This further confirms that the DHR architecture, under the conditions of infinite resources, cannot ensure the stable operation of the system when facing a memorization-based attack on a definite target under limited resources.

4.1.2. Game Model Based on Incomplete Information Conditions

Model Under the Condition of the Incomplete Information Game

Similarly in the game model $G = \{\Omega, T, P, U\}$. To obtain an equilibrium solution for the system, the information about k needs to be hidden, transforming the model into an incomplete information game. At the same time, although the system itself has two sets of equilibrium points—(T_{A1}, T_{D1}), (T_{A2}, T_{D2}) or (T_{A2}, T_{D1}), (T_{A1}, T_{D2})—the defender must choose one. In other words, for the defender's basic goal of maintaining the normal operation of the system, the equilibrium point needs to be among (T_{A2}, T_{D1}), (T_{A1}, T_{D2}) as much as possible.

By averaging the return expectations under the incomplete information condition, we can obtain the payoff matrix for this condition. This matrix is shown in Table 4.

Table 4. Payoff matrix under incomplete information.

	k Unknown	
	T_{D1}	T_{D2}
T_{A1}	$((1-\lambda)B - kb, \lambda c - kd)$	$(e - kb, 0)$
T_{A2}	$(e, c - kd)$	$(e, 0)$

Model Equilibrium Solving Under Incomplete Information Game

The equilibrium equation under the mixed strategy condition can be obtained using the return matrix in Table 3:

$$((1-\lambda)B - kb)\alpha = (e - kb)(1-\alpha) \tag{10}$$

$$(\lambda c - kd)\beta = (c - kd)(1-\beta) \tag{11}$$

From Equations (7) and (8), two equilibrium solutions can be obtained.

$$\alpha = \left\{ \frac{e-kb}{(1-\lambda)B - 2kb + e}, \frac{(1-\lambda)B - kb}{(1-\lambda)B - 2kb + e} \right\} \tag{12}$$

$$\beta = \left\{ \frac{kd-c}{(1-\lambda)c + 2kd}, \frac{(2-\lambda)c + kd}{(1-\lambda)c + 2kd} \right\} \tag{13}$$

It is necessary to put the desired equilibrium point at (T_{A2}, T_{D1}), so it is necessary to have the equilibrium solutions $\{\alpha, \beta\}$.

$$\frac{e-kb}{(1-\lambda)B - 2kb + e} \geq \frac{(1-\lambda)B - kb}{(1-\lambda)B - 2kb + e} \tag{14}$$

$$\frac{kd-c}{(1-\lambda)c + 2kd} \leq \frac{(2-\lambda)c + kd}{(1-\lambda)c + 2kd} \tag{15}$$

That is, from Equations (14) and (15), the constraints on the desired equilibrium point can be expressed by Equation (16).

$$e > (1-\lambda)B \tag{16}$$

For the adversary, when there exists a revenue constraint $e > (1-\lambda)B$, the adversary may not make an attack because of an insufficient revenue, and its strategic equilibrium point is α. But for the defender, as long as the adversary satisfies the constraint $e > (1-\lambda)B$ and the defender performs defensive scheduling, there exists a strategic equilibrium point β.

Redundant Scheduling Constraint Solving Based on Incomplete Information Game Models

We now derive the relationship between attack basic gain e and information entropy by combining with the metric formulas in Section 3. Consider a set of m executors $\{a_1 \ldots a_m\}$ with T states for each redundant executor. For any redundant executor a_i, it is randomly in the t-th state. We make the following two assumptions with the set:

Assumption 6. *For the set of executors $\{a_1 \ldots a_m\}$, the total benefit of a successful attack by the adversary is B. The metric of the information entropy value of $\{a_1 \ldots a_m\}$ under the condition of state t is $F_{PA}(t)$, and $B \approx F_{PA}(t)$.*

Assumption 7. *The base gain when the adversary is not traced is a constant value e and e is much larger than the attack cost of a single redundant executor b. The base gain is average and equal for all the T states, denoted as $e(t_0)$.*

Then, according to Equations (12) and (14), the equilibrium solution and constraints of the set of executors $\{a_1 \ldots a_m\}$ for the attacker can be expressed by Equation (17).

$$\begin{array}{l} \alpha = \frac{e-kb}{(1-\lambda)F_{PA}(t) - 2kb + e} \\ s.t. e > (1-\lambda)F_{PA}(t) \end{array} \tag{17}$$

In general, the gains available to the attacking party increase gradually as the attack continues. At state t, $F_{PA}(t) = mb$ can be taken. Since the objective function of the equilibrium solution α is a decreasing function of $F_{PA}(t)$ in the range of T, the maximum value of the model under the satisfied condition can be obtained and the objective function $\max\alpha$ satisfies Equation (18).

$$\max\alpha = \frac{e - kb}{(1-\lambda)mb - 2kb + e} \tag{18}$$

Meanwhile, according to Assumption 7, combined with the constraints of Equation (17), we obtain the constraints shown in Equation (19).

$$e(t_0) = e(\Delta t) \geq (1-\lambda)F_{PA}(\Delta t) \tag{19}$$

From Equations (18) and (19), we calculate the limiting value $\lim\limits_{e/b\to m} \max\alpha$ when the ratio of the base gain e to the single redundant executor gain b converges to the total number of executors m. The solution of $\lim\limits_{e/b\to m} \max\alpha$ with respect to the number of attacked redundant executors k within its definition domain is $[(m+1)/2]$ or $[(m-1)/2]$. That is, a scheduling algorithm is designed to make the attacker's gain in any t-state close to $[(m+1)/2]$ or $[(m-1)/2]$, and to satisfy that the change in the base gain from the t-state to $t+1$. The maximum attacker–defender equilibrium gain is guaranteed when the amount of state change satisfies Equation (19).

4.2. The Description of the Scheduling Algorithm

According to the analysis results in Section 4.1, we propose a redundant executor scheduling algorithm based on the information entropy of randomized weight: REWS (Random Entropy Weight Scheduling Algorithm).

The key steps of the algorithm are as follows. **Firstly**, select a collection of redundant executors, and construct a redundant executor's attacked state value interval for each of them, which can be a separate indicator such as the number of attacks or the number of scheduling, or a composite indicator of multiple elements. Then, construct the state and information entropy weight function, as well as design the information entropy weight decay rate function when the state changes. **Next**, perform random scheduling of the set of redundant executors with weight random update feedback so that the updated sum of the weights of each redundant executor is in the vicinity of $[(m+1)/2]$ or $[(m-1)/2]$ information entropy weights. That is, the information entropy weights satisfy the maximum value of the attacker's gain when the gains of the adversary and the defender are balanced. **Finally**, the calculation of the updated information entropy value makes the adversary unable to discern whether the attack result satisfies the gain or not, thus improving the reliability of the system. The flow chart of the algorithm is shown in Figure 5 and the three steps are detailed in the following:

Step 1. Initialization (**Algorithm 1**). First, in a redundancy pool with a margin of n, starting with the first redundant executor, set the range of the number of redundant executor states $\{t(a_i)|t(a_i) \in [1,T]\}$. Then, construct the weight function $w(F_{Pai}(t))$ of the redundant executor state and the information entropy value, construct the decay rate function $w(F_{Pai}(\Delta t))$ of the information entropy value when the state changes, and set the decay rate threshold of the information entropy value $e_{ai}(t_0)$.

Step 2. Randomized scheduling with weight updates (**Algorithm 2**). First, determine the total redundancy m of the set of redundant executors for this scheduling, and perform a random scheduling computation in the pool of redundant bodies if the state intervals are satisfied and the decay rate of the information entropy value satisfies the threshold condition of $e_{ai}(t_0)$. At each redundant executor scheduling, the adjudication result V is the product of each redundant executor's computation result di and its weights cumulatively. The computational results d_i are all compared with their previous settlement results, taking 1 if they are the same, and -1 if they are not.

Then, within the information entropy decay rate threshold, each redundant executor weight $w(F_{Pai}(t+1))$ that is scheduled is updated so that it is randomly fetched within the range of the offset ε_{ai}, i.e., it satisfies $w(F_{Pai}(t+1)) \in [w(F_{Pai}(t+1)) - \varepsilon_{ai}, w(F_{Pai}(t+1)) + \varepsilon_{ai}]$. The weights after taking values satisfy the conditions in Equation (20) or (21).

$$\sum_{i=1}^{m} \max w(F_{Pai}(t+1)) = \sum_{i=1}^{m} (w(F_{Pai}(t+1) + \varepsilon_{ai}) = w(\sum_{i=1}^{[(m+1)/2]} F_{Pai}(t)) \tag{20}$$

$$\sum_{i=1}^{m} \min w(F_{Pai}(t+1) = \sum_{i=1}^{m} (w(F_{Pai}(t+1) - \varepsilon_{ai}) = w(\sum_{i=1}^{[(m-1)/2]} F_{Pai}(t)) \tag{21}$$

Step 3. If a_i is not the last redundant executor, step 2 is repeated. Otherwise, a fictitious adjudication is performed based on the entropy weight value with the redundant executor calculation result. The resulting optimal V of the weight-based adjudication can indicate the reliability of the system as shown in Equation (22), i expresses the i-th redundant executor.

$$\begin{aligned} &\max V = \sum_{i=1}^{m} w(F_{Pai}(t))d_i \\ &s.t. \begin{cases} d_i = 1, d_{i+1} = \begin{cases} 1, if\ d_{i+1} \oplus d_i = 1 \\ -1, if\ d_{i+1} \oplus d_i = 0 \end{cases} \\ \sum_{i=1}^{m} \max w(F_{Pai}(t+1)) = \sum_{i=1}^{m} (w(F_{Pai}(t+1) + \varepsilon_{ai}) = w(\sum_{i=1}^{[(m+1)/2]} F_{Pai}(t)) \\ \sum_{i=1}^{m} \min w(F_{Pai}(t+1) = \sum_{i=1}^{m} (w(F_{Pai}(t+1) - \varepsilon_{ai}) = w(\sum_{i=1}^{[(m-1)/2]} F_{Pai}(t)) \\ F_{Pai}(\Delta t) \le e(t_0) \end{cases} \end{aligned} \tag{22}$$

Algorithm 1 *Initialization*

INPUT: redundancy pool n, Redundancy n, range of redundant executor states $\{t(a_i)|t(a_i) \in [1, T]\}$, information entropy weight function $w(F_{Pai}(t))$, decay rate function of the information entropy value $w(F_{Pai}(\Delta t))$, decay rate threshold of the information entropy value $e_{ai}(t_0)$.

OUTPUT: The set of redundant executor states *t_set*, initial weight set *w_set*, information entropy value decay rate set *rt_set*, and information entropy value decay rate threshold set *ct_set*.

for $1 \le I \le n$ do:
t_set = *t_set* + $\{t(a_i)\}$
w_set = *w_set* + $\{w(F_{Pai}(t))\}$
rt_set = *rt_set* + $\{F_{Pai}(\Delta t)\}$
ct_set = *ct_set* + $\{e_{ai}(t_0)\}$
endfor
output *t_set*,*w_set*,*rt_set*,*ct_set*

Algorithm 2 *Randomized scheduling with weight updates*

INPUT: Scheduled set of redundancies $A = \{a_1 \ldots a_m\}$, Residual degree m of set A, Stochastic scheduling function $C(m,n)$, the result of the redundant executor ai randomized scheduling $d(i)$, the result set D, the redundant executor ai weight update offset value ε_{ai}.

OUTPUT: mimetic adjudication result V.

Initialization

$D = C(m,n)$

for $d(i)$ in D do:

if ($t\_set(i) > T$) or ($rt\_set(i) > ct\_set(i)$) then

V = null

output V

break

end if

end for

if $V \neq 0$ then

for $d(i)$ in D do:

if $d(i) \oplus d(0) = 1$ then

$V = V + w\_set\ (i)*d(i)$

else if $d(i) \oplus d(0) = 0$ then

$V = V + (-w\_set\ (i))*d(i)$

end if

if $t\_set\ (i) + 1 \leq T$ then

$t\_set\ (i) = t\_set\ (i) + 1$

if w_set (I + 1) > 0 then

w_set (I + 1) = random $(w(F_{Pai}(t\_set(i+1))) \pm \varepsilon)$

end if

end if

end for

if (($\sum_{1}^{\lfloor(m+1)/2\rfloor}(w\_set(i)) == \sum_{1}^{m}(w\_set(i+1))$) or $\sum_{1}^{\lfloor(m-1)/2\rfloor}(w\_set(i)) == \sum_{1}^{m}(w\_set(i+1))$) and ($V$ = null) then

output V

else

output null

end if

end if

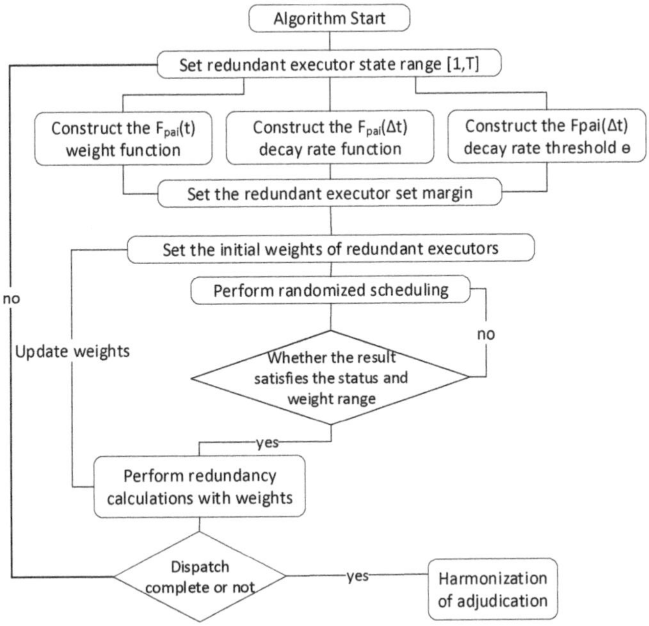

Figure 5. The flow chart of the algorithm.

5. Simulation Evaluation

In this section, we perform simulations to evaluate the scheduling algorithm REWS under memorization-enabled attacker and finite resource qualification conditions, as well as the metrics (defined in Section 3) related to the information entropy value. The experiments are conducted using the system with an Intel Core i7 7200 CPU, 16 GB DDR memory, and a Windows 11 Professional operating system. The software running environment is Python 3.9.

5.1. Experiment Setup

The experiment initialization design mainly includes basic conditions initialization, index initialization, and algorithm model initialization, detailed in the following:

(i) Basic conditions initialization

It is mainly set for the redundant resource pool and the set of redundant executables. In this paper, we set a redundant pool with a redundancy n of 9. The similarity between the redundant executors is randomly generated with a β-distribution with parameters (5, 15), and then the similarity matrix S_{ij} is obtained as shown in Equation (23).

$$\begin{pmatrix} 1 & 0.229 & 0.134 & 0.316 & 0.242 & 0.345 & 0.280 & 0.225 & 0.383 \\ 0.229 & 1 & 0.125 & 0.215 & 0.209 & 0.302 & 0.210 & 0.069 & 0.153 \\ 0.134 & 0.125 & 1 & 0.259 & 0.282 & 0.321 & 0.206 & 0.240 & 0.185 \\ 0.316 & 0.215 & 0.259 & 1 & 0.404 & 0.139 & 0.358 & 0.165 & 0.181 \\ 0.242 & 0.209 & 0.282 & 0.404 & 1 & 0.241 & 0.361 & 0.238 & 0.190 \\ 0.345 & 0.302 & 0.321 & 0.139 & 0.241 & 1 & 0.280 & 0.270 & 0.319 \\ 0.280 & 0.210 & 0.206 & 0.358 & 0.361 & 0.280 & 1 & 0.386 & 0.292 \\ 0.225 & 0.069 & 0.240 & 0.165 & 0.238 & 0.270 & 0.386 & 1 & 0.264 \\ 0.383 & 0.153 & 0.185 & 0.181 & 0.190 & 0.319 & 0.292 & 0.264 & 1 \end{pmatrix} \tag{23}$$

At the same time, according to the relationship between the redundancy and the safety gain in the existing research, we select the redundant executor set margin m as 3 and 4 for the computational research.

(ii) Metric normalization for the assessment of dynamism

In order to compare the algorithms and metrics in the experiments with those in the established research, it is necessary to normalize the metrics proposed in this paper with the traditional metrics. Consider a mimic defense system A. Among the traditional research metrics, the scheduling cycle metric T is generally used to evaluate the dynamics of the system.

We investigate the mainstream scheduling algorithms proposed in recent years, including the heterogeneity-based CRS algorithm [13], the heterogeneity-based extension of the history confidence-based HDCD [31], and the HHAC algorithm [29]. The average number of scheduling times for a single redundant executor of the system during one scheduling cycle is about 3.6 and 8.9 times at residuals m = 3 and 4, respectively. Therefore, for the purpose of metric normalization, we adopt the average number of times that a single redundant executor is dispatched within one scheduling cycle of these three algorithms as the upper limit of the state range of the redundant executor.

(iii) Initialization of the information entropy weight-based scheduling model

According to the study in Section 3, $w_t = w(F_{Pai}(t))$ is a composite function of the attacked state of the redundant executor, where $F_{Pai}(t)$ is a monotonically decreasing function on t. Meanwhile, the function for when there is a memory attack and as t increases, the information that can be mined is decreasing gradually, i.e., $\frac{dH(A)}{dt}$ decreases gradually and $\lim_{t\to\infty} \frac{dH(A)}{dt} = 0$. Therefore, in this paper, the function $w = e^{-\eta t}$ with similar properties is selected to replace the composite function for the approximate solution analysis. Where, η is the regulation parameter, w is the entropy weight, and t is the state of the redundant executor being attacked.

Meanwhile, from the conclusion of the above study, it is necessary to control the range of the scheduling state values within 4.6 and 9.9 times when the margin m is taken as 3 and 4. Therefore, we take 1 and 0.25, respectively, and the results are shown in Figure 6.

The maximum number of states is approximated as 5 and 10 in both cases and the values of each scheduling weight are shown in Tables 5 and 6.

Table 5. The entropy weights are taken at $w = e^{-t}$.

T	w
1	0.37
2	0.15
3	0.05
4	0.02
5	approximately equal to 0

Therefore, the weighting function parameters η can be taken as 0.5 and 0.25, respectively, and the decay rate thresholds θ for the overall information entropy value are 20% and 10%, respectively, for the comparison experiments.

Table 6. The entropy weights are taken at $w = e^{-0.25t}$.

t	w
1	0.78
2	0.61
3	0.47
4	0.37
5	0.29
6	0.22
7	0.17
8	0.14
9	0.11
10	approximately equal to 0

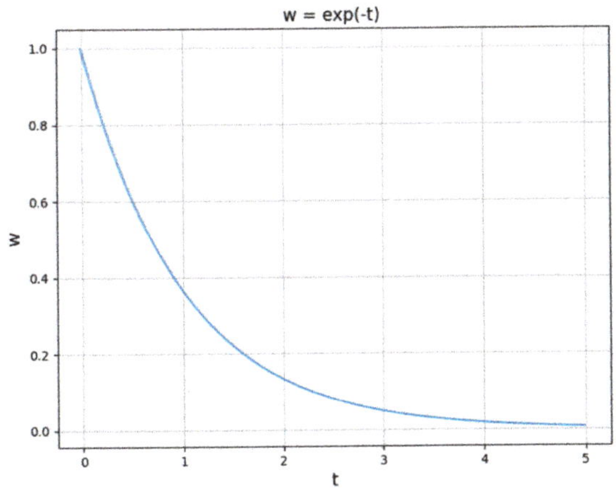

(a)

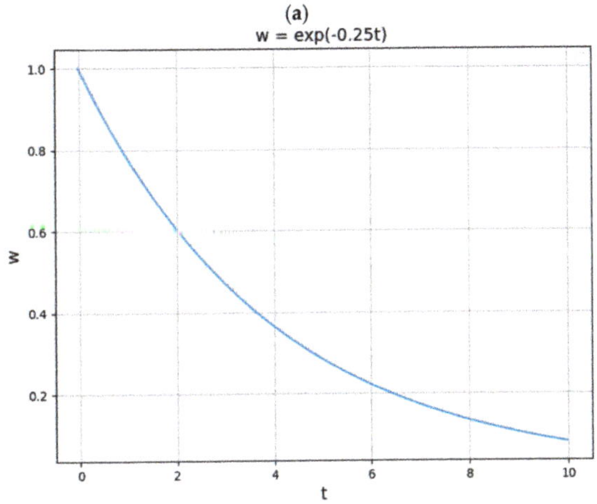

(b)

Figure 6. (**a**) Weights and scheduling time functions for η of 1. (**b**) Weights and scheduling times functions for η of 0.25.

5.2. Experimentation and Analysis of Algorithm Dynamics Under Limited Resource Conditions

We conduct simulation experiments to compare the CRS, HDCD, HHAC, and REWS algorithms under limited resources. To facilitate the comparison of the experimental results, this paper makes the following assumptions:

Assumption 8. *All the redundant executor program sets cannot be repeated with the initial program.*

Assumption 9. *Any redundancy set scheme that has been invoked is also unrepeatable (including HDCD, HHAC 2 algorithms with no increase in historical confidence or local confidence, Local Confidence (LC) and a decay rate of 100%).*

Under this condition, we conduct two experiments on dynamics, through which we expect to find the algorithm with the highest average scheduling period, the average number of states of the redundant executors, and the scheduling period to state ratio. Among them, the higher the average scheduling period, the stronger the system dynamics and the higher the reliability; a higher average number of states of the redundant executors indicates a higher initial information entropy value under the condition of limited resources, i.e., the stronger the reliability of the initial state; and the higher the ratio of the scheduling period to the state indicates that each scheduling under the condition of limited resources plays a bigger role in the reliability of the system. We conducted 100 independent experiments under simulated finite resource conditions and obtained the following results.

(i) At $m = 3$, the REWS algorithm is chosen as the weighting function for the experiments. The scheduling period T of the CRS algorithm, the HDCD algorithm, the HHAC algorithm, and the REWS algorithm is shown in Figure 7a–d.

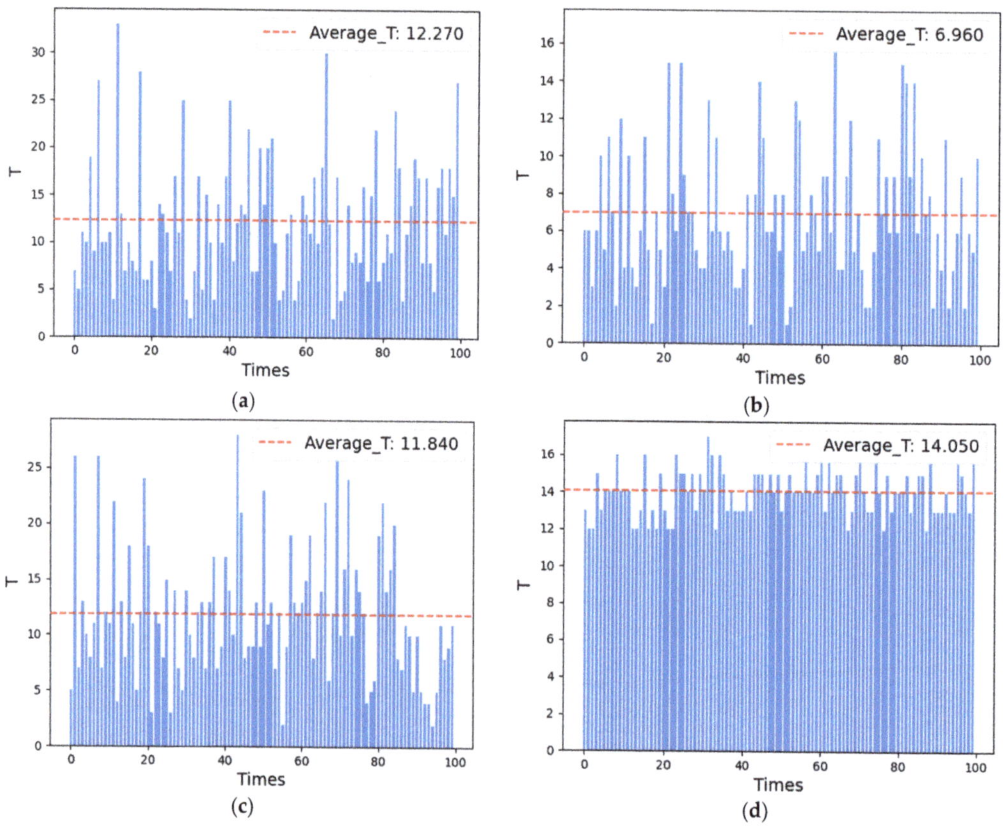

Figure 7. (**a**) CRS algorithm scheduling period for m = 3. (**b**) HCDC algorithm scheduling period for $m = 3$. (**c**) HHAC algorithm scheduling period for $m = 3$. (**d**) REWS algorithm scheduling period for $m = 3$.

The average number of scheduling states for the CRS algorithm, the HDCD algorithm, the HHAC algorithm, and the REWS algorithm for $m = 3$ is shown in Figure 8a–d.

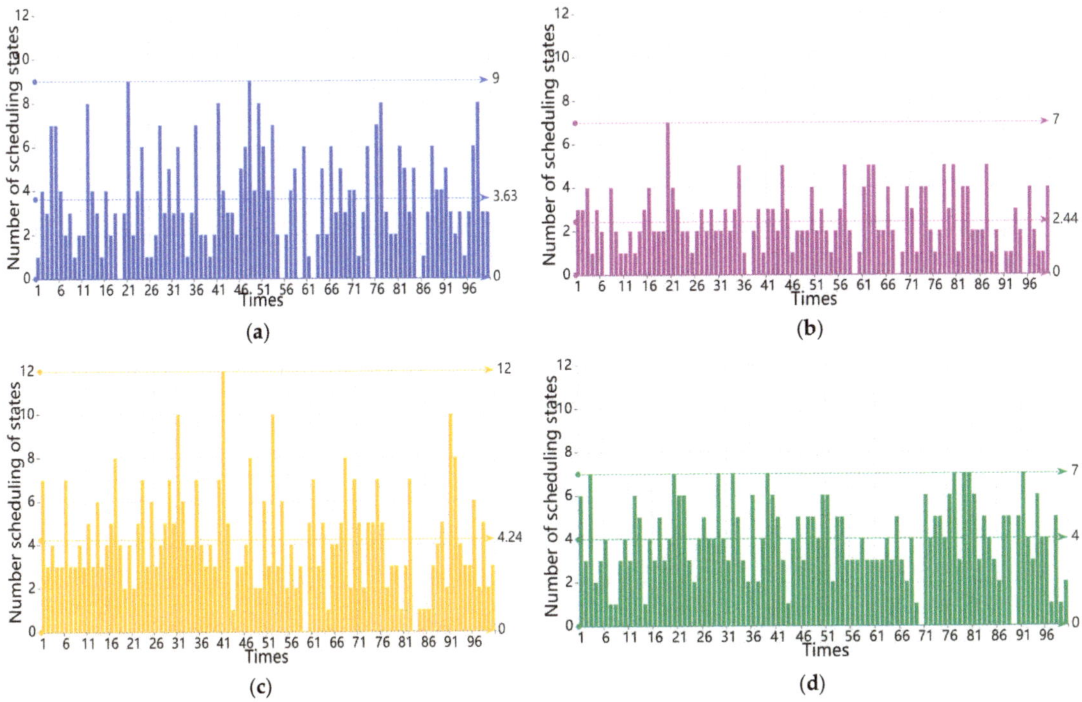

Figure 8. (**a**) Average number of scheduling states for the CRS algorithm for m = 3. (**b**) Average number of scheduling states for the HCDC algorithm for m = 3. (**c**) Average number of scheduling states for the HHAC algorithm for m = 3. (**d**) Average number of scheduling states for the REWS algorithm for m = 3.

(ii) The REWS algorithm selects $w = e^{-0.25t}$ as the weight function for the experiment at m = 4. The scheduling period T of the CRS algorithm, the HDCD algorithm, the HHAC algorithm, and the REWS algorithm is shown in Figure 9.

The average number of scheduling states for the CRS algorithm, the HDCD algorithm, the HHAC algorithm, and the REWS algorithm for m = 4 is shown in Figure 10a–d.

The comparison of the experimental results is shown in Table 7.

Table 7. Different scheduling algorithms scheduling **cycle** T. Average number of scheduling states, n; period-to-state ratio, T/n.

	Redundancy m = 3			Redundancy m = 4		
	Scheduling Cycle T	Average Number of Scheduling States n	Period-to-State Ratio T/n	Scheduling Cycle T	Average Number of Scheduling States n	Period-to-State Ratio T/n
CRS	12.27	3.63	3.38	14.26	9.04	1.57
HCDC	6.96	2.44	2.85	11.39	8.36	1.36
HHAC	11.84	4.24	3.01	15.55	9.71	1.60
REWS	**14.05**	**4.00**	**3.51**	**20.57**	**9.00**	**2.28**

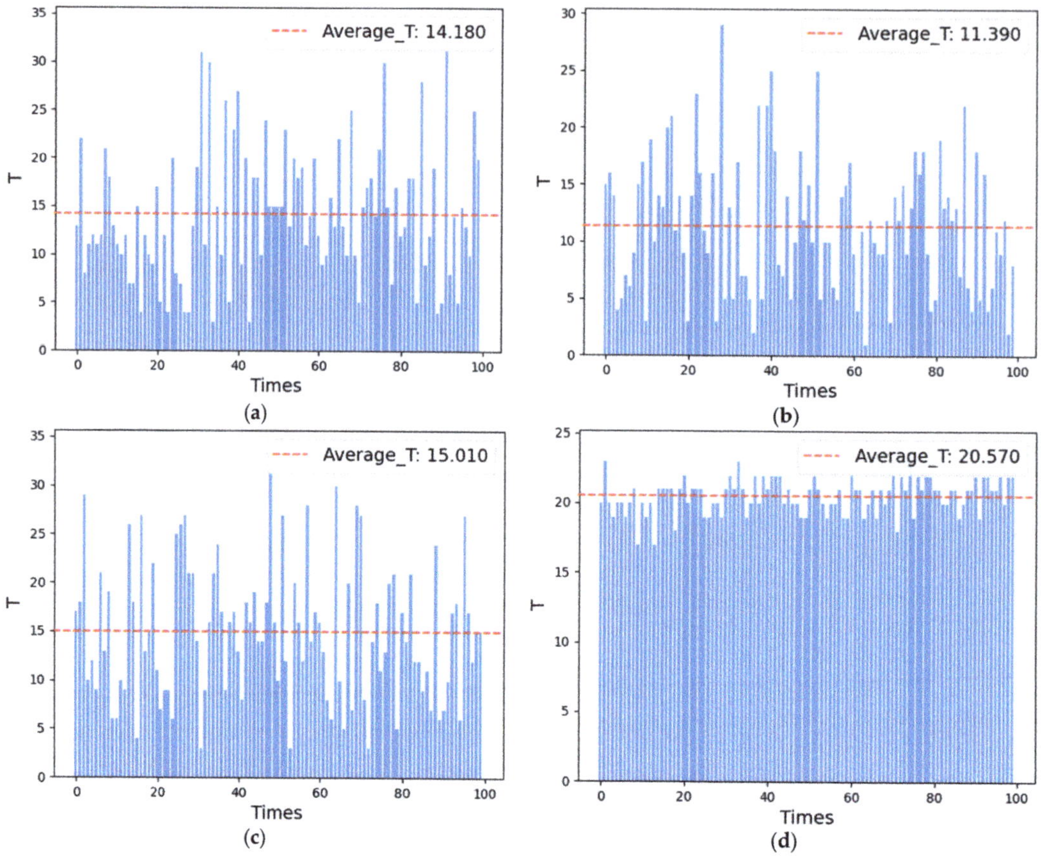

Figure 9. (**a**) CRS algorithm scheduling period for m = 4. (**b**) HCDC algorithm scheduling period for m = 4. (**c**) HHAC algorithm scheduling period for m = 4. (**d**) REWS algorithm scheduling period for m = 4.

From the experiments, it can be observed that the average scheduling period of the REWS algorithm is about 14.05 and 20.57 under the conditions of redundancy 3 and 4, respectively, even though the scheduling of the redundant system failure is about 14.05 and 20.47 times at this point. This result is 1.14 and 1.44 times more than the CRS algorithm, 2.01 and 1.8 times more than the HCDC algorithm, and 1.18 and 1.32 times more than the HHAC algorithm, respectively, and it also shows that the REWS algorithm has a better dynamic than the other algorithms under the condition of limited resources. Secondly, the average number of states of the REWS algorithm is 4 and 9, respectively, which is only slightly lower than the HHAC algorithm. This indicates that its initial reliability is better and only slightly worse than the HHAC algorithm. Finally, the period-to-state ratios of the REWS algorithm are 3.51 and 2.28, respectively, which are 1.03 and 1.45 times higher than those of the CRS algorithm, 1.23 and 1.67 times higher than those of the HCDC algorithm, and 1.17 and 1.43 times higher than those of the HHAC algorithm. This suggests that, even in the case of a less-than-optimal initial reliability, the scheduling of each time of the REWS algorithm plays a more significant role in the system reliability than the other algorithms. The system reliability is better than the other algorithms and the scheduling effectiveness of the system is higher.

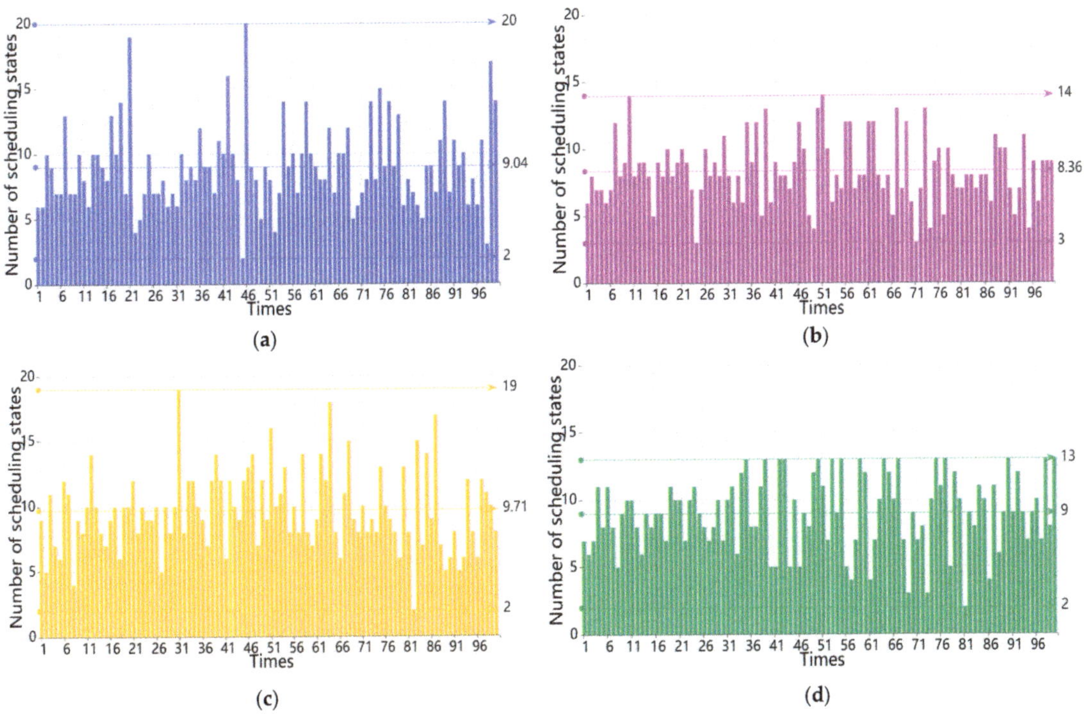

Figure 10. (**a**) Average number of scheduling states for the CRS algorithm for $m = 4$. (**b**) Average number of scheduling states for the HCDC algorithm for $m = 4$. (**c**) Average number of scheduling states for the HHAC algorithm for $m = 4$. (**d**) Average number of scheduling states for the REWS algorithm for $m = 4$.

5.3. Reliability Analysis Under a Memorization-Based Attack

For targeted memorization-based attacks, if an attacker discovers a high-threat 0-day vulnerability in a redundant executor, it is often difficult for the defender to quickly find an effective countermeasure. This means that all the scheduling strategies with respect to that redundant executor are at risk. Therefore, in this paper, we set the condition that a single redundant executor is unreliable after each scheduling, i.e., the decay rate of the information entropy is 100% to simulate the memorization-based attack for the experiments. We would like to experimentally find the algorithm that can resist the maximum number of memorized attacks under the condition of memorized attacks, and the experimental steps are specified as follows:

(i) First, still choosing the residual degree $m = 3, 4$, according to the similarity matrix constructed in Section 4.1, the average similarity of the above four algorithms is calculated as shown in Table 8.

Table 8. Average similarity of the four different scheduling algorithms.

Average Similarity	CRS	HCDC	HHAC	REWS
$m = 3$	0.254	0.170	0.144	0.254
$m = 4$	0.244	0.191	0.171	0.240

(ii) In order to simplify the calculation, let $f(s_{ij}) = s_{ij}$, then according to Equation (8), the initial information entropy values of the four algorithms can be calculated as shown in Table 9.

Table 9. Information entropy value of the different scheduling algorithms.

	CRS	HCDC	HHAC	REWS
Information entropy value	27.282	28.082	28.346	27.282

(iii) Finally, under the condition that the decay rate θ of the information entropy of a single redundant executor is 100% and according to the algorithmic process in Section 4, the scheduling is carried out at the residual degree of $m = 3$ and 4, respectively, then the trend of the information entropy is shown in Figure 11a,b.

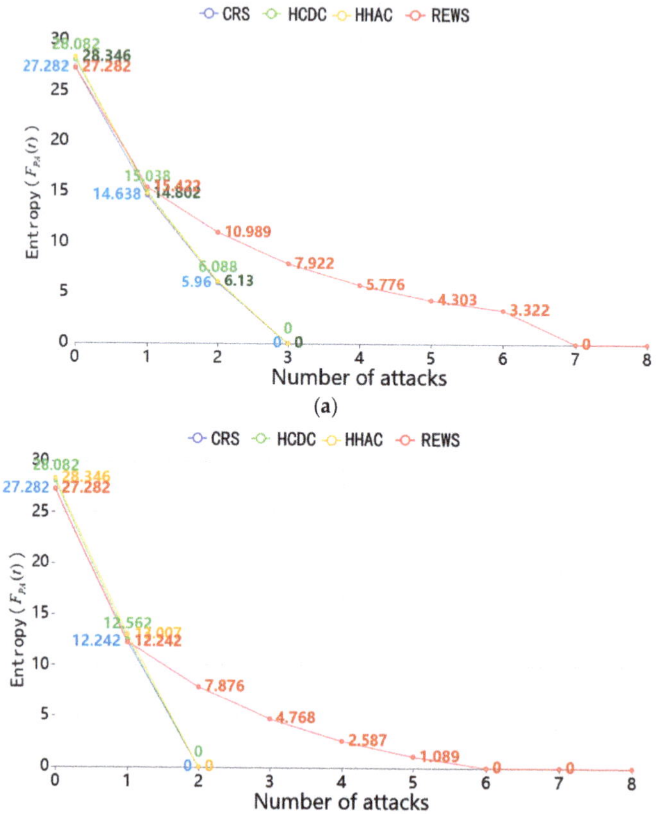

Figure 11. (**a**) Experiments on different algorithms against memorization-based attacks for $m = 3$. (**b**) Experiments on different algorithms against memorization-based attacks for $m = 4$.

From the experiments, it can be observed that the redundancy is permanently unreliable by the back side of the scheduling due to the memorization-based attack, which makes the traditional scheduling algorithms, such as the CRS algorithm, the HCDC algorithm, and the HHAC algorithm, unreliable by at most 3 and 2 attacks, respectively. As for the REWS algorithm, after the first scheduling, it can quickly adaptively adjust the adjudication strategy through the weights to make the attacker and the defender reach an equilibrium. This means that the subsequent scheduling in the case of the information entropy of the redundant executor that has been scheduled is 0, and it can still guarantee that the total information entropy value of the set of redundant executors is greater than 0, which in turn makes the whole system able to withstand 7 and 6 attacks to make the system unreliable.

5.4. Analysis of the Algorithm Time Complexity

According to the related literature, the time complexity of the CRS algorithm, the HCDC algorithm, the HHAC algorithm, and the main part of the REWS algorithm is shown in Table 10.

Table 10. The time complexity of the four different scheduling algorithms.

	CRS	HCDC	HHAC	REWS
Time complexity	$o(n^2)$	$o(n^2 \times Y)$	$o(n(n^2 + (n-1)n))$	$o(n(n \times t))$

The CRS algorithm has the smallest time complexity of $o(n^2)$, the REWS algorithm has a slightly larger time complexity than the CRS algorithm and a smaller time complexity than the HCDC algorithm and the HHAC algorithm, which is $o(n(n \times t))$, and the HCDC algorithm and the HHAC algorithm have the largest time complexity of $o(n^2 \times Y)$ and $o(n(n^2 + (n-1)n))$, respectively. Here, t is the number of scheduling times determined according to the different weight functions and Y is the number of redundant executor scheduling times based on the historical confidence.

6. Conclusions and Future Work

This paper aims to address the problem of a gradual decrease in the reliability of the scheduling cycle in the face of limited scheduling resources and a memorization-based attack environment. Based on the mimic defense system of the DHR architecture in the cloud service platform of the railroad internal service network, relying on the actual engineering and construction scenarios of the CRCC, we propose three reliability evaluation metrics of the CRCC-DHR architecture in terms of the number of scheduling states of the redundancy executors, the information entropy value, and the decay rate of the information entropy value. On this basis, the problem is modeled and solved based on the incomplete information game model, and at the same time, a random entropy weight redundant executor scheduling algorithm, namely, the REWS algorithm, is further proposed.

Then, based on the evaluation metrics proposed in this paper, simulations are conducted to verify and compare the dynamics of the system and the reliability capability against memorization-based attacks of the REWS algorithm, the CRS algorithm, the HCDC algorithm, and the HHAC algorithm under the conditions of a residual degree of 3 and 4. The experimental analysis shows that the average scheduling period of the REWS algorithm is 1.14 and 1.44 times that of the CRS algorithm, 2.01 and 1.8 times that of the HCDC algorithm, and 1.18 and 1.32 times that of the HHAC algorithm, respectively, under the conditions of residuals 3 and 4, i.e., it means that the REWS algorithm is a better dynamic under the conditions of limited resources. Meanwhile, the cycle state ratio of the REWS algorithm is 1.03 and 1.45 times the CRS algorithm, 1.23 and 1.67 times the HCDC algorithm, and 1.17 and 1.43 times the HHAC algorithm, which means that each scheduling of the REWS algorithm plays a greater role in the system reliability and the scheduling effectiveness of the system is higher. In terms of the reliability against memorization-based attacks, under the condition of margins of 3 and 4, the REWS algorithm can withstand 7 and 6 attacks, respectively, to make the system unreliable, while the traditional scheduling algorithm can be made unreliable at most 3 and 2 attacks, respectively, i.e., its reliability is higher due to the traditional scheduling algorithm.

Although the REWS algorithm improves the reliability of the DHR architecture under the conditions of limited scheduling resources and memorization-based attacks, the total information entropy of the system still gradually decreases. Further improvements to the REWS algorithm will be explored in future research, focusing on enhancing the information entropy model. In addition, scalability is a big limitation of our scheduling algorithm.

We will explore how to deal with this limitation and will also explore the reinforcement learning technique to design the scheduling algorithm. Moreover, we will explore how to collect data in the CRCC-DHR, establish a similarity matrix, and verify the effectiveness of our algorithm.

Author Contributions: Conceptualization, X.W. and M.W.; Methodology, X.W., Y.C., and X.C.; Data curation and system experimental, X.W. and Y.L.; Writing—original draft preparation, X.W.; Writing—review and editing, X.C., M.W., and Y.C. All authors have read and agreed to the published version of the manuscript.

Funding: This research was funded by the Scientific Research Project of the China Academy of Railway Sciences Co., Ltd. (No. 2024YJ224).

Data Availability Statement: No new data were created or analyzed in this study. Data sharing is not applicable to this article.

Conflicts of Interest: The authors declare no conflicts of interest.

References

1. Technical Expansion Requirements of the Railway Network-Security Protection of Railway Network Cloud Platform. Available online: https://www.ebiaozhun.com/std/513cd09e426641369584cec34c7bdff5.html (accessed on 16 August 2024).
2. The Rise of Zero-Day Vulnerabilities: Why Traditional Security Solutions Fall Short. Available online: https://thehackernews.com/2024/10/rise-of-zero-day-vulnerabilities.html (accessed on 16 August 2024).
3. Liu, S.; Yin, C.; Chen, D.; Lv, H.; Zhang, Q. Cascading Failure in Multiple Critical Infrastructure Interdependent Networks of Syncretic Railway System. *IEEE Trans. Intell. Transp. Syst.* **2022**, *23*, 5740–5753. [CrossRef]
4. Bešinović, N.; Ferrari Nassar, R.; Szymula, C. Resilience assessment of railway networks: Combining infrastructure restoration and transport management. *Reliab. Eng. Syst. Saf.* **2022**, *224*, 108538. [CrossRef]
5. Lu, Q.; Li, J.; Peng, Z.; Wu, L.; Ni, M.; Luo, J. Detecting the cyber-physical-social cooperated APTs in high-DER-penetrated smart grids: Threats, current work and challenges. *Comput. Networks* **2024**, *254*, 110776. [CrossRef]
6. Theisen, C.; Munaiah, N.; Al-Zyoud, M.; Carver, J.C.; Meneely, A.; Williams, L. Attack surface definitions: A systematic literature review. *Inf. Softw. Technol.* **2018**, *104*, 94–103. [CrossRef]
7. Stojanović, B.; Hofer-Schmitz, K.; Kleb, U. APT datasets and attack modeling for automated detection methods: A review. *Comput. Secur.* **2020**, *92*, 101734. [CrossRef]
8. Kumar, R.; Kela, R.; Singh, S.; Trujillo-Rasua, R. APT attacks on industrial control systems: A tale of three incidents. *Int. J. Crit. Infrastruct. Prot.* **2022**, *37*, 100521. [CrossRef]
9. Lakshminaraytana, S.; Yau, D. Cost-benefit analysis of moving target defense in power grids. *IEEE Trans. Power Syst.* **2020**, *36*, 1152–1163. [CrossRef]
10. Cho, J.-H.; Sharma, D.; Alavizadeh, H.; Yoon, S.; Ben-Asher, N.; Moore, T.; Kim, D.; Lim, H.; Nelson, F.F. Toward Proactive, Adaptive Defense: A Survey on Moving Target Defense. *IEEE Commun. Surv. Tutor.* **2020**, *22*, 709–745. [CrossRef]
11. Navas, R.E.; Cuppens, F.; Boulahia Cuppens, N.; Toutain, L.; Papadopoulos, G.Z. MTD, Where Art Thou? A Systematic Review of Moving Target Defense Techniques for IoT. *IEEE Internet Things J.* **2021**, *8*, 7818–7832. [CrossRef]
12. Zheng, Y.; Li, Z.; Xu, X.; Zhao, Q. Dynamic defenses in cyber security: Techniques, methods and challenges. *Digit. Commun. Netw.* **2022**, *8*, 422–435. [CrossRef]
13. Wu, J. DHR Architecture. In *Cyberspace Mimic Defense*; Springer: Berlin/Heidelberg, Germany, 2020; Volume 2, pp. 273–337.
14. Chen, Y.; Li, M.; Zhu, X.; Fang, K.; Ren, Q.; Guo, T.; Chen, X.; Li, C.; Zou, Z.; Deng, Y. An improved algorithm for practical byzantine fault tolerance to large-scale consortium chain. *Inf. Process. Manag.* **2022**, *59*, 102884. [CrossRef]
15. Zhan, Y.; Wang, B.; Lu, R.; Yu, Y. DRBFT: Delegated randomization Byzantine fault tolerance consensus protocol for blockchains. *Inf. Sci.* **2021**, *559*, 8–21. [CrossRef]
16. Zhang, J.; Rong, Y.; Cao, J.; Wu, W. DBFT: A Byzantine Fault Tolerance Protocol With Graceful Performance Degradation. *IEEE Trans. Dependable Secur. Comput.* **2022**, *19*, 3387–3400. [CrossRef]
17. Cai, M.; He, X.; Zhou, D. Self-Healing Fault-Tolerant Control for High-Order Fully Actuated Systems Against Sensor Faults: A Redundancy Framework. *IEEE Trans. Cybern.* **2024**, *54*, 2628–2640. [CrossRef]
18. Reghenzani, F.; Guo, Z.; Fornaciari, W. Software Fault Tolerance in Real-Time Systems: Identifying the Future Research Questions. *ACM Comput. Surv.* **2023**, *55*, 1–30. [CrossRef]
19. Wu, J. Cyberspace Endogenous Safety and Security. *Engineering* **2022**, *15*, 179–185. [CrossRef]

20. Ying, F.; Zhao, S.; Wang, J. A Security Information Transmission Method Based on DHR for Seafloor Observation Network. *Sensors* **2024**, *24*, 1147. [CrossRef]
21. Kang, Y.; Zhang, Q.; Jiang, B.; Bu, Y. A Differentially Private Framework for the Dynamic Heterogeneous Redundant Architecture System in Cyberspac. *Electronics* **2024**, *13*, 1805. [CrossRef]
22. Li, L.; Wu, J.; Hu, H. Secure Cloud Architecture for 5G Core Network. *Chin. J. Electron.* **2021**, *30*, 516–522. [CrossRef]
23. Wu, Q.; Wu, C.; Yan, X.; Cheng, Q. Intrinsic Security and Self-Adaptive Cooperative Protection Enabling Cloud Native Network Slicing. *IEEE Trans. Netw. Serv. Manag.* **2021**, *18*, 1287–1304. [CrossRef]
24. Wang, Z.; Jiang, D.; Lv, Z. AI-Assisted Trustworthy Architecture for Industrial IoT Based on Dynamic Heterogeneous Redundancy. *IEEE Trans. Ind. Inform.* **2023**, *19*, 2019–2027. [CrossRef]
25. Sepczuk, M. Dynamic Web Application Firewall Detection supported by Cyber Mimic. *J. Netw. Comput. Appl.* **2023**, *213*, 103596. [CrossRef]
26. Chen, G.; Shi, G.; Chen, L.; He, X.; Jiang, S. A Novel Model of Mimic Defense Based on Minimal L-Order Error Probability. *IEEE Access* **2020**, *8*, 180481–180490. [CrossRef]
27. Li, Q.; Meng, S.; Sang, X.; Zhang, H.; Wang, S.; Bashir, A.; Yu, K.; Tariq, U. Dynamic Scheduling Algorithm in Cyber Mimic Defense Architecture of Volunteer Computing. *ACM Trans. Internet Technol.* **2021**, *21*, 1–33. [CrossRef]
28. Zhu, Z.; Yu, H.; Liu, Q.; Liu, D.; Yu, H. An Adaptive Multiexecutors Scheduling Algorithm Based on Heterogeneity for Cyberspace Mimic Defense. *Secur. Commun. Netw.* **2022**, *13*, 2300407. [CrossRef]
29. Shao, S.; Ji, Y.; Zhang, W.; Liu, S.; Jiang, F.; Cao, Z.; Wu, F.; Zeng, F.; Zuo, J.; Zhou, L. A DHR executor selection algorithm based on historical credibility and dissimilarity clustering. *Sci. China* **2023**, *66*, 212304. [CrossRef]
30. Hu, H.; Wu, J.; Wang, Z.; Cheng, G. Mimic defense: A designed-in cybersecurity defense framework. *IET Inf. Secur.* **2018**, *12*, 226–237. [CrossRef]
31. Chen, Z.; Cui, G.; Zhang, L.; Yang, X.; Li, H.; Zhao, Y.; Ma, C.; Sun, T. Optimal Strategy for Cyberspace Mimic Defense Based on Game Theory. *IEEE Access* **2021**, *9*, 68376–68386. [CrossRef]
32. Shi, L.; Miao, Y.; Ren, J.; Liu, R. Game Analysis and Optimization for Evolutionary Dynamic Heterogeneous Redundancy. *IEEE Trans. Netw. Serv. Manag.* **2023**, *20*, 4186–4197. [CrossRef]
33. Hu, J.; Li, Y.; Li, Z.; Liu, Q.; Wu, J. Unveiling the Strategic Defense Mechanisms in Dynamic Heterogeneous Redundancy Architecture. *IEEE Trans. Netw. Serv. Manag.* **2024**, *21*, 4912–4926. [CrossRef]
34. Shao, S.; Gu, T.; Nie, Y.; Ji, Z.; Wu, F.; Ba, Z.; Ji, Y.; Ren, K.; Sun, G. An Active Defense Adjudication Method Based on Adaptive Anomaly Sensing for Mimic IoT. *IEEE Trans. Serv. Comput.* **2025**, *18*, 57–71. [CrossRef]
35. Wu, X.; Wang, M.; Shen, J.; Gong, Y. Towards Double-Layer Dynamic Heterogeneous Redundancy Architecture for Reliable Railway Passenger Service System. *Electronics* **2024**, *13*, 3592. [CrossRef]

entropy

MDPI

Article

HECM-Plus: Hyper-Entropy Enhanced Cloud Models for Uncertainty-Aware Design Evaluation in Multi-Expert Decision Systems

Jiaozi Pu [1,*] and Zongxin Liu [2]

1 School of Culture and Art, Chengdu University of Information Technology, Chengdu 610103, China
2 West China School of Medicine, Sichuan University, Chengdu 610041, China; liuzongxin@scu.edu.cn
* Correspondence: pjz@swjtu.edu.cn

Abstract

Uncertainty quantification in cloud models requires simultaneous characterization of fuzziness (via Entropy, *En*) and randomness (via Hyper-entropy, *He*), yet existing similarity measures often neglect the stochastic dispersion governed by *He*. To address this gap, we propose HECM-Plus, an algorithm integrating Expectation (*Ex*), *En*, and *He* to holistically model geometric and probabilistic uncertainties in cloud models. By deriving *He*-adjusted standard deviations through reverse cloud transformations, HECM-Plus reformulates the Hellinger distance to resolve conflicts in multi-expert evaluations where subjective ambiguity and stochastic randomness coexist. Experimental validation demonstrates three key advances: (1) Fuzziness–Randomness discrimination: HECM-Plus achieves balanced conceptual differentiation ($\delta C_1/C_4 = 1.76$, $\delta C_2 = 1.66$, $\delta C_3 = 1.58$) with linear complexity outperforming PDCM and HCCM by 10.3% and 17.2% in differentiation scores while resolving *He*-induced biases in HECM/ECM (C_1–C_4 similarity: 0.94 vs. 0.99) critical for stochastic dispersion modeling; (2) Robustness in time-series classification: It reduces the mean error by 6.8% (0.190 vs. 0.204, $*p* < 0.05$) with lower standard deviation (0.035 vs. 0.047) on UCI datasets, validating noise immunity; (3) Design evaluation application: By reclassifying controversial cases (e.g., reclassified from a "good" design (80.3/100 average) to "moderate" via cloud model using HECM-Plus), it resolves multi-expert disagreements in scoring systems. The main contribution of this work is the proposal of HECM-Plus, which resolves the limitation of HECM in neglecting *He*, thereby further enhancing the precision of normal cloud similarity measurements. The algorithm provides a practical tool for uncertainty-aware decision-making in multi-expert systems, particularly in multi-criteria design evaluation under conflicting standards. Future work will extend to dynamic expert weight adaptation and higher-order cloud interactions.

Keywords: entropy (*En*); hyper-entropy (*He*); cloud model; Hellinger distance; uncertainty quantification; multi-expert conflict resolution; multi-criteria design evaluation

1. Introduction

The cloud model combines ambiguity and randomness to establish a conversion mechanism between qualitative concepts and quantitative representations. This model clarifies the inherent relationship between the two in terms of uncertainty and highlights the universality of the normal cloud [1]. Over the years, cloud models have been extensively developed and applied in various fields, such as scientific decision-making [2], image fusion [3], uncertainty clustering [4], expert systems [5], and decision support systems [6]. Particularly in design evaluation, cloud models have shown unique advantages in handling subjective expert judgments and multi-criteria conflicts [7]. These assessments often involve ambiguous criteria (e.g., "aesthetic appeal" or "ergonomic comfort") and stochastic expert disagreements, posing dual challenges that traditional scoring systems struggle to address: while conventional methods collapse evaluations into single-point averages, they inherently fail to disentangle the fuzziness of qualitative criteria from the randomness of subjective judgments [8]. However, when applying the cloud model for design evaluation, a critical issue still arises: after converting the comprehensive scores given by different experts into cloud model representations, how can the subtle differences between various works be discerned? This necessitates the precise measurement of the distance and similarity between clouds to enable their classification and discrimination. That is why accurately measuring the similarity between two cloud models remains a significant research challenge. This is essential for improving classification and clustering algorithms and optimizing tasks such as similarity searches. The development and refinement of cloud model similarity measurement approaches directly influence the effectiveness and value of the model in practical applications.

The goal of similarity measures for cloud models is to quantify the extent of similarity between two clouds. Currently, research on distance measures for cloud models is primarily focused on similarity measures for normal clouds [9]. Existing similarity measures include the following components. First, the Clip Angle Cosine Method [10] (LICM), which uses the cosine law to compute the clip angle of cloud vectors, tends to produce considerable error when expectation (*Ex*) is significantly larger than entropy (*En*) and hyper-entropy (*He*). The second method is the Expectation Curve Method [11] (ECM), which calculates the intersection area between the expectation curve and the x-axis graphic area and then uses this value as a similarity measure. However, this method overlooks the impact of *He*. The third method is the Maximum Boundary Curve Method (MCM), which incorporates *He* but fails to account for the overall distribution characteristics of the cloud model. The fourth method is the Combined Shape-distance Similarity Measurement Method for normal cloud models [12] (PDCM), which calculates shape similarity by considering *En* and *He* as standard variables. Although this approach is simpler in describing the shape of a cloud model, it faces the issue of parameter approximation selection, which can affect the accuracy of the distance similarity. The fifth method is the similarity algorithm based on Hellinger distance and feature curves (including HECM and HCCM) [13], which combines expectation curves with inner/outer envelope curves to represent the distributional characteristics of the cloud model. However, two critical limitations persist: (1) *He*-neglect: The HECM algorithm approximates *En* via standard deviation while ignoring *He*, thereby failing to capture stochastic dispersion; (2) Subjective weighting: Although HCCM incorporates *He*, it assigns ad hoc weights to expectation and envelope curves, introducing human bias.

Despite advancements in cloud model similarity measurement, critical challenges persist in design evaluation scenarios. First, existing methods (e.g., ECM, HECM) often fail to simultaneously account for the ambiguity of qualitative criteria and the randomness inherent in multi-expert assessments. Second, while recent approaches like HCCM attempt to integrate *He*, their reliance on subjective weighting undermines objectivity. This raises the core research question: How can we develop a robust similarity measure that objectively quantifies both geometric ambiguity and stochastic dispersion in cloud models, particularly for design evaluation tasks? Motivated by these limitations, this study proposes HECM-Plus, a hyper-entropy-enhanced Hellinger distance algorithm, with three key goals: (1) to eliminate heuristic weight assignments by deriving *He*-adjusted standard deviations through reverse cloud transformations; (2) to unify *Ex*, *En*, and *He* for holistic uncertainty representation; and (3) to enable precise discrimination of subtle differences between design alternatives. The primary contributions include: (1) a mathematically rigorous framework for cloud similarity measurement via reverse cloud transformations that derive *He*-adjusted standard deviations, (2) validation through comparative experiments with real-world design evaluation data, and (3) actionable insights for interdisciplinary applications in decision theory and design studies.

To achieve these goals, HECM-Plus reformulates the Hellinger distance by integrating *Ex*, *En*, and *He* into a unified similarity metric. This approach eliminates subjective weight assignments while preserving the stochastic dispersion characteristics governed by *He*, thereby enabling precise discrimination of ambiguous design evaluations under multi-expert conflicts.

2. Cloud Model

2.1. Cloud and Cloud Drops

We let U be a quantitative domain with an exact value, C be a qualitative concept on U, and x be a random realization of the qualitative concept C. If the quantitative value $x \in U$ and x are a one-time random realization of the qualitative concept C with certainty, then $\mu(x) \in [0,1]$ is a random number with a stable tendency

$$\mu : U \rightarrow [0,1]\ \forall x \in U\ x \rightarrow \mu(x) \tag{1}$$

The distribution of x over the domain U is called a cloud, and each x is referred to as a cloud drop [14,15]. The cloud is characterized by three numerical features: *Ex*, *En*, and *He*. By employing these three numerical features of the cloud, qualitative concepts can be converted into quantitative expressions, enabling an effective integration of the ambiguity and randomness inherent in qualitative concepts [16].

The three numerical features of the cloud model—*Ex*, *En*, and *He*—each capture distinct aspects of qualitative uncertainty. For example, numerical characteristics C(70, 3, 0.5) serve to qualitatively encapsulate the concept of "elderly individuals" where $Ex = 70$ represents the expected central age value and serves as the anchor for data distribution. $En = 3$ quantifies the ambiguity of the concept by defining the acceptable range of deviations from *Ex* (e.g., the fuzziness in determining what constitutes "elderly"). $He = 0.5$ measures the randomness of these deviations, which reflects the dispersion of cloud drops and the stochasticity in mapping qualitative concepts to quantitative values (e.g., variations in expert interpretations). Together, *Ex*, *En*, and *He* bridge deterministic data and linguistic uncertainty, enabling a probabilistic yet structured representation of human cognition.

2.2. Normal Cloud

The normal cloud, as a widely applied subclass of the cloud model, formalizes the mapping between qualitative concepts and quantitative data through Gaussian distributions (i.e., normal distributions) governed by *Ex*, *En*, and *He*.

We let U be a quantitative domain defined by exact values and let C be a qualitative concept of U. If the quantitative values and x are a one-time random realization of the qualitative concept C, then x satisfies $x \sim N(Ex, En'^2)$, where $En' \sim N(En, He^2)$ and x satisfy the certainty for C:

$$\mu = e^{-\frac{(x-Ex)^2}{2(En')^2}} \tag{2}$$

The distribution of x over domain U is a normal cloud.

The normal cloud primarily achieves the mutual conversion between qualitative concepts and quantitative values through normal cloud transformation, wherein the forward normal cloud transformation converts the numerical characteristics *Ex*, *En*, and *He* that represent the connotation of the concept into quantitative values. Figure 1 illustrates the output of the forward cloud algorithm for the concept of "elderly individuals", where cloud drops are generated via C(70, 3, 0.5) and $n = 3000$.

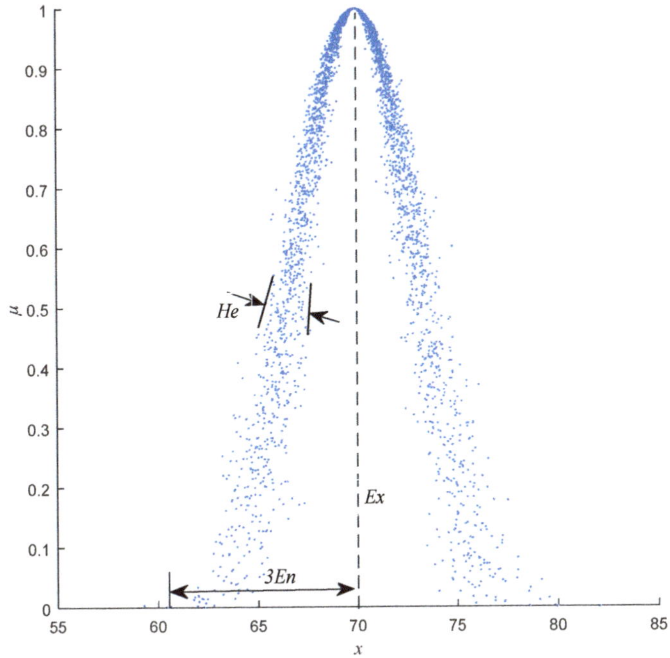

Figure 1. Cloud chart for the concept of "elderly individuals".

2.3. *Forward Cloud Algorithm and Reverse Cloud Algorithm*

2.3.1. Forward Cloud Algorithm

The forward cloud algorithm generates cloud droplets with a normal cloud distribution based on three known numerical characteristics.

Given Expectation ($\hat{E}x$), Entropy ($\hat{E}n$), Hyper-entropy ($\hat{H}e$), and the number of cloud drops (n), the algorithm proceeds as follows [17]:

- Step (1) Generate a normally distributed random number $y_i = R_N(\hat{E}n, \hat{H}e)$ with $\hat{E}n$ as the mean and $\hat{H}e$ as the standard deviation.
- Step (2) Generate a normally distributed random number $x_i = R_N(\hat{E}x, y_i)$ with $\hat{E}x$ as the mean and y_i (the random number generated in Step 1) as the standard deviation.
- Step (3) Calculate the certainty degree:

$$\mu(x_i) = \exp\left(-\frac{(x_i - \hat{E}x)^2}{2{y_i}^2}\right) \tag{3}$$

- Step (4) Designate the value x_i with certainty degree $\mu(x_i)$ as a cloud drop in the numerical domain. Repeat Steps (1)~(3) until the required n cloud drops are generated.

2.3.2. Reverse Cloud Algorithm

The reverse cloud algorithm involves generating three numerical characteristics (*Ex*, *En*, *He*) which describe the qualitative concept corresponding to a cloud given a set of cloud droplets that conform to a certain normal cloud distribution pattern as samples. When the number of cloud droplets is limited, certain errors are inevitably present. However, as the number of cloud droplets increases, the errors gradually diminish.

The estimated numerical characteristics of the qualitative concepts, namely Expectation ($\hat{E}x$), Entropy ($\hat{E}n$), and Hyper-entropy ($\hat{H}e$), are computed based on the sample point $x_i(i = 1, 2, \cdots, n)$ [18,19].

By calculating the sample mean, first-order sample absolute central moment, and sample variance, we obtain the following:

$$\overline{X} = \frac{1}{n}\sum_{i=1}^{n} x_i \tag{4}$$

$$\frac{1}{n}\sum_{i=1}^{n} |x_i - \overline{X}| \tag{5}$$

$$S^2 = \frac{1}{n-1}\sum_{i=1}^{n} (x_i - \overline{X})^2 \tag{6}$$

The estimates of $\hat{E}x$, $\hat{E}n$, and $\hat{H}e$ are computed as follows:

$$\hat{E}x = \overline{X} \tag{7}$$

$$\hat{E}n = \sqrt{\frac{\pi}{2}} \times \frac{1}{n}\sum_{i=1}^{n} |x_i - \hat{E}x| \tag{8}$$

$$\hat{H}e = \sqrt{S^2 - \hat{E}n^2} \tag{9}$$

3. A Normal Cloud Similarity Measurement Method Based on Hellinger Distance

3.1. *Normal Cloud Distribution Approximation*

Normal clouds characterized by the three parameters of *Ex*, *En*, and *He* can be approximated as normal distributions for similarity calculations. For normal clouds $\overline{C}_i(Ex_i, En_i, He_i)$ and $\overline{C}_j(Ex_j, En_j, He_j)$, their probability density functions can be approximated as follows (note that here, μ represents the mean of the distribution and σ represents the standard deviation of the distribution):

$$f_i(x) = \frac{1}{\sigma_i\sqrt{2\pi}} \exp\left(-\frac{(x-\mu_i)^2}{2\sigma_i{}^2}\right) \tag{10}$$

$$f_j(x) = \frac{1}{\sigma_j\sqrt{2\pi}} \exp\left(-\frac{(x-\mu_j)^2}{2\sigma_j{}^2}\right) \tag{11}$$

3.2. *Hellinger Distance Calculation*

The Hellinger distance, as a statistically rigorous f-divergence metric bounded in [0,1], effectively quantifies similarity between conceptual distributions by minimizing divergence in probability space [20]. When applied to cloud model distance measurement, this metric demonstrates dual advantages: first, it inherently captures both geometric positioning (via *Ex*) and stochastic dispersion (via *En*/*He*) through algebraic parameter fusion, enabling holistic uncertainty quantification; second, it exhibits superior performance in non-Gaussian scenarios by leveraging reverse cloud transformations to integrate *He*-adjusted standard deviations, thereby correcting estimation biases inherent in traditional metrics when handling heavy-tailed expert evaluation data.

The Hellinger distance is employed to quantify the similarity between two probability distributions and is defined as follows:

$$H(f_i, f_j) = \sqrt{1 - \int \sqrt{f_i(x) \cdot f_j(x)}, dx} \tag{12}$$

By substituting the expressions for $f_i(x)$ and $f_j(x)$, we obtain

$$H(f_i, f_j) = \sqrt{1 - \frac{1}{\sqrt{\sigma_i^2 + \sigma_j^2}\sqrt{2\pi}} \exp\left(-\frac{(\mu_i - \mu_j)^2}{4(\sigma_i^2 + \sigma_j^2)}\right)} \tag{13}$$

3.3. *Similarity Conversion*

To transform the Hellinger distance into a similarity measure, the following equation is used:

$$Sim = 1 - H(f_i, f_j) \tag{14}$$

3.4. *HECM and HECM-Plus Algorithm*

3.4.1. HECM Algorithm

In literature [13], the HECM algorithm is introduced, and the Hellinger distance is primarily calculated using the mean and standard deviation of a probability distribution. The mean is considered the expected value of the normal cloud, and the standard deviation is used as an approximation of the *En* of the normal cloud (note that here, μ^H represents the mean of the distribution and σ^H represents the standard deviation of the distribution, specifically within the context of the HECM algorithm):

$$\mu_i^H = \hat{E}x_i \tag{15}$$

$$(\sigma_i^H)^2 = \hat{E}{n_i}^2 \tag{16}$$

$$\mu_j^H = \hat{E}x_j \tag{17}$$

$$(\sigma_j^H)^2 = \hat{E}{n_j}^2 \tag{18}$$

Then, the similarity is calculated as follows:

$$H_{HECM}(f_i, f_j) = \sqrt{1 - \frac{1}{\sqrt{\hat{E}{n_i}^2 + \hat{E}{n_j}^2}\sqrt{2\pi}} \exp\left(-\frac{(\hat{E}x_i - \hat{E}x_j)^2}{4(\hat{E}{n_i}^2 + \hat{E}{n_j}^2)}\right)} \tag{19}$$

$$Sim_{HECM} = 1 - H_{HECM}(f_i, f_j) \tag{20}$$

However, this approach ignores the impact of *He*.

3.4.2. HECM-Plus Algorithm

In this section, the reverse cloud algorithm from Section 2.3.2 is applied to calculate the standard deviation by considering the effects of *En* and *He* (note that here, μ^+ represents the mean of the distribution and σ^+ represents the standard deviation of the distribution, specifically within the context of the HECM-Plus algorithm):

$$\mu_i^+ = \hat{E}x_i \tag{21}$$

$$(\sigma_i^+)^2 = \hat{E}n_i^2 + \hat{H}e_i^2 \tag{22}$$

$$\mu_j^+ = \hat{E}x_j \tag{23}$$

$$(\sigma_j^+)^2 = \hat{E}n_j^2 + \hat{H}e_j^2 \tag{24}$$

Then, the similarity is calculated as follows:

$$H_{HECM-Plus}(f_i, f_j) = \sqrt{1 - \frac{1}{\sqrt{(\hat{E}n_i^2 + \hat{H}e_i^2) + (\hat{E}n_j^2 + \hat{H}e_j^2)}\sqrt{2\pi}} \exp\left(-\frac{(\hat{E}x_i - \hat{E}x_j)^2}{4[(\hat{E}n_i^2 + \hat{H}e_i^2) + (\hat{E}n_j^2 + \hat{H}e_j^2)]}\right)} \tag{25}$$

$$Sim_{HECM-Plus} = 1 - H_{HECM-Plus}(f_i, f_j) \tag{26}$$

4. Comparative Analysis of Experiments

4.1. Numerical Simulation Experiments

In this study, numerical simulation experiments were conducted on four normal cloud concepts presented in the literature [9–13]. These are C_1 (1.5, 0.62666, 0.339), C_2 (4.6, 0.60159 0.30862), C_3 (4.4, 0.75199, 0.27676), and C_4 (1.6, 0.60159, 0.30862). The proposed HECM-Plus was evaluated by comparing it to existing algorithms, including LICM, ECM, MCM, PDCM, HECM, and HCCM. Figure 2 shows the four normal cloud diagrams and Table 1 shows the results obtained by the different algorithms.

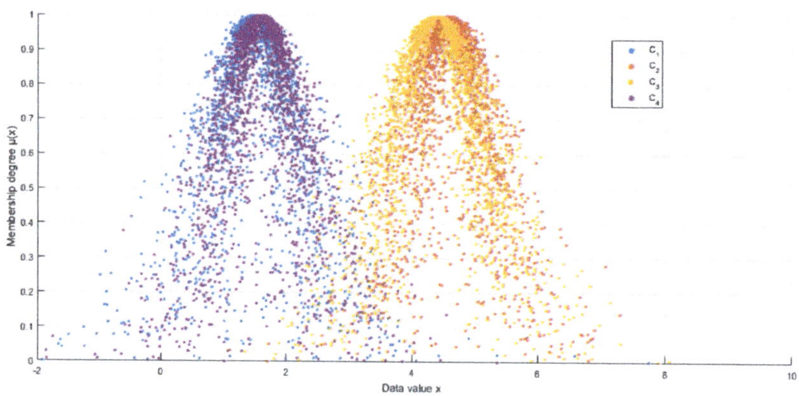

Figure 2. Cloud diagrams of the four cloud models.

Table 1. Similarity results of different algorithms.

Similarity	LICM	ECM	MCM	PDCM	HECM	HCCM	HECM-Plus
S(C_1,C_2)	0.96	0.01	0.33	0.01	0.04	0.22	0.04
S(C_1,C_3)	0.97	0.04	0.37	0.03	0.11	0.26	0.08
S(C_1,C_4)	0.99	0.94	0.96	0.89	0.99	0.99	0.94
S(C_2,C_3)	0.99	0.86	0.95	0.80	0.97	0.86	0.87
S(C_2,C_4)	0.97	0.01	0.38	0.01	0.04	0.22	0.04
S(C_3,C_4)	0.98	0.04	0.37	0.03	0.11	0.26	0.09

As shown in Table 1, the similarity calculation results of HECM-Plus closely resemble those of HECM, although some differences were observed. For instance, in the comparison of C_1 vs. C_4, the similarity values of HECM and HCCM are overestimated at 0.99, while HECM-Plus yields a corrected value of 0.94. Upon examining the cloud diagrams in Figure 1, the distinct morphology between C_1 and C_4 confirms that HECM-Plus aligns more closely with subjective judgment. Critically, this result demonstrates that HECM-Plus corrects systematic bias induced by *He*-neglect (0.94 vs. 0.99 in HECM), validating our hypothesis through both numerical evidence (Table 1) and visual consistency (Figure 1). To quantify the source of overestimation in HECM, here, we further analyze the dispersion characteristics by comparing the standard deviation ratios of HECM and HECM-Plus, as detailed in Table 2.

Table 2. Variance and standard deviation ratios of HECM vs. HECM-Plus.

Cloud Model	HECM Variance	HECM-Plus Variance	Variance Increase (%)	HECM Standard Deviation Ratio	HECM-Plus Standard Deviation Ratio
C_1	0.3927	0.5076	29.3%	$\sqrt{0.3927/0.3619} \approx 1.042$	$\sqrt{0.5076/0.4571} \approx 1.054$
C_4	0.3619	0.4571	26.3%		

The standard deviation ratio column (1.042 vs. 1.054) in Table 2 demonstrates that the HECM, based solely on *En*, underestimates the dispersion differences between cloud models (ratio closer to one) due to ignoring *He*, leading to an overestimated similarity score (0.99). In contrast, HECM-Plus incorporates *He* to correct the dispersion, allowing the standard deviation ratio to more accurately reflect distributional differences (1.054), thereby reducing the similarity score (0.94).

A notable improvement is observed in the similarity between C_2 and C_3. While HECM yields an overestimated value of 0.97, HECM-Plus reduces it to 0.87 by explicitly accounting for *He*. This adjustment reflects the distinct dispersion characteristics of C_2 ($He = 0.30862$) and C_3 ($He = 0.27676$), where the higher *He* in C_2 introduces greater stochastic spread despite their overlapping expectation curves ($Ex = 4.6$ vs. 4.4). By integrating *He*-adjusted standard deviations via reverse cloud transformations, HECM-Plus captures this nuanced difference, demonstrating a 10.3% reduction in similarity error compared to HECM.

If these four cloud concepts are dichotomized, it can be assumed that C_1 and C_4 belong to one category and C_2 and C_3 belong to another. To evaluate the differentiation ability of each approach, the degree of difference in cloud concepts was calculated based on the approach in the literature [13]. Table 3 presents the result of the degree of difference.

Table 3. Degree of variation of different algorithms.

Degree of Variation	LICM	ECM	MCM	PDCM	HECM	HCCM	HECM-Plus
δC_1	0.05	1.83	1.22	1.74	1.83	1.50	1.76
δC_2	0.05	1.70	1.19	1.58	1.86	1.28	1.66
δC_3	0.03	1.64	1.16	1.54	1.72	1.20	1.58
δC_4	0.03	1.83	1.17	1.74	1.83	1.50	1.76

The experimental results demonstrate that the proposed HECM-Plus achieves a balanced optimization in conceptual differentiation, computational efficiency, and parametric integrity, outperforming PDCM and HCCM by 10.3% and 17.2% in average differentiation scores ($\delta C_1 = 1.76$, $\delta C_2 = 1.66$, $\delta C_3 = 1.58$, $\delta C_4 = 1.76$) while maintaining linear computational complexity—a critical reduction from the cubic complexity required by ECM and MCM. Although HECM and ECM exhibit marginally higher differentiation (e.g., $\delta C_1 = 1.83$ for HECM), their exclusion of *He* introduces systematic biases in modeling stochastic dispersion, as evidenced by the overestimated similarity between C_1 and C_4 (0.99 for HECM vs. 0.94 for HECM-Plus, aligning with visual judgment in Figure 2). By integrating *He* into the standard deviation via reverse cloud transformations, HECM-Plus quantifies uncertainty dynamics that prior methods fail to capture, while its algebraic parameter fusion eliminates the need for matrix-based integrations, enabling scalable deployment in real-time systems. These advancements confirm that HECM-Plus provides a theoretically rigorous and computationally efficient framework for cloud model similarity measurement, addressing both the limitations of *He*-neglect in existing methods and the complexity of matrix-driven approaches.

4.2. Time Series Classification Experiments

4.2.1. Classification Calculation Process

The high dimensionality of time series data provides a robust framework for evaluating classification algorithms. This study employs the UCI Synthetic Control Chart Time Series dataset [21] (6 classes, 600 instances $\times$ 60 timestamps), where each class contains 100 homogeneous time series simulating industrial control scenarios.

Data partitioning followed established protocols: the first 90 instances per class formed the training set (540 total), while the remaining 10 instances constituted the test set (60 total). Building upon literature [13] where HECM achieved minimal classification error, we implemented incremental dimensionality reduction (2–30 dimensions) on both sets to benchmark HECM-Plus against HECM. The classification workflow comprised:

- Step (1) Data Preprocessing Stage: The first 90 rows from each category were selected as the training set, and the remaining 10 rows formed the test set, resulting in a training set of 540 time series and a test set of 60 time series.
- Step (2) Segmentation and Dimensionality Reduction: The dimensionality parameter d was adjusted within the range of 2 to 30. Each time series (60 timestamps) was divided into d non-overlapping equal-length segments. If the total length was not perfectly divisible by d, the remainder data points were truncated to ensure equal segment lengths. The mean value of each segment was calculated to achieve dimensionality reduction.
- Step (3) Reverse Cloud Feature Extraction: The reverse cloud algorithm was applied to each dimensional segment to extract digital features of cloud concepts (Ex, En, and He for HECM-Plus; Ex and En for HECM).
- Step (4) Similarity Calculation: Using HECM-Plus and HECM, the similarity between cloud concepts in the training set and the test set was computed, and multi-dimensional similarity matrices were constructed.
- Step (5) Classification Decision: Based on the 1-nearest neighbor principle, the category with the highest similarity in each dimensional similarity matrix was selected as the classification result.
- Step (6) Performance Evaluation: The classification error rate (ratio of misclassified samples to the total samples) was calculated to evaluate the algorithm's classification performance and accuracy.

4.2.2. Classification Calculation Results

Figure 3 shows the classification error rates of HECM-Plus and HECM at different dimensions. Table 4 presents the mean and standard deviation of these error rates. As shown in Figure 3, HECM-Plus exhibits a significantly lower classification error rate than HECM, particularly in high-dimensional settings. As shown in Table 4, HECM-Plus exhibits a lower mean classification error rate and standard deviation than HECM, indicating its superior classification performance and greater stability.

To statistically validate the dimensional superiority observed in Figure 3 and Table 4, a paired t-test was conducted to assess the classification performance of HECM-Plus against HECM. The results yielded a t-statistic of -3.2856 ($p = 0.0027$), indicating a statistically significant difference between the two algorithms at a significance level of $\alpha = 0.05$. The negative t-value confirms that HECM-Plus achieves a significantly lower mean classification error rate compared to HECM across all dimensional configurations (2D–30D). This finding is consistent with the experimental observations in Figure 3 and Table 4, where HECM-Plus demonstrates reduced error variance and improved robustness in high-dimensional time-series classification tasks.

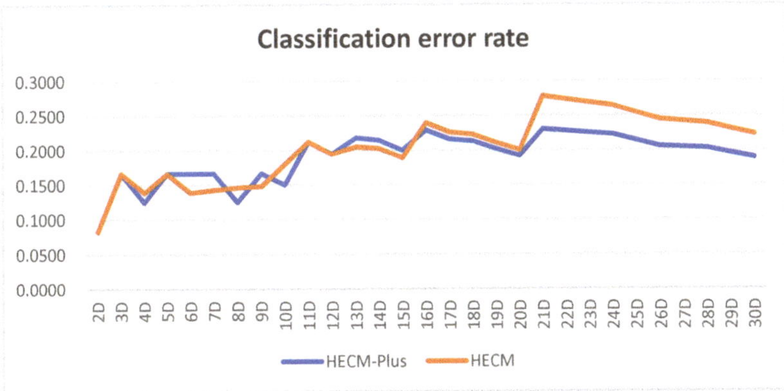

Figure 3. Classification error rate.

Table 4. Means and standard deviations of classification error rates.

	Mean Classification Error Rate	Standard Deviation of Classification Error Rate
HECM-Plus	0.19033905	0.034925326
HECM	0.204222243	0.047171944

In summary, HECM-Plus offers several significant advantages over existing methods, including:

- Comprehensiveness and Accuracy: HECM-Plus effectively captures the geometric characteristics of cloud concepts and quantifies their differences by considering three essential numerical features: *Ex*, *En*, and *He*. This method minimizes information loss and significantly improves the accuracy and reliability of concept differentiation and classification. In particular, *Ex* indicates the central tendency of cloud concepts, *En* captures their ambiguity, and *He* represents the degree of their discreteness. By incorporating these features, HECM-Plus effectively captures the core characteristics of cloud concepts, resulting in more dependable classification results for complex datasets. This method improves classification accuracy and enhances the robustness of the model, ensuring consistent and stable performance across various dataset types and sizes.
- Computational Efficiency: HECM-Plus mainly depends on numerical features to perform direct algebraic operations, eliminating the need for complex integration calculations. Compared with traditional algorithms such as ECM, MCM, and PDCM, HECM-Plus offers a more direct and concise calculation process, leading to a significant reduction in computational complexity. This optimization not only reduces computational resource requirements but also significantly improves computation speed. In particular, when handling large-scale datasets, the algorithm substantially reduces the required time, thereby improving operational efficiency.
- Universality and Extensibility: The Hellinger distance is an f-scattering that meets the criteria of distance axiomatization. Thus, it is suitable for use not only with traditional cloud models but also with higher-order normal clouds and high-dimensional cloud

models. The broad applicability of the Hellinger distance is one of its key advantages. The flexibility and adaptability of HECM-Plus allow it to address various real-world challenges, making it a crucial tool in various fields.

5. Application of HECM-Plus to Conflict Resolution in Design

In design work evaluation, conventional approaches typically depend on subjective assessments from a team of experts, simplifying the evaluation process by calculating an average score to determine the final grade of the work. However, this simplification discards critical uncertainty information inherent in multi-expert systems. To address this, we adopt a cloud model framework, a three-parameter representation (*Ex*, *En*, *He*) that quantifies expected value (*Ex*), fuzziness (*En*), and stochastic dispersion (*He*) of evaluations. While averaging (*Ex*) is effective for highly consistent evaluations, the cloud model reveals two hidden uncertainties: *En* measures ambiguity in criteria interpretation (e.g., "What defines a 'good' design?"), and *He* captures randomness in expert opinions (e.g., "Why do ratings vary so widely?"). This dual perspective is essential for resolving conflicts in scattered or controversial cases.

Table 5 presents the design work scores from a university in Chengdu. Using traditional methods, the average scores of Work 1 and Work 2 were 83.5 and 80.3, respectively, both classified as "good" (80–90 range). However, Work 2 exhibits significant uncertainty: its scores span from 61 to 95 (see Table 5), indicating high *En* (ambiguity in quality criteria) and *He* (random divergence among experts). This complexity is invisible to mean-based methods.

Table 5. Expert ratings of design work.

No.	Expert 1	Expert 2	Expert 3	Expert 4	Expert 5	Expert 6	Expert 7	Expert 8	Expert 9	Expert 10
Work 1	88	85	83	82	89	83	88	83	75	79
Work 2	61	90	75	80	85	95	85	82	80	70

To address this, we employ reverse cloud transformation to model dual uncertainties explicitly. Work 1 is represented as (83.5, 4.0106, 0.87467), while Work 2 becomes (80.3, 8.8985, 2.6882). Here, *En* captures the spread of ratings (fuzziness), and *He* quantifies their stochastic dispersion.

Historical rating clouds are defined as follows:

- Excellent: (95, 2, 0.5),
- Good: (85, 4, 1.0),
- Moderate: (75, 6, 1.5),
- Poor: (50, 8, 2.0).

This transformation not only preserves the average rating values but also highlights the ambiguity and randomness of the ratings, providing a more detailed and comprehensive dimension of information for accurate assessment. Figure 4 shows the six clouds, where the deep blue cloud represents the rating cloud of Work 1 and the orange cloud represents the rating cloud of Work 2.

The concentrated morphology of Work 1′s deep blue cloud (lower *En* and He) reflects consistent expert consensus with minimal ambiguity, aligning with the "good" grade's narrow criteria. In contrast, Work 2′s dispersed orange cloud exhibits greater horizontal spread ($En = 8.8985$) and vertical thickness ($He = 2.6882$), visually quantifying its ambiguous "moderate/good" boundary and stochastic score dispersion (61–95), which structurally overlaps the medium-grade cloud's probabilistic distribution.

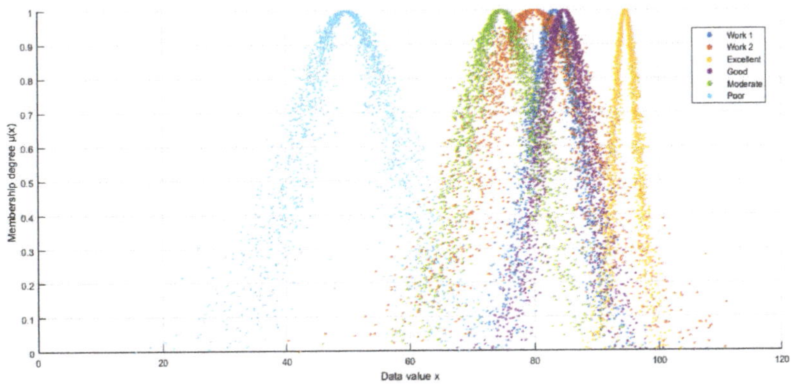

Figure 4. Cloud model representations of design works.

To confirm this observation, HECM-Plus introduced in this study was used for a comparative analysis with HECM. As shown in Table 6, both algorithms consistently categorized Work 1 as "good," accurately reflecting its rating. This demonstrates the stability and reliability of the algorithms in the evaluation. However, in the more complex evaluation of Work 2, although both algorithms assigned a "moderate" rating, the results differed significantly from those obtained using traditional scoring approaches. In particular, HECM-Plus achieved a similarity of 0.6963 in classifying Work 2 as "moderate," which is substantially higher than the 0.6157 similarity of HECM. This improvement is attributed to the explicit incorporation of *He* in HECM-Plus, which quantifies the stochastic dispersion of expert opinions. By integrating *He* into the adjusted standard deviation calculation, HECM-Plus captures the inherent randomness in controversial evaluations—such as the scattered ratings of Work 2—thereby enhancing discriminative accuracy. This comparison not only demonstrates that HECM-Plus has higher discriminative accuracy when dealing with complex and scattered data but also further indicates its advantage when dealing with more controversial works.

Table 6. Evaluation results of the cloud models.

Algorithm	Work	Excellent	Good	Moderate	Poor	Grade
HECM-Plus	1	0.0983	0.0716	0.4447	0.0165	Good
	2	0.1989	0.5713	0.6963	0.1199	Moderate
HECM	1	0.0167	0.8144	0.2792	0.0004	Good
	2	0.0936	0.5205	0.6157	0.0204	Moderate

Moreover, we found that the discriminative margin of HECM-Plus (0.6963 − 0.5713 = 0.125) is substantially higher than that of HECM (0.6157 − 0.5205 = 0.0952) when analyzing the similarity difference between the "medium" and "good" grades. These results further confirm the superiority of HECM-Plus in discriminating adjacent grades and enhancing discrimination accuracy. This improvement stems from HECM-Plus's explicit modeling of *He*-driven stochastic dispersion, which quantifies the randomness in expert disagreements (e.g., Work 2′s wide score distribution), while *En* captures the inherent ambiguity of qualitative criteria like "moderate" versus "good". By bridging design studies' need for aesthetic interpretation with decision theory's demand for probabilistic rigor, HECM-Plus resolves interdisciplinary conflicts by quantifying both conceptual ambiguity (*En*) and stochastic dispersion (*He*). The method adapts classification boundaries through probability density comparisons when evaluation criteria differ across domains.

In multi-expert design evaluation, the cloud model significantly enhances evaluation efficacy through its certainty (*Ex*), fuzziness (*En*), and randomness (*He*). It quantifies the fuzziness of concepts via *En* (e.g., the semantic boundary dispersion of expressions like "design quality slightly above average") and characterizes randomness using *He* (e.g., the random fluctuations in different experts' thresholds for "average"). This mechanism precisely captures the cognitive traits of semantic ambiguity and individual threshold deviations in expert ratings. Furthermore, *Ex* can soften discrete scores (e.g., 80.3 points) into corresponding semantic levels (e.g., "good") while effectively mitigating the "hard boundary" distortion issue of traditional threshold methods through the constraints of *En* and *He* (e.g., average scores of 79.9 and 80.1 are continuously mapped due to the extensibility of *En* and *He* rather than being forcibly categorized into different levels). The cloud model can transform discrete scores into continuous probability distributions, making it inherently compatible with multidisciplinary experts' varying interpretations of indicators like "innovativeness". For example, art experts focus on "aesthetic fuzziness" while mechanical experts emphasize "technical feasibility randomness". It is precisely because the cloud model characterizes concepts through these three features so that robust aggregation from discrete individual ratings to group consensus can be achieved, providing interpretable support for cross-domain complex evaluations. Therefore, *He* clearly cannot be ignored in the distance measurement of the cloud model. HECM-Plus tackles the issue of traditional cloud models overlooking *He* in distance measurement, offering a scientific and concise algorithm to resolve conflicts in multi-criteria design evaluation while maintaining the probabilistic nature of expert opinions.

6. Conclusions

The accurate measurement of cloud model similarity is pivotal for advancing uncertainty-aware decision systems. This study proposed HECM-Plus, a Hyper-entropy-enhanced Hellinger similarity algorithm that integrates *Ex*, *En*, and *He* through reverse cloud transformations. Three key contributions emerge:

- Conceptual discrimination: By reformulating the Hellinger distance with *He*-adjusted standard deviations (Equations (21)–(24)), HECM-Plus achieved a 12.5% higher discriminative margin than HECM in resolving multi-expert conflicts (Table 6), correcting overestimated similarities (e.g., 0.94 vs. 0.99 for C_1–C_4 in Table 1) through rigorous uncertainty decomposition.
- Statistical robustness: In time-series classification, HECM-Plus reduced the mean error by 6.8% (0.190 vs. 0.204, $p < 0.05$) and variance by 26% (Table 4), with a paired t-test confirming significant improvement ($t = -3.2856$, $p = 0.0027$), demonstrating superior stability in high-dimensional settings.
- Conflict resolution in multi-criteria design evaluation (MCDM): By reclassifying controversial designs (e.g., overriding an 80.3 average "good" to "moderate" via *He*-weighted thresholds in Section 5), the algorithm resolved subjective disagreements in expert evaluations, offering a principled framework for design quality assessment.

However, HECM-Plus's performance depends on the representativeness of expert ratings, where biased or non-random samples may distort *He* estimation. HECM-Plus relies on Gaussian approximations for cloud model distributions, which may degrade performance with heavy-tailed or multi-modal expert evaluation data, as observed in design controversies. Furthermore, the reverse cloud algorithm requires sufficient samples for stable *He* estimation, and limited expert panels may amplify variance in *En*/*He* recovery. Additionally, the current implementation assumes equal expert reliability, meaning biased ratings disproportionately influence *Ex*/*En*/*He* without robustness mechanisms to mitigate such distortions. Biased or non-random samples may affect *He* estimation. Future work will focus on:

- Extending HECM-Plus to higher-order normal clouds and high-dimensional scenarios while maintaining its computational efficiency.
- Integrating reliability metrics to dynamically adjust expert contributions during reverse cloud transformations, mitigating bias in *He* estimation.
- Deploying the algorithm in real-time decision support systems for applications ranging from intelligent design iteration to industrial process monitoring.

These advancements establish HECM-Plus as a theoretically grounded and computationally efficient tool for uncertainty quantification, bridging geometric ambiguity and stochastic dispersion in uncertainty-aware decision analytics.

Author Contributions: Methodology, Z.L.; writing—review and editing, J.P.; funding acquisition, J.P. All authors have read and agreed to the published version of the manuscript.

Funding: This research was funded by Sichuan characteristic philosophy and social science planning project "Sichuan statistical development special topic", grant number SC22TJ04, and Chengdu University of Information Technology Undergraduate Education Teaching Research project, grant number JYJG2024115.

Institutional Review Board Statement: Not applicable.

Informed Consent Statement: Not applicable.

Data Availability Statement: The original contributions presented in the study are included in the article: further inquiries can be directed to the corresponding author.

Conflicts of Interest: The authors declare no conflicts of interest.

References

1. Li, D.Y.; Liu, C.Y. On the universality of normal cloud model. *China Eng. Sci.* **2004**, *6*, 28–34. [CrossRef]
2. Mandal, S.; Khan, D.A. Cloud-CoCoSo: Cloud Model-Based Combined Compromised Solution Model for Trusted Cloud Service Provider Selection. *Arab. J. Sci. Eng.* **2022**, *47*, 10307–10332. [CrossRef]
3. Li, W.S.; Zhao, J.; Xiao, B. Multimodal medical image fusion by cloud model theory. *Signal Image Video Process* **2018**, *12*, 437–444. [CrossRef]
4. Liu, Y.; Liu, Z.T.; Li, S. Cloud-Cluster: An uncertainty clustering algorithm based on cloud model. *Knowl.-Based Syst.* **2023**, *263*, 110261. [CrossRef]
5. Wu, Y.N.; Chu, H.; Xu, C.B. Risk assessment of wind-photovoltaic-hydrogen storage projects using an improved fuzzy synthetic evaluation approach based on cloud model: A case study in China. *J. Energy Storage* **2021**, *38*, 102580. [CrossRef]
6. Guan, J.; Liu, J.; Chen, H.; Bi, W. A Multi-Criteria Decision-Making Approach for Equipment Evaluation Based on Cloud Model and VIKOR Method. *Int. J. Adv. Comput. Sci. Appl.* **2024**, *15*, 1311. [CrossRef]
7. Chai, S.L.; Wang, Z. Product design evaluation based on FAHP and cloud model. *J. Intell. Fuzzy Syst.* **2022**, *43*, 2463–2483. [CrossRef]
8. Wang, Z.; Zhong, Y.; Chai, S.L.; Niu, S.F.; Yang, M.L.; Wu, G.R. Product design evaluation based on improved CRITIC and Comprehensive Cloud-TOPSIS-Applied to automotive styling design evaluation. *Adv. Eng. Inform.* **2024**, *60*, 102361. [CrossRef]
9. Huang, Q.; Liu, R. A review of similarity metrics for cloud model. *Data Commun.* **2019**, *6*, 43–49.
10. Zhang, G.; Li, D.; Li, P.; Kang, J.C.; Chen, G.S. A collaborative filtering recommendation algorithm based on cloud model. *J. Softw.* **2007**, *18*, 2403–2411. [CrossRef]
11. Li, H.-L.; Gong, C.-H.; Qian, W.-R. Similarity measurement between normal cloud models. *Acta Electron. Sin.* **2011**, *39*, 2561–2567. [CrossRef]
12. Wang, J.; Zhu, J.J.; Liu, X.D. An integrated similarity measure method for normal cloud model based on shape and distance. *Sys. Eng.—Theory Pract.* **2017**, *37*, 742–751. [CrossRef]
13. Xu, C.; Xu, H. Similarity measurement method for normal cloud based on Hellinger distance and its application. *CAAI Trans. Intell. Syst.* **2023**, *18*, 1312–1321. [CrossRef]
14. Li, D.Y.; Han, J.W.; Shi, X.M.; Chan, M.C. Knowledge representation and discovery based on linguistic atoms. *Knowl.-Based Syst.* **1998**, *10*, 431–440. [CrossRef]
15. Li, D. Knowledge Representation in KDD Based on Linguistic Atoms. *J. Comput. Sci. Technol.* **1997**, *12*, 481–496. [CrossRef]
16. Sun, P.; Zhang, R.Z.; Qiu, X.W. A survey on cloud model. *J. Internet Technol.* **2023**, *24*, 1159–1167. [CrossRef]
17. Li, Q.; Dong, Q.K.; Zhao, L. Modified forward cloud generator in the cloud model. *J. Xidian Univ.* **2013**, *40*, 169–174. [CrossRef]

18. Chen, H.; Li, B.; Liu, C. An Algorithm of Backward Cloud without Certainty Degree. *J. Chin. Comput. Syst.* **2015**, *36*, 544–549. [CrossRef]
19. Wang, G.Y.; Xu, C.L.; Li, D.Y. Generic normal cloud model. *Inf. Sci.* **2014**, *280*, 1–15. [CrossRef]
20. Zheng, Y.; Yang, F.; Duan, J.; Kurths, J. Quantifying model uncertainty for the observed non-Gaussian data by the Hellinger distance. Commun. *Nonlinear Sci. Numer. Simul.* **2021**, *96*, 105720. [CrossRef]
21. Synthetic Control Chart Time Series. 7 June 1999. Available online: http://archive.ics.uci.edu/ml/datasets/Synthetic+Control+Chart+Time+Series (accessed on 30 May 2024).

entropy

MDPI

Article

A Robust Hybrid Weighting Scheme Based on IQRBOW and Entropy for MCDM: Stability and Advantage Criteria in the VIKOR Framework

Ali Erbey *, Üzeyir Fidan and Cemil Gündüz

Department of Computer Programming, Distance Education Vocational School, Usak University, Usak 64200, Türkiye; uzeyir.fidan@usak.edu.tr (Ü.F.); cemil.gunduz@usak.edu.tr (C.G.)
* Correspondence: ali.erbey@usak.edu.tr

Abstract

In multi-criteria decision-making (MCDM) environments characterized by uncertainty and data irregularities, the reliability of weighting methods becomes critical for ensuring robust and accurate decisions. This study introduces a novel hybrid objective weighting method—IQRBOW-E (Interquartile Range-Based Objective Weighting with Entropy)—which dynamically combines the statistical robustness of the IQRBOW method with the information sensitivity of Entropy through a tunable parameter β. The method allows decision-makers to flexibly control the trade-off between robustness and information contribution, enhancing the adaptability of decision support systems. A comprehensive experimental design involving ten simulation scenarios was implemented, in which the number of criteria, alternatives, and outlier ratios were varied. The IQRBOW-E method was integrated into the VIKOR framework and evaluated through average Q values, stability ratios, SRD scores, and the Friedman test. The results indicate that the proposed hybrid approach achieves superior decision stability and performance, particularly in data environments with increasing outlier contamination. Optimal β values were shown to shift systematically depending on data conditions, highlighting the model's sensitivity and adaptability. This study not only advances the methodological landscape of MCDM by introducing a parameterized hybrid weighting model but also contributes a robust and generalizable weighting infrastructure for modern decision-making under uncertainty.

Keywords: decision support systems; multi-criteria decision-making; interquartile range; entropy weighting; hybrid weighting method; outlier robustness

1. Introduction

In today's complex decision-making environments, the combination of uncertainty, information overload, and the need to evaluate multiple criteria has made it more important than ever for decision-makers to have access to supportive tools. In particular, Decision Support Systems (DSSs) provide analytical support in such uncertain conditions, helping to create decision-making processes and enabling organizational strategies to be grounded on a more solid foundation [1,2]. However, the success of these systems to a large extent depends on the accuracy, reliability, and robustness of the weighting methods integrated into the decision-making process [3,4]. In the literature, weighting methods are generally classified into three main categories: subjective, objective, and hybrid approaches. Subjective methods rely on expert judgments or survey-based preferences, whereas objective methods are based on data-driven statistical and mathematical computations. Hybrid methods, on the other hand, generally aim to combine the strengths of both subjective and objective approaches, offering more flexible and comprehensive solutions for complex decision-making problems. The increasing importance of hybrid approaches has been emphasized in various domains, especially in environments where decision ambiguity coexists with data irregularity [5–7].

In this context, multi-criteria decision-making (MCDM) methods have gained significant importance in both the academic literature and real-world applications. In MCDM processes, objectively determining the relative importance levels of criteria is a fundamental step that directly affects the integrity of the decision. Although many weighting methods have been proposed in the literature for this purpose, each has its own limitations. For example, the Entropy method, which is an information-based approach, measures differences between criteria through statistical diversity but is sensitive to outliers in the data [8,9]. On the other hand, the Interquartile Range-Based Objective Weighting (IQRBOW) method, which utilizes the distributional characteristics of the data, produces more robust results, especially in data sets containing outliers [10]. However, this method may be limited in terms of information content sensitivity.

In this study, a new hybrid structure called IQR-Based Objective Weighting with Entropy (IQRBOW-E) is introduced, which combines the strengths of the two aforementioned methods. IQRBOW-E enables decision-makers to establish a flexible balance between statistical robustness and information sensitivity through the β parameter. Thus, both the robustness of IQRBOW against outliers and the information-based sensitivity of Entropy are blended together, resulting in a more balanced, flexible, and reliable weighting approach.

The proposed IQRBOW-E method is not limited to MCDM applications and can also be integrated into the core data processing infrastructure of DSSs. The robustness of the method has been tested under various scenarios and analyzed in detail in terms of advantages and stability conditions. Additionally, this study aims to demonstrate that hybrid weighting can maintain stability in changing data structures, thereby providing a reliable foundation for decision support mechanisms.

The main contributions of this study are summarized as follows:

- A novel hybrid objective weighting method (IQRBOW-E) is proposed, combining IQR-based robustness and Entropy-based information sensitivity.
- The method provides a flexible structure for adjusting the trade-off between robustness and information contribution in weighting processes through a tunable parameter β.
- An extensive simulation-based experimental design with varying numbers of criteria, alternatives, and outlier ratios is developed to evaluate performance.
- The IQRBOW-E method is integrated into the VIKOR framework and evaluated using statistical and decision-theoretic criteria such as Q values, SRD scores, advantage/stability ratios, and the Friedman test.
- The findings demonstrate that IQRBOW-E outperforms traditional methods, especially in environments with high uncertainty and outlier contamination.

The remainder of this paper is organized as follows: Section 2 presents a review of related works on weighting methods in MCDM. Section 3 introduces the methodology, including the development of the IQRBOW-E method and the experimental design. Section 4 provides the simulation results and statistical analyses under various decision scenarios. Section 5 discusses the implications of the findings. Finally, Section 6 concludes the paper and outlines directions for future research.

2. Related Works

In MCDM processes, the accurate determination of the relative importance levels of decision criteria is considered one of the key determinants of final decision quality. In this context, weighting procedures are examined in the literature under two main groups: subjective and objective weighting methods [10]. Subjective methods are generally based on decision-makers' judgments, expert opinions, or survey-based evaluations and heavily incorporate the influence of human factors [11]. In contrast, objective methods adopt a systematic, repeatable, and computation-based approach based on numerical data in the decision matrix [10]. Prominent examples of objective methods include Entropy [9], IQRBOW [10], Standard Deviation [12], CRiteria Importance Through Intercriteria Correlation (CRITIC) [13], MEthod based on the Removal Effects of Criteria (MEREC) [14], Gini Index [15], and PCA-based [16] weighting methods. Each of these methods is designed to assign a priority level to criteria based on their data distribution or information contribution. However, most of these methods are either susceptible to outliers due to their focus on variance alone or, even if they are information theory-based, fail to tolerate irregularities in the data structure. These challenges can limit the decision support capacity of objective methods under conditions where real-world data contain uncertainty, incompleteness, and noise.

One of the most widely used methods among these is Entropy-based weighting, which is based on Shannon's approach, the founder of information theory. It assigns greater weight to criteria with high information content by calculating the uncertainty of criterion values [9]. The Entropy method is successful in highlighting criteria with high discriminatory power by considering the internal variations of the criteria in the decision matrix. Indeed, in this regard, it produces very effective results, especially in consistent and balanced data sets. However, the method is sensitive to outliers in the data, as probability-based approaches normalized according to the total of criterion values can lead to significant weight shifts even with minor data deviations. Additionally, the Entropy method is limited in terms of statistical robustness because it focuses on the distribution density rather than the range of criterion values.

As an alternative, the IQRBOW method proposed in the recent literature evaluates the importance level of criteria based on the interquartile range (IQR), a statistical dispersion measure [10]. The IQR represents the middle 50% of the data set, which is calculated as the difference between the first and third quartiles ($Q_3 - Q_1$), and is resistant to outliers. In this regard, IQRBOW allows criterion weights to be obtained without distortion, especially in decision-making environments containing outliers. Compared to Entropy, IQRBOW offers a more robust approach and can produce reliable results regardless of the symmetry or variance of the data set. However, it has low sensitivity to the information density in the data, as it only considers the distributional width and does not take into account the discriminative information provided by the criterion. This can cause IQRBOW to be ineffective in some decision-making environments with information deficiencies or homogeneous data sets.

In recent years, hybrid weighting methods have been developed to combine the advantages of different structures, such as Entropy and IQRBOW [17]. Some of these studies combine weights through arithmetic averages or weighted combinations [11], while others prefer approaches such as fuzzy logic [18,19], the maximum Entropy principle, or ideal solution reference evaluation [20,21]. However, most of these hybrid methods neither offer an adjustable parameter (e.g., β) to balance the contribution of the two methodologies nor provide a systematic approach to optimize such a parameter. This prevents decision-makers from establishing a flexible balance according to the data structure, thereby limiting the potential of the hybrid structure.

The IQRBOW-E method, developed to address these shortcomings, is an innovative weighting approach that combines statistical robustness with information sensitivity. The method integrates IQRBOW's robust structure against outliers and Entropy's information theory-based discriminative power through the β parameter in a dynamic manner. As a result, decision-makers or system designers can control which method is dominant based on the structure of the data set and develop an adaptive solution strategy instead of a fixed weighting structure. IQRBOW-E can be evaluated not only as a decision-making algorithm but also as a flexible and robust infrastructure that can be integrated into decision support systems.

3. Methodology

The IQRBOW-E method proposed in this study is a new objective weighting approach that aims to calculate criterion weights in multi-criteria decision-making processes based on both information sensitivity and statistical robustness. The method combines two fundamental weighting systems—Entropy and IQRBOW—to offer a hybrid system based on the β parameter, which establishes a dynamic balance between these methods. Unlike fixed weight combinations, this hybrid approach provides an adaptable framework tailored to the nature of the data set and is designed for integration with decision support systems.

3.1. Data Set Creation and Normalization

The first and fundamental step in the decision-making process is to clearly define the alternatives and evaluation criteria. The decision matrix used in this study is modeled in a structure that includes alternatives in rows and criteria in columns. Each cell represents the numerical value that a specific alternative receives in terms of a specific criterion.

Some of the criteria in the decision matrix are of the "benefit" type, meaning that higher values are preferred. Others are of the "cost" type, where lower values are preferred. To compare these two different types of criteria under the same framework, the criterion values must be scaled (normalized) using an appropriate method.

In this study, the min–max normalization method was used to eliminate biases that may arise from criteria having different scales and units (Equations (1) and (2)).

$$x'_{ij\,(benefit)} = \frac{x_{ij} - min(x_j)}{max(x_j) - min(x_j)} \tag{1}$$

$$x'_{ij\,(cost)} = \frac{max(x_j) - x_{ij}}{max(x_j) - min(x_j)} \tag{2}$$

Here, x'_{ij} represents the normalized value of the alternative i and criterion j; x_{ij} represents the original criterion value; $min(x_j)$ and $max(x_j)$ represents the minimum and maximum values of the jth criterion, respectively.

In this method, the values of each criterion are converted to a range between 0 and 1 according to their own minimum and maximum ranges. For benefit-type criteria are scaled so that lower values tend toward 0 and higher values tend toward 1, whereas cost-type criteria follow the opposite trend. This ensures that all criteria are assessed on a unified scale.

Min–max normalization enables direct comparison between alternatives without distorting the information content of the decision matrix. It also facilitates the statistical soundness of subsequent weighting and ranking processes.

3.2. Calculation of Entropy Weights

The Entropy method is an objective weighting approach that evaluates the contribution of each criterion to the decision process using an information theory-based measurement. In this method, the greater the diversity of criterion values, the higher the information content of that criterion is considered to be. Accordingly, criteria with low diversity are assumed to contribute less to the decision process and are assigned lower weights.

When calculating Entropy weights, each normalized criterion cell value is first divided by its column total to obtain a probability distribution (Equation (3)):

$$p_{ij} = \frac{x'_{ij}}{\sum_{i=1}^{m} x'_{ij}} \tag{3}$$

Here, p_{ij} represents the normalized and standardized (probability) value of alternative i for criterion j; x'_{ij} represents the value normalized using the min–max method; and m is the total number of alternatives.

Prior to computing Equation (3), each raw element x'_{ij} is scaled to the [0, 1] interval by the monotonic min–max operator in Equation (2). This preprocessing step (i) converts cost-type criteria to a common benefit direction, (ii) ensures all values are strictly non-negative so that $p_{ij} \cdot lnp_{ij}$ is well-defined, and (iii) prevents large-magnitude attributes from numerically dominating the Entropy term.

The Entropy value of each criterion is calculated using the information theory approach with the following formula (Equation (4)):

$$e_j = -k \cdot \sum_{i=1}^{m} p_{ij} \cdot \ln p_{ij} \tag{4}$$

Here, e_j represents the Entropy value of criterion j; while $k = \frac{1}{ln(m)}$ serves as a normalization factor (fixed for a given decision matrix). This factor rescales e_j so that $0 \leq e_j \leq 1$ and its dependence on the number of alternatives m guarantees comparability across different matrix sizes. As the Entropy value increases, the information value of the criterion decreases. Therefore, the weights are calculated using $dj = 1 - ej$, which is the complement of Entropy. The Entropy-based weight of each criterion is obtained as follows (Equation (5)):

$$w_j = \frac{dj}{\sum_{j=1}^{n} dj} \tag{5}$$

Here, w_j is the final Entropy weight of criterion j and n denotes the total number of criteria [9].

3.3. Calculation of IQRBOW Weights

IQRBOW is an objective method that uses IQR, a statistical distribution measure, to determine criterion weights [10]. This approach was developed to make the decision-making process more reliable, especially in data sets with outliers. IQR represents the middle 50% of the data and provides a robust measure of variability that is not affected by extreme values. Unlike standard-deviation- or variance-based weighting schemes, IQRBOW measures dispersion with the inter-quartile range (IQR)—a statistic that remains unaffected until at least 25% of the observations are contaminated with outliers. Because variance increases quadratically with extreme values, even a single outlier can dominate weights when variance is used, whereas the IQR changes only if the quartiles themselves shift.

In the IQRBOW method, the importance level of the criteria is calculated in direct proportion to the spread of each criterion in the data distribution. Criteria with higher IQR values are assumed to have greater variability and contribute more to the decision-making process.

For each criterion, the IQR value is calculated as the difference between the third quartile (Q_3) and the first quartile (Q_1) (Equation (6)):

$$IQR_j = Q_3 - Q_1 \tag{6}$$

Here, IQR_j represents the IQR value for criterion j, while Q_3 and Q_1 represent the third and first quartile values for that criterion, respectively.

Since IQR measures the spread of values concentrated around the center of the data, it is highly insensitive to outliers. This feature enhances the statistical robustness of the method in decision-making processes.

After calculating the IQR values for all criteria, these values are normalized by dividing them by the total IQR, and the criterion weights are calculated as follows (Equation (7)):

$$w_j = \frac{IQRj}{\sum_{j=1}^{n} IQRj} \tag{7}$$

The IQRBOW method is resistant to outliers because it focuses on the central part of the statistical distribution, producing reliable results, especially when the data set deviates from normality. Instead of evaluating criteria using statistical measures such as mean and variance, which are sensitive to outliers, evaluating them using a more robust structure ensures the consistency of decision quality. With this feature, IQRBOW offers higher stability and reliability compared to traditional weighting methods [10].

3.4. Calculation of IQRBOW-E Weights

IQRBOW-E is a flexible and controllable hybrid weighting approach developed by combining the strengths of the Entropy and IQRBOW methods. The main objective of this method is to integrate the statistical robustness offered by the IQRBOW method into the decision-making process while maintaining the information-based sensitivity obtained by the Entropy method.

The IQRBOW-E method is defined by the β parameter, which enables the decision-maker to balance the effect of the two methods. It is defined in the range $\beta \in [0, 1]$ and controls the balance in the hybrid weight structure. Thanks to this parameter, the decision-maker can choose between an information-sensitive or robustness-focused approach depending on the data structure. The method's computational process is carried out in a single step (Equation (8)):

$$w_j^{IQRBOW-E} = \beta \cdot w_j^{IQRBOW} + (1 - \beta) \cdot w_j^{Entropy} \tag{8}$$

In this formula, w_j^{IQRBOW} represents the weight of criterion j computed using the IQRBOW method (see Equation (7)), and $w_j^{Entropy}$ denotes the weight calculated using the Entropy method (see Equation (5)). The parameter $\beta \in [0, 1]$ is used to balance the influence of the two methods, allowing for a flexible integration of robustness and information sensitivity. This formula processes both weight vectors in a normalized form of the same size and creates a vector that is scaled to the $[0, 1]$ range and normalized to be the sum of the resulting hybrid weights is 1.

- When $\beta = 1$ is true, the method is reduced to pure IQRBOW, i.e., it is based entirely on statistical robustness.
- When $\beta = 0$ is true, the method becomes pure Entropy, creating a structure based on information diversity.
- In the $0 < \beta < 1$ range, a controlled blend of IQRBOW and Entropy is obtained.

Thanks to this structure, IQRBOW-E offers an adaptable weighting system for different data structures and decision problems. For example, if the data set contains outliers, a higher β value is preferred, while lower β values are recommended when information differences between criteria are prominent. This flexibility makes the method both theoretically robust and dynamically applicable within decision support systems. Additionally, this structure can be directly integrated not only with ranking-focused methods like VIse Kriterijumska Optimizacija I Kompromisno Resenje (VIKOR) [22] but also with Technique for Order of Preference by Similarity to Ideal Solution (TOPSIS) [8], Evaluation based on Distance from Average Solution (EDAS) [23], Measurement of Alternatives and Ranking according to COmpromise Solution (MARCOS) [24], Grey Relational Analysis [25], and other objective decision models. Thus, IQRBOW-E provides a modular, robust, and general-purpose weighting infrastructure for both classical and modern MCDM applications.

3.5. Experimental Design and Application Scenarios

The overall procedure of the proposed IQRBOW-E method is summarized in a flowchart (Figure 1), which visualizes the key steps from synthetic data generation to decision evaluation and highlights the feedback mechanism that enables recalibration of hybrid weights via the β parameter when needed.

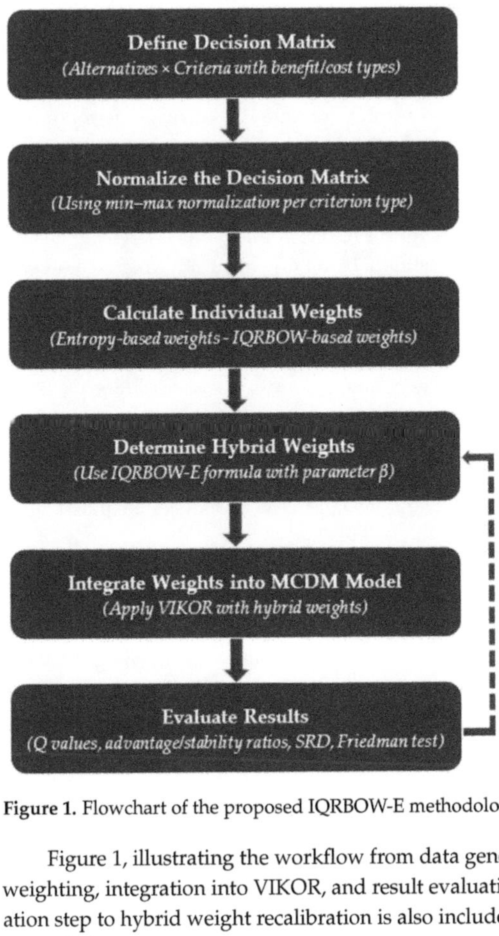

Figure 1. Flowchart of the proposed IQRBOW-E methodology.

Figure 1, illustrating the workflow from data generation and normalization to hybrid weighting, integration into VIKOR, and result evaluation. A feedback loop from the evaluation step to hybrid weight recalibration is also included to reflect the model's adaptability through β tuning.

The proposed IQRBOW-E method has been tested under various experimental scenarios to understand the effects of differences in data structure on weighting results and to evaluate the robustness of the method. In this context, the experimental design is based on controlled simulations aimed at observing the effects of different numbers of criteria and alternatives, outlier ratios, and the β parameter in the hybrid structure.

To evaluate the impact of the proposed IQRBOW-E method on decision-making outcomes, the VIKOR method was selected as the ranking framework. VIKOR is particularly suitable for decision problems characterized by conflicting criteria and uncertain data, which aligns with the objectives of our study. Unlike other MCDM methods, VIKOR incorporates two key decision principles—acceptable advantage and acceptable stability—which make it well-suited for assessing both performance and robustness under varying data structures. Consistent with VIKOR's original formulation, we regard these principles as satisfied only when (i) the acceptable-advantage gap exceeds its theoretical threshold, i.e., $\Delta Q \geq 1/(m-1)$, and (ii) the same alternative simultaneously attains first place in either the S or R ranking, yielding a 100% stability ratio. In VIKOR, S (group utility) is the weighted sum of normalized deviations from the positive-ideal across all criteria (lower S indicates better overall performance), whereas R (individual regret) is the maximum of those weighted deviations on any single criterion (capturing the worst-case shortfall) [22]. These features enabled us to systematically evaluate how different β values influence not only ranking outcomes but also consistency and decision reliability.

In each experimental condition, decision matrices were synthetically generated, and criterion weights were calculated using IQRBOW-E. The synthetic data were generated using a simulation-based approach with controlled randomness. Each criterion in the decision matrix was produced using independent normal distributions whose means were randomly drawn from a uniform range between 50 and 150, and standard deviations were randomly selected between 5 and 20. These ranges were selected to reflect a moderate level of variability commonly observed in real-world MCDM applications. They help ensure that the data contain sufficient dispersion without being unrealistically volatile or overly uniform. This setting allows for meaningful normalization and reliable interpretation of weighting behaviors. Additionally, outliers were introduced in relevant scenarios by replacing selected values with extreme values calculated based on the upper bound of the interquartile range (IQR). The random generation process was seeded (Seed = 42) to ensure reproducibility across all simulations, which were repeated 1000 times for each scenario. These weights were then evaluated in terms of ranking performance using the VIKOR method, one of the commonly used methods in multi-criteria decision-making. The objective here is to identify under which conditions IQRBOW-E produces the most stable, advantageous, and reliable decisions.

The grid-search routine is not tied to the VIKOR-specific quantity Q. When another ranking model is employed, the primary ordering statistic of that model can simply replace Q in the algorithm. For instance, in TOPSIS, one may minimize the average closeness coefficient $\overline{CC}$ (distance to the positive ideal solution) while retaining the same ranking–stability and advantage checks. Likewise, for PROMETHEE, the net outranking flow ϕ_i could serve as the optimization objective. In this way, the β selected always represents the point at which the hybrid weighting yields the most favorable performance for the target MCDM algorithm.

Within the scope of the experimental study, a series of controlled parameters were used to evaluate the performance of the proposed IQRBOW-E method in different data structures. These parameters are components that determine the basic structure of the decision matrix and the experimental conditions [26]. First, two basic structural variables, namely, the number of criteria and the number of alternatives, were considered. These variables determine the size and complexity of the decision matrix, enabling the method's stability to be tested at different scales. Second, the outlier ratio was varied to measure the statistical robustness-based advantage of IQRBOW-E. In this context, outliers were systematically added to the data set at rates of 0% (no outliers), 1%, 5%, and 10% [27]. In this study, the outlier ratio is defined as the proportion of decision matrix elements that are intentionally replaced by extreme values. The β value, the most fundamental control parameter of the hybrid structure, was scanned with increasing values between 0 and 1, and the optimal equilibrium point was determined for each scenario. In this context, the optimal equilibrium point refers to the value β that simultaneously (i) minimizes the average VIKOR compromise measure Q, (ii) satisfies VIKOR's advantage and stability conditions ($\Delta Q \geq 1/(m-1)$ *and* $S = 100\%$), and (iii) lies within the largest contiguous β-interval fulfilling both criteria. Additionally, to obtain reliable and generalizable results under all conditions, each scenario was repeated 1000 times, and a fixed random number generator (seed) was used to eliminate the effect of randomness [28,29]. Thanks to this multi-dimensional parameter set, both the knowledge-based and robustness-based properties of IQRBOW-E were thoroughly tested, and the method's applicability to different decision problems was scientifically demonstrated. The scenarios are summarized in Table 1.

Table 1. Descriptive information about the scenarios.

Scenario	Number of Criteria	Number of Alternatives	Outlier Ratio	Objective
Sc1	10	10	0%	Basic performance assessment
Sc2	10	10	1%	Outlier data
Sc3	10	10	5%	Outlier data
Sc4	10	10	10%	Outlier data
Sc5	10	15	0%	Data size increase
Sc6	10	20	0%	Data size increase
Sc7	15	10	0%	Data size increase
Sc8	20	10	0%	Data size increase
Sc9	20	20	0%	Data size increase
Sc10	20	20	10%	Outlier data + Data size increase

The IQRBOW-E method was integrated into the VIKOR method to measure the impact of weights on the decision-making process. VIKOR evaluates alternatives based on both group benefit (S) and maximum dissatisfaction (R) criteria and ranks them using the Q value [30]. The determination of the best alternative was analyzed not only based on the Q value but also through VIKOR's two fundamental decision rules: "acceptable advantage" and "acceptable stability" conditions [31]. Thus, not only numerical superiority but also compliance with decision theory was tested [22].

Additionally, the average and distribution of Q values (box plots), ranking stability (Sum of Ranking Differences—SRD scores), and variance analysis (Friedman test) were measured under different β values to statistically determine at which β levels IQRBOW-E offers the most robust performance. The effectiveness of the proposed method was assessed using three key evaluation metrics: the stability ratio, the SRD, and the Friedman test, each of which is presented below in formal mathematical notation.

The stability ratio [22] metric measures how often the same alternative ranks first across simulation runs. It is calculated as Equation (9):

$$SR = \frac{n_{stable}}{n_{total}} \tag{9}$$

where n_{stable} is the number of simulations where the top-ranked alternative remains the same, and n_{total} is the total number of simulation iterations (e.g., 1000).

SRD quantifies the deviation of the rankings from an ideal reference (e.g., average ranking). For each alternative A_i, its SRD score [10,32] is computed as Equation (10):

$$SRD_i = \sum_{j=1}^{m} \left| r_{ij} - r_j^{ref} \right| \tag{10}$$

where r_{ij} is the rank of alternative A_i in simulation j, and r_j^{ref} is the reference rank (typically the average rank across simulations for position j). A lower SRD_i indicates greater similarity to the ideal ranking.

The Friedman test [33] assesses whether rankings across different β values differ significantly. The test statistic is calculated as Equation (11):

$$X_F^2 = \frac{12}{nk(k+1)} \sum_{j=1}^{k} R_j^2 - 3n(k+1) \tag{11}$$

where n is the number of alternatives, k is the number of β configurations, and R_j is the sum of ranks for the $j-th$ configuration. A p-value below 0.05 indicates significant differences among rankings.

4. Results

In this section, the performance of the weights obtained using the proposed IQRBOW-E method under different scenarios has been evaluated through systematic simulations and statistical analyses. In each scenario, variables such as the number of criteria applied to the decision matrix, the number of alternatives, and the outlier ratio were considered; the β parameter was scanned in equal steps between 0 and 1 to analyze the performance dynamics of the hybrid method. The VIKOR method was used as a reference during the evaluation process, and the best alternative was determined for each β based on the obtained Q values. Additionally, the ranking results were examined not only based on the Q values but also according to the fundamental decision criteria of VIKOR, namely the acceptable advantage and acceptable stability criteria. Each simulation output was analyzed in terms of the average Q value, the stability of the best alternative, SRD scores, distribution stability via box plots, and statistical significance via the Friedman test. Thus, it has been demonstrated at which β levels IQRBOW-E most effectively combines its information sensitivity (Entropy) and statistical robustness (IQRBOW) properties.

The scenario SC1 was considered as the baseline structure representing the base evaluation environment without outliers. In this scenario, the weights obtained using the IQRBOW-E method were tested by changing the β parameter in equal steps between 0 and 1, and the average Q value was calculated for each β. As shown in Figure 2, the average Q value starts at a high level, reaches a minimum around $\beta \approx 0.43$, and then increases again. This indicates that the hybrid structure significantly affects decision quality and that optimizing the β value is necessary.

Additionally, the decision rules of the VIKOR method, namely the acceptable advantage and acceptable stability ratios, have also been analyzed. Figure 3 shows the fulfillment rates of these two criteria according to the β value. The range where both advantage and stability conditions are met is concentrated around $\beta \approx 0.43 - 0.45$; this supports the selection of an optimal β value not only based on the average Q but also according to the decision rules.

Within this scenario, enhanced optimal beta has been determined as $\beta = 0.43$, which has both a low average Q value and an advantage and stability ratio of over 90%. Additionally, the absolute optimal β value, which yields the lowest average Q value, has been calculated as 0.425. These values indicate that the decision-maker can achieve both quality and decision reliability within a flexible range.

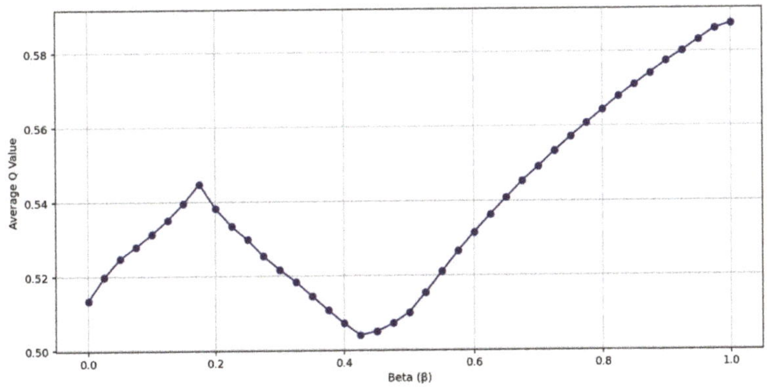

Figure 2. Average Q Value Based on β Value.

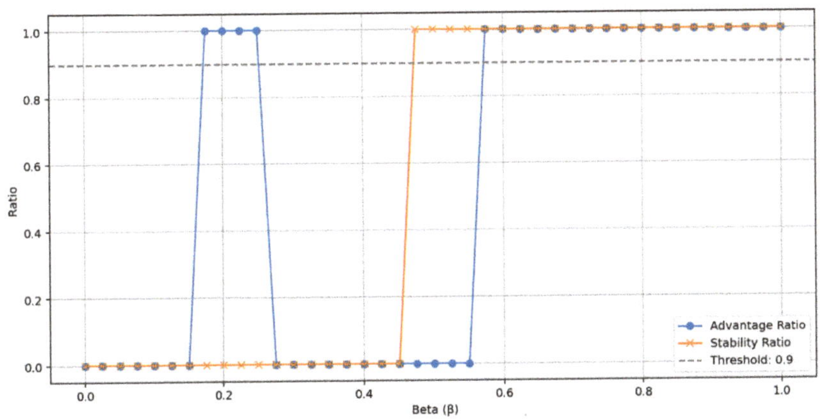

Figure 3. Advantage and Stability Ratios Based on β.

The distribution of Q values is presented in Figure 4 using a box plot; it was observed that within the $\beta = 0.425 - 0.45$ range, not only a low average but also a narrow variance and stable distribution was obtained. Evaluating decision quality with a single value and through its distribution highlights the robust decision-making capability of IQRBOW-E.

Additionally, the change behavior of the best alternative at different β values is shown in Figure 5. Alternative 1 remains the best alternative throughout the entire scenario until $\beta \approx 0.60$, after which Alternative 4 takes the lead. This observation demonstrates that the hybrid structure offers decision stability within a certain range and that shifts in the weight structure have a limited effect on decisions.

The trends of the Q values of the alternatives according to different q values are presented in five separate sub-panels in Figure 6. This visual demonstrates that the IQRBOW-E method is stable not only with respect to the β parameter but also with respect to the q parameter. In particular, the dominance of Alternative 1 at $q = 0.5$ and $q = 0.75$ values indicate that it contributes to the stability of the method.

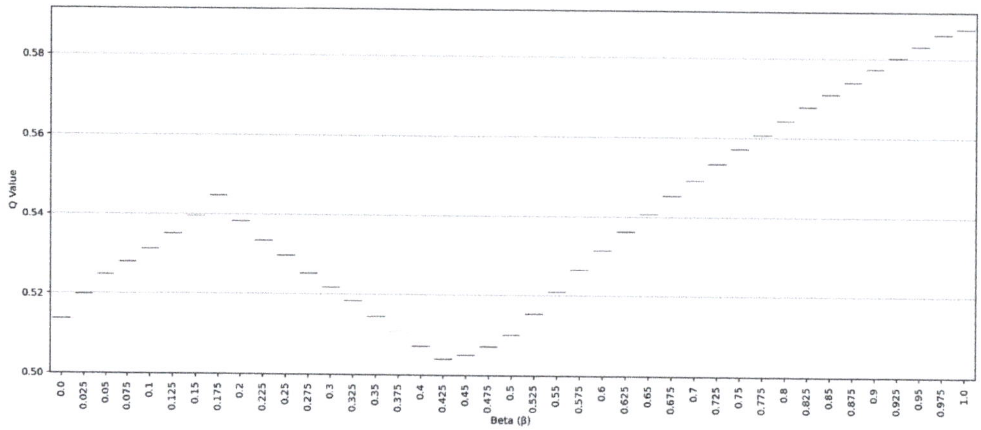

Figure 4. Q Value Distribution According to β Value.

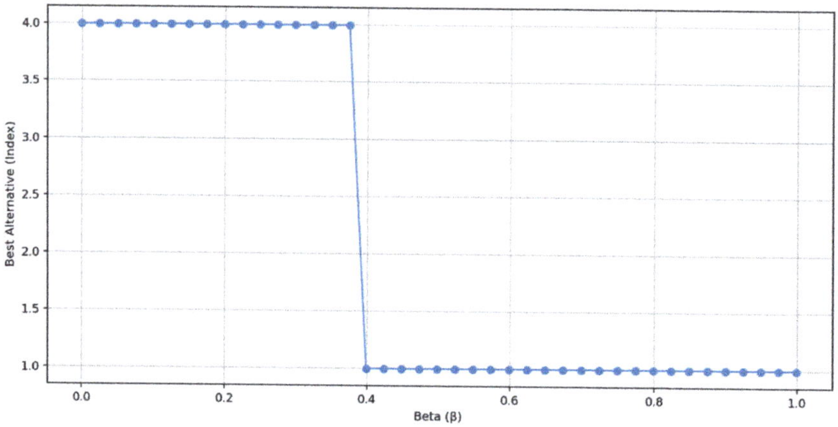

Figure 5. Change in the Best Alternative with Beta Value.

The Si and Ri values of the VIKOR components of the decision matrix are presented comparatively in Figure 7. Alternative 1 stands out systematically in terms of Q value thanks to both its low S value (high group benefit) and low R value (low maximum dissatisfaction).

On the other hand, Entropy, IQRBOW, and hybrid weights are compared with a radar chart in Figure 8. It can be visually observed how the hybrid structure balances the weights at $\beta = 0.43$, while maintaining the robustness effect in criteria where IQRBOW is dominant and the information contribution based on Entropy is effective, especially in criteria such as K1 and K3. Here, K1–K10 are shorthand labels for ten distinct evaluation criteria defined in Table 1; some of these criteria are cost-type and others are benefit-type, as specified in the corresponding scenarios.

The stability of decision rankings was measured using SRD scores. SRD is an important measure of decision consistency because it is based on average rankings. As shown in Figure 9, Alternative 1 has the lowest SRD value and is the most stable alternative.

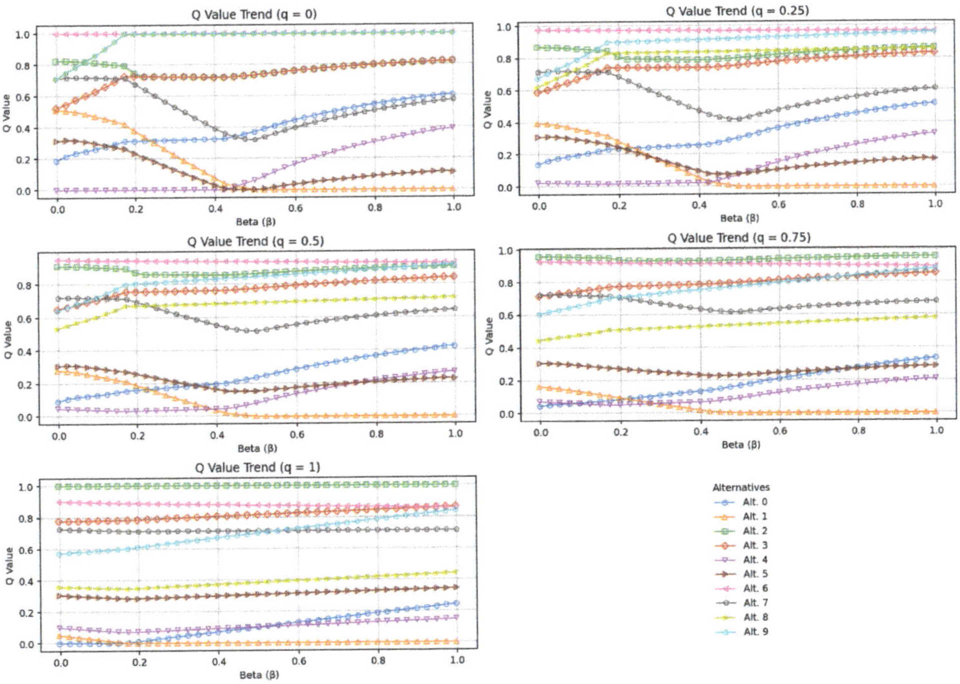

Figure 6. Alternative-Based Q Trends According to Different q Values.

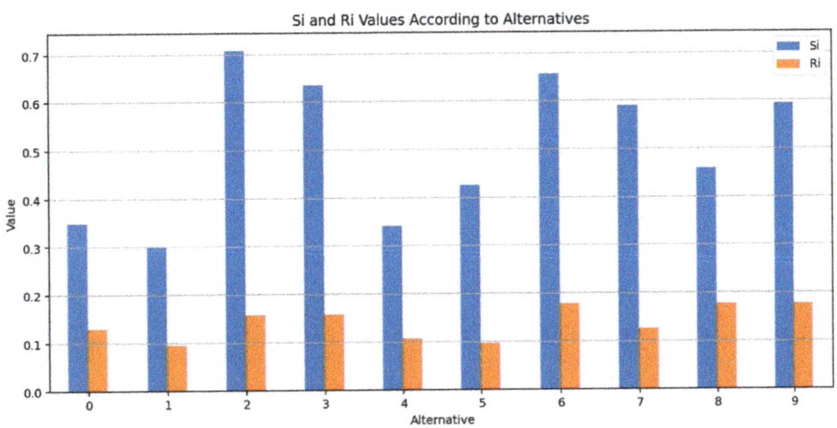

Figure 7. Si and Ri Values According to Alternatives.

Finally, the Friedman test was used to determine the statistical difference between the rankings, and the results were significant ($\chi^2 = 350.0075$, $p = 0.0000$). This indicates that different β values significantly affect the ranking and that the selection of the optimal β is not only theoretically but also statistically justified.

The impact of the weights obtained using the proposed IQRBOW-E method under various data sets on the decision-making process was evaluated through ten different experimental scenarios. The scenarios included increases in the number of criteria and alternatives, outlier ratios, and combinations of these factors (see Table 2). For each scenario, the β parameter was scanned in equal steps between 0 and 1, and the optimal β

was determined based on the obtained Q values. Additionally, decision rules within the VIKOR method, such as acceptable advantage and stability ratios, were also included in the analysis process.

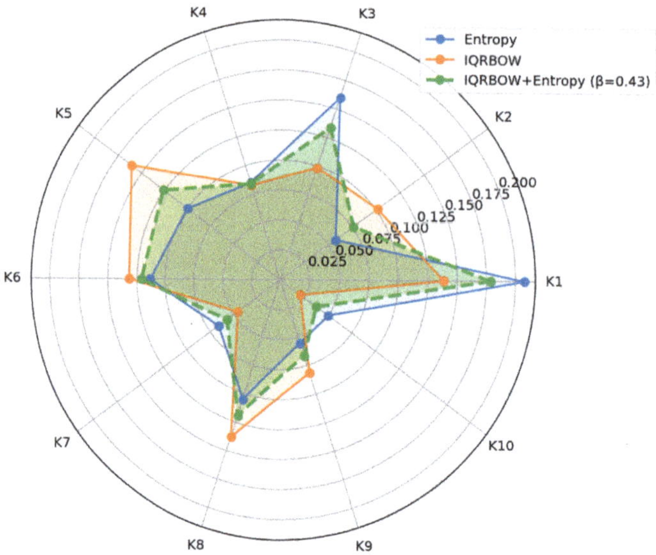

Figure 8. Comparison of Criteria Weights.

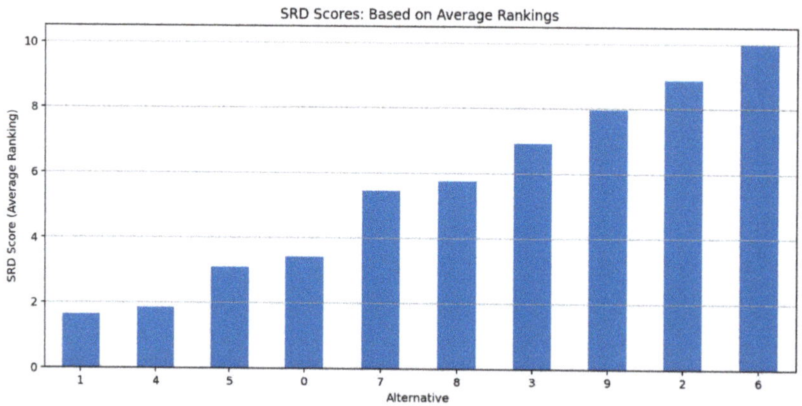

Figure 9. SRD Scores: Based on Average Rankings.

According to the analysis results, it was observed that the optimal β value generally concentrated in the range of 0.4–0.8 in scenarios without outliers (Sc1 and Sc5–Sc9) and low-scale scenarios (10 criteria, 10 alternatives, etc.). This range adequately represents both information-based sensitivity and distributional robustness. When the outlier ratio exceeds 5% (Sc3, Sc4, and Sc10), the optimal β value was observed to increase steadily, highlighting the effect of the IQRBOW-E method. This confirms that IQRBOW-E offers a data-sensitive and adaptive structure.

β optimization, decision stability, and ranking statistics for all scenarios are summarized in Table 2. As the outlier ratio increases, the optimal β value systematically rises, and SRD scores generally become more volatile.

When all scenarios are considered, it was observed that the optimal β value obtained using the IQRBOW-E method not only reduced the average Q scores but also increased ranking stability. The best alternative's protection ratio remained high, especially in the $\beta = 0.43 - 0.80$ range; the results with the lowest variance in terms of SRD scores were also obtained in this range. Friedman test results revealed significant differences across all scenarios ($p < 0.001$), indicating that the β parameter statistically influences ranking. These findings suggest that the optimal β value should be determined systematically and based on the data structure, rather than randomly.

Table 2. Summary table of scenarios.

Scenario	Optimal β	Average Q	Advantage (%)	Stability (%)	Min SRD	Friedman p
Sc1	0.425	0.0747	100	100	1.634	<0.001
Sc2	1	0.0496	100	100	1.195	<0.001
Sc3	1	0.0496	100	100	1.195	<0.001
Sc4	1	0.1136	0	100	1.634	<0.001
Sc5	0.8	0.0281	100	100	1	<0.001
Sc6	0.675	0.0124	100	100	1.22	<0.001
Sc7	0.95	0.0018	100	100	1	<0.001
Sc8	1	0	100	100	1	<0.001
Sc9	0.9	0.2571	100	100	1.268	<0.001
Sc10	0.975	0.3638	100	100	2.902	<0.001

5. Discussion

This study has demonstrated that the IQRBOW-E method developed for use in decision support systems is not merely a theoretical proposal, but also capable of producing highly flexible, robust, and relevant outputs under varying data sets. The findings clearly demonstrate that hybrid approaches with parametric controllability offer much more reliable decision-making processes than classical single-source weighting methods. In particular, the balance achieved between information sensitivity (Entropy) and statistical robustness (IQRBOW) through the β parameter can be evaluated not only as a mathematical optimization element within the method but also as a flexibility tool capable of modeling the decision-maker's strategic preferences.

In practical applications, the choice between IQRBOW, Entropy, or their hybrid form (IQRBOW-E) should depend on the characteristics of the data and decision environment. The IQRBOW method is advantageous in scenarios where robustness against outliers and noise is crucial. On the other hand, the Entropy method is more appropriate when discriminating information among criteria is prioritized in a clean, structured data set. The hybrid weighting model (Equation (8)) enables decision-makers to dynamically adjust this trade-off via the β parameter. For instance, higher β values (e.g., $\beta \geq 0.7$) are recommended in volatile environments, whereas lower β values may suit contexts emphasizing informational clarity.

One of the most striking findings worthy of discussion is that, even at low outlier rates, the optimal β value converges toward 1.0 in some scenarios. This indicates that the information-based Entropy approach can systematically break down in the presence of outliers, while IQR-based robustness consistently maintains decision quality.

On the other hand, the width of the optimal β range that satisfies the advantages and stability conditions shows that the method can work without being confined to a narrow optimization window, i.e., it offers a wide range of applications to decision-makers. This structure, integrated with ranking methods such as VIKOR, is consistent with decision rules and also stands out in terms of ranking stability measured by SRD scores.

This demonstrates that IQRBOW-E not only achieves a low Q value but also possesses a structure that enhances the repeatability and reliability of decisions. Therefore, IQRBOW-E can be regarded not only as a methodological improvement but also as a tool that enhances confidence in the reliability and integrity of decision-making processes.

6. Conclusions

This study focuses on the structural nature of weighting in decision-making processes and proposes IQRBOW-E, a parametrically adjustable hybrid method that balances information sensitivity and robustness. Comprehensive experimental analyses conducted under various scenarios demonstrate that this method not only achieves high performance in average success measures but also in ensuring decision rules and ranking stability.

The adaptability of IQRBOW-E to data structures and its flexible β parameter are the most fundamental features that distinguish the method from fixed-structure classical approaches. The results of this study demonstrate that a scalable and modular weighting method capable of responding to the dynamic needs of decision support systems is feasible.

In this context, IQRBOW-E has the potential to offer reliable, adaptable, and interpretable solutions not only within the MCDM framework but also in more complex, multi-dimensional decision environments characterized by uncertainty and data irregularities. By enabling a tunable balance between robustness and information sensitivity through the β parameter, the method allows decision-makers to adjust weighting strategies dynamically based on the characteristics of the data. Future research could build on this flexibility by integrating IQRBOW-E with fuzzy logic, interval-based representations, or hierarchical decision models. Additionally, comparative analyses involving real-world data sets and alternative MCDM methods such as TOPSIS, MARCOS, or EDAS would further enrich the applicability and generalizability of the proposed approach.

This study operates under certain assumptions and within specific limitations that should be acknowledged. The simulation-based evaluation was conducted using synthetically generated decision matrices with normally distributed values and assumed independence among criteria. While this design provides a controlled environment for testing robustness, it may not fully capture the complexities of real-world decision problems. Moreover, the current analysis focused solely on quantitative performance indicators—such as average Q values, SRD scores, and decision stability—without addressing computational cost or decision-making efficiency. These limitations present valuable directions for future work, particularly for studies seeking to validate the method using empirical data or assess its performance across a broader spectrum of decision-making contexts.

Author Contributions: Conceptualization, A.E. and Ü.F.; methodology, Ü.F.; software, C.G.; validation, A.E. and C.G.; formal analysis, Ü.F.; investigation, C.G.; resources, A.E.; data curation, Ü.F.; writing—original draft preparation, C.G.; writing—review and editing, A.E.; visualization, Ü.F.; project administration, A.E. All authors have read and agreed to the published version of the manuscript.

Funding: This research received no external funding.

Institutional Review Board Statement: This study fully complies with all ethical guidelines. The research process was conducted in accordance with the principles of the Declaration of Helsinki, and all procedures related to the data produced in the study have been transparently disclosed.

Data Availability Statement: The raw data supporting the conclusions of this article will be made available by the authors upon request.

Conflicts of Interest: The authors declare no conflicts of interest.

References

1. Gupta, S.; Modgil, S.; Bhattacharyya, S.; Bose, I. Artificial intelligence for decision support systems in the field of operations research: Review and future scope of research. *Ann. Oper. Res.* **2022**, *308*, 215–274. [CrossRef]
2. Marchau, V.A.; Walker, W.E.; Bloemen, P.J.; Popper, S.W. *Decision Making Under Deep Uncertainty: From Theory to Practice*; Springer Nature: Cham, Switzerland, 2019; p. 405. [CrossRef]
3. Odu, G.O. Weighting methods for multi-criteria decision-making technique. *J. Appl. Sci. Environ. Manag.* **2019**, *23*, 1449–1457. [CrossRef]
4. Paradowski, B.; Wątróbski, J.; Sałabun, W. Novel coefficients for improved robustness in multi-criteria decision analysis. *Artif. Intell. Rev.* **2025**, *58*, 1–41. [CrossRef]
5. Duan, Y.; Cai, Y.; Wang, Z.; Deng, X. A novel network security risk assessment approach by combining subjective and objective weights under uncertainty. *Appl. Sci.* **2018**, *8*, 428. [CrossRef]
6. Jiang, J.; Liu, X.; Wang, Z.; Ding, W.; Zhang, S.; Xu, H. Large group decision-making with a rough integrated asymmetric cloud model under multi-granularity linguistic environment. *Inf. Sci.* **2024**, *678*, 120994. [CrossRef]
7. Liu, X.; Zhang, S.; Wang, Z.; Zhang, S. Classification and identification of medical insurance fraud: A case-based reasoning approach. *Technol. Econ. Dev. Econ.* **2025**, 1–27. [CrossRef]
8. Hwang, C.L.; Yoon, K. Methods for multiple attribute decision making. In *Multiple Attribute Decision Making*; Springer: Berlin/Heidelberg, Germany, 1981; pp. 58–191. [CrossRef]
9. Shannon, C.E. A mathematical theory of communication. *Bell Syst. Tech. J.* **1948**, *27*, 379–423. [CrossRef]
10. Fidan, Ü. Basic statistical methods in determining criteria weights. *Int. J. Inf. Technol. Decis. Mak.* **2025**, *24*, 1103–1124. [CrossRef]
11. Lescauskiene, I.; Bausys, R.; Zavadskas, E.K.; Juodagalviene, B. VASMA weighting: Survey-based criteria weighting methodology that combines ENTROPY and WASPAS-SVNS to reflect the psychometric features of the VAS scales. *Symmetry* **2020**, *12*, 1641. [CrossRef]
12. Roth, P.L.; Pritchard, R.D.; Stout, J.D.; Brown, S.H. Estimating the impact of variable costs on SDy in complex situations. *J. Bus. Psychol.* **1994**, *8*, 437–454. [CrossRef]
13. Diakoulaki, D.; Mavrotas, G.; Papayannakis, L. Determining objective weights in multiple criteria problems: The critic method. *Comput. Oper. Res.* **1995**, *22*, 763–770. [CrossRef]
14. Keshavarz-Ghorabaee, M.; Amiri, M.; Zavadskas, E.K.; Turskis, Z.; Antucheviciene, J. Determination of objective weights using a new method based on the removal effects of criteria (MEREC). *Symmetry* **2021**, *13*, 525. [CrossRef]
15. Li, G.; Chi, G. A new determining objective weights method-gini coefficient weight. In Proceedings of the 2009 First International Conference on Information Science and Engineering, Nanjing, China, 26–28 December; pp. 3726–3729. [CrossRef]
16. Wu, R.M.X.; Zhang, Z.; Yan, W.; Fan, J.; Gou, J.; Liu, B.; Gide, E.; Soar, J.; Shen, B.; Fazal-E-Hasan, S.; et al. A comparative analysis of the principal component analysis and entropy weight methods to establish the indexing measurement. *PLoS ONE* **2022**, *17*, e0262261. [CrossRef]
17. Wang, H.Y.; Wang, J.S.; Wang, G. Combination evaluation method of fuzzy c-mean clustering validity based on hybrid weighted strategy. *IEEE Access* **2021**, *9*, 27239–27261. [CrossRef]
18. Aktaš, A.; Ecer, B.; Kabak, M. A hybrid hesitant fuzzy model for healthcare systems ranking of European countries. *Systems* **2022**, *10*, 219. [CrossRef]
19. Aliyeva, K.; Aliyeva, A.; Aliyev, R.; Özdeşer, M. Application of Fuzzy Simple Additive Weighting Method in Group Decision-Making for Capital Investment. *Axioms* **2023**, *12*, 797. [CrossRef]
20. Esangbedo, M.O.; Tang, M. Evaluation of Enterprise Decarbonization Scheme Based on Grey-MEREC-MAIRCA Hybrid MCDM Method. *Systems* **2023**, *11*, 397. [CrossRef]
21. Özceylan, E.; Erbaş, M.; Tolon, M.; Kabak, M.; Durğut, T. Evaluation of freight villages: A GIS-based multi-criteria decision analysis. *Comput. Ind.* **2016**, *76*, 38–52. [CrossRef]
22. Opricovic, S.; Tzeng, G.H. Extended VIKOR method in comparison with outranking methods. *Eur. J. Oper. Res.* **2007**, *178*, 514–529. [CrossRef]
23. Keshavarz Ghorabaee, M.; Zavadskas, E.K.; Olfat, L.; Turskis, Z. Multi-criteria inventory classification using a new method of evaluation based on distance from average solution (EDAS). *Informatica* **2015**, *26*, 435–451. [CrossRef]
24. Stević, Ž.; Pamučar, D.; Puška, A.; Chatterjee, P. Sustainable supplier selection in healthcare industries using a new MCDM method: Measurement of alternatives and ranking according to COmpromise solution (MARCOS). *Comput. Ind. Eng.* **2020**, *140*, 106231. [CrossRef]
25. Julong, D. Application of grey system theory in China. In Proceedings of the First International Symposium on Uncertainty Modeling and Analysis, College Park, MD, USA, 3–5 December 1990; pp. 285–291. [CrossRef]
26. Wang, P.; Meng, P.; Zhai, J.Y.; Zhu, Z.Q. A hybrid method using experiment design and grey relational analysis for multiple criteria decision-making problems. *Knowl. Based Syst.* **2013**, *53*, 100–107. [CrossRef]
27. Hubert, M.; Van der Veeken, S. Outlier detection for skewed data. *J. Chemom. Soc.* **2008**, *22*, 235–246. [CrossRef]

28. Stipčević, M.; Koç, Ç. True Random Number Generators. In *Open Problems in Mathematics and Computational Science*; Koç, Ç., Ed.; Springer: Cham, Switzerland, 2014. [CrossRef]
29. Kietzmann, P.; Schmidt, T.C.; Wählisch, M. A guideline on pseudorandom number generation (PRNG) in the IoT. *ACM Comput. Surv.* **2021**, *54*, 1–38. [CrossRef]
30. Kansal, D.; Kumar, S. Multi-criteria decision-making based on intuitionistic fuzzy exponential knowledge and similarity measure and improved VIKOR method. *Granul. Comput.* **2024**, *9*, 26. [CrossRef]
31. Fidan, Ü. Can Bitcoin be an alternative for portfolio diversification decisions? MEREC-based VIKOR approach. *J. Acad. Approaches* **2022**, *13*, 526–545. [CrossRef]
32. Kollár-Hunek, K.; Héberger, K. Method and model comparison by sum of ranking differences in cases of repeated observations (ties). *Chemom. Intell. Lab. Syst.* **2013**, *127*, 139–146. [CrossRef]
33. Friedman, M. The use of ranks to avoid the assumption of normality implicit in the analysis of variance. *J. Am. Stat. Assoc.* **1937**, *32*, 675–701. [CrossRef]

entropy

MDPI

Article

Distributed Data Classification with Coalition-Based Decision Trees and Decision Template Fusion

Katarzyna Kusztal [1] and Małgorzata Przybyła-Kasperek [1,2,*]

1 Institute of Computer Science, University of Silesia in Katowice, Będzińska 39, 41-200 Sosnowiec, Poland; katarzyna.kusztal@us.edu.pl

2 Department of Informatics, Faculty of Natural Sciences and Informatics, Constantine the Philosopher University in Nitra, Tr. A. Hlinku 1, 949 01 Nitra, Slovakia

* Correspondence: malgorzata.przybyla-kasperek@us.edu.pl

Abstract

In distributed data environments, classification tasks are challenged by inconsistencies across independently maintained sources. These environments are inherently characterized by high informational uncertainty. Our framework addresses this challenge through a structured process designed for the reduction of entropy in the overall decision-making process. This paper proposes a novel framework that integrates conflict analysis, coalition formation, decision tree induction, and decision template fusion to address these challenges. The method begins by identifying compatible data sources using Pawlak's conflict model, forming coalitions that aggregate complementary information. Each coalition trains a decision tree classifier, and the final decision is derived through decision templates that fuse probabilistic outputs from all models. The proposed approach is compared with a variant that does not use coalitions, where each local source is modeled independently. Additionally, the framework extends previous work based on decision rules by introducing decision trees, which offer greater modeling flexibility while preserving interpretability. Experimental results on benchmark datasets from the UCI repository demonstrate that the proposed method consistently outperforms both the non-coalition variant and the rule-based version, particularly under moderate data dispersion. The key contributions of this work include the integration of coalition-based modeling with decision trees, the use of decision templates for interpretable fusion, and the demonstration of improved classification performance across diverse scenarios.

Keywords: distributed data; classification; decision trees; hierarchical system; conflict analysis; coalition formation; decision templates; interpretability

1. Introduction

Contemporary systems for data processing and analysis operate in environments where information originates from multiple independently managed sources. Such fragmentation is a natural consequence of the organization of institutions, business processes, or research units collecting and storing their records according to internal procedures. On the one hand, this provides flexibility and allows data collection methods to be tailored to specific needs and conditions; on the other, it introduces serious challenges. Individual sources may represent reality differently–by applying distinct measurement protocols, storing datasets in heterogeneous formats, or maintaining varying levels of detail. As a result, simple aggregation is often impossible or leads to contradictory conclusions, which undermines the reliability of analyses. Consequently, the integration of distributed data has become one of the central concerns of modern data science.

This problem is universal and arises across many practical domains. In medicine, patient records are often stored in different healthcare providers, each relying on its own diagnostic procedures and laboratory tests. As a result, examination outcomes and the medical decisions derived from them may vary between hospitals. It is not uncommon for the same patient to be treated in more than one facility, which can lead to inconsistencies and discrepancies in diagnoses. In the financial sector, independent institutions maintain separate databases, where information about the same client may be differ depending on the applied risk assessment methods, directly influencing credit and investment decisions. Comparable difficulties also occur in business, where individual company branches analyze sales locally, focusing on the specifics of their market. This local perspective hinders the creation of a coherent organizational picture and limits the ability to make effective strategic decisions.

In response to these difficulties, the literature presents a variety of approaches to distributed data classification [1,2]. Broadly, they can be divided into interpretable models, such as decision trees and rule-based classifiers [3–6], and black-box models, including neural networks and deep learning techniques [7]. While the latter often achieve very high accuracy, the lack of explainability limits their usefulness in applications that require transparency of the classification process. Ensemble methods such as bagging, boosting, and stacking [8,9] represent another important research direction. However, these techniques mainly focus on improving predictive performance rather than integrating knowledge across multiple sources. More recently, federated learning has gained attention [10,11], allowing decentralized model training while preserving the privacy of local data. Although this approach addresses increasing demands for data protection, it typically relies on complex black-box models, without providing interpretability. Another line of research involves hierarchical classification schemes [12], where local models are combined within a higher-level structure; however, these methods do not directly resolve the issue of divergent predictions between sources. Managing uncertainty in multi-source and distributed environments has been a central topic in information fusion and decision-making research. Among the most influential frameworks, Dempster–Shafer evidence theory provides a flexible approach for representing and combining uncertain information, extending classical probability theory by allowing belief assignments to subsets of hypotheses rather than singletons [13,14]. This property makes Dempster–Shafer theory particularly suitable for applications in sensor fusion, fault diagnosis, and risk analysis [15–17]. However, the transformation of basic probability assignments into actionable probability distributions remains a critical challenge. Traditional methods such as the pignistic probability transformation redistribute mass uniformly across focal elements [18], while optimization-based approaches aim to minimize entropy for improved decisiveness [19]. Recent research introduces graph-based models to capture structural relationships among focal elements. For example, the ordered visibility graph probability method constructs a directed graph based on basic probability assignments ordering [20], while its weighted variant integrates belief entropy to improve interpretability [21]. Paper [17] proposes an enhanced probabilistic transformation using weighted visibility graph networks combined with advanced entropy measures, such as Jiroušek's decomposable entropy [22]. Comparative studies show that these methods outperform classical probability transformation. Consequently, this research aligns with the fundamental principles of information theory, specifically focusing on maximizing information gain through classification model synergy and minimizing overall decision entropy across the distributed architecture.

Against this background, methods for the formal analysis of conflicts in distributed data are gaining growing relevance. One of the foundation approaches is Pawlak's conflict analysis model [23], which enables the identification and description of dependencies between agents. This idea was subsequently extended, among others, within the framework of rough set theory [24], and also linked to three-way decision theory [25]. A study [26] demonstrated the possibility of broadening classical models by considering analysis across two universes. More recent research [27] has also shown that the approach can be applied in hierarchical systems, where scenarios of disagreement are constructed using methods inspired by cluster analysis.

In parallel, research has advanced on methods fusing classification results, aimed at producing a consistent decision from the predictions of multiple local models. The simplest strategies include majority voting and averaging, but these typically overlook relationships between classifiers and fail to capture more complex decision patterns. To overcome this limitations, decision templates were proposed by Kuncheva [28], which capture the characteristic behavior of ensembles and serve as a reference for evaluating new cases.

This paper introduces a new approach to the classification of distributed data, which combines conflict analysis, the construction of tree-based models, and the mechanism of decision templates. In the first stage, data sources are grouped into coalitions, enabling their collaboration and better utilization of complementary information. Next, decision trees are trained for each coalition. The final component is the application of decision templates, which provide stable result integration and robustness against local inconsistencies.

In the authors' earlier study [29], conflict analysis was integrated with rule-based classification. Decision rules were induced using four algorithms: exhaustive search, covering, genetic, and LEM2. For classification purposes, three alternative strategies were applied: (1) the choice of the class of the first matching rule, (2) the assignment of the most frequent decision among matching rules, and (3) the selection of the class with the highest sum of covering rule weights. The analysis focused on comparing different induction-classification configurations. In a subsequent work [30], the same rule-based framework was further developed, where the classification process relied on the decision template mechanism. Building on this line of research, the current study extends the coalition- and template-based framework to decision trees. Replacing rules with trees broadens the ability to model complex, hierarchical dependencies between attributes, offering greater flexibility and integration potential, while preserving the interpretability of the classification process.

The contribution of this work is threefold:

- A novel framework for distributed data classification that integrates coalition formation based on conflict analysis with decision tree induction and decision template fusion.
- An interpretable modeling approach, where decision trees are used instead of rule-based classifiers, enabling the representation of complex attribute dependencies while maintaining transparency.
- A robust fusion mechanism, which leverages decision templates to integrate predictions from multiple coalition-based models, improving classification accuracy and consistency across diverse data sources.

The organization of the paper is as follows. Section 2 presents the proposed method, covering the construction of local models and the use of decision templates. The datasets and the experimental procedure are described as well. Section 3 reports and analyzes the obtained results. The implications of the findings and the study's limitations are discussed in Section 4. Finally, Section 5 concludes with a summary of contributions and prospects for future work.

2. Materials and Methods

This section introduces the data representation used in the study and the proposed framework for distributed data. It also includes an illustrative example to demonstrate the operation of the method, followed by the description of the experimental setup used for evaluation.

2.1. Data Representation and Notation

Formally, we assume that the distributed data are represented as a set of local decision tables $T = \{T_i : i \in \{1, \ldots, n\}\}$. Each $T_i = (U_i, A, d)$ consists of a set of objects U_i, a set of conditional attributes A, and a decision attribute d. Within this study, the local tables are considered to be described by the same set of conditional attributes. As they originate from the same domain, the decision attribute is also common to all of them. This formalization ensures a consistent basis for further analysis and enables subsequent modeling and classification procedures.

2.2. Proposed Classification Framework

The proposed method can be outlined in four main stages:

1. Forming coalitions of sources using conflict analysis;
2. Combining data within each coalition and training a decision tree model on the aggregated set;
3. Deriving prediction vectors for training instances and generating a decision template corresponding to each decision class;
4. Conducting the final classification, where prediction vectors of test samples are matched against the decision templates using normalized Euclidean distance.

The workflow of the proposed framework is summarized in Figure 1.

Initially, coalitions of local tables are identified using Pawlak's conflict analysis model [23]. For this purpose, each conditional attribute is expressed in a simplified form by assigning it one of three values from the set $\{-1, 0, 1\}$. This transformation provides a uniform representation of local tables, which is then used for constructing the information system $S = (T, A)$. The assignment procedure differs depending on the type of attribute.

The use of simple quantisation into $\{-1, 0, 1\}$ follows the original formulation of Pawlak's conflict analysis model [23], which emphasizes symbolic representation and interpretability over numerical precision. This approach enables a clear and intuitive comparison of local data sources by reducing attribute values to a common scale of deviation from the global norm. While more nuanced encoding or adaptive discretisation methods could retain richer data characteristics, they often introduce additional complexity and may obscure the interpretability of the conflict relations. In contrast, the three-valued representation preserves the transparency of the model and aligns with the foundational principles of conflict analysis in distributed environments.

For each quantitative attribute $a_{quan} \in A$, we assign to every local table T_i its mean value, written as $\overline{Val}^{i}_{a_{quan}}$. Subsequently, the global mean $\overline{Val}_{a_{quan}}$ and the global standard deviation $SD_{a_{quan}}$ are calculated over the entire collection of tables. Based on these statistics, we introduce a mapping $a_{quan} : T \to \{-1, 0, 1\}$, specified as follows:

$$a_{quan}(T_i) = \begin{cases} 1 & \text{if } \overline{Val}_{a_{quan}} + SD_{a_{quan}} < \overline{Val}^{i}_{a_{quan}} \\ 0 & \text{if } \overline{Val}_{a_{quan}} - SD_{a_{quan}} \leq \overline{Val}^{i}_{a_{quan}} \leq \overline{Val}_{a_{quan}} + SD_{a_{quan}} \\ -1 & \text{if } \overline{Val}^{i}_{a_{quan}} < \overline{Val}_{a_{quan}} - SD_{a_{quan}} \end{cases} \quad (1)$$

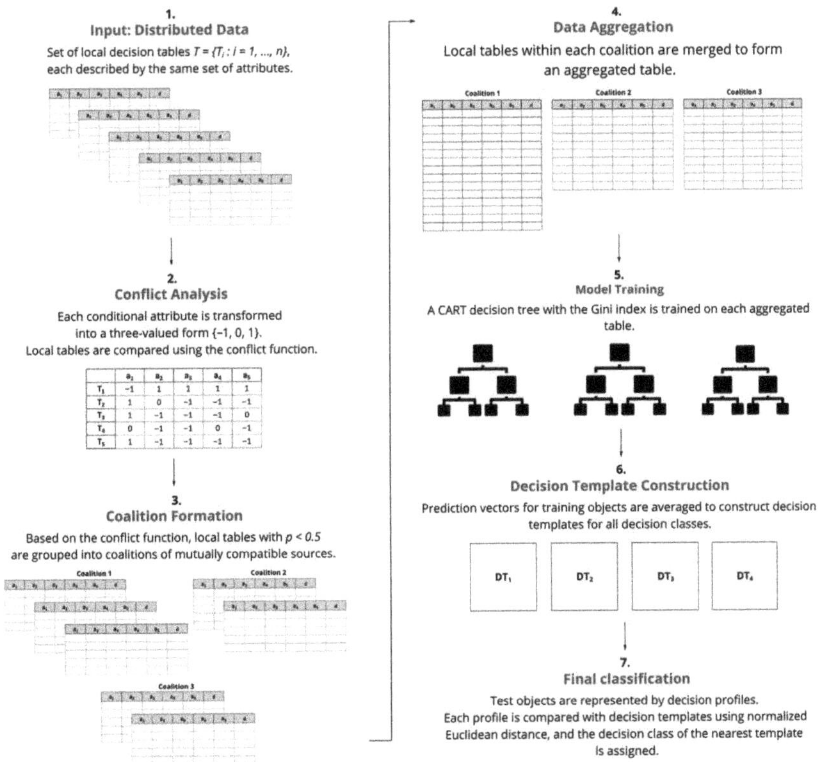

Figure 1. Workflow of the proposed classification framework for distributed data.

A value of 0 indicates that the attribute in the considered table remains within the typical range observed across all tables. A value of 1 means that it exceeds the global tendency, whereas -1 corresponds to lower-than-usual values.

In contrast, for a qualitative attribute $a_{qual} \in A$, we describe its distribution within each local table T_i. If a_{qual} admits c distinct categories $val_1, \ldots, val_c$, we define the vector $Val^i_{a_{qual}} = (n^i_1, \ldots, n^i_c)$, where each component n^i_j denotes the number of objects in T_i taking the value val_j. Each vector is then normalized. Subsequently, to reduce this representation, the 3-means clustering algorithm with Euclidean distance is applied to the set of such vectors. The obtained centroids are then sorted in descending order according to the value of their first coordinate. The clusters are assigned the values 1, 0, and -1, respectively. As a result, three groups of tables are obtained, characterized by similar distributions of attribute values.

With conditional attributes represented in the three-valued form, we define a conflict function $\rho : T \times T \rightarrow [0, 1]$ describing the relation of two local tables. It is given by

$$\rho(T_i, T_j) = \frac{card\{a \in A : a(T_i) \neq a(T_j)\}}{card\{A\}}. \tag{2}$$

The value of $\rho(T_i, T_j)$ corresponds to the proportion of attributes on which the tables disagree. A lower value indicates higher similarity, while a higher value reflects stronger divergence. Tables satisfying $\rho(T_i, T_j) < 0.5$ are considered compatible and are grouped into the coalition. Hence, each coalition consists of tables that are mutually consistent in at least half of the attributes.

The compatibility threshold of 0.5 originates from Pawlak's original conflict analysis model [23], which interprets agreement in more than half of the attributes as sufficient for establishing compatibility. This simple and intuitive criterion ensures interpretability and aligns with the foundational principles of conflict-based reasoning. Previous studies introduced parameterized extensions with adjustable thresholds to give more flexibility in coalition formation. For example, ref. [31] examined the effect of such parameters in a dispersed data classification framework based on allied relations, which is conceptually different from the approach used in this work. While the present study adopts the classical threshold for consistency with the original model, future work will explore parameterized variants to assess their influence on coalition structure and classification performance.

Next, an aggregation decision table $T_j^{aggr} = (U_j^{aggr}, A, d)$ is created by merging the data from all local tables belonging to that coalition. The universe U_j^{aggr} is defined as the union of objects from the constituent tables. The sets of conditional attributes A and the decision attribute d are retained from the original representation. For every object $x \in U_i$, the corresponding attribute values in the aggregated table are obtained directly from its source table T_i.

For each coalition, a decision tree model following the classification and regression tree (CART) algorithm with the Gini index as the splitting criterion [32] is trained on the aggregated table T_j^{aggr}. Although the Gini index is used, it is a measure of impurity functionally related to the concept of information entropy often employed in decision tree induction. Both measures aim to achieve the maximum information gain (i.e., the largest possible reduction in classification uncertainty) at each node split, thereby explicitly grounding the model construction in information theory principles. Entropy and information gain will be utilized in future research as key criteria for determining the optimal partitioning of tree structures. The Gini index was selected due to its computational efficiency and its proven effectiveness in classification tasks involving dispersed data. In particular, previous research has shown that the Gini index performs comparably to other criteria such as entropy and twoing in distributed environments. For example, ref. [33] conducted a comparative study of splitting criteria for decision trees applied to dispersed data, demonstrating that while entropy and twoing offer alternative perspectives on impurity, the Gini index remains a robust and interpretable choice. Its simplicity and speed make it especially suitable for large-scale distributed systems, which aligns with the goals of this framework.

Since the decision template fusion method [28] operates on probability-based predictions, each classifier produces outputs at the measurement level for both training and test objects. For an object x, these probabilities are obtained in Python 3.13.0 using the `predict_proba` function from the `scikit-learn` library [34] and are represented as a normalized vector $[\mu_{j,1}(x), \cdots, \mu_{j,i}(x), \cdots, \mu_{j,c}(x)]$, where c denotes the number of decision classes.

In the next step, probability outputs from all coalition-based classifiers are used to construct decision templates. The process of constructing templates DT_i by averaging prediction vectors (Equation (3)) serves as a fusion mechanism designed to minimize the collective uncertainty (or output entropy) of the ensemble. By integrating probabilistic outputs from all coalition models, this approach effectively extracts a consensus informational profile, which increases the stability and reduces the entropy of the final classification decision compared to individual local predictions. For each decision class i, a template DT_i is built by averaging the prediction vectors of training objects that belong to this class:

$$DT_i = \frac{1}{card\{X_i\}} \sum_{x \in X_i} \begin{bmatrix} \mu_{1,1}(x) & \cdots & \mu_{1,i}(x) & \cdots & \mu_{1,c}(x) \\ & & \cdots & & \\ \mu_{j,1}(x) & \cdots & \mu_{j,i}(x) & \cdots & \mu_{j,c}(x) \\ & & \cdots & & \\ \mu_{L,1}(x) & \cdots & \mu_{L,i}(x) & \cdots & \mu_{L,c}(x) \end{bmatrix}, \quad (3)$$

where X_i denotes the set of training objects labeled with class i, and L is the number of coalition-based models.

To classify a new (test) object $\bar{x}$, a decision profile is generated from its probability predictions across all classifiers:

$$DP(\bar{x}) = \begin{bmatrix} \mu_{1,1}(\bar{x}) & \cdots & \mu_{1,i}(\bar{x}) & \cdots & \mu_{1,c}(\bar{x}) \\ & & \cdots & & \\ \mu_{j,1}(\bar{x}) & \cdots & \mu_{j,i}(\bar{x}) & \cdots & \mu_{j,c}(\bar{x}) \\ & & \cdots & & \\ \mu_{L,1}(\bar{x}) & \cdots & \mu_{L,i}(\bar{x}) & \cdots & \mu_{L,c}(\bar{x}) \end{bmatrix}. \quad (4)$$

The final decision is made by comparing the decision profile $DP(\bar{x})$ with each decision template DT_i using the normalized Euclidean distance:

$$s(DP(\bar{x}), DT_i) = \frac{1}{L \cdot c} \sum_{m=1}^{L} \sum_{l=1}^{c} (DP^{m,l}(\bar{x}) - DT_i^{m,l})^2, \quad (5)$$

where $DP^{m,l}(\bar{x})$ and $DT_i^{m,l}$ refer to the values at the m-th row and l-th column of $DP(\bar{x})$ and DT_i, respectively. The object $\bar{x}$ is then assigned to the class whose template yields the smallest distance, indicating the closest match between the prediction patterns.

For clarity, the pseudo-code of the proposed framework is presented in Algorithm 1. The computational complexity can be determined by analyzing the operations carried out within its individual components. The creation of the information system involves deriving summary statistics for all conditional attributes across the collection of local tables. This operation requires $O((N+n) \cdot m)$ time, where $N = \sum_{i=1}^{n} card\{U_i\}$, $n = card\{T\}$, and $m = card\{A\}$. Because typically $N \geq n$, the contribution of the n-dependent part is marginal relative to the effort associated with processing all objects. Pairwise conflict function values are next obtained by comparing the three-valued attribute representations of each pair of local tables. With $n(n-1)$ ordered pairs, this stage scales as $O(n^2 \cdot m)$. Coalition formation proceeds by identifying subsets of local tables that satisfy the compatibility condition ($\rho < 0.5$); in the worst case, determining all admissible groupings entails examining all subsets of the n tables, leading to an exponential upper bound of $O(2^n)$. After the coalition structure has been established, the data within each coalition are aggregated by concatenating the objects originating from its constituent local tables. Across the framework, this operation is linear in the total number of instances, yielding $O(N)$. Training a CART model for each coalition requires $O(N_j \cdot m \log N_j)$ for a dataset of size $N_j = card\{U_j^{aggr}\}$. Summing these contributions over all coalitions gives a total cost of $O\big(\sum_j N_j \cdot m \log N_j\big)$. Since $N_j \leq N$ for all j, this term can be upper-bounded by $O\big((\sum_j N_j) \cdot m \log N\big)$. Decision templates are then constructed by averaging the prediction vectors produced by the k coalition models over the training objects assigned to each decision class. Since each probability vector contains c components, this stage runs in $O(N \cdot k \cdot c)$. Finally, classifying a new object consists in generating its decision profile from the predictions of all coalition-based models and comparing it with each decision template. Each distance computation takes $O(k \cdot c)$, so the classification of a single object proceeds in $O(k \cdot c^2)$.

Taken together, the overall computational complexity of the proposed framework is dominated by the exponential cost of coalition formation, while all remaining stages operate in polynomial or linear time. In practical scenarios, however, compatible coalitions tend to emerge earlier in the process, so only part of the possible subsets is explored. Thus, the final coalition structure is obtained faster than the theoretical upper bound suggests.

Algorithm 1 Pseudo-code of the proposed classification framework for distributed data

Input: A set of local decision tables $T = \{T_i = (U_i, A, d)\}_{i=1}^{n}$.
Output: Final classification result for a test object $\bar{x}$.

Creation of information system
for each conditional attribute $a \in A$, define the function $a(T_i) \in \{-1, 0, 1\}$:
 if a is quantitative then
  Use Equation (1)
 else
  Apply the procedure described for qualitative attributes
Form the information system $S = (T, A)$.

Coalition formation
for each pair $(T_i, T_j) \in T \times T$:
 Use Equation (2) to compute the conflict function value $\rho(T_i, T_j)$
Group local tables into coalitions $C_1, \ldots, C_k$ (where k denotes the number of coalitions) so that tables within each coalition satisfy $\rho(T_i, T_j) < 0.5$.

Data aggregation
for each coalition C_j:
 Combine local tables into the aggregated table $T_j^{aggr} = (U_j^{aggr}, A, d)$

Model training
for each aggregated table T_j^{aggr}:
 Train a CART decision tree model CT_j^{aggr} using the Gini index

Construction of decision templates
for each training object x:
 for each coalition model CT_j^{aggr}:
  Obtain the class-probability vector $\mu_j(x) = [\mu_{j,1}(x), \ldots, \mu_{j,i}(x), \ldots, \mu_{j,c}(x)]$ (where c is the number of decision classes)
for each decision class i:
 Average prediction vectors of training objects belonging to class i to generate the decision template DT_i according to Equation (3)

Final classification
for a (new) test object $\bar{x}$:
 for each coalition model CT_j^{aggr}:
  Obtain the class-probability vector $\mu_j(\bar{x}) = [\mu_{j,1}(\bar{x}), \ldots, \mu_{j,i}(\bar{x}), \ldots, \mu_{j,c}(\bar{x})]$
 Form the decision profile $DP(\bar{x})$ using Equation (4)
 Compute normalized Euclidean distances $s(DP(\bar{x}), DT_i)$ as defined in Equation (5)
 Return the decision class i corresponding to the smallest distance $s(DP(\bar{x}), DT_i)$

2.3. Illustrative Example

To demonstrate the operation of the proposed framework, consider a symbolic, practice-oriented example reflecting a business environment. Three local decision tables, denoted as T_1, T_2, and T_3, represent customer purchasing activity recorded by different regional branches, as summarized in Table 1. All local tables share the same set of conditional attributes $A = \{a_1, a_2, a_3\}$ and a common decision attribute d. Attributes a_1 and a_2 are quantitative, while a_3 is qualitative. Specifically, a_1 denotes the customer's average number of transactions per month, a_2 represents the average purchase value (expressed in relative units), and a_3 indicates the dominant shopping channel (online, retail, or business). The decision attribute d indicates the customer satisfaction level, where 1 corresponds to low and 2 to high satisfaction. This dataset is entirely synthetic and was designed solely for explanatory purposes.

Table 1. Example of local tables.

T_1				
U_1	a_1	a_2	a_3	d
x_1	8	10	online	1
x_2	9	10	online	1
x_3	8	11	retail	2
T_2				
U_2	a_1	a_2	a_3	d
x_1	9	11	retail	1
x_2	8	12	business	2
x_3	9	10	retail	2
T_3				
U_3	a_1	a_2	a_3	d
x_1	13	7	business	1
x_2	13	7	retail	1
x_3	14	8	business	2

Following the procedure described in Section 2.2, all conditional attributes are transformed into the three-valued representation $\{-1, 0, 1\}$ according to Pawlak's conflict analysis model. This process varies depending on whether the attribute is quantitative or qualitative. Table 2 presents the resulting information system obtained for the local tables T_1, T_2, and T_3.

Table 2. Information system.

	a_1	a_2	a_3
T_1	0	0	-1
T_2	0	0	0
T_3	1	-1	1

Based on the information system, the conflict function is computed in line with Pawlak's model. The generated conflict matrix is shown in Table 3, where each element quantifies the degree of disagreement between two local tables in terms of their symbolic attribute representations.

Table 3. Conflict matrix.

	T_1	T_2	T_3
T_1	0.00	0.33	1.00
T_2	0.33	0.00	1.00
T_3	1.00	1.00	0.00

With the threshold $\rho < 0.5$, local tables T_1 and T_2 are compatible and form coalition $\mathcal{C}_1 = \{T_1, T_2\}$, whereas T_3 remains separate as $\mathcal{C}_2 = \{T_3\}$. For each coalition, data are aggregated and a CART decision tree is constructed using the Gini index.

Afterward, the coalition-based classifiers produce class-probability predictions for two decision classes ($c = 2$) and two coalitions ($L = 2$). In accordance with Equation (3), averaging the predictions across training objects within each decision class yields two decision templates, DT_1 and DT_2, associated with classes 1 and 2, respectively:

$$DT_1 = \begin{bmatrix} 0.80 & 0.20 \\ 0.40 & 0.60 \end{bmatrix}, \quad DT_2 = \begin{bmatrix} 0.25 & 0.75 \\ 0.00 & 1.00 \end{bmatrix}.$$

As can be seen, in DT_1 the first coalition assigns a higher probability to class 1 (0.80 vs. 0.20), indicating a stronger association with this class. In contrast, the second coalition within DT_1 shows a higher probability for class 2 (0.60 vs. 0.40), suggesting partial disagreement between coalitions in terms of class preference. In DT_2, both coalitions assign higher probabilities to class 2, which indicates a more consistent representation of this class across the coalitions.

For a test object $\bar{x}$ described by the attributes $a_1 = 9$, $a_2 = 11$, and $a_3 = retail$, the prediction profile obtained across the coalitions is given by:

$$DP(\bar{x}) = \begin{bmatrix} 1.00 & 0.00 \\ 0.00 & 1.00 \end{bmatrix}.$$

The first coalition assigns the test object $\bar{x}$ entirely to class 1, while the second coalition assigns it to class 2, providing conflicting predictions. To determine the final classification, the similarity between the decision profile and each decision template is computed using the normalized Euclidean distance (Equation (5)). The resulting distances are:

$$s\big(DP(\bar{x}), DT_1\big) = 0.1, \quad s\big(DP(\bar{x}), DT_2\big) = 0.28125.$$

As the smaller distance reflects greater similarity between the decision profile and the corresponding decision template, the test object $\bar{x}$ is assigned to class 1. Interpreted in business terms, the model predicts that the customer belongs to the low-satisfaction group.

2.4. Experimental Setup and Evaluation Procedure

The experiments, intended to assess the effectiveness of the proposed method, were performed on three datasets—Balance Scale, Vehicle Silhouettes [35], and Car Evaluation [36]—all sourced from the UCI Machine Learning Repository [37]. Each dataset was divided into two non-overlapping subsets using a stratified sampling strategy: 70% of the instances were assigned to the training set, while the remaining 30% formed the test set. The Balance Scale dataset includes 625 instances, with 437 used for training and 188 for testing, defined by four categorical attributes and three decision classes representing balance states: B (balanced), L (titled left), and R (titled right). The Vehicle Silhouettes dataset contains 846 instances, of which 592 were used for training and 254 for testing.

These are described by 18 numerical attributes and grouped into four decision classes corresponding to different vehicle types: bus, opel, saab, and van. Finally, the Car Evaluation dataset comprises 1728 records (1209 for training and 519 for testing), characterized by six categorical attributes and four decision labels reflecting car acceptability levels: unacc (unacceptable), acc (acceptable), good, and vgood (very good).

Although the data are not originally distributed, they were divided into several local tables to simulate the presence of multiple data sources that describe the same decision problem. Four configurations were tested, with 5, 7, 9, and 11 local tables. These settings provide a gradual increase in data fragmentation, allowing the analysis of the method's robustness and coalition formation behavior. Consequently, twelve versions of the datasets were generated. All local tables retained the complete set of attributes but contained only a portion of the training data. The stratified sampling ensured that, for each decision class, instances were proportionally assigned to the tables. Such a setup enables meaningful comparison and coalition formation, as the observed differences between sources result from the intrinsic properties of the data rather than from variations in class composition.

Classification performance was evaluated on the test set of each dataset. A diverse set of indicators was used to provide a multidimensional view of the results, namely accuracy (Acc), balanced accuracy (BAcc), precision (Prec.), recall, F-measure (F.m.), and geometric mean (G-mean). In general, accuracy expresses how many observations were correctly assigned to their true categories. When focusing on specific classes, precision measures the correctness of positive predictions, while recall indicates the proportion of real class members that were successfully detected. Their joint behavior is captured by the F-measure, calculated as the harmonic mean of these two quantities:

$$\text{F-measure} = 2 \cdot \frac{\text{Precision} \cdot \text{Recall}}{\text{Precision} + \text{Recall}}. \tag{6}$$

Since the analyzed datasets differ in class distribution, additional measures were incorporated. Balanced accuracy summarizes the average recall obtained for all classes, while G-mean evaluates the uniformity of performance, rewarding models that achieve comparable recall across categories.

The experiments were structured according to the main principles of the proposed framework, and consisted of the following steps:

- Creation of coalitions among local decision tables;
- Training decision tree models using the data combined within each coalition;
- Construction of prediction vectors for training and test instances with reference to the built decision trees;
- Generation of class-specific decision templates;
- Final classification of test samples based on normalized Euclidean distance to the decision templates.

To provide a reference for performance evaluation, a baseline approach was also implemented. In this variant, conflict analysis and coalition formation were omitted, and each local table was used to train an independent decision tree model.

3. Results

This section presents the obtained results and their analysis. The evaluation is structured around three main aspects. The first part concerns the performance and execution time of the proposed method in comparison with the baseline approach, the second addresses its interpretability through the examination of the generated decision templates, and the third focuses on the findings in relation to those achieved for the rule-based variant of this framework [30].

3.1. Comparison with the Baseline Approach

As presented in Table 4, the proposed approach generally yields higher classification results than the baseline method. In the case of the Balance Scale dataset, results for 5 local tables are not included due to the absence of coalitions in this configuration. For other tested dispersion levels, the proposed framework consistently outperforms the baseline across all dispersion levels, achieving higher values in most evaluation metrics. This observation highlights the robustness of the method, which demonstrates stable and reliable predictive performance for this dataset.

In contrast, the findings for the remaining data collections reveal a more diverse pattern. While the proposed approach often surpasses the baseline, its performance varies with the level of data dispersion. The framework tends to produce stronger results under moderate dispersion, suggesting that coalition formation is particularly effective when each local table retains sufficient information for meaningful conflict analysis. Moreover, metrics such as F-measure and G-mean follow a similar trend, confirming that the proposed method provides more balanced predictions across decision classes. As the degree of dispersion increases and local tables become smaller and less representative, a slight decline in performance can be observed.

Table 4. Results of classification accuracy (Acc), balanced accuracy (BAcc), precision (Prec.), recall, F-measure (F-m.), and geometric mean (G-mean) for the proposed and baseline approaches across datasets and dispersion levels.

Dataset	# Local Tables	Proposed Approach Acc/BAcc/Prec./Recall/F-m./G-Mean	Baseline Approach Acc/BAcc/Prec./Recall/F-m./G-Mean
Balance Scale	7	**0.739**/0.627/0.819/0.739/0.772/0.816	0.670/0.633/0.866/0.670/0.741/0.791
	9	**0.686**/0.644/0.867/0.686/0.752/0.801	0.654/0.676/0.893/0.654/0.731/0.788
	11	**0.739**/0.738/0.889/0.739/0.791/0.838	0.670/0.688/0.902/0.670/0.746/0.800
Vehicle Silhouettes	5	**0.752**/0.745/0.751/0.752/0.750/0.832	0.693/0.675/0.688/0.693/0.688/0.791
	7	0.709/0.691/0.714/0.709/0.709/0.804	0.709/0.696/0.710/0.709/0.705/0.804
	9	**0.780**/0.766/0.786/0.780/0.781/0.853	0.760/0.750/0.770/0.760/0.756/0.840
	11	0.689/0.673/0.682/0.689/0.681/0.787	**0.717**/0.698/0.707/0.717/0.706/0.807
Car Evaluation	5	**0.767**/0.670/0.786/0.767/0.774/0.779	0.755/0.697/0.777/0.755/0.763/0.765
	7	**0.765**/0.750/0.792/0.765/0.773/0.782	0.742/0.741/0.782/0.742/0.753/0.775
	9	0.751/0.702/0.783/0.751/0.761/0.775	**0.769**/0.769/0.810/0.769/0.780/0.811
	11	0.757/0.760/0.795/0.757/0.768/0.791	**0.776**/0.797/0.823/0.776/0.787/0.822

Figure 2 presents box plots comparing the distribution of classification accuracy and F-measure for the proposed coalition-based approach and the approach without coalition formation. The plots reveal that the coalition-based method achieves higher median values for both metrics (0.751 for accuracy and 0.768 for F-measure) compared to the non-coalition variant (0.717 and 0.746, respectively). Moreover, the interquartile range for the proposed approach is narrower, indicating greater stability and less variability across different data dispersion scenarios. The lower whisker for the non-coalition approach extends to substantially smaller values, suggesting that this method is more sensitive to unfavorable configurations of distributed data.

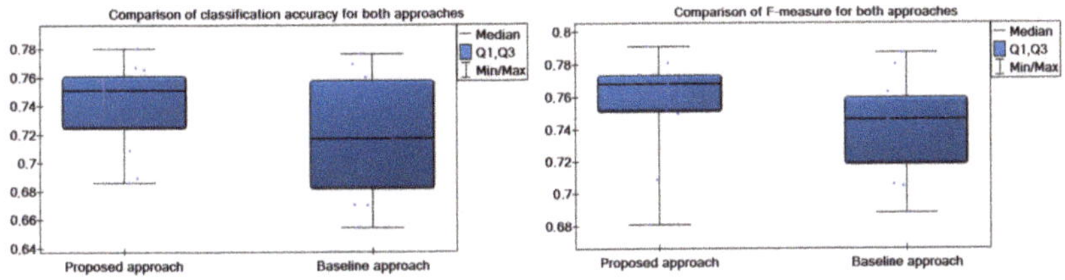

Figure 2. Comparison of accuracy and F-measure obtained for the proposed and the baseline approaches.

Additionally, to complement the theoretical complexity analysis, the execution time of the proposed framework was compared with that of the baseline model. All computations were performed on a portable computer equipped with an AMD Ryzen 5 4600H processor, 32 GB RAM and Microsoft Windows 11. The algorithms were implemented in Python. Table 5 reports the exact running times (in seconds) for all three datasets and dispersion levels. Across all configurations, the proposed method consistently runs faster than the baseline, with differences becoming more pronounced as the number of local tables increases. These results demonstrate that, despite the exponential worst-case complexity of coalition formation, the observed runtime stays within practical limits for all tested settings (up to 11 local tables).

Table 5. Execution time (in seconds) of the proposed and baseline approaches across datasets and dispersion levels.

Dataset	# Local Tables	Proposed Approach	Baseline Approach
Balance Scale	7	**1.975**	3.555
	9	**2.980**	4.077
	11	**2.678**	5.003
Vehicle Silhouettes	5	**3.181**	3.889
	7	**3.262**	5.211
	9	**3.327**	6.400
	11	**2.848**	7.747
Car Evaluation	5	**5.756**	6.951
	7	**8.209**	9.213
	9	**9.367**	11.977
	11	**10.904**	14.278

3.2. Interpretability Analysis

An important feature of the proposed approach is its interpretability, which allows for a detailed examination of how individual local models contribute to the final class assignment. This property makes it possible to identify patterns of specialization and the impact of coalition-based aggregation. To illustrate this aspect and provide a clearer insight into the behavior of the ensemble framework, Tables 6–8 present exemplary decision templates corresponding to one selected dispersion level for each dataset. The configurations were chosen based on the largest observed difference in classification accuracy between the proposed and baseline approaches, making them the most informative for further analysis. Specifically, the templates were obtained for the following numbers of local tables: 7 for Balance Scale, 5 for Vehicle Silhouettes, and 7 for Car Evaluation. In the tables, decision templates are denoted by the class labels (e.g., DT_B for class B), which are denoted as DT_i in Equation (3). Each local model CT_j^{aggr} is derived, in the proposed approach, from the

Table 8. Decision templates for the Car Evaluation dataset (7 local tables) for the proposed and baseline approaches. The values in the columns p(class) represent the averaged class membership probabilities $\mu_{j,i}(x)$ for each local model.

Proposed Approach					
Decision Template	**Local Model**	***p*(acc)**	***p*(Good)**	***p*(unacc)**	***p*(vgood)**
DT_{acc}	CT_1^{aggr}	0.704	0.019	0.277	0.000
	CT_2^{aggr}	0.692	0.017	0.280	0.011
	CT_3^{aggr}	0.652	0.017	0.314	0.017
	CT_4^{aggr}	0.599	0.041	0.346	0.015
	CT_5^{aggr}	0.599	0.043	0.325	0.033
	CT_6^{aggr}	0.665	0.032	0.281	0.022
DT_{good}	CT_1^{aggr}	0.229	0.510	0.219	0.042
	CT_2^{aggr}	0.219	0.552	0.208	0.021
	CT_3^{aggr}	0.104	0.549	0.285	0.062
	CT_4^{aggr}	0.292	0.458	0.229	0.021
	CT_5^{aggr}	0.188	0.469	0.240	0.104
	CT_6^{aggr}	0.104	0.490	0.240	0.167
DT_{unacc}	CT_1^{aggr}	0.093	0.010	0.890	0.007
	CT_2^{aggr}	0.097	0.009	0.882	0.011
	CT_3^{aggr}	0.077	0.009	0.896	0.018
	CT_4^{aggr}	0.119	0.019	0.845	0.017
	CT_5^{aggr}	0.103	0.014	0.870	0.014
	CT_6^{aggr}	0.135	0.005	0.836	0.024
DT_{vgood}	CT_1^{aggr}	0.122	0.000	0.278	0.600
	CT_2^{aggr}	0.022	0.044	0.278	0.656
	CT_3^{aggr}	0.022	0.067	0.144	0.767
	CT_4^{aggr}	0.311	0.044	0.267	0.378
	CT_5^{aggr}	0.000	0.222	0.156	0.622
	CT_6^{aggr}	0.111	0.233	0.167	0.489
Baseline Approach					
Decision Template	**Local Model**	***p*(acc)**	***p*(Good)**	***p*(unacc)**	***p*(vgood)**
DT_{acc}	CT_1	0.599	0.041	0.346	0.015
	CT_2	0.558	0.024	0.392	0.026
	CT_3	0.665	0.032	0.281	0.022
	CT_4	0.550	0.056	0.394	0.000
	CT_5	0.654	0.071	0.268	0.007
	CT_6	0.617	0.098	0.285	0.000
	CT_7	0.599	0.043	0.325	0.033
DT_{good}	CT_1	0.292	0.458	0.229	0.021
	CT_2	0.271	0.458	0.271	0.000
	CT_3	0.104	0.490	0.240	0.167
	CT_4	0.208	0.479	0.271	0.042
	CT_5	0.271	0.521	0.125	0.083
	CT_6	0.229	0.444	0.243	0.083
	CT_7	0.188	0.469	0.240	0.104
DT_{unacc}	CT_1	0.119	0.019	0.845	0.017
	CT_2	0.083	0.006	0.901	0.009
	CT_3	0.135	0.005	0.836	0.024
	CT_4	0.164	0.015	0.812	0.008
	CT_5	0.112	0.030	0.849	0.009
	CT_6	0.133	0.015	0.837	0.014
	CT_7	0.103	0.014	0.870	0.014
DT_{vgood}	CT_1	0.311	0.044	0.267	0.378
	CT_2	0.178	0.222	0.289	0.311
	CT_3	0.111	0.233	0.167	0.489
	CT_4	0.178	0.000	0.289	0.533
	CT_5	0.311	0.044	0.133	0.511
	CT_6	0.200	0.111	0.156	0.533
	CT_7	0.000	0.222	0.156	0.622

As can be observed for the Balance Scale dataset, the most noticeable difference between the two approaches appears in the decision template corresponding to class B. In the baseline approach, none of the local models assign the highest probability to this class; instead, the dominant probabilities are associated with other classes. In contrast, in the proposed approach, CT_1^{aggr} clearly indicates class B with the highest probability (0.588), demonstrating the emergence of a localized specialization for this class. This effect is directly linked to the coalition underlying CT_1^{aggr}, which aggregates information from multiple local tables and strengthens the model's ability to capture class-specific patterns. For the templates DT_L and DT_R, both approaches show generally consistent results. However, the proposed approach produces sharper probability peaks (e.g., 0.955 for CT_1^{aggr} in DT_R compared to 0.871 for CT_5 in the baseline), reflecting stronger class assignment within coalitions. For the Vehicle Silhouettes dataset, the proposed approach also reinforces class assignment, but the differences between the two approaches are more subtle. This is due to the fact that only one coalition is multi-table, while the remaining coalitions consist of single tables. Notably, for the Car Evaluation dataset, more pronounced enhancement effects are observed, particularly for the templates corresponding to classes vgood and good, where the average probability increases from 0.482 to 0.585 and from 0.474 to 0.505, respectively.

These observations confirm that the decision templates offer a transparent perspective, highlighting the role of coalition structures in shaping the final classification outcomes. In the baseline approach, each model is trained on an individual local table, which may lead to fragmented class patterns. In contrast, coalition-based models, built on merged and compatible data sources, capture more coherent decision tendencies, resulting in clearer and more stable class-related behaviors, thus improving interpretability.

3.3. Comparison with Rule-Based Models

To better understand the effect of the chosen local modeling strategy, the proposed tree-based approach was also compared with its variant relying on decision rule induction [30]. Table 9 summarizes the classification results obtained with rule-based models for each dataset and dispersion level. These results come directly from [30], which used the same datasets as in the present study. In that work, four rule induction algorithms were considered: the exhaustive search algorithm, the covering algorithm, the genetic algorithm, and LEM2. For each configuration, the method achieving the highest classification accuracy was selected and reported in the table. The abbreviations Exh and Gen refer to the exhaustive search and genetic algorithms, respectively, while Exh/Gen indicates identical results for both methods. The last column, ΔAcc, shows the difference in accuracy (in percentage points) between the proposed tree-based framework and its rule-based counterparts. Positive values indicate that the tree-based approach outperformed the rule-based variant, whereas negative values correspond to the opposite case. For the Balance Scale dataset, results for 5 local tables are again not included due to the absence of coalitions in this configuration.

A closer look at the results reveals that the use of decision trees as local models often leads to better classification performance compared to rule-based models. The most evident differences are observed for the Vehicle Silhouettes and Car Evaluation datasets under moderate dispersion levels. In these configurations, higher values of ΔAcc are obtained–for instance, for Vehicle with 9 local tables, the accuracy increases by 0.079, corresponding to an 11.27% relative gain. In addition, the improvements are also visible in other evaluation metrics, including G-mean, balanced accuracy, and F-measure. For Vehicle, these effects appear across most dispersion levels (e.g., an increase in G-mean from 0.797 to 0.853 for 9 local tables), and for Car, particularly at lower dispersion levels, with G-mean improving in all tested configurations. These tendencies suggest that decision trees adapt better to the underlying structure of the data, resulting in more balanced predictions across decision classes. This, in turn, strengthens the coalition-based framework by improving its overall classification reliability, especially under favorable dispersion conditions.

Table 9. Results of classification accuracy (Acc), balanced accuracy (BAcc), precision (Prec.), recall, F-measure (F-m.), and geometric mean (G-mean) for the coalition approach using decision rule models across datasets and dispersion levels, as reported in [30].

Dataset	# Local Tables	Best Rule Induction Method	Acc/BAcc/Prec./Recall/F-m./G-Mean	ΔAcc
Balance Scale	7	Exh/Gen	0.745/0.742/0.890/0.745/0.795/0.841	−0.006
	9	Exh/Gen	0.686/0.681/0.856/0.686/0.745/0.798	0.000
	11	Exh/Gen	0.697/0.670/0.863/0.697/0.756/0.806	**+0.042**
Vehicle Silhouettes	5	Exh	0.713/0.700/0.711/0.713/0.706/0.803	**+0.039**
	7	Exh	0.701/0.686/0.697/0.701/0.693/0.796	**+0.008**
	9	Exh	0.701/0.695/0.707/0.701/0.693/0.797	**+0.079**
	11	Gen	0.701/0.690/0.706/0.701/0.696/0.796	−0.012
Car Evaluation	5	Gen	0.744/0.674/0.761/0.744/0.750/0.745	**+0.023**
	7	Exh/Gen	0.748/0.641/0.760/0.748/0.752/0.743	**+0.017**
	9	Exh/Gen	0.765/0.726/0.786/0.765/0.772/0.774	−0.014
	11	Exh/Gen	0.765/0.758/0.790/0.765/0.773/0.783	−0.008

4. Discussion

The experimental results demonstrate that the proposed tree-based framework often achieves better classification performance compared to both the baseline approach and the rule-based variant. The improvements are most visible when the local tables preserve enough informative structure to enable meaningful collaboration between models. This cooperation allows the models to better exploit complementary knowledge available across local sources. These outcomes highlight the potential of coalition-based mechanisms to enhance the robustness of the classification process and support more balanced and reliable decision-making in distributed data settings.

A key factor behind this improvement is the way coalition formation increases the representativeness of the training data and, consequently, the reliability of the classification process. By aggregating similar local tables into larger coalitions, the method reduces the negative impact of limited sample size and local variability. As a result, the decision tree models can better capture underlying patterns and improve their generalization capability. The use of decision templates also provides a clear and interpretable view of how coalition-level models contribute to the final classification outcome. This is particularly valuable in scenarios where transparency and explainability are essential.

Another important observation concerns the method's behavior under different levels of data dispersion. The best results are achieved mainly at moderate dispersion, where the balance between local variability and shared structure is optimal for coalition formation. At this level, local tables contain enough distinct yet complementary information to make aggregation meaningful, while not being too fragmented to undermine the learning process. As dispersion increases, the representativeness of individual tables decreases, which naturally limits the gains from aggregation. In such settings, the performance of the method declines, but in a predictable manner, reflecting the reduced informational value of the local sources. Although other approaches may outperform it at the highest dispersion level, the proposed strategy maintains a reasonable level of effectiveness, highlighting its robustness to data fragmentation. These observations are consistent with information theory principles: lower uncertainty enables more efficient knowledge integration, while higher entropy constraints the capacity for meaningful collaboration between distributed models.

Although this study focuses exclusively on the Gini index, future work will explore the use of alternative splitting criteria such as entropy and twoing. These criteria may offer different insights into data structure and classification performance, particularly in the context of dispersed data. Comparative experiments involving multiple impurity measures could help identify optimal strategies for specific data distributions and application domains. Such extensions would enhance the generalizability and adaptability of the proposed approach.

An additional factor contributing to the effectiveness of the approach is the use of decision trees as local models. Their ability to capture complex relationships and produce well-structured decision boundaries enhances the quality of the coalition aggregation, leading to more coherent and informative decision templates. This suggests that the selection of flexible and expressive local models can play a crucial role in maximizing the benefits of coalition-based mechanisms in distributed classification settings.

Despite these promising results, the proposed approach has several limitations that should be acknowledged. First, its effectiveness depends on the number and size of the local tables. When the tables become too small or unbalanced, the benefits of coalition formation are reduced. Second, the method introduces an additional computational overhead associated with building and maintaining coalition structures, which may become relevant for large-scale applications. Although the theoretical complexity grows exponentially with the number of local tables, the empirical results (Section 3.1) indicate that the execution time remains reasonable even for the largest tested configuration (11 local tables). This suggests that the proposed approach is computationally feasible in moderately distributed environments and that its practical scalability is more favorable than implied by the theoretical analysis. Third, the current evaluation was conducted on a limited number of datasets and controlled data partitioning scenarios. Although these benchmark datasets allow for a transparent and interpretable assessment of the framework's behavior, more complex, noisy, or domain-specific data will be considered in future work, as they are likely to require further methodological refinement to ensure scalability and robustness.

From a practical perspective, the proposed coalition-based framework may be particularly beneficial in scenarios where data are inherently fragmented or decentralized. Such settings frequently occur in areas where direct data integration is difficult or impossible due to technical, organizational, or legal constraints. By enabling more effective aggregation of knowledge from multiple sources without requiring full data centralization, the approach provides a flexible solution for improving classification performance in distributed environments. Furthermore, the use of decision templates supports a higher level of interpretability, which can be advantageous in domains where transparency and explainability are critical, such as healthcare, finance, or business.

5. Conclusions

This work introduced a distributed data classification method that integrates conflict analysis, coalition formation, decision tree induction, and decision template fusion. The proposed framework enables knowledge to be combined from multiple sources while keeping the resulting model transparent and effective across data sources. Furthermore, by utilizing the Gini index to maximize information gain during tree induction and employing Decision Templates to minimize decision entropy during final fusion, this framework offers a methodology that is deeply rooted in information theory for uncertainty management in decentralized systems.

The approach was experimentally evaluated on three benchmark datasets from the UCI Machine Learning Repository: Balance Scale, Vehicle Silhouettes, and Car Evaluation. Its performance was compared with a baseline method that does not involve coalition formation as well as with a rule-based variant proposed in previous work by the authors. The results demonstrated that the proposed method often achieved better classification performance, with the improvement observed at moderate levels of data dispersion. In addition, the study also analyzed the generated decision templates, showing that they strengthen the specialization of class predictions and provide a transparent representation of coalition-level behavior.

The proposed coalition-based approach provides a practical and transparent way to integrate distributed knowledge through partial aggregation of local data, without requiring full centralization. This makes it particularly relevant in domains such as healthcare, finance, or business, where information is often fragmented across multiple independent entities. By supporting more coherent and explainable decision-making, the method has the potential to address key challenges associated with decentralized data environments.

Future research will focus on extending the proposed approach to scenarios in which local tables are defined over partially different feature sets. Such an extension will make it possible to evaluate the robustness and adaptability of coalition-based mechanisms under more realistic and heterogeneous data conditions.

Author Contributions: Conceptualization, K.K. and M.P.-K.; methodology, K.K. and M.P.-K.; software, K.K.; validation, K.K.; formal analysis, K.K. and M.P.-K.; investigation, K.K. and M.P.-K.; writing—original draft preparation, K.K.; writing—review and editing, K.K. and M.P.-K.; visualization, K.K. and M.P.-K.; supervision, M.P.-K. All authors have read and agreed to the published version of the manuscript.

Funding: This research received no external funding.

Institutional Review Board Statement: Not applicable.

Informed Consent Statement: Not applicable.

Data Availability Statement: Publicly available datasets were analyzed in this study. These data can be found at the UCI Machine Learning Repository [37].

Conflicts of Interest: The authors declare no conflicts of interest.

References

1. Pękala, B.; Kosior, D.; Rząsa, W.; Garwol, K.; Czuma, J. Unique Method for Prognosis of Risk of Depressive Episodes Using Novel Measures to Model Uncertainty Under Data Privacy. *Entropy* **2025**, *27*, 162. [CrossRef]
2. Bentkowska, U.; Gałka, W.; Mrukowicz, M.; Wojtowicz, A. Ensemble Classifier Based on Interval Modeling for Microarray Datasets. *Entropy* **2024**, *26*, 240. [CrossRef]
3. Bollaert, H.; Palangetić, M.; Cornelis, C.; Greco, S.; Słowiński, R. FRRI: A novel algorithm for fuzzy-rough rule induction. *Inf. Sci.* **2025**, *686*, 121362. [CrossRef]
4. Durdymyradov, K.; Moshkov, M. Deterministic and Nondeterministic Decision Trees for Recognition of Properties of Decision Rule Systems. In *International Joint Conference on Rough Sets*; Springer Nature: Cham, Switzerland, 2025; pp. 426–435.
5. Faliszewski, P.; Gawron, G.; Kusek, B. Robustness of approval-based multiwinner voting rules. *Rev. Econ. Des.* **2025**, 1–37. [CrossRef]
6. Rudin, C. Stop explaining black box machine learning models for high stakes decisions and use interpretable models instead. *Nat. Mach. Intell.* **2019**, *1*, 206–215. [CrossRef] [PubMed]
7. Pouyanfar, S.; Sadiq, S.; Yan, Y.; Tian, H.; Tao, Y.; Reyes, M.P.; Shyu, M.L.; Chen, S.C.; Iyengar, S.S. A survey on deep learning: Algorithms, techniques, and applications. *ACM Comput. Surv. (CSUR)* **2018**, *51*, 1–36. [CrossRef]
8. Krawczyk, B.; Minku, L.L.; Gama, J.; Stefanowski, J.; Woźniak, M. Ensemble learning for data stream analysis: A survey. *Inf. Fusion* **2017**, *37*, 132–156. [CrossRef]
9. Yang, Y.; Lv, H.; Chen, N. A survey on ensemble learning under the era of deep learning. *Artif. Intell. Rev.* **2023**, *56*, 5545–5589. [CrossRef]
10. Dyczkowski, K.; Pękala, B.; Szkoła, J.; Wilbik, A. Federated learning with uncertainty on the example of a medical data. In Proceedings of the IEEE International Conference on Fuzzy Systems (FUZZ-IEEE), Padua, Italy, 18–23 July 2022; IEEE: Piscataway, NJ, USA, 2022; pp. 1–8.
11. Saeed, N.; Ashour, M.; Mashaly, M. Comprehensive review of federated learning challenges: A data preparation viewpoint. *J. Big Data* **2025**, *12*, 153. [CrossRef]

12. Valmadre, J. Hierarchical classification at multiple operating points. *Adv. Neural Inf. Process. Syst.* **2022**, *35*, 18034–18045.
13. Dempster, A.P. Upper and lower probabilities induced by a multivalued mapping. *Ann. Math. Stat.* **1967**, *38*, 325–339. [CrossRef]
14. Shafer, G. *A Mathematical Theory of Evidence*; Princeton University Press: Princeton, NJ, USA, 1976.
15. Huo, Z.; Martínez-García, M.; Zhang, Y.; Shu, L. A multisensor information fusion method for high-reliability fault diagnosis of rotating machinery. *IEEE Trans. Instrum. Meas.* **2021**, *71*, 1–12. [CrossRef]
16. Pan, Y.; Zhang, L.; Li, Z.; Ding, L. Improved fuzzy Bayesian network-based risk analysis with interval-valued fuzzy sets and D-S evidence theory. *IEEE Trans. Fuzzy Syst.* **2020**, *28*, 2063–2077. [CrossRef]
17. Tang, Y.; Wu, K.; Li, R.; Guan, H.; Zhou, D.; Huang, Y. Probabilistic transformation of basic probability assignment based on weighted visibility graph networks. *Appl. Soft Comput.* **2025**, *184*, 113821. [CrossRef]
18. Smets, P.; Kennes, R. The transferable belief model. *Artif. Intell.* **1994**, *66*, 191–234. [CrossRef]
19. Han, D.; Dezert, J.; Han, C.; Yang, Y. Is entropy enough to evaluate the probability transformation approach of belief function? In Proceedings of the 13th International Conference on Information Fusion, Edinburgh, UK, 26–29 July 2010; IEEE: Edinburgh, UK, 2010.
20. Li, M.; Zhang, Q.; Deng, Y. A new probability transformation based on the ordered visibility graph. *Int. J. Intell. Syst.* **2016**, *31*, 44–67 [CrossRef]
21. Chen, L.; Deng, Y.; Cheong, K.H. Probability transformation of mass function: A weighted network method based on the ordered visibility graph. *Eng. Appl. Artif. Intell.* **2021**, *105*, 104438. [CrossRef]
22. Jiroušek, R.; Shenoy, P.P. A new definition of entropy of belief functions in the Dempster–Shafer theory. *Int. J. Approx. Reason.* **2018**, *92*, 49–65. [CrossRef]
23. Pawlak, Z. An inquiry into anatomy of conflicts. *Inf. Sci.* **1998**, *109*, 65–78. [CrossRef]
24. Deja, R.; Ślęzak, D. Rough set theory in conflict analysis. In *Annual Conference of the Japanese Society for Artificial Intelligence*; Springer: Berlin/Heidelberg, Germany, 2001; pp. 349–353.
25. Yao, Y. Three-way decision and granular computing. *Int. J. Approx. Reason.* **2018**, *103*, 107–123. [CrossRef]
26. Sun, B.; Ma, W.; Zhao, H. Rough set-based conflict analysis model and method over two universes. *Inf. Sci.* **2016**, *372*, 111–125. [CrossRef]
27. Przybyła-Kasperek, M.; Deja, R.; Wakulicz-Deja, A. Hierarchical system in conflict scenarios constructed based on cluster analysis-inspired method for attribute significance determination. *Appl. Soft Comput.* **2024**, *167*, 112304. [CrossRef]
28. Kuncheva, L.I.; Bezdek, J.C.; Duin, R.P. Decision templates for multiple classifier fusion: An experimental comparison. *Pattern Recognit.* **2001**, *34*, 299–314. [CrossRef]
29. Przybyła-Kasperek, M.; Kusztal, K. Integrating Conflict Analysis and Rule-Based Systems for Dispersed Data Classification. In Proceedings of the ICCS 2025 Conference, Singapore, 24–26 June 2025; Springer: Cham, Switzerland, 2025.
30. Kusztal, K.; Przybyła-Kasperek, M. Coalition-Based Rule Induction and Decision Template Matching for Distributed Tabular Data. In Proceedings of the ISD 2025 Conference, Belgrade, Serbia, 3–5 September 2025; AIS eLibrary: Belgrade, Serbia, 2025.
31. Przybyła-Kasperek, M.; Kusztal, K.; Addo, B.A. Dispersed Data Classification Model with Conflict Analysis and Parameterized Allied Relations. *Procedia Comput. Sci.* **2024**, *246*, 2215–2224. [CrossRef]
32. Mienye, I.D.; Jere, N. A survey of decision trees: Concepts, algorithms, and applications. *IEEE Access* **2024**, *12*, 86716–86727. [CrossRef]
33. Aning, S.; Przybyła-Kasperek, M. Comparative study of twoing and entropy Criterion for decision tree classification of dispersed data. *Procedia Comput. Sci.* **2022**, *207*, 2434–2443. [CrossRef]
34. Pedregosa, F.; Varoquaux, G.; Gramfort, A.; Michel, V.; Thirion, B.; Grisel, O.; Blondel, M.; Prettenhofer, P.; Weiss, R.; Dubourg, V.; et al. Scikit-learn: Machine Learning in Python. *J. Mach. Learn. Res.* **2011**, *12*, 2825–2830.
35. Siebert, J.P. *Vehicle Recognition Using Rule Based Methods*; Turing Institute: London, UK, 1987.
36. Bohanec, M.; Rajkovič, V. Knowledge acquisition and explanation for multi-attribute decision making. In Proceedings of the 8th International Workshop on Expert Systems and their Applications, Avignon, France, 30 May–3 June 1988.
37. Dua, D.; Graff, C. *UCI Machine Learning Repository*; University of California, School of Information and Computer Science: Irvine, CA, USA, 2019.

entropy

MDPI

Article

Entropy and Normalization in MCDA: A Data-Driven Perspective on Ranking Stability

Ewa Roszkowska

Faculty of Computer Science, Bialystok University of Technology, Wiejska 45A, 15-351 Bialystok, Poland; e.roszkowska@pb.edu.pl

Abstract

Normalization is a critical step in Multiple-Criteria Decision Analysis (MCDA) because it transforms heterogeneous criterion values into comparable information. This study examines normalization techniques through the lens of entropy, highlighting how criterion data structure shapes normalization behavior and ranking stability within TOPSIS (Technique for Order Preference by Similarity to Ideal Solution). Seven widely used normalization procedures are analyzed regarding mathematical properties, sensitivity to extreme values, treatment of benefit and cost criteria, and rank reversal. Normalization is treated as a source of uncertainty in MCDA outcomes, as different schemes can produce divergent rankings under identical decision settings. Shannon entropy is employed as a descriptive measure of information dispersion and structural uncertainty, capturing the heterogeneity and discriminatory potential of criteria rather than serving as a weighting mechanism. An illustrative experiment with ten alternatives and four criteria (two high-entropy, two low-entropy) demonstrates how entropy mediates normalization effects. Seven normalization schemes are examined, including vector, max, linear Sum, and max–min procedures. For vector, max, and linear sum, cost-type criteria are treated using either linear inversion or reciprocal transformation, whereas max–min is implemented as a single method. This design separates the choice of normalization form from the choice of cost-criteria transformation, allowing a cleaner identification of their respective contributions to ranking variability. The analysis shows that normalization choice alone can cause substantial differences in preference values and rankings. High-entropy criteria tend to yield stable rankings, whereas low-entropy criteria amplify sensitivity, especially with extreme or cost-type data. These findings position entropy as a key mediator linking data structure with normalization-induced ranking variability and highlight the need to consider entropy explicitly when selecting normalization procedures. Finally, a practical entropy-based method for choosing normalization techniques is introduced to enhance methodological transparency and ranking robustness in MCDA.

Keywords: Multiple-Criteria Decision Analysis; normalization techniques; TOPSIS; entropy; ranking stability; rank reversal; data distribution; cost and benefit criteria; uncertainty

1. Introduction

Multiple-Criteria Decision Analysis (MCDA) is a fundamental methodological framework for evaluating and ranking alternatives characterized by multiple, often conflicting criteria [1,2]. MCDA has been widely applied in the social sciences, including economics, management, business, finance, and public policy [3–7], among others.

The MCDA process typically includes constructing a decision matrix, normalizing criteria, weighting, and aggregating into a final preference score [1,8]. Among these steps, normalization is pivotal. It allows for a comparison of criteria measured on different scales and directly affects both the stability and interpretability of ranking results [9,10]. Normalization is not a trivial methodological choice but a decision-analytic component with substantive implications. Normalization interacts with the intrinsic characteristics of the data. This interaction can further influence ranking outcomes. Criteria with larger magnitudes or broader numerical ranges may disproportionately affect aggregation results if normalization is inadequately selected. This can lead to biased rankings and potentially misleading decisions [11–14].

Consequently, normalization is increasingly viewed not merely as a technical preprocessing step, but as a decision-analytic component with substantive implications for ranking outcomes, robustness, and rank reversal phenomena [15–18]. In this sense, normalization contributes to decision-making uncertainty, since alternative normalization procedures may generate different rankings even when all other elements of the MCDA model remain unchanged. This highlights uncertainty as an inherent methodological feature of MCDA rather than simply stemming from data constraints.

Over the past two decades, a substantial body of research has examined normalization techniques in MCDA, addressing their formal properties [11,19], effects on rankings [20–22], and robustness across decision contexts [15,23–25]. Despite its recognized importance, the choice of normalization technique in many MCDA applications is rarely theoretically justified, and sensitivity analyses with respect to normalization are often omitted or only superficially discussed.

Entropy, introduced by Shannon [26], quantifies uncertainty or dispersion within a dataset. In this study, uncertainty is understood in a structural sense, arising from the informational heterogeneity of criterion data and its interaction with normalization procedures. In MCDA, entropy is often employed as an objective weighting technique. Criteria with higher variability and lower entropy are assigned higher weights. Criteria with more uniform values receive lower weights [27,28]. Extensions such as Tsallis [29] and Rényi entropy [30] have been proposed to handle incomplete, noisy, or highly complex decision data. Beyond weighting, entropy provides insight into the structural properties of criterion data. It reflects the intrinsic informational content of a criterion and distinguishes between low-entropy criteria, which exhibit pronounced disparities and high discriminatory potential, and high-entropy criteria, which show near-uniform values and limited discrimination power. This distinction is particularly important for normalization, as different techniques respond differently to data dispersion, extreme values, and skewness.

Despite extensive research, a methodological gap remains: the role of entropy as a mediator between data structure and normalization behavior has not been systematically examined. Specifically, it is unclear how criteria with different entropy levels respond to various normalization procedures and how this interaction affects ranking robustness.

This study addresses this gap by providing a structured theoretical and empirical analysis of normalization techniques in MCDA, explicitly considering the influence of criterion entropy on normalization outcomes. Rather than using entropy as a weighting mechanism, we treat it as a descriptive measure of data distribution, which helps explain and interpret the behavior of normalized values and resulting rankings.

This study addresses the following research question:

How does the entropy level of criterion data influence the behavior of different normalization techniques and the resulting ranking stability in MCDA methods such as TOPSIS?

Normalization techniques are not distribution-neutral transformations. Their effects depend critically on the underlying data structure, particularly on the degree of dispersion

https://doi.org/10.3390/e28010114

and the presence of extreme values. Ranking stability is understood here as the consistency of alternative ordering under different normalization techniques, measured through rank correlation and rank reversal analysis.

To illustrate the proposed framework, an empirical experiment is conducted using a decision matrix of ten alternatives and four criteria, comprising two high-entropy and two low-entropy criteria. Seven widely used normalization procedures are applied, including vector normalization, max normalization, linear sum normalization, linear cost inversion, reciprocal cost transformation, and linear max–min normalization. Cost-type criteria are handled according to the specific formulation of each normalization method. This controlled example allows for examining how entropy and cost treatment interact with normalization, providing a practical context for the theoretical analysis without implying that the observed effects are universally generalizable.

This study contributes to the literature in several ways. First, it synthesizes existing normalization research by organizing methods according to their mathematical properties and sensitivity to data distribution. Second, it introduces entropy as a unifying descriptive concept linking raw data structure with normalization behavior and ranking stability. Third, it provides a systematic comparative analysis of selected normalization techniques and illustrates their effects through an empirical example based on TOPSIS (Technique for Order Preference by Similarity to Ideal Solution) [8]. TOPSIS was chosen due to its popularity and extensive application across various decision-making contexts [8,31,32]. Originally developed with vector normalization, TOPSIS has since been extended with alternative normalization methods to enhance ranking consistency and discriminatory power [33]. Moreover, this study develops a conceptual link between entropy, data distribution, and normalization behavior. It demonstrates that normalization is not distribution-neutral and that entropy mediates its impact on ranking stability. These contributions advance methodological transparency and offer practical guidance for selecting normalization procedures in entropy-diverse decision problems.

The paper is organized as follows. Section 2 introduces entropy as a descriptor of the criterion data distribution. Section 3 presents a detailed theoretical analysis of selected normalization techniques and their properties. Sections 4 and 5 provides an illustrative empirical example using TOPSIS. Section 6 concludes with a discussion of findings and directions for future research.

2. Entropy in Multiple-Criteria Decision Analysis

2.1. *Shannon Entropy as a Descriptor of Criterion Information*

Entropy, a fundamental concept from information theory introduced by Shannon [26], quantifies uncertainty, disorder, or information content in a system. In MCDA, it characterizes the distributional structure and uncertainty inherent in criterion values across alternatives. From this perspective, entropy captures the uncertainty inherent in criterion distributions, which affects the stability of normalized rankings. Unlike classical dispersion measures such as variance or range, which focus on the spread of values around the mean and largely depend on their magnitude, entropy captures the evenness of the distribution. In other words, entropy evaluates how uniformly values are distributed across categories or alternatives, regardless of their absolute size. This allows entropy to reveal subtle differences in the structure of the data that may remain hidden when using traditional dispersion measures [34]. Such characteristics make entropy particularly useful in MCDA, as it helps to better capture the relative differences among criteria and alternatives, where decision matrices involve heterogeneous criteria in different units and diverse data distributions [8,35,36].

https://doi.org/10.3390/e28010114

Let a decision problem consist of m alternatives $A_1, A_2, \ldots, A_m$ evaluated with respect to n criteria $C_1, C_2, \ldots, C_n$. The decision matrix is denoted as

$$D = [x_{ij}], \tag{1}$$

where x_{ij} represents the performance of alternative A_i under criterion C_j.

To evaluate the informational structure of a given criterion, the original values are transformed into non-negative proportions:

$$p_{ij} = \frac{x_{ij}}{\sum_i^m x_{ij}} (i = 1, 2 \ldots, m;\ j = 1, 2, \ldots n). \tag{2}$$

This formulation implicitly assumes non-negative criterion values and reflects relative rather than absolute performance differences.

The Shannon entropy of criterion C_j is defined as:

$$E_j = -\frac{1}{\ln m} \sum_{i=1}^m p_{ij} \ln p_{ij},\ j = 1, 2, \ldots, n. \tag{3}$$

Here, the factor $-\frac{1}{\ln m}$ serves as a normalization factor, ensuring that the entropy value E_j lies in the range $[0, 1]$.

High entropy values indicate a relatively uniform distribution, implying limited discriminatory power. Low entropy reflects stronger dispersion and higher informational content. When $x_{ij} = 0$, the term $p_{ij} \ln p_{ij} = 0$ is conventionally assumed to be zero. To avoid zero values in practical applications, Ref. [28] proposed a modified formulation that introduces a small positive constant C, ensuring strictly positive proportions.

Entropy measures the informational capacity of a criterion to differentiate alternatives rather than its importance or preference weight. This distinction is crucial in methodological studies that aim to analyze the behavior of MCDA models under varying data structures, independently of decision-maker preferences [13,25].

Several generalized entropy measures have been proposed to capture uncertainty under different assumptions, including Rényi entropy [30], Tsallis entropy [29], and fuzzy entropy [37]. These formulations differ in sensitivity to extreme values, tail behavior, and dominance effects, and have been applied in MCDA to address incomplete, noisy, or non-extensive data environments [36,38]. Despite these developments, Shannon entropy remains widely used for its strong theoretical foundation, simplicity, intuitive interpretation, and lack of tuning parameters, enhancing transparency and reproducibility. Accordingly, this study adopts it as a representative measure of criterion data dispersion.

2.2. Entropy-Based Weighting: Applications and Limitations

In MCDA literature, entropy is most commonly employed as an objective weighting technique, referred to as the entropy weight method (EWM). The underlying assumption is that criteria exhibiting greater variability (lower entropy) contain more decision-relevant information and should therefore receive higher weights, whereas criteria with more uniform values (higher entropy) contribute less information and are assigned lower weights. This approach reduces the influence of subjective judgment [29,36,39,40].

Two computational schemes are commonly used for EWM: direct entropy estimation from the original criterion values and entropy estimation following normalization, typically using max–min scaling. The choice between these approaches affects the resulting entropy values and criterion weights [13,41].

The EWM has been widely applied across a broad range of domains, including management-oriented analyses [42], financial performance evaluation [43], environmen-

https://doi.org/10.3390/e28010114

tal quality assessment [44], sustainable energy systems [45,46], water resources management [47], facility and location selection problems [48], urban air quality evaluation [49], and tourism performance analysis [46,50]. In these studies, EWM is frequently integrated with established multi-criteria methods such as TOPSIS, VIKOR (VIekriterijumsko KOmpromisno Rangiranje), AHP (Analytic Hierarchy Process), COPRAS (Complex Proportional Assessment), and others, to support objective criterion weighting and ranking.

The entropy method, commonly applied for objective weight determination [51], exhibits several limitations. It assumes that greater variability implies higher criterion importance, which may not reflect decision-makers' priorities, as criteria with low dispersion can still be essential in practice. As a result, entropy-based weights may inadequately represent strategic or policy-related relevance. In addition, entropy weights are sensitive to data preprocessing, particularly normalization and scaling procedures, which can substantially affect the resulting weight distribution. This sensitivity raises concerns regarding the robustness and reproducibility of results [13]. Moreover, the method assumes independence among criteria and does not account for potential interrelationships, which may distort importance assessment in complex decision contexts. Finally, the purely data-driven nature of entropy excludes expert judgment, suggesting that entropy-based weighting is more effective when combined with subjective or hybrid approaches rather than used as a standalone method [52–55].

These limitations motivate a broader interpretation of entropy beyond its traditional role in weighting and justify its use as a descriptive analytical tool in methodological MCDA research.

2.3. Entropy as a Descriptive Characteristic of Criterion Data Structure and Its Methodological Role in Normalization

Beyond weighting, entropy can be interpreted as a descriptive characteristic of the decision matrix, capturing the internal distribution of criterion values. From this perspective, entropy does not prescribe importance but provides a systematic explanation of:

- the inherent discriminatory power of the criteria before aggregation,
- similarities and differences in data structure across decision problems,
- the sensitivity of MCDA results to data characteristics rather than preferences.

This interpretation is particularly relevant in methodological studies focusing on normalization, ranking stability, and rank reversal, where the objective is to analyze how MCDA techniques respond to varying data conditions rather than to support a single decision-making case.

Normalization is a fundamental step in MCDA, transforming heterogeneous criteria into comparable, dimensionless scales. Since entropy captures the distributional structure of criterion values before normalization, it provides a natural framework for analyzing how normalization interacts with data characteristics. Different techniques respond differently to dispersion, skewness, and extreme values. Consequently, criteria with identical ranges but different entropy levels may produce substantially different normalized values and inter-alternative distances, even when the original matrix is unchanged. Importantly, entropy does not modify normalization formulas directly but influences outcomes indirectly through its interaction with the mathematical properties of the methods [11].

Entropy mediates the effects of normalization on ranking stability. By capturing the structural characteristics and inherent uncertainty of criterion distributions, entropy helps explain why alternative normalization schemes may produce different rankings, even when weights and decision-maker preferences remain unchanged. Consequently, joint consideration of entropy and normalization provides a theoretically grounded framework for evaluating ranking robustness in MCDA. This perspective directly motivates the em-

https://doi.org/10.3390/e28010114

pirical analysis that follows and underpins the comparative assessment of normalization techniques presented in the next section.

In this study, entropy is used solely as a descriptive measure of data structure, distinct from its traditional role in objective weighting in MCDM, to avoid potential confusion.

3. Normalization Techniques in MCDA—Overview and Conceptual Framework

3.1. Conceptual Foundations of Normalization in MCDA

Normalization is a fundamental preprocessing step in MCDA, transforming criterion values expressed in different units, ranges, or magnitudes into a common and comparable scale. Without proper normalization, criteria with larger numerical values may dominate aggregation results, regardless of their actual importance. Effective normalization, therefore, ensures balance, interpretability, and fairness in multi-criteria evaluation.

From a methodological perspective, normalization techniques can be broadly classified into vector, linear, and non-linear transformations [33]. Vector normalization scales criterion values with respect to the overall magnitude of observations for a given criterion, preserving relative proportions while accounting for differences in units. Linear normalization methods, such as max, max–min, and sum-based transformations, are widely used due to their simplicity, transparency, and ease of implementation. Non-linear normalization approaches, although less frequently applied, are particularly useful for data characterized by strong skewness, exponential growth, or logarithmic relationships, allowing for more flexible handling of extreme values.

In this study, seven normalization techniques commonly applied in MCDA are examined, with particular emphasis on their use within the TOPSIS framework (see Appendix A). Normalization methods have been applied in TOPSIS studies, depending on the authors and the problem context. Non-linear vector normalization has been used in two main variants: N1, applied in [11,25,56–58], and N2, used by [11,59]. Among linear normalization methods, the max method has been employed in variants N3 [23,25,57,59] and N4 [11,58]. The max–min method (N5) has been used in [11,25,59]. Finally, the sum method has been applied in variants N6 [23,58] and N7 [25,57,59].

Each normalization procedure explicitly distinguishes between benefit and cost criteria. A criterion is classified as a benefit criterion when higher values indicate more desirable performance, whereas a cost criterion represents situations in which lower values are preferred. For each method, the corresponding formulations for both criterion types are analyzed in the subsequent sections. This analysis will provide insights into the strengths and weaknesses of each normalization technique.

The analysis focuses on the comparative characteristics of normalization techniques, including the range of normalized values, sensitivity to extreme observations, dependence on the number of alternatives, and invariance under linear and positive affine transformations. Particular attention is devoted to the issue of rank reversal, which may arise when alternatives are added to or removed from the decision set, potentially affecting ranking stability [60,61]. As emphasized by Aires & Ferreira [62], rank reversal constitutes a central and unresolved issue in MCDM, involving diverse methods and scenarios, and continues to motivate research on the modeling and robustness of rankings.

In addition to scale and range, the internal distribution of criterion values influences normalization outcomes. Even with similar numerical ranges, criteria can differ in how uniformly their values are distributed across alternatives. This characteristic can be described using entropy, which here serves solely as a descriptor of data distribution rather than a weighting mechanism. Entropy highlights the discriminatory power of criteria and helps explain differences in normalization effects, particularly regarding ranking stability and sensitivity to rank reversal.

A normalization formula N is said to satisfy the Linear Transformation property if, for criteria C_i and C_j, where $y_{ij} = ax_{ij}$ with $a > 0$, it holds that

$$N(y_{ij}) = N(x_{ij}). \tag{4}$$

Similarly, a normalization formula N satisfies the Positive Affine Transformation property if, for criteria C_i and C_j, where $y_{ij} = ax_{ij} + b$ with, $a > 0$ and $b \neq 0$, it holds that

$$N(y_{ij}) = N(x_{ij}). \tag{5}$$

These properties describe whether normalization outcomes remain invariant under rescaling or shifting of criterion values. Overall, this analysis will provide insights into the strengths and weaknesses of each normalization technique.

3.2. Literature Review on Normalization Techniques and Ranking Stability in MCDA

This section reviews the main research streams on normalization techniques in MCDA, with particular emphasis on their mathematical properties, effects on ranking outcomes, and implications for ranking stability. The review provides the methodological background for the comparative analysis of normalization procedures presented in the subsequent sections.

The first direction focuses on the classification and formal properties of normalization techniques. Foundational studies distinguished vector-based, linear, and non-linear methods and analyzed their mathematical characteristics, including sensitivity to extreme values, scale dependence, and invariance under linear and affine transformations [11,19]. Jahan and Edwards [57] provided a comprehensive overview, identifying thirty-one normalization techniques and discussing their advantages and limitations in engineering decision problems. More recent surveys further systematize these methods, highlight implementation pitfalls, and propose guidelines for their appropriate use [10,18,19].

The second direction examines how normalization affects ranking outcomes. Empirical studies show that applying different normalization techniques to the same data can produce substantially different preference values and alternative rankings, even when weighting and aggregation procedures remain unchanged [20–22]. These differences are often due to varying sensitivity to extreme values, the number of alternatives, and the treatment of cost and benefit criteria. Rank reversal, where the relative ordering of alternatives changes due to normalization choices or modifications in the decision set, has emerged as a key concern in this research [10,60,63].

The third direction considers normalization within specific MCDA methods. Different techniques have been applied and compared across TOPSIS [8,12,13,25,64], VIKOR [65], AHP [66], COPRAS [22], SAW (Simple Additive Weighting) [11,15], ELECTRE (ÉLements pour laaide à la DÉCision-REcherche et ELimination) [11,67], PROMETHEE II (Preference Ranking Organization Method Enrichment Evaluations) [68], the Hellwig method [69], and others.

The fourth direction involves empirical evaluation and robustness analysis. Comparative studies use correlation measures, ranking consistency indices, and simulation-based experiments to assess how normalization choices influence ranking stability under different decision scenarios [15,23–25,70]. Max–min, vector, sum, and max normalization are among the most frequently used techniques, but are also highly sensitive to data distribution and extreme values [18]. Ranking stability is frequently assessed using ranking consistency in-

https://doi.org/10.3390/e28010114

dices, Kendall and Spearman coefficients, and mean error measures, providing quantitative support for the choice of normalization [24,56,71].

Finally, a key research stream focuses on normalization techniques in TOPSIS and offers guidance for their selection. Vector normalization is generally considered the most consistent across different problem sizes and data ranges [24,35,56,59]. However, sum normalization can serve as an effective alternative depending on data characteristics [21,28,56].

3.3. Normalization Procedures and Their Properties

Let $C = \{C_1, \ldots, C_n\}$ denote the set of criteria and $A = \{A_1, \ldots, A_m\}$ the set of alternatives. The performance score of alternative A_i with respect to criterion C_j is denoted by x_{ij} where $i = 1, 2, \ldots, m$ and $j = 1, 2, \ldots, n$.

Each normalization method provides distinct formulations for benefit and cost criteria and exhibits different mathematical properties, sensitivity to data distribution, and implications for ranking stability.

3.3.1. Vector Normalization (N1, N2)

Vector normalization scales the performance ratings of alternatives relative to the Euclidean norm of the vector formed by all alternatives for a given criterion.

For benefit criteria, the normalized value n_{ij} is calculated as:

$$n_{ij} = \frac{x_{ij}}{\sqrt{\sum_{i=1}^{m} (x_{ij})^2}} \quad \text{(N1, N2)} \tag{6}$$

For cost criteria, two commonly used variants exist. In the first variant (N1), lower values are preferred by subtracting the normalized value from one [57]:

$$n_{ij} = 1 - \frac{x_{ij}}{\sqrt{\sum_{i=1}^{m} (x_{ij})^2}} \quad \text{(N1)} \tag{7}$$

In the second variant (N2), reciprocal values are used [8]:

$$n_{ij} = \frac{1/x_{ij}}{\sqrt{\sum_{i=1}^{m} (1/x_{ij})^2}} \quad \text{(N2)} \tag{8}$$

N2 cannot be applied if any $x_{ij} = 0$, as this results in division by zero.

Vector normalization rescales values according to their relative contribution to the overall magnitude of the criterion vector. As a consequence, normalized values depend not only on the absolute magnitude of each alternative. They also depend on the relative distribution of values across all alternatives. The normalized values are dimensionless and lie within the interval $[0, 1]$, although the effective range depends on the ratio between extreme values.

For benefit criteria, the range of normalized values is:

$$\left[\frac{\min_i x_{ij}}{\sqrt{\sum_{i=1}^{m} (x_{ij})^2}}; \frac{\max_i x_{ij}}{\sqrt{\sum_{i=1}^{m} (x_{ij})^2}} \right] \tag{9}$$

For cost criteria, the ranges differ between N1 and N2. In the case of N1:

$$\left[1 - \frac{\max_i x_{ij}}{\sqrt{\sum_{i=1}^{m} (x_{ij})^2}}; 1 - \frac{\min_i x_{ij}}{\sqrt{\sum_{i=1}^{m} (x_{ij})^2}} \right] \tag{10}$$

https://doi.org/10.3390/e28010114

whereas for N2:

$$\left[\frac{1/\max\limits_{i} x_{ij}}{\sqrt{\sum_{i=1}^{m}(1/x_{ij})^2}};\frac{1/\min\limits_{i} x_{ij}}{\sqrt{\sum_{i=1}^{m}(1/x_{ij})^2}}\right]. \tag{11}$$

These expressions indicate that both the distribution of criterion values and the number of alternatives directly influence the normalization outcome. As the ratio $\frac{\max_i x_{ij}}{\min_i x_{ij}}$ or $\frac{\min_i x_{ij}}{\max_i x_{ij}}$ decreases, normalized values are compressed into a narrower portion of the $[0,1]$ interval. Moreover, for a fixed distribution of values, increasing the number of alternatives tends to reduce the length of the effective normalized interval [11].

Vector normalization satisfies the Linear Transformation property but not the Positive Affine Transformation property [11]. Changes in the domain of criterion values, such as adding or removing alternatives, may influence normalized scores and potentially lead to rank reversal, affecting ranking stability [60].

Vector normalization is moderately sensitive to extreme values, especially in the reciprocal-based N2 variant. For criteria where most values are clustered near one end of the range (low-entropy), vector normalization compresses the differences among the remaining alternatives, making them harder to distinguish. In contrast, for criteria with a wider spread of values (high-entropy), the normalization better preserves the relative distances between alternatives. Overall, the impact on ranking stability is medium compared to other normalization methods.

Despite these limitations, vector normalization remains one of the most widely adopted approaches in MCDA due to its conceptual simplicity and compatibility with distance-based aggregation methods [11,25,56–58]. It should be noted that in the standard TOPSIS method [8], the normalization Equation (6) is applied to cost criteria as well. The positive and negative ideal solutions can be determined directly, without converting cost-type criteria into benefit-type criteria.

3.3.2. Linear Max Normalization (N3, N4)

Linear max normalization rescales criterion values relative to the maximum observed performance.

For benefit criteria, the normalized value n_{ij} is defined as:

$$n_{ij} = \frac{x_{ij}}{\max\limits_{i} x_{ij}} \quad \text{(N3, N4.)} \tag{12}$$

For cost criteria, two alternative formulations are employed to reflect the preference for lower values. In the N3 variant, the normalized value is computed as [57]:

$$n_{ij} = 1 - \frac{x_{ij}}{\max\limits_{i} x_{ij}} \quad \text{(N3)} \tag{13}$$

In contrast, the N4 variant uses a reciprocal relation with respect to the minimum observed value [11,58]:

$$n_{ij} = \frac{\min\limits_{i} x_{ij}}{x_{ij}} \quad \text{(N4)} \tag{14}$$

While N3 preserves linear proportionality, N4 introduces nonlinear penalization of higher costs. These formulations cannot be applied if $\max_i x_{ij} = 0$, as division by zero would occur. Here, $\max_i x_{ij}$ and $\min_i x_{ij}$ denote the maximum and minimum performance ratings, respectively, among all alternatives for the j-th criterion.

https://doi.org/10.3390/e28010114

A key advantage of linear max normalization is its linearity. The transformation preserves proportional differences between alternatives by scaling all values directly with respect to the maximum (or minimum in the case of N4 for cost criteria). Consequently, the relative ordering of alternatives is maintained without distortion of proportional relationships [23]. For benefit criteria, the range of normalized values obtained using linear max normalization is:

$$\left[\frac{\min\limits_i x_{ij}}{\max\limits_i x_{ij}};1\right]. \tag{15}$$

For cost criteria, the normalized ranges differ depending on the selected variant. In the case of N3, the range is:

$$\left[0;1-\frac{\min\limits_i x_{ij}}{\max\limits_i x_{ij}}\right] \tag{16}$$

whereas for N4 it becomes:

$$\left[\frac{\min\limits_i x_{ij}}{\max\limits_i x_{ij}};1\right] \tag{17}$$

All these ranges lie within the interval $[0,1]$. Importantly, their length depends solely on the ratio $\frac{\min_i x_{ij}}{\max_i x_{ij}}$ or $\frac{\max_i x_{ij}}{\min_i x_{ij}}$, between the minimum and maximum values, rather than on the internal distribution of criterion values. Unlike vector normalization, linear max normalization, the normalized range does not reflect the full internal distribution of the data. Linear max normalization satisfies the Linear Transformation property and does not satisfy the Positive Affine Transformation property [11].

Linear max normalization is highly sensitive to extreme values due to reliance on maximum or minimum scores. Low-entropy criteria amplify contrasts among alternatives with extreme values, enhancing discrimination, while high-entropy criteria yield clustered normalized scores. The overall impact on ranking stability is relatively high compared to vector normalization and shows the role of entropy in interpreting N3 and N4 [60].

The method is simple, fast, and intuitive, making it suitable when extreme values are meaningful. However, reliance on maximum and minimum values requires caution in the presence of outliers or changing alternative sets.

3.3.3. Linear Max–Min Normalization (N5)

Linear max–min normalization (N5), unlike linear max normalization, max–min normalization maps all criterion values linearly onto $[0,1]$, considering both maximum and minimum values. The worst observed performance is assigned a normalized value of 0, while the best observed performance receives a value of 1. Relative differences between alternatives are preserved proportionally within the normalized scale.

For benefit criteria, the normalized value n_{ij} is defined as:

$$n_{ij}=\frac{x_{ij}-\min\limits_i x_{ij}}{\max\limits_i x_{ij}-\min\limits_i x_{ij}} \quad \text{(N5)} \tag{18}$$

For cost criteria, where lower values are preferred, the normalization is adjusted accordingly [11]:

$$n_{ij}=1-\frac{x_{ij}-\min\limits_i x_{ij}}{\max\limits_i x_{ij}-\min\limits_i x_{ij}} \quad \text{(N5)} \tag{19}$$

https://doi.org/10.3390/e28010114

In these formulas, $\max_i x_{ij}$ and $\min_i x_{ij}$ denote the maximum and minimum performance ratings, respectively, across all alternatives for the j-criterion.

This property ensures direct comparability across criteria, regardless of their original units or magnitudes, and greatly facilitates interpretation in subsequent aggregation and ranking procedures [23]. N5 satisfies both the Linear Transformation property and the Positive Affine Transformation property [11]. This distinguishes N5 from vector, max, and sum-based normalization techniques and provides a degree of robustness with respect to simple rescaling of the original data. However, when comparing linear max normalization (N3) and max–min normalization (N5), we can observe that N3 can be regarded as a special case of N5, in which the minimum of the scale is set to a conventional absolute zero, independent of the observed data. Nevertheless, N3 and N5 are generally treated as distinct normalization methods in the literature.

Max–min normalization preserves wide dispersion for low-entropy criteria and produces clustered scores for high-entropy criteria, reflecting its interaction with data structure. While it is invariant to rescaling, the method remains sensitive to extreme values. Outliers define the maximum and minimum, which can compress other scores and affect discrimination. The fixed [0, 1] range maps values proportionally. Low-entropy criteria yield widely dispersed normalized scores, while high-entropy criteria produce tightly clustered values, reducing effective resolution. Changes in the set of alternatives may alter maxima or minima, potentially causing rank reversal. Techniques such as introducing extreme fictitious alternatives [62,72] can help stabilize rankings.

In practice, N5 is widely used in SAW and other linear aggregation methods due to its simplicity and interpretability, though careful handling of outliers and alternative set changes is required.

3.3.4. Linear Sum Normalization (N6, N7)

Linear sum normalization rescales values relative to the total sum of a criterion. Larger original values dominate the normalized sum, while smaller values contribute proportionally less.

For benefit criteria, the normalized value n_{ij} is computed as:

$$n_{ij} = \frac{x_{ij}}{\sum_{i=1}^{m} x_{ij}} \quad \text{(N6, N7)} \tag{20}$$

For cost criteria, two variants are typically used. In the first variant (N6), the normalized value is inverted to reflect preference for lower values.

Linear: Sum (N6) [58]:

$$n_{ij} = 1 - \frac{x_{ij}}{\sum_{i=1}^{m} x_{ij}} \quad \text{(N6)} \tag{21}$$

In the second variant (N7), reciprocal values are employed [57]:

$$n_{ij} = \frac{1/x_{ij}}{\sum_{i=1}^{m} (1/x_{ij})} \quad \text{(N7)} \tag{22}$$

N7 cannot be applied when $x_{ij} = 0$ as this would result in division by zero. Consequently, careful preprocessing or alternative normalization methods are required when zero values occur in cost criteria.

Normalized values sum to one, making it suitable for assessing relative contributions. As a result, sum-based normalization is frequently employed in weighted aggregation models and proportional evaluation frameworks [58].

https://doi.org/10.3390/e28010114

The range of normalized values depends on the original distribution of criterion values. For benefit criteria, the normalized values lie within:

$$\left[\frac{\min_i x_{ij}}{\sum_{i=1}^m x_{ij}}; \frac{\max_i x_{ij}}{\sum_{i=1}^m x_{ij}}\right] \tag{23}$$

For cost criteria, the ranges differ between N6 and N7.

In N6, the range is:

$$\left[1 - \frac{\max_i x_{ij}}{\sum_{i=1}^m x_{ij}}; 1 - \frac{\min_i x_{ij}}{\sum_{i=1}^m x_{ij}}\right] \tag{24}$$

whereas in N7 it becomes:

$$\left[\frac{1/\max_i x_{ij}}{\sum_{i=1}^m 1/x_{ij}}; \frac{1/\min_i x_{ij}}{\sum_{i=1}^m 1/x_{ij}}\right] \tag{25}$$

Linear sum normalization (N6, N7) rescales criterion values relative to the total sum. Reciprocal transformations can be optionally applied for cost criteria. Similar to vector normalization, sum-based normalization is influenced by both the distribution of criterion values and the number of alternatives. The method is sensitive to extreme or zero values. Such values can compress other scores and reduce discrimination.

Low-entropy criteria produce asymmetric distributions that favor alternatives with extreme values. High-entropy criteria, in contrast, yield nearly uniform or clustered scores, which affects effective resolution. N6 is suitable for simple proportional inversion of cost criteria. N7 uses reciprocal scaling for stronger cost dominance. Both variants satisfy the Linear Transformation property but not the Positive Affine Transformation property [11].

The impact on ranking stability ranges from medium to high, depending on the data distribution and the set of alternatives. Both N6 and N7 normalizations are intuitive and widely used. However, care is required when handling outliers, zeros, or changes in the alternative set [58].

3.4. Comparison of Normalization Methods—Integrated View

All normalization methods satisfy the fundamental requirement of scale comparability by transforming heterogeneous criterion values into dimensionless measures suitable for comparison across alternatives.

Normalization mechanism. The underlying mechanisms differ across methods. Vector normalization (N1, N2) scales values relative to the Euclidean norm of the vector formed by all alternatives for a given criterion. Linear max normalization (N3, N4) scales values relative to the maximum (or minimum) observed value. Max–min normalization (N5) uses both the maximum and minimum to linearly map values into the $[0, 1]$ interval. Linear sum normalization (N6, N7) rescales values relative to the total sum of the criterion, optionally employing reciprocal transformations for cost criteria (N2, N7).

Linearity and invariance. Only max–min normalization (N5) satisfies both the Linear Transformation and Positive Affine Transformation properties, making it invariant to rescaling and shifting of criterion values. Vector normalization (N1, N2), linear max normalization (N3, N4), and linear sum normalization (N6, N7) satisfy only the Linear Transformation property; adding a constant to all values shifts normalized scores and may affect rankings.

Sensitivity to extreme values. Methods relying on maximum or minimum values (N3–N5) are highly sensitive to outliers, which may compress or distort normalized scores. Sum-based normalization (N6, N7) is also sensitive to extreme values, particularly when a small number of alternatives dominate the total sum. Vector normalization (N1, N2) is

https://doi.org/10.3390/e28010114

moderately less sensitive, as scaling is performed relative to the Euclidean norm. Overall, vector normalization (N1, N2) shows medium sensitivity to extreme values, max-based normalization (N3, N4) shows high sensitivity, max–min normalization (N5) moderate, and sum-based normalization (N6, N7) medium to high, depending on data distribution.

Interaction with zero values. Zero or very small values pose challenges for methods using division or reciprocal transformations. Vector normalization (N2) and sum normalization (N7) cannot be directly applied when $x_{ij} = 0$ without prior adjustment. Max-based (N3, N4) and max–min (N5) methods handle zero values more robustly, although caution is still required when zeros coincide with extreme values. In practice, preprocessing or introducing a small positive constant may be necessary to avoid division-related issues.

Dependence on data distribution and entropy. Vector and sum-based normalizations (N1, N2, N6, N7) are strongly influenced by the internal distribution of criterion values. Low-entropy criteria dominated by a few alternatives tend to produce compressed or asymmetric normalized values, reducing discriminatory power, whereas high-entropy criteria yield more uniform scores. Max-based methods (N3, N4) preserve contrasts among dominant alternatives in low-entropy criteria. Max–min normalization (N5) maintains wide dispersion for low-entropy criteria and clustered values for high-entropy criteria, indicating that entropy governs effective resolution rather than the formal $[0, 1]$ scaling.

Sensitivity to the number of alternatives and rank reversal. All normalization methods may be affected by changes in the set of alternatives. Vector (N1, N2) and sum-based (N6, N7) methods respond to both the number of alternatives and the data distribution. In max-based and max–min normalization methods (N3–N5), the most common source of rank reversal is the change in the maximum or minimum value. This contrasts with sum-based normalization (N6–N7), where adding a new alternative alters the total sum and may cause rank reversal even without modifying the extrema [62].

Cost-type criteria treatment. Two main approaches are commonly applied for cost criteria. The first approach, linear cost inversion, rescales the original values by subtracting them from one. This preserves proportional differences and ensures that lower costs receive higher normalized values (N1, N3, N5, N6). The second approach, reciprocal cost transformation, rescales values using the reciprocal function. It increases the relative differences among higher costs while still reflecting the preference for lower values (N2, N4, N7). This distinction is relevant because linear inversion and reciprocal transformation produce different relative score distributions, especially when cost values vary considerably. As a result, the relative ordering and separation of alternatives may differ across MCDM methods employing these normalizations and may lead to different ranking outcomes.

Practical implications. Vector normalization is simple and compatible with distance-based methods, though it requires caution when handling zero or very small values (N2). Max-based normalization (N3, N4) is computationally efficient and intuitive but highly sensitive to outliers. Max–min normalization (N5) ensures uniform scaling and invariance to rescaling, although extreme values may still distort rankings. Sum-based normalization (N6, N7) emphasizes relative contributions but is sensitive to extreme or zero values, potentially affecting ranking stability.

Overall, the choice of a normalization method should consider its linearity properties, sensitivity to extreme and zero values, interaction with data entropy, and potential for rank instability. Normalization should therefore be regarded as a structural modeling decision rather than a purely technical preprocessing step. These conceptual differences form the basis for the empirical comparison of normalization-induced ranking stability presented in the next section. Selecting an appropriate normalization method involves balancing mathematical properties, data characteristics, expected ranking stability, and the practical interpretation of the transformed scale by decision-makers.

https://doi.org/10.3390/e28010114

4. Data and Experimental Design

4.1. Research Framework and Objectives

The empirical part of this study systematically examines the impact of normalization methods and entropy structure on the stability of rankings in MCDA. This analysis builds on the theoretical discussion in the previous section. It focuses on how different normalization methods transform the same decision matrix and how these transformations interact with criterion distributions to influence rankings.

The primary objective of the empirical investigation is to assess ranking robustness under different normalization schemes. In particular, the study identifies conditions under which rankings remain stable and conditions that lead to ranking instability when normalization methods vary. Special attention is given to the role of entropy as a descriptive measure of criterion heterogeneity, hypothesized to moderate the sensitivity of normalized values to scale transformations and extreme observations.

Rather than treating normalization as a neutral preprocessing step, the empirical framework explicitly models it as a methodological factor that can alter inter-alternative distances and, consequently, decision outcomes. This perspective allows a more nuanced evaluation of MCDA results and contributes to the broader discussion on methodological robustness and transparency in multi-criteria decision support.

4.2. Decision Matrix and Data Structure

The empirical analysis is based on a decision matrix comprising ten alternatives evaluated against four criteria. Criteria C1 and C2 are benefit-type criteria, where higher values indicate better performance, whereas C3 and C4 are cost-type criteria, for which lower values are preferred. This framework reflects typical decision-making problems that consider both gains and losses simultaneously. The dataset was deliberately constructed to include both high-entropy and low-entropy criteria in order to examine normalization-induced effects under controlled conditions, rather than to model a specific real-world decision problem.

Table 1 presents the original decision matrix together with basic descriptive statistics and Shannon entropy values for each criterion.

Table 1. Decision matrix with basic descriptive statistics and Shannon entropy values.

Alternative	C1	C2	C3	C4
A1	10	5	40	6
A2	20	21	30	8
A3	24	20	28	10
A4	10	20	26	12
A5	24	80	22	50
A6	10	22	24	8
A7	26	5	26	10
A8	22	21	28	9
A9	20	23	10	10
A10	30	20	28	8
mean	19.60	23.70	26.20	13.10
variability	34.99	83.63	26.98	94.63
min	10.00	5.00	10.00	6.00
max	30.00	80.00	40.00	50.00
max/min ratio	3.00	16.00	4.00	8.33
entropy	0.9712	0.8824	0.9824	0.8743

https://doi.org/10.3390/e28010114

The dataset is characterized by substantial heterogeneity in scale, dispersion, and distributional form. Shannon entropy values are computed for each criterion (Table 1). In this study, entropy is not employed as a weighting mechanism but exclusively as a descriptive indicator of the data structure, capturing the degree of heterogeneity and dominance within each criterion. High-entropy criteria distribute information evenly across alternatives, whereas low-entropy criteria concentrate information in a few observations, which amplifies sensitivity to normalization methods.

Criteria C1 and C3 exhibit relatively high entropy values, indicating a fairly uniform distribution of performance values across alternatives. Although these criteria display moderate variability, no single alternative consistently achieves the highest values across all alternatives. As a result, their informational content is evenly spread, and differences among alternatives are gradual rather than abrupt.

In contrast, criteria C2 and C4 are characterized by low entropy values combined with high variability and pronounced extreme observations. In both cases, a small number of alternatives concentrate a large share of the total informational content. For C2, exceptionally high benefit values strongly differentiate a limited subset of alternatives, while for C4, extreme cost values introduce strong asymmetry into the distribution. Such low-entropy structures are expected to amplify the effects of normalization, particularly for methods that depend on extreme values or proportional scaling.

Importantly, the original decision matrix remains unchanged throughout the analysis. All observed differences in normalized values, TOPSIS scores, and rankings arise exclusively from the application of alternative normalization procedures and their interaction with the entropy structure of the criteria.

4.3. Experimental Design and Procedure

The experimental design follows a controlled, stepwise procedure. First, the original decision matrix is normalized using seven normalization techniques (N1–N7), as defined in the methodological section. Benefit and cost criteria are treated according to the formulations specific to each normalization method.

Next, the TOPSIS method (see Appendix A) is applied to each normalized decision matrix using identical criterion weights (equal weights) and aggregation rules. By keeping all other modeling components constant, the experimental setup isolates the effects of normalization and entropy on ranking outcomes. Finally, ranking stability is evaluated by comparing the positions of alternatives across different normalization methods, with particular attention to instability and consistent ranking patterns.

In addition to the baseline experiment, a controlled sensitivity scenario is introduced to examine how small changes in low-entropy criteria influence ranking stability across normalization methods. Specifically, the value of the benefit-type criterion C2 for alternative A5 is reduced from 80 to 40, increasing its entropy from 0.8824 to 0.9466. This modification is intentionally limited and targets an alternative previously identified as sensitive due to extreme performance.

5. Results and Discussion

5.1. Effects of Normalization on TOPSIS Scores and Rankings

This section analyzes ranking variability induced solely by normalization choice, with all other modeling components held constant. Ranking stability is interpreted not as a normative criterion of correctness but as an indicator of methodological robustness under controlled variation. Table 2 reports the TOPSIS coefficients TN1–TN7 and Table 3 the corresponding rankings obtained under normalization methods N1–N7.

https://doi.org/10.3390/e28010114

Table 2. TOPSIS coefficients obtained under normalization methods N1–N7.

Alternative	TN1	TN2	TN3	TN4	TN5	TN6	TN7
A1	0.462	0.301	0.391	0.391	0.366	0.489	0.270
A2	0.539	0.327	0.502	0.409	0.500	0.557	0.305
A3	0.536	0.313	0.524	0.393	0.540	0.549	0.291
A4	0.495	0.233	0.441	0.258	0.418	0.516	0.226
A5	0.511	0.590	0.545	0.503	0.549	0.493	0.632
A6	0.531	0.317	0.477	0.369	0.453	0.552	0.300
A7	0.489	0.278	0.498	0.379	0.529	0.497	0.246
A8	0.542	0.321	0.520	0.401	0.528	0.556	0.300
A9	0.574	0.487	0.596	0.525	0.615	0.578	0.454
A10	0.559	0.377	0.563	0.480	0.592	0.568	0.347

Table 3. Rankings obtained by TOPSIS under normalization methods N1–N7.

Alternative	Range TN1	Range TN2	Range TN3	Range TN4	Range TN5	Range TN6	Range TN7
A1	10	8	10	7	10	10	8
A2	4	4	6	4	7	3	4
A3	5	7	4	6	4	6	7
A4	8	10	9	10	9	7	10
A5	7	1	3	2	3	9	1
A6	6	6	8	9	8	5	6
A7	9	9	7	8	5	8	9
A8	3	5	5	5	6	4	5
A9	1	2	1	1	1	1	2
A10	2	3	2	3	2	2	3

To evaluate the consistency and correlation of results obtained from TN1–TN7 based on normalization techniques N1–N7, both Pearson and Spearman correlation coefficients were calculated. The results are presented in Table 4.

Table 4. Pearson and Spearman Correlation Coefficients between TN1–TN7 under normalization methods N1–N7.

Pearson Coefficients	TN1	TN2	TN3	TN4	TN5	TN6	TN7	Spearman Coefficient	TN1	TN2	TN3	TN4	TN5	TN6	TN7
TN1	1.000							TN1	1.000						
TN2	0.368	1.000						TN2	0.673	1.000					
TN3	0.844	0.651	1.000					TN3	0.794	0.806	1.000				
TN4	0.553	0.857	0.756	1.000				TN4	0.673	0.915	0.867	1.000			
TN5	0.785	0.581	0.984	0.737	1.000			TN5	0.661	0.697	0.964	0.782	1.000		
TN6	0.935	0.056	0.614	0.314	0.559	1.000		TN6	0.939	0.491	0.612	0.479	0.503	1.000	
TN7	0.294	0.989	0.590	0.779	0.514	−0.02	1	TN7	0.673	1.000	0.806	0.915	0.697	0.491	1.000

Despite identical data, equal weights, and aggregation procedures, noticeable differences emerge in TOPSIS scores and final rankings. This confirms that normalization choice alone can materially affect decision outcomes.

At an aggregate level, alternatives A9 and A10 consistently occupy the top positions across all normalization methods. Their strong and well-balanced performance across both benefit and cost criteria results in high closeness coefficients regardless of the normalization

https://doi.org/10.3390/e28010114

scheme. This convergence indicates that alternatives with robust multi-criteria profiles are less sensitive to normalization-induced distortions.

In contrast, alternatives with mixed or asymmetric performance profiles exhibit substantial ranking variability. The most pronounced example is alternative A5, which displays the widest range of ranking positions across normalization methods. A5 achieves an exceptionally high value on the low-entropy benefit criterion C2, but simultaneously performs poorly on the low-entropy cost criterion C4. Consequently, its final ranking strongly depends on how normalization methods amplify benefit dominance and penalize extreme costs. Methods that preserve or emphasize extreme benefit values generally result in higher rankings for A5, while methods that apply stronger penalties to high cost values, particularly those using reciprocal transformations, tend to lower its ranking. This illustrates how low-entropy criteria drive ranking instability and magnify the methodological role of normalization.

Beyond these extremes, the remaining alternatives exhibit intermediate and more nuanced ranking behavior. Alternatives A2 and A8 generally occupy upper-middle positions across normalization methods, reflecting relatively strong performance combined with moderate sensitivity to normalization choice. Alternative A3 shows moderate variability, typically remaining in the middle of the ranking. Alternatives A6 and A7 consistently appear in the lower-middle part of the rankings. Although their positions shift slightly depending on the normalization method, these shifts are relatively minor compared to those observed for A5. Finally, alternatives A1 and A4 remain at the bottom across all normalization methods, confirming that normalization effects are least influential for the lowest-scoring alternatives.

Figures A1–A7 (Appendix B) present the normalized criteria values N1–N7, the distances to the positive and negative ideal solutions, and the TN1–TN7 closeness coefficients. Normalized values differ according to the selected method. Differences are particularly noticeable between methods using linear cost inversion and those employing reciprocal cost transformations. The spread of TN1–TN7 values varies substantially, with the smallest spread observed for TN1 and TN6 (0.112 and 0.089, respectively) and the largest for TN2 and TN7 (0.358 and 0.407, respectively).

Reducing A5's value in criterion C2 from 80 to 40 causes noticeable ranking shifts across normalization methods, highlighting TOPSIS's sensitivity to data structure and normalization choice (see Table 5). A comparison of the two experimental settings shows that ranking changes are uneven across alternatives. A5 consistently drops in all normalization methods, losing between one and four positions, while other alternatives shift only slightly, typically by one position at most. This asymmetric response shows that alternatives performing very well on benefit criteria but poorly on cost criteria are the most sensitive to normalization. The pronounced drop of A5 confirms that alternatives near the decision frontier are particularly affected by small data changes, while balanced or lower-performing alternatives remain largely stable. This asymmetric response indicates that sensitivity is concentrated on alternatives that previously combined strong benefit dominance with poor cost performance.

https://doi.org/10.3390/e28010114

Table 5. Rankings obtained under normalization methods N1–N7 after modification of criterion C2 for alternative A5.

Alternative	Range TN1	Range TN2	Range TN3	Range TN4	Range TN5	Range TN6	Range TN7
A1	9	8	10	8	10	9	8
A2	5	4	5	4	5	4	4
A3	4	7	3	6	3	5	7
A4	7	10	9	10	9	7	10
A5	10	2	7	3	6	10	2
A6	6	6	6	7	8	6	6
A7	8	9	8	9	7	8	9
A8	3	5	4	5	4	3	5
A9	1	1	1	1	1	1	1
A10	2	3	2	2	2	2	3

5.2. Ranking Convergence, Divergence, and Ranking Stability

Analysis of ranking agreement reveals a structured pattern of convergence and divergence among the considered normalization methods. The strongest convergence occurs for rankings TN2 and TN7, which produce identical rank orders (Spearman = 1.000). High agreement is also observed between TN3 and TN5 (Spearman = 0.964), indicating that these normalization approaches lead to very similar evaluations of alternatives despite differences in their mathematical formulations.

More broadly, TN3 shows the highest overall consistency with the remaining methods, exhibiting strong correlations across a wide range of comparisons (Spearman = 0.612–0.964). This suggests that TN3 provides a balanced transformation of criterion values, preserving relative differences between alternatives while avoiding excessive amplification of extreme values, which contributes to stable ranking behavior.

In contrast, TN6 exhibits the weakest overall agreement with the other normalization methods. Its rankings show particularly low correlations with TN2, TN4, TN5, and TN7 (Spearman = 0.491, 0.479, 0.503, and 0.491, respectively). This divergence can be attributed to the combination of linear sum normalization and linear cost inversion, which respond differently to dominant observations and low-entropy criteria.

These patterns indicate that normalization differences are not merely technical. They reflect how each method processes extreme values, total sums, and cost-type criteria. Methods that handle costs nonlinearly or rely on proportional scaling tend to respond more strongly to low-entropy criteria, increasing ranking variability.

Given this structured pattern of convergence and divergence, a natural next step is to move beyond pairwise correlation analysis and provide formal support for selecting normalization methods that yield robust and representative rankings. For this purpose, a procedure for supporting multi-criteria method selection is applied (see Appendix A.2). This procedure is based on average similarity scores computed across rankings obtained with different normalization techniques. The resulting similarity measures are as follows: TN1—0.700, TN2—0.733, TN3—0.733, TN4—0.727, TN5—0.667, TN6—0.640, and TN7—0.733. These values indicate that TN2, TN3, and TN7 show the greatest agreement with the remaining methods. Notably, TN3 also achieves the highest average Spearman rank correlation (0.808) between the TOPSIS-based ranking and the other approaches. In the modified example, the similarity values increase to TN1—0.733, TN2—0.746, TN3—0.773, TN4—0.767, TN5—0.733, TN6—0.740, and TN7—0.747. Here, TN3 clearly stands out, demonstrating the strongest overall consistency. This result is further confirmed by the highest average Spearman rank correlation (0.882) with the remaining methods.

https://doi.org/10.3390/e28010114

5.3. Role of Entropy in Explaining Normalization Effects

Entropy provides a unifying explanatory framework for interpreting the observed results. High-entropy criteria (C1 and C3) contribute to ranking stability, as their uniform distributions limit the impact of normalization-induced rescaling. Differences among alternatives remain relatively proportional across methods. In contrast, low-entropy criteria (C2 and C4) amplify normalization effects by concentrating informational content in a small number of observations. When such criteria are normalized, especially using methods sensitive to extreme values or total sums, small methodological differences translate into large changes in normalized values, distances to ideal solutions, and final rankings.

Correlation analysis confirms the role of entropy in shaping normalization outcomes. High-entropy criteria show strong alignment across normalization methods. This is reflected in high Spearman and Pearson correlations for alternatives with relatively uniform performance. In contrast, low-entropy criteria amplify the effects of methodological choices, such as the type of normalization and cost treatment. As a result, they contribute to greater ranking variability. Entropy, therefore, works together with these factors: it moderates sensitivity to extreme values, interacts with the normalization method, and, combined with cost-type treatment, affects how differences between alternatives are preserved. This confirms that ranking instability is structurally driven rather than random. Weaker correlations, such as those between TN2 and TN6, illustrate how low-entropy criteria, when combined with specific normalization and cost-handling approaches, increase sensitivity for certain alternatives.

The sensitivity experiment further confirms this mechanism: reducing the extreme value of criterion C2 for alternative A5 weakens its dominance under low-entropy conditions and leads to a consistent rank decline across all normalization methods, with the magnitude of this decline reflecting the specific sensitivity of each normalization technique.

5.4. Treatment of Cost Criteria and Directional Effects

The handling of cost-type criteria plays a critical role in shaping TOPSIS outcomes. Linear cost inversion, applied in TN1, TN3, TN5, and TN6, rescales cost values proportionally, ensuring consistent penalties for high-cost alternatives across normalization methods. This proportional treatment contributes to strong alignment of closeness coefficients and rankings, as reflected in high Spearman correlations between TN3 and TN5 (0.964) and between TN1 and TN6 (0.939). Whether normalization is max-based or max–min, the relative differences in costs among alternatives are preserved, leading to stable rankings even for alternatives influenced by low-entropy criteria (see also Figures A1–A7 in Appendix B). The reciprocal cost transformation used in TN2, TN4, and TN7 imposes non-linear penalties on high-cost alternatives. TN7 aligns perfectly with TN2 (Spearman = 1.000), while correlations with TN4 are slightly lower but still high (Spearman = 0.915), indicating generally consistent effects with minor differences in ranking outcomes.

This dual effect of nonlinear cost handling and differing normalization method increases sensitivity to low-entropy or extreme-value alternatives, resulting in weaker correlations and notable differences in absolute TOPSIS scores, as seen in TN2/TN6 (0.491).

These observations demonstrate that both the type of cost transformation and the normalization method jointly shape ranking stability, interacting with entropy to determine the sensitivity of alternatives to methodological choices. High correlations occur when cost differences are preserved proportionally, whereas nonlinear cost penalties or differing normalization bases amplify ranking variability and highlight the structural sensitivity of certain alternatives.

https://doi.org/10.3390/e28010114

5.5. Summary of Empirical Findings

The empirical analysis demonstrates that normalization techniques significantly influence TOPSIS rankings, especially in the presence of low-entropy criteria and extreme observations. Equally important is the treatment of cost-type criteria, which interacts with entropy and normalization to determine ranking stability. While some alternatives exhibit strong ranking robustness, others are highly sensitive to normalization choice, leading to rank reversal.

These results support the central premise of this study: normalization is a substantive modeling decision rather than a purely technical preprocessing step. Entropy serves as a powerful diagnostic tool for anticipating normalization effects, assessing ranking stability, and evaluating the influence of cost treatment, thereby clarifying the impact of methodological decisions and improving robustness in MCDA applications.

5.6. Discussion

The primary objective of this study is not to identify a universally optimal normalization method. Rather, it seeks to demonstrate that normalization constitutes a substantive methodological choice whose effects depend on the distributional properties of criteria—quantified here through Shannon entropy—and on the treatment of cost-type indicators. By systematically examining how entropy structure interacts with different normalization schemes, the study provides diagnostic insights into ranking stability and methodological robustness in MCDA applications. In this framework, ranking stability is not interpreted as correctness or decision optimality, but as an indicator of methodological robustness with respect to controlled variations in normalization and data characteristics.

The results of the empirical experiment provide clear evidence that normalization techniques play a decisive methodological role in MCDA, especially when combined with aggregation procedures such as TOPSIS. Although normalization is often treated as a routine preprocessing step, it fundamentally shapes inter-alternative distances, affects extreme observations, and ultimately determines ranking stability.

A key insight is the explanatory power of entropy as a descriptor of the criteria data structure. High-entropy criteria exhibit relatively uniform value distributions. This limits the impact of normalization-induced rescaling and preserves proportional differences across alternatives. This effect is evident for C1 and C3, whose high entropy corresponds to consistent contributions to TOPSIS scores under all normalization schemes.

Low-entropy criteria, dominated by extreme values and strong asymmetries (C2 and C4), amplify the sensitivity of normalized values to the chosen normalization method. Methods relying on extreme values, total sums, or reciprocal transformations respond differently to these dominant observations. As a result, substantial variation occurs in TOPSIS scores and rankings.

The observed TN1–TN7 rankings confirm that ranking instability is a systematic consequence of interactions among data structure, normalization approach, and cost criterion treatment. Alternatives with balanced performance, such as A9 and A10, remain robust across methods. In contrast, alternatives with extreme benefit and extreme cost values, like A5, exhibit pronounced ranking variability. This observation is practically relevant because, in many real-world MCDA applications, the analyst begins with a performance table—crisp, interval, or fuzzy—and normalization constitutes the first modeling operation that propagates data structure into ranking outcomes.

The treatment of cost-type criteria is a critical methodological issue. Linear inversion, reciprocal transformation, and sum-based normalization impose different penalty structures on high-cost values. Differences may be negligible for high-entropy criteria but

https://doi.org/10.3390/e28010114

become decisive under low-entropy conditions. This reinforces that cost criteria cannot be treated as mere inversions of benefit criteria.

Overall, entropy, normalization approach, and cost-type treatment jointly mediate ranking stability. This finding underscores the need for transparent diagnostic analysis in MCDA applications and cautions against treating normalization as a neutral preprocessing step.

Building on the theoretical analysis and empirical findings, this study proposes an entropy-informed diagnostic procedure to support the selection of normalization techniques in MCDA. Although the empirical investigation was conducted using TOPSIS, the framework is not method-specific. It can be applied to other MCDA approaches that rely on normalized decision matrices and ranking-based outputs.

Proposed diagnostic procedure for selecting normalization methods in MCDA:

Step 1. Entropy assessment. Compute Shannon entropy for all criteria. Identify low-entropy criteria that may dominate the ranking. This step helps anticipate potential sensitivity to normalization and highlights the criteria for which normalization choice is most consequential (see Section 2).

Step 2. Normalization verification. Apply several normalization techniques representing different mathematical principles (e.g., linear, reciprocal, sum-based). Evaluate each method with respect to desirable theoretical properties, such as sensitivity to extreme values, preservation of proportional differences, cost-type treatment, and robustness to changes in the alternative set (see Section 3).

Step 3. Selection of candidate methods. Based on the verification, select a subset of normalization techniques that best balance robustness, discrimination, and interpretability given the structure of the decision problem.

Step 4. Comparative ranking analysis. Apply the selected normalization methods to the decision matrix. Generate rankings using the chosen MCDA method (e.g., TOPSIS or other ranking-based techniques). Compare rankings to identify alternatives exhibiting high variability. Detect systematic sensitivity patterns, particularly in the presence of low-entropy criteria and extreme performance values (see Section 4).

Step 5. Optional formal method selection. For a more formal assessment, apply the procedure described in Appendix A.2. This approach uses inter-ranking similarity measures to compare rankings obtained from multiple MCDA methods. It identifies those producing results most consistent with the others. Additionally, alternative selection criteria may be considered, such as the average Spearman rank correlation or other rank-based agreement measures.

After Step 5, the procedure does not prescribe a single mandatory decision rule. Depending on the decision context, the analyst may either:

(i) select one normalization method as representative,

(ii) adopt a consensus ranking based on several highly consistent methods, or

(iii) report a stability profile to emphasize the uncertainty of rankings.

The choice depends on whether the priority is methodological parsimony, robustness, or transparency for stakeholders.

This diagnostic framework provides a practical tool for evaluating normalization effects, verifying methodological properties, and selecting normalization techniques aligned with the informational structure of the decision problem. Explicitly incorporating entropy and cost-type treatment, it supports more transparent, robust, and interpretable MCDA outcomes. The procedure is presented as a step-wise flowchart in Figure 1.

https://doi.org/10.3390/e28010114

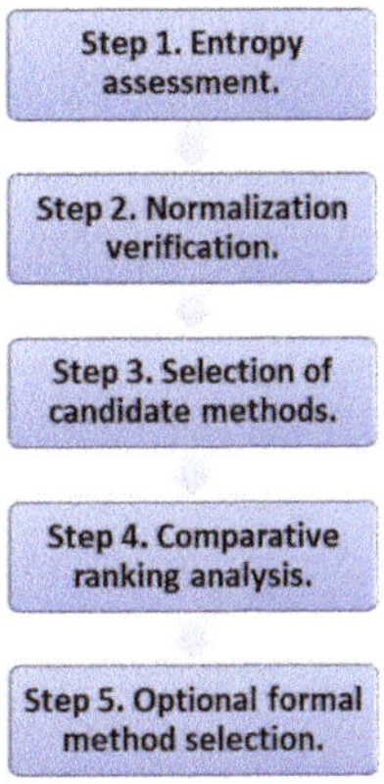

Figure 1. Proposed step-wise diagnostic procedure for selecting normalization methods in MCDA.

6. Conclusions

This study examined the role of normalization techniques in MCDA, focusing on the interplay between criterion entropy, cost-type treatment, and ranking stability. A central contribution is the use of Shannon entropy as a descriptive indicator of data structure rather than a weighting mechanism. Normalization is shown to be a substantive methodological choice that influences preference values, relative distances, and final rankings. High-entropy criteria support stable rankings, while low-entropy criteria increase sensitivity to normalization. Alternatives with extreme performances are particularly affected, as demonstrated in the TOPSIS experiment and controlled sensitivity scenario. Cost-type treatment, linear inversion, reciprocal, or sum-based normalization, further shapes rankings, especially under low-entropy conditions. The findings highlight the need to consider entropy, normalization method, and cost-type treatment jointly for transparent and robust MCDA results. The practical, entropy-based procedure for selecting normalization methods is also proposed.

This study also emphasizes the practical implications for decision-makers: by assessing entropy and understanding the sensitivity of rankings to normalization, analysts can better anticipate which alternatives are likely to experience rank reversals. This approach supports more informed and defensible decision-making, particularly in contexts where extreme values or asymmetric data are present.

Despite these contributions, the study has several limitations that suggest directions for future research. First, the analysis used a single dataset and focused on TOPSIS; extending the framework to other MCDA methods, such as PROMETHEE, VIKOR, ELECTRE, or COPRAS, would clarify its generality. Second, criterion weights were held constant; exploring interactions between entropy-based weighting and normalization represents a natural extension. Third, only Shannon entropy was considered, which captures statistical dispersion but may not fully represent uncertainty in highly skewed or heavy-tailed datasets. Alternative measures, such as Rényi or Tsallis entropy, may provide complementary insights. Fourth, the methodology assumes non-negative data, which can restrict applicability in contexts with negative or mixed-scale criteria. Finally, although synthetic data support controlled experimentation, they may not capture all complexities of real decision problems, and thus generalization should be approached cautiously.

Future research should address these limitations through systematic robustness analyses across diverse decision matrices, varying the number of alternatives and criteria, distributional characteristics, and the presence of extreme or missing values. Large-scale

https://doi.org/10.3390/e28010114

simulations and empirical studies would help validate the observed effects and refine practical guidance for normalization selection.

It is also important to note that the current findings are based on a synthetic dataset, which allows controlled experimentation but may not capture all complexities of real-world decision problems. Future work using diverse empirical datasets would help validate the generalizability of the observed effects.

Additionally, the proposed entropy-informed diagnostic procedure could be integrated into decision support software or applied as a preliminary step in organizational decision-making processes, providing a systematic way to anticipate and mitigate potential ranking instabilities.

Funding: The contribution was supported by the grant WZ/WI-IIT/2/25 from Bialystok University of Technology and funded by the Ministry of Science and Higher Education.

Institutional Review Board Statement: Not applicable.

Informed Consent Statement: Not applicable.

Data Availability Statement: All data are available in the manuscript.

Conflicts of Interest: The author declares no conflicts of interest.

Appendix A.

Appendix A.1. The TOPSIS Procedure

TOPSIS [8] is a multi-criteria decision-making method for ranking alternatives based on their distances from an ideal and an anti-ideal solution. TOPSIS starts by defining a finite set of alternatives $A = \{A_1, \ldots, A_m\}$ and criteria $C = \{C_1, \ldots, C_n\}$, which together form the decision matrix:

$$D = [x_{ij}]_{m\times n}.$$

The criteria are divided into benefit and cost types, and weights w_j are assigned to the criteria such that

$$\sum_{i=1}^{n} w_i = 1.$$

The decision matrix is normalized (using one of the normalization procedures N1–N7) to obtain the normalized matrix:

$$\overline{D} = [\overline{x}_{ij}]_{m\times n}$$

The decision matrix is weighted to obtain the weighted normalized matrix:

$$\tilde{D} = \left[\tilde{x}_{ij}\right]_{m\times n}, \tilde{x}_{\mathrm{ij}} = w_j \overline{x}_{ij}.$$

Based on $\tilde{D}$, the positive ideal solution and the negative ideal solution are defined as

$$A^+ = [\max_i \tilde{x}_{ij} \text{ for the benefit criteria; } \min_i \tilde{x}_{ij} \text{ for the cost criteria}]$$

and

$$A^- = [\min_i \tilde{x}_{ij} \text{ for the benefit criteria; } \max_i \tilde{x}_{ij} \text{ for the cost criteria}].$$

For each alternative A_i, the distances from the ideal d_i^+ and anti-ideal solutions d_i^- are computed (using the Euclidean metric):

$$d_i^+ = \sqrt{\left(\tilde{x}_{ij} - \tilde{x}_j^+\right)^2} \text{ and } d_i^- = \sqrt{\left(\tilde{x}_{ij} - \tilde{x}_j^-\right)^2}.$$

https://doi.org/10.3390/e28010114

Finally, the relative closeness to the ideal solution is determined as

$$T_i = \frac{d_i^-}{d_i^- + d_i^+}$$

and alternatives are ranked in descending order of T_i.

Appendix A.2. Procedure for Supporting Multicriteria Method Selection [73]

The procedure is based on inter-ranking similarity measures. It involves comparing the rankings of a set of m alternatives, $A_1, A_2, \ldots, A_m$, obtained by applying v different multi-criteria methods. As a result, v distinct rankings are generated. These rankings are then compared pairwise. The comparison outcomes are interpreted as inter-ranking similarities, quantified using the ranking similarity measure m_{pq}, defined as follows:

$$m_{pq} = 1 - \frac{2\sum_{i=1}^{m} \left| c_{ip} - c_{iq} \right|}{m^2 - z}, \; p, \, q = 1, \, 2, \, \ldots, v,$$

where c_{ip}—represents the position of the i—th alternative in the ranking generated by the p—th method; c_{iq}—represents the position of the i—th alternative in the ranking generated by the q—th method; $z = \begin{cases} 0, & m \in P \\ 1, & m \notin P \end{cases}$ where P denotes the set of even natural numbers.

All pairwise inter-ranking similarities can be aggregated into the matrix M:

$$M = \left[m_{pq} \right] = \begin{bmatrix} 1 & m_{12} & m_{13} & \ldots & m_{1v} \\ m_{21} & 1 & m_{23} & \ldots & m_{2v} \\ \vdots & \vdots & \vdots & \vdots & \vdots \\ m_{v1} & m_{v2} & m_{v3} & \ldots & 1 \end{bmatrix}$$

To assess the overall similarity of the ranking obtained using the p—th multi-criteria method with respect to all remaining rankings, it is sufficient to compute the average of the elements in the p—row (or column) of matrix M, excluding the diagonal element.

This value, denoted by u_p, is given by:

$$u_p = \frac{1}{v-1} \sum_{\substack{q=1 \\ p \neq q}}^{v} m_{pq}, \; p, \, q = 1, \, 2, \, \ldots, v,$$

Finally, the multicriteria method corresponding to the highest average similarity value is selected:

$$\overline{u}_p = \max_p u_p$$

This approach ensures that the chosen method produces rankings most consistent with the others.

Appendix B.

Figures A1–A7 present normalized criterion values for alternatives A1–A10, their distances to the positive and negative ideal solutions, and the corresponding TOPSIS closeness coefficients (TN1–TN7) under normalization methods N1–N7.

https://doi.org/10.3390/e28010114

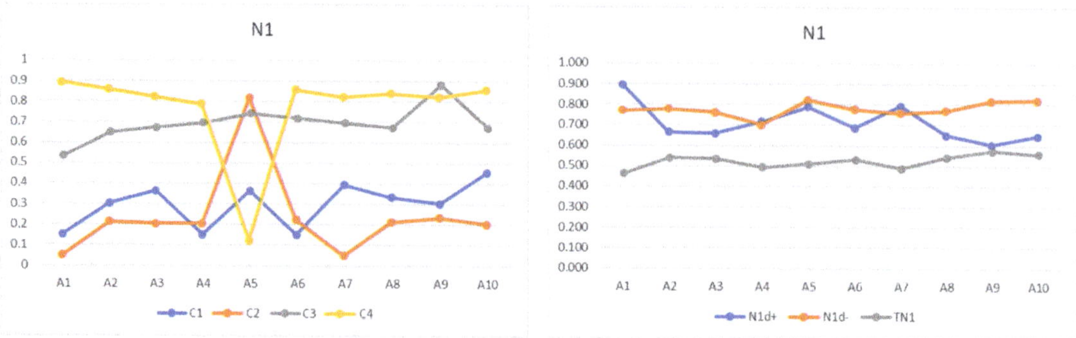

(**a**) Normalized criteria values for alternatives

(**b**) Distances to positive and negative ideal solutions and TOPSIS closeness coefficients

Figure A1. Normalization N1.

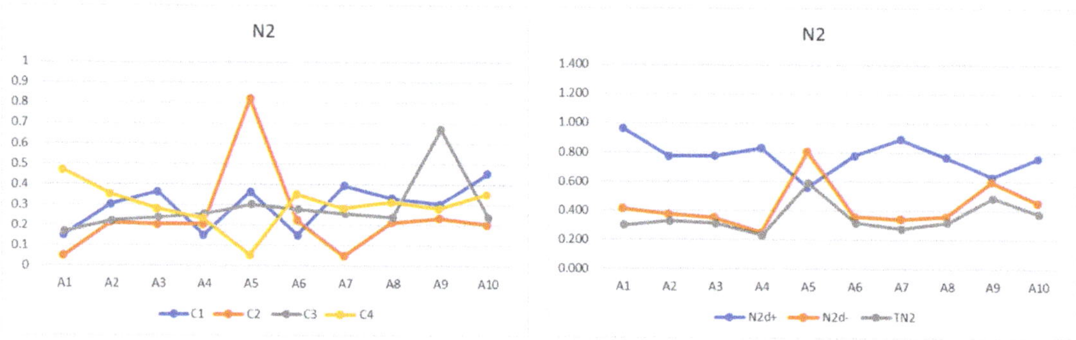

(**a**) Normalized criteria values for alternatives

(**b**) Distances to positive and negative ideal solutions and TOPSIS closeness coefficients

Figure A2. Normalization N2.

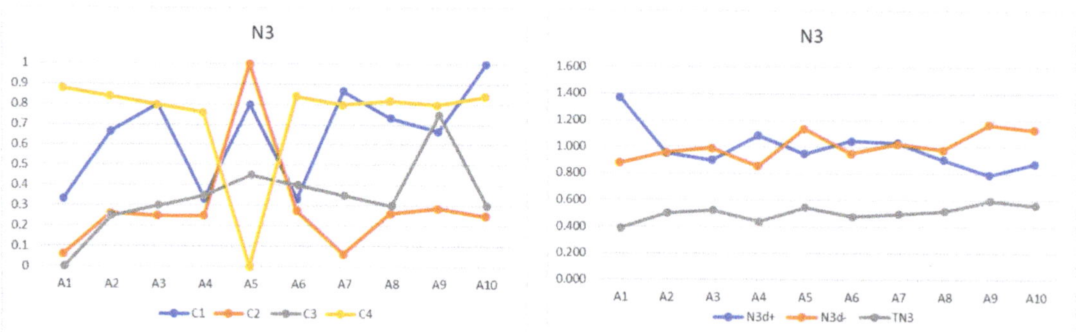

(**a**) Normalized criteria values for alternatives

(**b**) Distances to positive and negative ideal solutions and TOPSIS closeness coefficients

Figure A3. Normalization N3.

https://doi.org/10.3390/e28010114

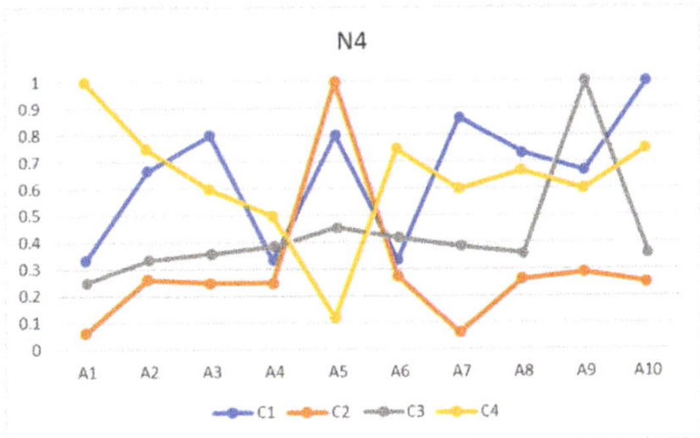

(**a**) Normalized criteria values for alternatives

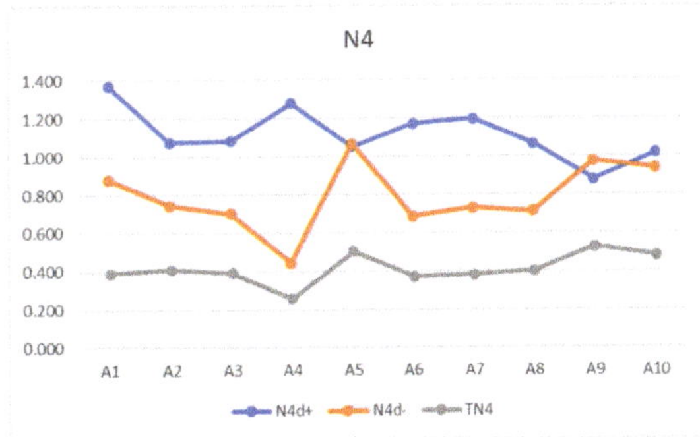

(**b**) Distances to positive and negative ideal solutions and TOPSIS closeness coefficients

Figure A4. Normalization N4.

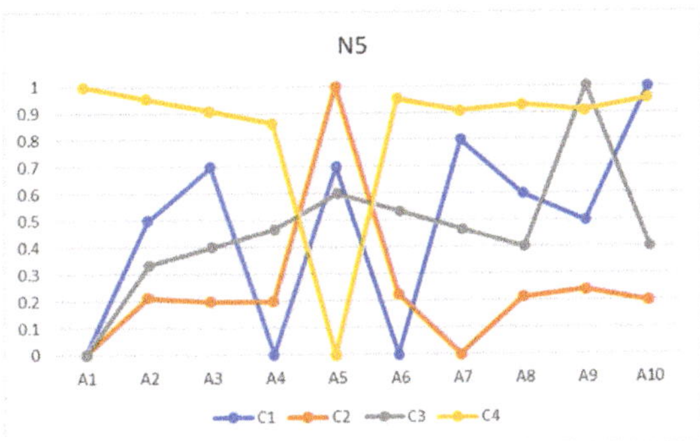

(**a**) Normalized criteria values for alternatives

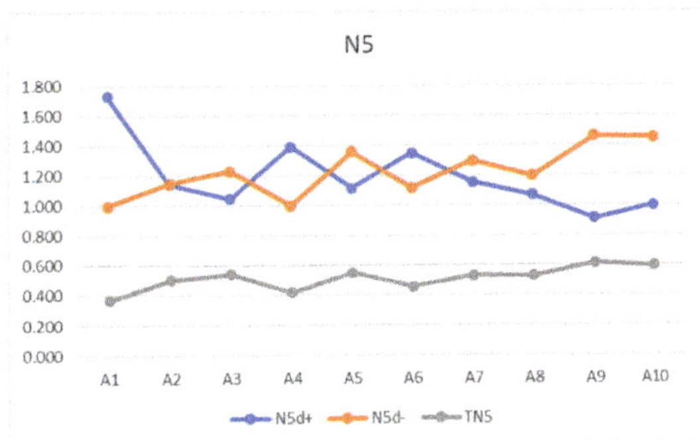

(**b**) Distances to positive and negative ideal solutions and TOPSIS closeness coefficients

Figure A5. Normalization N5.

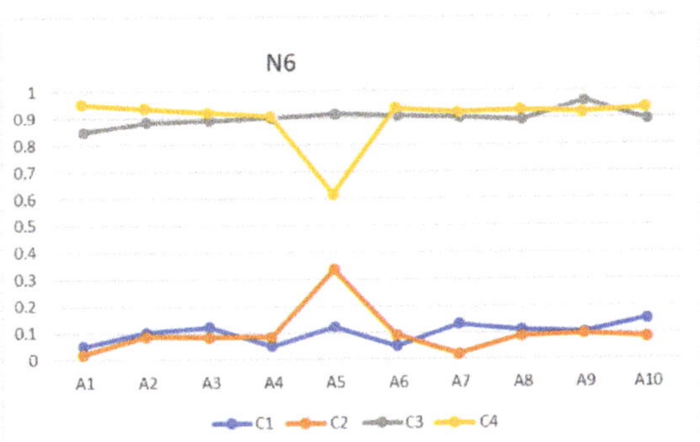

(**a**) Normalized criteria values for alternatives

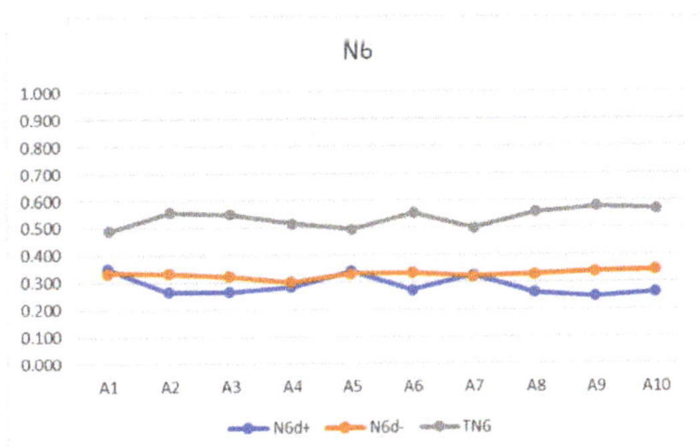

(**b**) Distances to positive and negative ideal solutions and TOPSIS closeness coefficients

Figure A6. Normalization N6.

https://doi.org/10.3390/e28010114

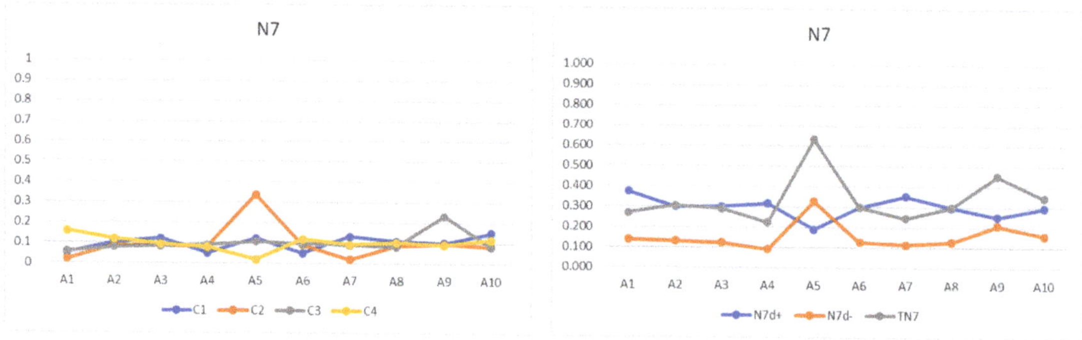

(**a**) Normalized criteria values for alternatives

(**b**) Distances to positive and negative ideal solutions and TOPSIS closeness coefficients

Figure A7. Normalization N7.

References

1. Greco, S.; Ehrgott, M.; Figueira, J.R. (Eds.) *Multiple Criteria Decision Analysis: State of the Art Surveys*, 2nd ed.; International Series in Operations Research & Management Science; Springer: New York, NY, USA, 2016.
2. Doumpos, M.; Zopounidis, C. Disaggregation Approaches for Multicriteria Classification: An Overview. In *Preference Disaggregation in Multiple Criteria Decision Analysis: Essays in Honor of Yannis Siskos*; Matsatsinis, N., Grigoroudis, E., Eds.; Multiple Criteria Decision Making; Springer International Publishing: Cham, Switzerland, 2018; pp. 77–94.
3. Zavadskas, E.K.; Turskis, Z. Multiple Criteria Decision Making (MCDM) Methods in Economics: An Overview. *Technol. Econ. Dev. Econ.* **2011**, *17*, 397–427. [CrossRef]
4. Zopounidis, C.; Galariotis, E.; Doumpos, M.; Sarri, S.; Andriosopoulos, K. Multiple Criteria Decision Aiding for Finance: An Updated Bibliographic Survey. *Eur. J. Oper. Res.* **2015**, *247*, 339–348. [CrossRef]
5. Siksnelyte, I.; Zavadskas, E.K.; Streimikiene, D.; Sharma, D. An Overview of Multi-Criteria Decision-Making Methods in Dealing with Sustainable Energy Development Issues. *Energies* **2018**, *11*, 2754. [CrossRef]
6. Stojčić, M.; Zavadskas, E.K.; Pamučar, D.; Stević, Ž.; Mardani, A. Application of MCDM Methods in Sustainability Engineering: A Literature Review 2008–2018. *Symmetry* **2019**, *11*, 350. [CrossRef]
7. Sahoo, S.K.; Goswami, S.S. A Comprehensive Review of Multiple Criteria Decision-Making (MCDM) Methods: Advancements, Applications, and Future Directions. *Decis. Mak. Adv.* **2023**, *1*, 25–48. [CrossRef]
8. Hwang, C.-L.; Yoon, K. *Methods for Multiple Attribute Decision Making*; Hwang, C.-L., Yoon, K., Eds.; Lecture Notes in Economics and Mathematical Systems; Springer: Berlin/Heidelberg, Germany, 1981.
9. Aytekin, A. Comparative Analysis of the Normalization Techniques in the Context of MCDM Problems. *Decis. Mak. Appl. Manag. Eng.* **2021**, *4*, 1–25. [CrossRef]
10. Chakraborty, S.; Chatterjee, P.; Das, P.P. Normalization Techniques. In *Multi-Criteria Decision-Making Methods in Manufacturing Environments*; Apple Academic Press: Palm Bay, FL, USA, 2024; pp. 351–353.
11. Pavličić, D. Normalization Affects the Results of MADM Methods. *Yugosl. J. Oper. Res.* **2001**, *11*, 251–265.
12. Milani, A.S.; Shanian, A.; Madoliat, R.; Nemes, J.A. The Effect of Normalization Norms in Multiple Attribute Decision Making Models: A Case Study in Gear Material Selection. *Struct. Multidiscip. Optim.* **2005**, *29*, 312–318. [CrossRef]
13. Chen, P. Effects of Normalization on the Entropy-Based TOPSIS Method. *Expert Syst. Appl.* **2019**, *136*, 33–41. [CrossRef]
14. Acuña-Soto, C.; Liern, V.; Pérez-Gladish, B. Normalization in TOPSIS-Based Approaches with Data of Different Nature: Application to the Ranking of Mathematical Videos. *Ann. Oper. Res.* **2021**, *296*, 541–569. [CrossRef]
15. Vafaei, N.; Ribeiro, R.A.; Camarinha-Matos, L.M. Selection of Normalization Technique for Weighted Average Multi-Criteria Decision Making. In *Proceedings of the Technological Innovation for Resilient Systems*; Camarinha-Matos, L.M., Adu-Kankam, K.O., Julashokri, M., Eds.; Springer International Publishing: Cham, Switzerland, 2018; pp. 43–52.
16. Wen, Z.; Liao, H.; Zavadskas, E.K. MACONT: Mixed Aggregation by Comprehensive Normalization Technique for Multi-Criteria Analysis. *Informatica* **2020**, *31*, 857–880. [CrossRef]
17. Shekhovtsov, A.; Kaczyńska, A.; Sałabun, W. Why Does the Choice of Normalization Technique Matter in Decision-Making. In *Multiple Criteria Decision Making*; Kulkarni, A.J., Ed.; Studies in Systems, Decision and Control; Springer Nature: Singapore, 2022; Volume 407, pp. 107–120.
18. Krishnan, A.R. Past Efforts in Determining Suitable Normalization Methods for Multi-Criteria Decision-Making: A Short Survey. *Front. Big Data* **2022**, *5*, 990699. [CrossRef] [PubMed]

https://doi.org/10.3390/e28010114

19. Mukhametzyanov, I.Z. *Normalization of Multidimensional Data for Multi-Criteria Decision Making Problems: Inversion, Displacement, Asymmetry*; International Series in Operations Research & Management Science; Springer International Publishing: Cham, Switzerland, 2023; Volume 348.
20. Shih, H.-S. Rank Reversal in TOPSIS. In *TOPSIS and Its Extensions: A Distance-Based MCDM Approach*; Shih, H.-S., Olson, D.L., Eds.; Springer International Publishing: Cham, Switzerland, 2022; pp. 159–175.
21. Simanavičienė, R.; Jakučionytė, V.; Deltuvienė, D. Sensitivity Study of TOPSIS and COPRAS Methods with Respect to Normalization Techniques. *Balt. J. Mod. Comput.* **2022**, *10*, 105–120. [CrossRef]
22. Malefaki, S.; Markatos, D.; Filippatos, A.; Pantelakis, S. A Comparative Analysis of Multi-Criteria Decision-Making Methods and Normalization Techniques in Holistic Sustainability Assessment for Engineering Applications. *Aerospace* **2025**, *12*, 100. [CrossRef]
23. Chakraborty, S.; Yeh, C.-H. A Simulation Comparison of Normalization Procedures for TOPSIS. In *Proceedings of the 2009 International Conference on Computers and Industrial Engineering (CIE39), Troyes, France, 6–9 July 2009*; IEEE Institute of Electrical and Electronics Engineers: New York, NY, USA, 2009; pp. 1815–1820.
24. Liao, Y.P.; Liu, L.; Xing, C. Investigation of Different Normalization Methods for TOPSIS. *Beijing Ligong Daxue Xuebao* **2012**, *32*, 871–875+880.
25. Vafaei, N.; Ribeiro, R.A.; Camarinha-Matos, L.M. Assessing Normalization Techniques for TOPSIS Method. In *Technological Innovation for Applied AI Systems*; Camarinha-Matos, L.M., Ferreira, P., Brito, G., Eds.; IFIP Advances in Information and Communication Technology; Springer International Publishing: Cham, Switzerland, 2021; Volume 626, pp. 132–141.
26. Shannon, C.E. A Mathematical Theory of Communication. *Bell Syst. Tech. J.* **1948**, *27*, 379–423. [CrossRef]
27. Yue, C. Entropy-Based Weights on Decision Makers in Group Decision-Making Setting with Hybrid Preference Representations. *Appl. Soft Comput.* **2017**, *60*, 737–749. [CrossRef]
28. Zhu, Y.; Tian, D.; Yan, F. Effectiveness of Entropy Weight Method in Decision-Making. *Math. Probl. Eng.* **2020**, *2020*, 3564835. [CrossRef]
29. Tsallis, C. Entropy. *Encyclopedia* **2022**, *2*, 264–300. [CrossRef]
30. Rényi, A. On Measures of Entropy and Information. In *Proceedings of the Fourth Berkeley Symposium on Mathematical Statistics and Probability, Volume 1: Contributions to the Theory of Statistics, Berkeley, CA, USA, 20 June–30 July 1960*; University of California Press: Oakland, CA, USA, 1961; Volume 4, pp. 547–562.
31. Zavadskas, E.K.; Mardani, A.; Turskis, Z.; Jusoh, A.; Nor, K.M. Development of TOPSIS Method to Solve Complicated Decision-Making Problems—An Overview on Developments from 2000 to 2015. *Int. J. Inf. Technol. Decis. Mak.* **2016**, *15*, 645–682. [CrossRef]
32. Zyoud, S.H.; Fuchs-Hanusch, D. A Bibliometric-Based Survey on AHP and TOPSIS Techniques. *Expert Syst. Appl.* **2017**, *78*, 158–181. [CrossRef]
33. Shih, H.-S.; Shyur, H.-J.; Lee, E.S. An Extension of TOPSIS for Group Decision Making. *Math. Comput. Model.* **2007**, *45*, 801–813. [CrossRef]
34. Chen, B.; Wang, J.; Zhao, H.; Principe, J.C. Insights into Entropy as a Measure of Multivariate Variability. *Entropy* **2016**, *18*, 196. [CrossRef]
35. Zavadskas, E.K.; Zakarevicius, A.; Antucheviciene, J. Evaluation of Ranking Accuracy in Multi-Criteria Decisions. *Informatica* **2006**, *17*, 601–618. [CrossRef]
36. Mukhametzyanov, I. Specific Character of Objective Methods for Determining Weights of Criteria in MCDM Problems: Entropy, CRITIC and SD. *Decis. Mak. Appl. Manag. Eng.* **2021**, *4*, 76–105. [CrossRef]
37. Chen, T.-Y.; Li, C.-H. Determining Objective Weights with Intuitionistic Fuzzy Entropy Measures: A Comparative Analysis. *Inf. Sci.* **2010**, *180*, 4207–4222. [CrossRef]
38. Wu, J.; Li, P.; Qian, H.; Chen, J. On the Sensitivity of Entropy Weight to Sample Statistics in Assessing Water Quality: Statistical Analysis Based on Large Stochastic Samples. *Environ. Earth Sci.* **2015**, *74*, 2185–2195. [CrossRef]
39. He, D.; Xu, J.; Chen, X. Information-Theoretic-Entropy Based Weight Aggregation Method in Multiple-Attribute Group Decision-Making. *Entropy* **2016**, *18*, 171. [CrossRef]
40. Kumar, R.; Singh, S.; Bilga, P.S.; Jatin; Singh, J.; Singh, S.; Scutaru, M.-L.; Pruncu, C.I. Revealing the Benefits of Entropy Weights Method for Multi-Objective Optimization in Machining Operations: A Critical Review. *J. Mater. Res. Technol.* **2021**, *10*, 1471–1492. [CrossRef]
41. Roszkowska, E.; Wachowicz, T. Impact of Normalization on Entropy-Based Weights in Hellble Development in Thewig's Method: A Case Study on Evaluating Sustaina Education Area. *Entropy* **2024**, *26*, 365. [CrossRef]
42. Dong, Q.; Ai, X.; Cao, G.; Zhang, Y.; Wang, X. Study on Risk Assessment of Water Security of Drought Periods Based on Entropy Weight Methods. *Kybernetes* **2010**, *39*, 864–870. [CrossRef]
43. Aras, G.; Tezcan, N.; Kutlu Furtuna, O.; Hacioglu Kazak, E. Corporate Sustainability Measurement Based on Entropy Weight and TOPSIS: A Turkish Banking Case Study. *Meditari Account. Res.* **2017**, *25*, 391–413. [CrossRef]

44. Dang, V.T.; Dang, W.V.T. Multi-Criteria Decision-Making in the Evaluation of Environmental Quality of OECD Countries: The Entropy Weight and VIKOR Methods. *Int. J. Ethics Syst.* **2019**, *36*, 119–130. [CrossRef]
45. Wang, Z.-X.; Li, D.-D.; Zheng, H.-H. The External Performance Appraisal of China Energy Regulation: An Empirical Study Using a TOPSIS Method Based on Entropy Weight and Mahalanobis Distance. *Int. J. Environ. Res. Public Health* **2018**, *15*, 236. [CrossRef]
46. Wang, J.-J.; Jing, Y.-Y.; Zhang, C.-F.; Zhao, J.-H. Review on Multi-Criteria Decision Analysis Aid in Sustainable Energy Decision-Making. *Renew. Sustain. Energy Rev.* **2009**, *13*, 2263–2278. [CrossRef]
47. Zardari, N.H.; Ahmed, K.; Shirazi, S.M.; Yusop, Z.B. *Weighting Methods and Their Effects on Multi-Criteria Decision Making Model Outcomes in Water Resources Management*; Springer: Berlin/Heidelberg, Germany, 2015.
48. Şahin, M. Location Selection by Multi-Criteria Decision-Making Methods Based on Objective and Subjective Weightings. *Knowl. Inf. Syst.* **2021**, *63*, 1991–2021. [CrossRef]
49. Lin, H.; Pan, T.; Chen, S. Comprehensive Evaluation of Urban Air Quality Using the Relative Entropy Theory and Improved TOPSIS Method. *Air Qual. Atmos. Health* **2021**, *14*, 251–258. [CrossRef]
50. Dehdashti Shahrokh, Z.; Nakhaei, H. An Entropy (Shannon) Based Approach for Determining Importance Weights of Influencing Factors in Selecting Medical Tourism Destinations. *Int. J. Travel Med. Glob. Health* **2016**, *4*, 115–121. [CrossRef]
51. Tzeng, G.-H.; Chen, T.-Y.; Wang, J.-C. A Weight-Assessing Method with Habitual Domains. *Eur. J. Oper. Res.* **1998**, *110*, 342–367. [CrossRef]
52. Duckstein, L.; Gershon, M.E.; McAniff, R. Model Selection in Multiobjective Decision Making for River Basin Planning. *Adv. Water Resour.* **1982**, *5*, 178–184. [CrossRef]
53. Ma, J.; Fan, Z.-P.; Huang, L.-H. A Subjective and Objective Integrated Approach to Determine Attribute Weights. *Eur. J. Oper. Res.* **1999**, *112*, 397–404. [CrossRef]
54. Dai, N.T.; Kuang, X.; Tang, G. Differential Weighting of Objective Versus Subjective Measures in Performance Evaluation: Experimental Evidence. *Eur. Account. Rev.* **2018**, *27*, 129–148. [CrossRef]
55. Qu, W.; Li, J.; Song, W.; Li, X.; Zhao, Y.; Dong, H.; Wang, Y.; Zhao, Q.; Qi, Y. Entropy-Weight-Method-Based Integrated Models for Short-Term Intersection Traffic Flow Prediction. *Entropy* **2022**, *24*, 849. [CrossRef]
56. Chakraborty, S.; Yeh, C.-H. A Simulation Based Comparative Study of Normalization Procedures in Multiattribute Decision Making. In *Proceedings of the 6th Conference on 6th WSEAS Int. Conf. on Artificial Intelligence, Knowledge Engineering and Data Bases*; Citeseer: New York, NY, USA, 2007; Volume 6, pp. 102–109.
57. Jahan, A.; Edwards, K.L. A State-of-the-Art Survey on the Influence of Normalization Techniques in Ranking: Improving the Materials Selection Process in Engineering Design. *Mater. Des.* **2014**, *65*, 335–342. [CrossRef]
58. Zaidan, B.B.; Zaidan, A.A. Comparative Study on the Evaluation and Benchmarking Information Hiding Approaches Based Multi-Measurement Analysis Using TOPSIS Method with Different Normalisation, Separation and Context Techniques. *Measurement* **2018**, *117*, 277–294. [CrossRef]
59. Çelen, A. Comparative Analysis of Normalization Procedures in TOPSIS Method: With an Application to Turkish Deposit Banking Market. *Informatica* **2014**, *25*, 185–208. [CrossRef]
60. García-Cascales, M.S.; Lamata, M.T. On Rank Reversal and TOPSIS Method. *Math. Comput. Model.* **2012**, *56*, 123–132. [CrossRef]
61. Aires, R.F.d.F.; Ferreira, L. A New Approach to Avoid Rank Reversal Cases in the TOPSIS Method. *Comput. Ind. Eng.* **2019**, *132*, 84–97. [CrossRef]
62. Aires, R.F.D.F.; Ferreira, L. The Rank Reversal Problem in Multi-Criteria Decision Making: A Literature Review. *Pesqui. Oper.* **2018**, *38*, 331–362. [CrossRef]
63. Pena, J.C.; Nápoles, G.; Salgueiro, Y. Normalization Method for Quantitative and Qualitative Attributes in Multiple Attribute Decision-Making Problems. *Expert Syst. Appl.* **2022**, *198*, 116821. [CrossRef]
64. Wachowicz, T.; Roszkowska, E. Enhancing TOPSIS to Evaluate Negotiation Offers with Subjectively Defined Reference Points. *Group Decis. Negot.* **2025**, *34*, 715–749. [CrossRef]
65. Więckowski, J.; Sałabun, W. How the Normalization of the Decision Matrix Influences the Results in the VIKOR Method? *Procedia Comput. Sci.* **2020**, *176*, 2222–2231. [CrossRef]
66. Vafaei, N.; Ribeiro, R.A.; Camarinha-Matos, L.M. Normalization Techniques for Multi-Criteria Decision Making: Analytical Hierarchy Process Case Study. In *Proceedings of the Technological Innovation for Cyber-Physical Systems*; Camarinha-Matos, L.M., Falcão, A.J., Vafaei, N., Najdi, S., Eds.; Springer International Publishing: Cham, Switzerland, 2016; pp. 261–269.
67. Alencar, L.H.; Almeida, A.T.d.; Morais, D.C. A Multicriteria Group Decision Model Aggregating the Preferences of Decision-Makers Based on Electre Methods. *Pesqui. Oper.* **2010**, *30*, 687–702. [CrossRef]
68. Palczewski, K.; Sałabun, W. Influence of Various Normalization Methods in PROMETHEE II: An Empirical Study on the Selection of the Airport Location. *Procedia Comput. Sci.* **2019**, *159*, 2051–2060. [CrossRef]
69. Roszkowska, E.; Filipowicz-Chomko, M.; Łyczkowska-Hanćkowiak, A.; Majewska, E. Extended Hellwig's Method Utilizing Entropy-Based Weights and Mahalanobis Distance: Applications in Evaluating Sustainable Development in the Education Area. *Entropy* **2024**, *26*, 197. [CrossRef]

https://doi.org/10.3390/e28010114

70. Sałabun, W.; Wątróbski, J.; Shekhovtsov, A. Are MCDA Methods Benchmarkable? A Comparative Study of TOPSIS, VIKOR, COPRAS, and PROMETHEE II Methods. *Symmetry* **2020**, *12*, 1549. [CrossRef]
71. Sałabun, W. The Mean Error Estimation of TOPSIS Method Using a Fuzzy Reference Models. *J. Theor. Appl. Comput. Sci.* **2013**, *7*, 40–50.
72. Kong, F. Rank Reversal and Rank Preservation in TOPSIS. *Adv. Mater. Res.* **2011**, *204*, 36–41. [CrossRef]
73. Kukuła, K.; Luty, L. Propozycja Procedury Wspomagającej Wybór Metody Porządkowania Liniowego. *Przegląd Stat.* **2015**, *62*, 219–231. [CrossRef]

https://doi.org/10.3390/e28010114

MDPI AG
Grosspeteranlage 5
4052 Basel
Switzerland
Tel.: +41 61 683 77 34

Entropy Editorial Office
E-mail: entropy@mdpi.com
www.mdpi.com/journal/entropy

www.ingramcontent.com/pod-product-compliance
Lightning Source LLC
Chambersburg PA
CBHW061554210926
51850CB00009B/2096
* 9 7 8 3 7 2 5 8 7 0 3 2 5 *